Good-bye to the
MERMAIDS

To DR. Sawyer
hoping you'll enjoy
the book.
with gratitude for your
medical care —
Yes! thank you —

Karin Finell

Feb. 9, 2022

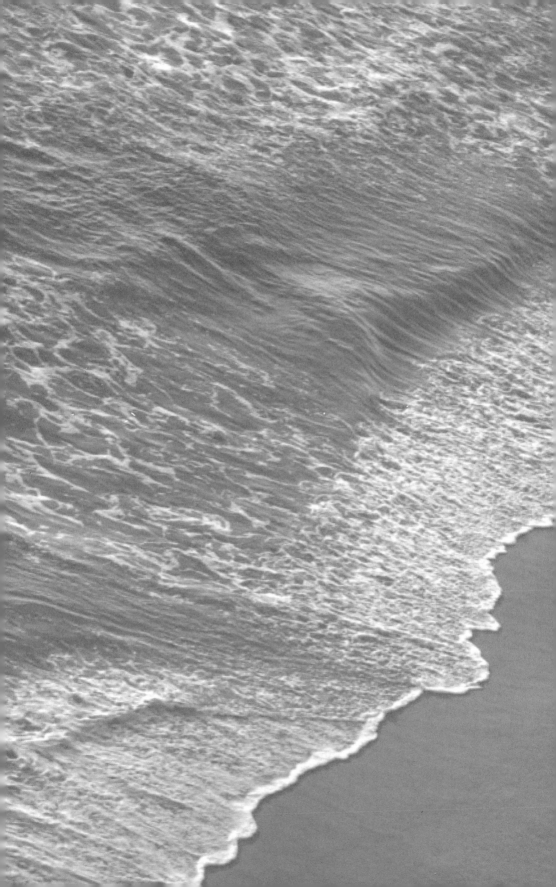

Good-bye to the
MERMAIDS

A Childhood Lost in
Hitler's Berlin

KARIN FINELL

University of Missouri Press
Columbia and London

Library of Congress Cataloging-in-Publication Data

Finell, Karin.
    Good-bye to the mermaids : a childhood lost in Hitler's
Berlin / Karin Finell.
          p.   cm.
    Summary: "Memoir of a child living in Berlin during World War II.
Tells how the war affected three generations of middle-class German
women who lived through the bombing of Berlin, the Russian and
Allied occupation, the Berlin Airlift, and the postwar recovery"
—Provided by publisher.
    Includes index.
    ISBN-13: 978-0-8262-1690-8 (alk. paper)
    ISBN-10: 0-8262-1690-0 (alk. paper)
  1. Finell, Karin—Childhood and youth. 2. World War, 1939–
1945—Germany—Berlin. 3. World War, 1939–1945—Children—
Germany—Berlin—Biography. 4. World War, 1939–1945—Personal
narratives, German. 5. Berlin (Germany)—History—Blockade,
1948–1949—Personal narratives.   I. Title.
    D757.9.B4F56 2006
    940.53'161—dc22
    [B]
                                                      2006017988

Designer: Jennifer Cropp
Typesetter: Crane Composition, Inc.
Printer and binder: Thomson-Shore, Inc.
Typefaces: Bembo and Eplica

*The University of Missouri Press offers its grateful acknowledgment to the M.
B. Seretean Foundation, Inc. for its generous contribution in support of the
publication of this volume.*

*The University of Missouri Press offers its grateful acknowledgment to
Ava Astaire McKenzie for her generous contribution in support of the
publication of this volume.*

*To my grandmother, my mother, and Aunt Margaret
. . . and to the women of Berlin.*

Contents

ACKNOWLEDGMENTS

Where to begin?

There are so many who deserve my gratitude for having helped me on the long road to publication. A big thank you goes to my agent, Robert Diforio, who believed in *Good-bye to the Mermaids.* It was in Anne Lowenkopf's class at Adult Ed that I discovered my voice and the courage to write about those times of war. In "The Lions' Den," a workshop led by Shelly Lowenkopf and Leonard Tourney, I gained confidence and was encouraged by these two maestros of the written word. Shelly suggested the title *Good-bye to the Mermaids,* which he thought accurately conveyed the loss of the innocence of childhood.

I owe much to the Santa Barbara Writers Conference and its high caliber workshop leaders. Its founder, Barnaby Conrad, has been my unwavering supporter. My first memoir piece won first prize at the conference of nonfiction and is now a chapter in my book. Charles Champlin, a former *Los Angeles Times* book critic, championed my individual war stories and encouraged me to expand them into a book. Grace Rachow, the editor and publisher of "Community of Voices" anthologies, praised my writing and published several of my war stories.

There are so many writers and friends who were of help, but I can only name a few. My gratitude goes to the members of our "Thursday Writers" group, with special thanks to Susan Chiavelli, who diligently read rewritten pages again and again and whose suggestions for combining scenes were invaluable. My thanks go to Linda Stewart-Oaten, who mercilessly red-lined hyperbole, and to Fran Davis, who corrected sentence structure. And Carrie Brown, Susan Gulbranson, Katie Ingram, Janis Jennings, Toni Lorien, and Sheila Tenold, I thank you! You gave me invaluable advice and buoyed me up with your unfailing encouragement.

My gratitude extends to Gloria Hamilton, who enthusiastically opened the door to Beverly Jarrett, the director and editor-in-chief of the University of Missouri Press. And my thanks go to Gary Kass, the acquisitions editor who championed my book to the Press's Faculty Press Committee. There were many people at the Press who became involved with the book, Karen Renner, Sara Davis, Jenny Cropp, who designed the inspired title page, and numerous others, and to all of them I want to say thank you.

Everyone was efficient and helpful, and it was a pleasure to work with them. During the book's journey to the published page, Susan King became its editor. She deserves all the accolades I can muster, but I will restrain the hyperbole. Susan has shown great patience, and I am grateful for her eagle eye, which caught many minor inconsistencies. The various spellings of names and nouns in German and in anglicized German would drive most editors mad, but Susan survived. And so did I.

And to my husband, Martin Dent, I want to extend my foremost gratitude. His British schooling and insistence on historical accuracy was of enormous help to me when we were going over the manuscript one last time. Martin's drawings of preliminary maps and family trees helped enormously. Again, thank you Martin.

And my thanks also to Aldo, my 130-pound German shepherd, who faithfully snored at my feet. Whether I sat at my computer or at the table strewn with papers and books, his mere presence was a calming influence on me.

I think with gratitude of family members and friends who appear in the book, but who are no longer alive. I know they would be pleased to be remembered in these pages. Without the love of my grandmother, I would not be the person I am today. I loved my mother, but I learned to fully understand her only after she had died and I had written about the times she endured in this book. I have experienced much in my life, good and bad, and I am grateful for those lessons. They opened my mind to others' suffering.

The names of family members and most friends have not been changed, and the names of historical figures are accurate. Some names have been changed to protect the privacy of those still alive.

Father's Family Tree

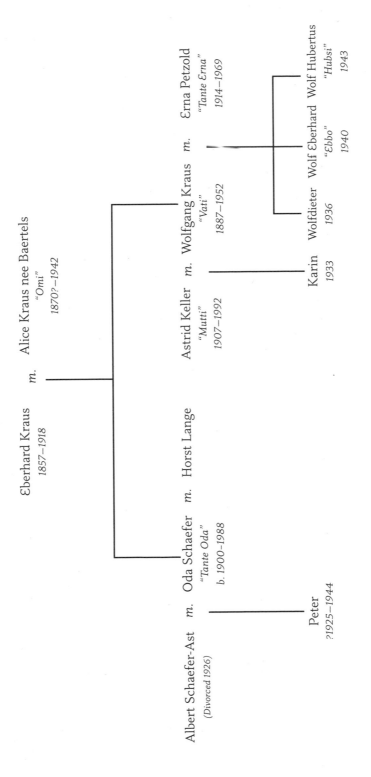

Eberhard Kraus
1857–1918

m.

Alice Kraus nee Baertels
"Omi"
1870?–1942

Albert Schaefer-Ast
(Divorced 1926)

m.

Oda Schaefer
"Tante Oda"
b. 1900–1988

Horst Lange

Astrid Keller
"Mutti"
1907–1992

m.

Wolfgang Kraus
"Vati"
1887–1952

m.

Erna Petzold
"Tante Erna"
1914–1969

Peter
?1925–1944

Karin
1933

Wolfdieter
1936

Wolf Eberhard
"Ebbo"
1940

Wolf Hubertus
"Hubsi"
1943

MOTHER'S FAMILY TREE

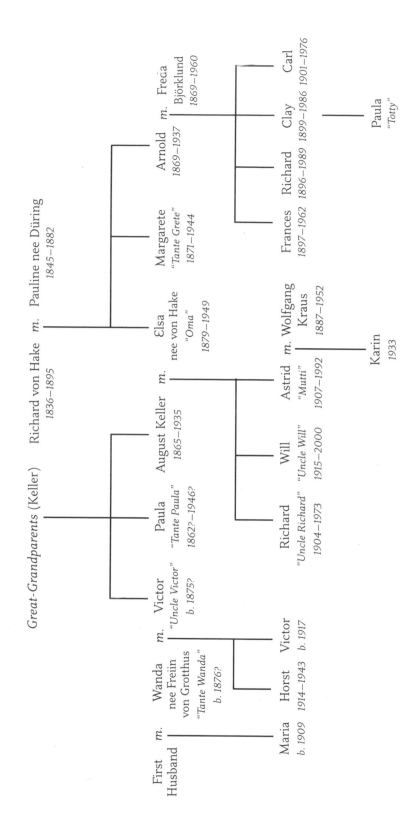

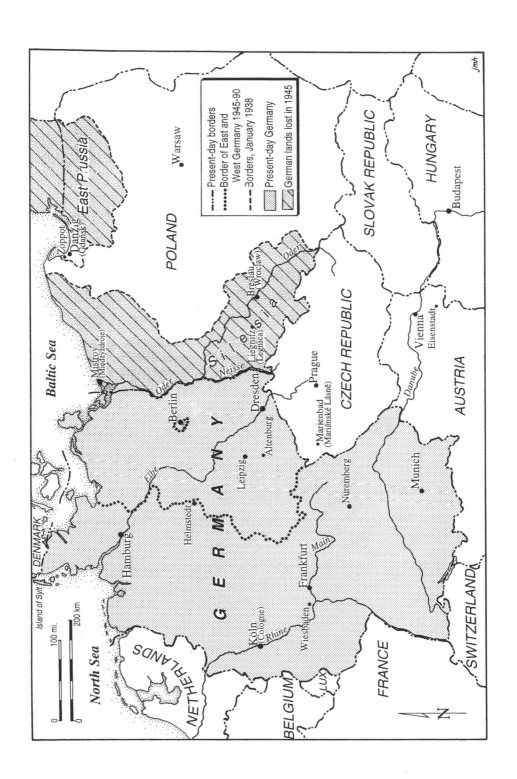

FRENCH SECTOR

EAST GERMANY

Tegeler See

Tegel Airport

BRITISH SECTOR

EAST BERLIN

River Spree

SOVIET SECTOR

CHARLOTTENBURG

TIERGARTEN

WEST

BERLIN

River Spree

Kurfürstendamm

Havel River

Halensee

GRUNEWALD

(Autobahn)

WILMERSDORF

Avus

Clay Allee

DAHLEM

STEGLITZ

Tempelhof Airport

Gatow Airport

Wannsee

Schlachtensee

ZEHLENDORF

AMERICAN SECTOR

WANNSEE

NIKOLASSEE

Dreilinden Checkpoint

Potsdam

EAST GERMANY

jmh

Good-bye to the
MERMAIDS

Prologue

In the early years after World War II only historians wrote about the fall of Berlin. Now, sixty years later, literature documenting the suffering of German civilians is emerging from the tombs of silence. Susan Sontag noted the lack of contemporary accounts of the torment German women and children endured when their cities burned. She wrote, "We can't imagine how dreadful, how terrifying war is" and "Remembering is an ethical act." W. S. Sebald called this, "A conspiracy of silence in every German household," which he attributed to "a numbness of spirit and the guilt of a Nazi past still bearing down on the German psyche." Years have passed and most of the eyewitnesses are now dead. It is too late for me to ask my mother what she remembered. It is up to people whose memories are still clear and who lived through the bombings, the artillery fire, and the rapes to bear witness to the many who suffered and died.

During my early years in America, I too tried to forget the terror of my youth. There were occasions when an airplane flying low overhead would make me duck for cover. Memories were mere reflexes then, not to be brought back into consciousness. I never talked to my mother about those times. I, like many others who had lived through the war years in Berlin, tried to erase those memories.

But memory is not a slate that can be erased with ease. Memories are like fleeting shades or like dreams, which can be recalled in great detail upon awakening, but then retreat into the shadows and are soon forgotten. Mine had only retreated; they had never been forgotten. Little by little my memories and the stories emerged. In the early 1990s, I watched the BBC movie *Christabel* and found myself in tears as "my" Berlin was bombed. Afterward I went to the computer to write down what I remembered. I was working on a novel at the time, but these war memories kept intruding, demanding to be written down. Gradually, on warm, moonlit California nights—an atmosphere so opposite to war-torn Berlin—I began to tell my war stories to friends. Lingering over coffee or wine, my guests prodded me to tell one more tale. Story after story emerged, as if sprouting from a root cellar of memory. Scenes formed in my mind, and remembering my grandmother led me to think of her sister, my beloved aunt Margaret. She seemed to be in the same room with me, and I could almost smell her scent of camphor and peppermint and see her with my inner eye as clearly as if we had said good-bye only yesterday. More and more friends and relatives elbowed their way into my consciousness, asking me to tell their story.

Readers may ask, "How can dialogue be remembered verbatim?" Of course, it can't, but I can remember my grandmother's voice and what she or my mother would have said under given circumstances. The conversations in my book are "re-remembered," and the individual scenes are as faithfully rendered as memory allows.

When I was well into writing this book, I went to Berlin to revisit a few places. The scenes playing out in my mind were so dramatic that I thought perhaps my memory was playing tricks on me. One drizzly autumn evening I took the bus down Kurfürstendamm to the street where we had lived. From there I decided to walk across the Halenseebrücke, a bridge spanning a network of train tracks. It was an eerie feeling: I was walking alone but at the same time I held the hand of the little girl I once had been. I broke out in tears, feeling a great sadness for the horrors that child had seen. I arrived at what used to be our neighborhood butcher shop. It had become a small sausage factory, but the white tiled walls were smeared with blood as they had been then, and the odor was much the same.

The next day I went to the Hochmeister Church. After the fall of Berlin, the Russians had been holed up in this church, and one day as I walked down the street, they had shot at me. I remembered them shooting from the tower, but I wondered, how could they have climbed up when the interior of the church had been burned by incendiary bombs? It was a Tuesday afternoon, and the doors of the church were wide open. Upon entering, I noticed a flight of stone stairs winding up to the tower. Of course, I thought, stone doesn't burn. A gracious woman, too young to have known the war, greeted me. I told her I was visiting from California but had lived a block down the street as a child and attended services here. I asked if she knew anyone who had lived in this neighborhood in April 1945, during the Russians' conquest. I explained that I wanted to speak with women older than myself about their experiences in war-torn Berlin and to ask them questions for a book I was writing. "You're in luck," she said with a smile. "Our seniors are here on Tuesday afternoons for coffee and cake. Would you like to join us? I'm sure many of them will be happy to talk to a former neighbor who comes from so far away."

I learned that many of these women had lived on my former street since before 1945. They had shoveled rubble, more than likely alongside my mother, my grandmother, and me. When I told the women that I was writing about the last weeks of the war in Berlin and that I would like to ask some questions, they shook their heads. I went on talking about my own experiences, but not one of them would talk about hers. Most of them became agitated. A woman at the far end of the table threw up and then fainted, and others fell into accusations and arguments about whether this one or that one had voted for "him," meaning Hitler. I soon left. Once outside I breathed deeply, to loosen a constriction in my chest. Looking at the building across the street, my eyes were drawn to the lower part of the stone foundation where I noticed small round holes. Were they the bullet holes from the time when the Russians shot at me?

In one of her ballads, Hildegard Knef calls Berlin, "A woman in an apron": a simple woman, not made-up, strong, robust, and ready to tackle all calamities. In the center of Berlin's coat of arms is the figure of a bear standing on its hind feet. In my mind, I replaced that symbol with a woman in an apron: a brave Berlin woman became my heraldic figure. Sadly, it seemed that many of these brave women had not come to terms with their guilt about the Holocaust and the shame of having been raped by Russian soldiers. Added to this mixture was the guilt of having supported, or tolerated, Hitler at one point or another. I kept remembering the words of the women in the Hochmeister Church: "You should forget those times," a chorus of them had said, "We all want to forget them."

"No, this period should be remembered," I told them. "You were brave women. You should not be ashamed of what the Russians did to you, and your guilt for what the Germans did to others should not obscure your own stories. They too must be told."

I vowed not to forget and also to write down what I remembered and let the women live again in the pages of my book. The women of Berlin were the unsung heroes of that ungodly time. They fought and some died, but many persevered. And out of ashes and rubble, they helped rebuild their city.

Women of Berlin, I salute you.

PART I

Mother and me on Sylt, 1939.

CHAPTER I

Good-bye to the Mermaids

I ran ahead of my mother, skipping along the hot sand—a blonde, pig-tailed six-year-old with sunbaked skin. Beyond the dunes sat the ancient fisherman's cottage, with a straw roof and a garden full of sunflowers, where we were staying that summer on the island of Sylt in the North Sea. I knew Mother would be following me, carrying our towels and the large beach ball with its sections of yellow and red. Dune grass scraped my legs, and the white sand burned the soles of my feet as I ran toward the damp strip where sand meets sea. I cooled my feet in the water, inhaled the iodine sea smell, and looked far out to where seabirds dove for fish.

Mother forbade me to go into the water by myself, but there was always that irresistible pull. I waded into the surf, slowly, the sea lapping at my knees. In the distance the cresting waves looked like white horses with curling manes. I wished I could swim out and ride those horses of the sea. Closer to shore the waves changed, and this made me sad. Their breaking foam was made of mermaids' souls. I knew this to be true. Had someone told me, or did I learn this from Hans Christian Andersen? As I watched the patterns of the spuming surf, I could not help but think about the many mermaids dying before me, leaving their souls in the foam of the sea.

Behind me my mother called, "Karin, Karin . . ." Her voice pulled me out of my daydream. I watched her come to a stop. She stood tall against the sun and looked slender like a statue made of bronze. Then she began to run toward me with her arms outstretched, and at that moment I knew something was wrong.

She pulled me into her arms, and we sank onto the sand. Mother was shaking and crying. She pressed me against her chest so hard that I couldn't breathe, and I wondered who had died?

I squirmed from her arms and backed away. "Mutti, what is it?"

"It's that . . . that madman." She looked over her shoulder, lowered her voice, and half-whispered, "*Ach,* this is crazy, Karin." She pulled me close, wiping her eyes.

"What is it? Tell me."

"We're at war. At WAR! Germany has marched into Poland. Hitler won't get away with it. France and England will attack us."

"Our Führer? But Mutti, he knows what's best. He's all powerful."

"Ha. Knows what's best. No one is all powerful." She lowered her voice and shook her head. "I shouldn't be talking to you. You're so young." I freed myself from her suffocating grip, but she held me tight by my wrist. Her large gray eyes studied me. "You're all I have, Karin. I wish Oma were here, or your uncles. I need to talk to someone, someone who understands."

"I understand."

"Oh, Karin." Then she held her fingers to her lips and made a *shh* sound. "Remember. Whatever I say is a secret. Between you and me."

Part of me felt grown up and honored to be so trusted, but I was also angry with her for having broken up my mermaid fantasy, replacing it with visions of soldiers marching.

Could Mother be right? Would we soon be at war with England and France? England, I knew, was an island, maybe a little larger than the one we were on. My friend Guggi's mother came from England. And just a few months ago, my friend Esther, from across the street, had moved to England with her parents. I was still upset with her for not telling me that she was moving. Esther didn't even say good-bye. One day her father's corner grocery was closed, and she was gone.

Why would France attack us? Mother's white leather gloves and perfumes came from France, as did the champagne my family drank on special occasions.

War. What did that mean? My grandmother had told me tales of the Great War. Even potatoes were scarce, she said, and the bread hard and almost inedible because the flour used for baking was mixed with sawdust. Would this war be as bad as the one so long ago? Would we go hungry?

On that Friday in September, we did not swim. Mother dragged me back to the fisherman's house, past the forest of sunflowers standing tall like sentries, into the kitchen with its walls tiled with fishing scenes of delft blue on white. On the sideboard sat a brown box with big round knobs called a *Volksempfänger.* These radios were quite affordable, and they made it possible for most Germans to listen to Adolf Hitler's speeches right in their own living rooms.

Mother turned on one of the knobs, and marches shrilled from the box. Then we heard the harsh and gravelly voice of our Führer, talking with hard-rolling *r*'s and the Austrian accent he tried so hard to disguise. To me, his accent sounded gruff. Although I had a hard time understanding his words, he sounded serious and caring, and I simply believed whatever he said.

I understood that Germany had lost many lands after the Great War. Now the Führer said this was a shame no German could live with any longer. Then his voice grew louder, and he shouted, "Poland has refused to negotiate the return of German lands. Today our troops have invaded Poland. We are taking back what is rightfully ours." I sat with my eyes fixed on the brown box. Mother cried.

Friends of ours, neighboring vacationers from Frankfurt and Berlin, came by in the evening, bringing schnapps and pretzels. I sat quietly in a corner, hoping I could stay up late and listen to the adults talk. One woman told of a recent train trip to East Prussia through the German-Polish corridor. When she went through Poland, formerly Germany, all of the windows were boarded up and the passengers were told not to peer out. At a train stop, she was not allowed to leave the compartment because, as she said, "The Poles would attack us." "Why?" someone asked. "They hate us," she answered. "They fed you propaganda," Mother said. "Why would they attack? You traveled a month ago. *Now* they'd have a reason."

Mother sent me to bed, promising she'd be up soon to kiss me goodnight. I could hear them arguing and talking about this new war, agitated voices rose through the warm summer air to my little room. Was our Führer right to march into Poland? The adults said no, but I disagreed. *He* knew what was right for us.

"He's crazy. He's *crazy,*" Mother cried out. One of the neighbors tried to shush her. Another said, "Astrid is too outspoken. One of these days she'll wind up in jail." When I heard that I felt a cold chill. Then Mother shouted, "The man suffers from *Grössenwahn.*" I knew that meant someone was "feeling too big for his britches." A man's voice cautioned her, "God, you're stubborn, Astrid. The windows are wide open. If you don't care about yourself, at least think of your child upstairs in bed."

That scared me. I waited for her to perform her nightly routine. I listened for her footsteps, taking two steps at a time, clicking on the wooden stairs. All remained silent. But then I heard her voice again, informing one and all that Hitler was insane. Her voice was loud and was not filled with her usual musical ring. I wanted to run downstairs and overwhelm Mother with kisses and beg her to shush up. But I stayed in bed, too scared to move.

I had never felt fear like this before. I'd been afraid of "night animals" growling in the room next to mine, keeping me awake, until I discovered it was my grandmother's snoring. I had suffered from nightmares in which I was running away from a man in a trench coat. Just before he caught up with me, I would lift off into the night sky and fly away. But this was no dream; I could not fly away. It was as if my fear were alive, hovering over me, a fear of something big and evil I could not understand.

The next day brought warmth and sunshine, but somehow the island had changed; the tranquility and the calm were gone. Mother's worries were catching, and like an illness they infected me. She longed to be with my grandmother and her two brothers. She told me we were returning to Frankfurt as soon as possible.

It was Saturday, usually the busiest day for the small arts and crafts gallery that Mother managed during the summer months on Sylt. She nervously started packing boxes to be shipped back to Frankfurt. There was no time for her to take me down to the beach. I was forgotten. Quietly slipping away, I walked to the water's edge. It was already dark, but the sea held the day's reflection in it like a mirror. I dipped my toes into the foaming waves, drawing small phosphorescent circles in the starlight. I said good-bye.

Good-bye to the mermaids.

Later, in my attic room, I knelt on the bed where a narrow window allowed me to peer out beyond the dunes to the water. Straw from the roof covered half of the glass like unkempt yellow hair. I wanted to brush the hair aside, to see more of the water.

Then I slipped under the cover on my cot, careful not to bang my head on the ceiling beneath the pitched roof. I loved it here. I felt free in the blowing wind and felt the rhythm of the tides, as if they were ebbing and flowing inside of me. I loved to look far out into the distance, beyond the sea, to the stars.

But that night in September I buried my face in the pillow and wept.

Black Boots and Quetzal Feathers

Two days later, on September 3, 1939, England and France declared war on Germany. Our train went straight through to Frankfurt, but I was impatient; the stopover in Hamburg seemed to take forever. The station buzzed with people just like the big Wertheim store in Frankfurt did every year before Christmas. The many noises made me dizzy: the tooting of locomotives, the clanking of engines, and the booming voice on the loudspeaker announcing track number seven or track number fifty, all of the different platforms from which trains would leave to their many destinations. Mother saw me fidget and told me to sit still. "Karin, be patient. Now that we're at war, lots of people want to go home, just like us. That's why it's so crowded."

Through the window I saw an ice milk vendor. My mouth watered. "Mutti, could you please give me ten pfennig so I can buy an ice lolly?"

Mother looked at me, her gray eyes stern. "No. You might get shoved and get lost, there are too many people."

"Please." I begged. "I'll be right back. You can watch me from right here. See! The man's right over there."

She took note of the vendor and gave in, digging in her purse for coins. "All right," she said, dropping the change into my palm. "But come straight back."

I thanked her with an air kiss and rushed off, jumping down the high steps of the carriage. I ran to the vendor, but when I turned around to wave at Mother, I found myself surrounded by tall, shiny black boots that were almost as tall as I was. The heavy steps of thick soles resounded—*clack-boom-clack*—on the station platform, soldiers marching in step to the terse commands of the sergeant in charge. Were all these men in gray uniforms getting onto our train? I peered up at the faces. They looked so young and happy, going off to war. Maybe war was not as bad as I thought. It might be a great adventure. For a moment I forgot my fear and wished I were a boy, and older, so I could join the soldiers.

I bought my chocolate ice lolly, licking it fast so that it wouldn't drip onto my good dress. But I wasn't successful. Mother would be upset. One of the soldiers smiled and winked at me, this skinny blue-eyed girl wearing a chocolate-ice mustache. I wiped my mouth with the back of my hand and squeezed through the unending line of marching soldiers.

When I reached the train, Mother stood waiting for me by the door. She pulled me up the two high steps and held me tight, saying she'd been worried when she lost sight of me behind the soldiers. I leaned out of the window to catch a last glimpse of them, as they climbed onto the newly attached cars at the end of the train.

A whistle sounded. Now the crowd—held back earlier by the soldiers—jostled and pushed to get onto the train. Our comfortable compartment was now overfilled. Mother had chosen two seats facing each other so she could exchange one with me, since I often got motion sickness. Two young girls shared one seat, giggling and, I thought, acting foolish. A fat woman balanced a fat child on her knees. The child sucked on a *Schnuller,* then threw it on the dirty floor. Mother hated these pacifiers, big rubbery things with a large yellow rim. The mother picked up the pacifier, wiped it on her spotted sleeve, and shoved it back into the child's mouth. An old woman in another seat coughed and spat into her handkerchief. A pockmarked man smelling of onions and sweat squeezed in next to me. I grew queasy. People who had not been able to get seats crowded the corridor. They sat on their suitcases, blocking the path to the water closet.

Mother said, "Wait here, just a moment, Karin. Keep my seat. I'll be right back." Her georgette dress, navy blue with a pattern of small white flowers, flipped around her slender knees as she clicked out of sight on high-heeled strappy shoes. A little later she returned wearing a big grin. She grabbed the few pieces of luggage we had with us in the compartment and handed me a small cosmetic case. With her gloved hand she straightened out the small triangular hat perched on her chestnut hair, which threatened to slide over one eye, smoothed her spidery little veil, and smiled good-bye to the passengers.

Mother had done it. Her good looks and proper dress convinced the conductor that we belonged in first class. Mother paid no additional money, but it was understood that we would occupy the dining car for most of the trip. That was just fine with me. That was exactly where I wanted to be, and I ordered my favorite: Wiener schnitzel.

The dining car was a peaceful haven; its walls were paneled in shiny mahogany and the tables were covered with white linen. I sipped black currant juice. Then I found the courage to ask, "Mutti, why didn't you marry Uncle Ossie? I liked him. By now we could be in Guatemala."

"I didn't love Oswald. I didn't want to marry him just to get out of Germany."

"But when you sat on the sofa with him and held hands . . ."

"Did you spy on me?"

Yes, I had spied on her, but I couldn't admit it. "No, I just saw you holding hands with him. Oma was there with me, remember? He told us about his country and . . . it sounded so wonderful. I wanted to go there. So much."

Mother softened her look, as if part of her wished we were in Guatemala now.

Less than a year ago, Oswald, the brother of my godmother Tante Gwendolyn, visited us. I had watched them through the keyhole, almost giving myself away with a loud *aah,* when I heard him ask Mother to marry him. They sat near each other on a striped, silken Biedermeier sofa. He put his hand on her knee, and she scooted a few centimeters away from him. I understood that she was pleased, but at the same time she clearly wasn't comfortable sitting so close to him.

He was short and square with a jutting chin, stubby fingers, and hands that were rough and brown from farming in the Guatemalan sun. He told us about his finca, about coffee growing high, lush, and green, about riding horses through sloping hills to the bluest of lakes right next to a volcano. He bought me a baby doll, my first doll with sleeping eyes, and he promised me a white pony and high black boots so the snakes wouldn't bite me.

Between bites of Wiener schnitzel and the jostling movement of the train, I thought of the excitement I'd felt then. I wanted to go to Guatemala and live among people who wore costumes in joyful colors. He'd shown us hand-colored postcards of native people clad in *huipiles* and fancy headgear in purple, pink, and orange. The words *The Land of Eternal Spring* were printed across the landscape and the faces of smiling people. I wanted to go to this land, but when I asked my mother, she shook her head.

"No, Karin," she said. "Oswald is a good man and I've known him since I was a child, but I don't love him."

I had been angry with her a year ago, and I was still angry with her. She was in charge, and I was helpless. Other people said I was smart for my age. I knew what was best for us, so why couldn't she listen to me once in a while? How could she do this to me? Mother had left my father when I was two years old, and we had moved in with Oma, her recently widowed mother. I wanted a new father, especially one who would give me a white horse. I wouldn't need a prince to carry me off. I could gallop off all on my own.

"It's unfair," I said.

"What's unfair?"

"Why do *you* have to decide who'll be my next father? You say you love me. Can't we both decide what's best for *us*?"

Mother laughed. I didn't like the way it sounded. Was she laughing at me? "I do love you, *meine kleine Pröpenine*." She was calling me one of her silly pet names. "But I alone will choose whom I'll marry. I'd have to be very much in love. Even if you love someone as I loved your father, marriage can fail."

"Why couldn't you love someone I love? What's so hard about that?"

Mother looked out the window, ignoring me. "Remember when you two talked?" I pulled on her sleeve so she would pay attention to me. "Uncle Ossie said you had to decide. Time was running out. There might be a war, he said. A big war, like the one you and Oma were in."

"Your memory is pretty good. That was after Austria and Czechoslovakia were annexed. Yes, Oswald said Poland would be next. And then there would be an all-out war, not mere annexation. He was right."

The train rattled on as I put another piece of Wiener schnitzel in my mouth. I chewed while thinking of Oma's tales of the Great War: the hunger they had suffered, and the soldiers who had died. Would those terrible things happen again? Guatemala seemed like a magical kingdom that was now lost to me.

Mother took a sip of her Mosel wine, swirling the pale yellow liquid in the glass, letting the sun's rays transform the wine into gold like the magic potions in my fairy-tale books. I made a silent wish for such a potion. I would drink it, fall asleep, and awaken in Guatemala, the country beautiful.

I had asked my grandmother if that country was as beautiful as Utah, where she grew up. Oma said that it might be even more lovely because Guatemala was tropical, with palm trees, parrots, and monkeys in the forests. Monkeys! Parrots! And quetzals, birds with long sweeping feather trains.

"What are you thinking, Karin? Day dreaming again?"

"Guatemala," I said. "How beautiful it must be. And you stopped us from going there. I'm still mad at you."

The waiter came to the table and asked if we wanted dessert. Oh yes, I wanted *Schwarzwälder Kirschtorte*. The taste of rich dark chocolate with cherries and whipped cream made me forget Guatemala and my unhappiness with my mother.

At least for a while.

Spinach and Studs

We returned to our large, sunny corner apartment on the second floor of a cream-colored building on Hansa Allee, a quiet street in Frankfurt. The allee was divided in the center by a walking path with inviting wrought iron benches and rows of horse chestnut trees. I often perched on the balcony above the sidewalk with my girlfriend Guggi. We leaned against the greenish black, scrolled ironwork, waiting for late summer rains. It was fun to spit plum pits onto the umbrellas of passersby, keeping score of whose pit made more hops or skips when it hit. When someone happened to look up and shake his finger at us, we would run inside giggling so hard that we would pee in our pants.

That was one of the bad things I still did after Nunu had become my best friend. Nunu was several years older than I, and she taught me how to play with dolls and to act more ladylike. Before I met her, I was more at home in a tree, roughing it up with boys. Mother should have thanked Nunu and her satin-and-lace bedroom for having a civilizing effect on me, because, about a year earlier, there had been the horrible incident with Frau Winterfeld and the spinach.

I was five years old at the time, and Oma considered me to be a quiet child, since I spent much of my time drawing with crayons or reading. I played with Guggi or with Esther, the grocers' daughter, but I found it more exciting to play cowboys and Indians with the neighborhood boys. When Oma questioned me about my scabby knees and scraped arms, I told her that the boys had made me play the role of a squaw, and that they had tied me to a tree and whooped around me. But I didn't tell her that I had bitten them and pulled their hair when they got too rough—which was why Oma believed me to be quiet and angelic.

When Herta Winterfeld came to visit us, though, I gave Oma a surprise. She was our guest for the mid-day meal, our *Mittagessen,* and when she swept into the entrance hall, she brushed my sweet aunt Margaret aside as if she were a piece of furniture. I shook hands with Frau Winterfeld, said "*guten Tag,*" and curtsied, but I felt an instant dislike for the woman. Her name—Winter-feld—said it all, for she resembled a cold field in winter. I could not understand why Oma was friends with this gaunt, sticklike woman who had forgotten how to smile. What a contrast to my grandmother, who was warm and gracious. And I didn't like Frau Winterfeld's pearls. They were big white globes that were strung on a long dangling chain and hung from her bony neck and fell past a nonexistent bosom to her waist.

Mother asked if it wasn't dangerous to travel by train wearing those pearls, for they were *real* Oriental pearls. It made me wonder what they were talking about. Frau Winterfeld shook her head and said that no one would ever suspect they were genuine. They were so big they looked like paste. (What kind of paste? I wondered. I was familiar with tomato paste and anchovy paste, but paste made into pearls?) "No," Frau Winterfeld repeated, "I'm perfectly safe wearing them." Mutti, Oma, and my aunt Margaret eyed the pearls and then smiled strangely, the corners of their mouths pulled down. Even at my age, I sensed a feeling of disapproval there.

Oma was the only person in our family who liked Frau Winterfeld. She insisted that Herta was her oldest and best friend. They had known each other since boarding school, when grandmother—age fifteen—first returned to Germany from Utah and had to learn German. The two became friends, and Herta helped Oma with her grammar. When they were older they attended many cotillions together, and it was Oma who gave this would-be spinster the advice that eventually landed Herta a husband.

That story, of course, I learned much later. The Winterfelds had no children, and I thought this was a good thing. I would have pitied any child born to that woman.

We were all seated at the dining table, the damask cloth forming a white island in the room. The wine sparkled in the crystal glasses, and the silver gleamed. Mother had arranged flowers that added splashes of blue, red, and pink to the white, making the table look festive.

I sat across from Frau Winterfeld. I could feel her eyes on me while I ate my soup, her steely gray eyes narrowing whenever the slightest slurp could be heard. I tried to eat without making a sound. Then the potatoes, the roast, and the early springtime spinach were served. I was given a generous heap of green and promptly shoved it to the side on my plate.

"The child doesn't want to eat her spinach," this pearl-dangling enemy said.

The child. I have a name, I thought, why doesn't she use it?

Oma, embarrassed that her friend had found fault with me, chided me and pointed to the spinach on my plate. I stuffed a bite into my mouth, felt those narrow-steel eyes on every chewing move of my jaws, and gagged. Then I managed to choke the green stuff down. I played with the rest of the spinach and ate all of the potatoes, careful not to make one smacking sound.

Everyone had finished. I looked forward to the dessert. My plate still displayed a green mound on the blue of the onion pattern.

"The child must eat her spinach, Elsa," Frau Winterfeld now said, "Do you let children rule your family?"

Mother intervened for Oma, commanding, "Karin, eat your spinach."

I pushed the plate a bit further toward the bouquet of flowers.

"The child has no manners," said Frau Winterfeld. "Now, eat your spinach, child!" She waved a bony finger in my direction, and suddenly her face changed to that of the witch in *Hänsel und Gretel,* right out of my Grimm's *Märchenbuch.* I stared at her, then slowly rose from my seat, and—as if a demon had possessed me—I grabbed the plate and hurled it, spinach and all, right at Frau Winterfeld.

There she sat, with spinach dripping from her eyebrows, spinach coloring her gray face green, spinach encrusting her pearls, spinach on her gray silk blouse, and spinach dripping onto the table cloth and onto the shattered Meissen plate lying on the red Persian carpet. Oma, Aunt Margaret, and Mother all stared at the green ghastliness our guest had become.

I sat down again. Should I run? Where could I hide? A week earlier, I had gone to see a Shirley Temple movie. During the movie, the film strip had torn, and the action had stopped abruptly when Heidi showed something to her grandfather. Everything on the screen looked frozen, the movement, the moment. Now it felt as if the same thing had happened to me. A moving picture had suddenly stopped and the image on the screen remained still. Painfully still. The characters' mouths were wide open and their bulging eyes were all looking at me.

I stood up and yelled, "She can't tell me anything. She's a stranger. I hate spinach!" I'm glad I didn't also blurt out, "I hate her." I ran from the room, half falling over my grandmother's favorite leather armchair and slammed the door.

Oma and Mother made a commotion trying to clean up Frau Winterfeld, then someone called a taxi, and she left.

This would not have happened if Nunu had lived next door. She and her aging parents moved into an adjoining apartment after my sixth birthday. Nunu had the type of toys little girls dream of. She had a small walk-in grocery store, complete with diminutive scales, a cash register that rang, and counters with tiny drawers. The shelves were stacked with replicas of food items in miniature. She had a dollhouse that took up half of the space of her room. Whereas I had only one doll to play with, Nunu had at least six or seven. At Nunu's house the dolls were our children, hers and mine, since she shared everything with me.

But on one particular day, Nunu was visiting relatives with her mother, and I was alone and bored. Thinking about the "war effort" and of Germany's need for metals, I decided to take the silvery studs out of Oma's favorite leather arm chair and donate them to the cause. It was fun to poke them out, and I had done a thorough job. There were only a few studs left. Suddenly, as I sat quietly on the floor of the dining room, next to the chair, the parquet floor shook and the rosettes on the dark red of the Sarouk carpet wavered. Uncle Richard's voice made me drop the last stud I had pulled, and I watched as it rolled over the scroll pattern on the carpet.

"What are you doing?" his voice bellowed. "Have you gone crazy?" He yanked me off the floor, making me drop a rain of ornamental studs. He pointed to the wine-colored leather of the Jugendstil chair. "You are . . ." He flushed red with anger. Then just when he looked as if he would explode, he pulled me across his knees to spank me. I felt his hand hit my bottom—*wham,* and again *wham*—and I wailed.

At that moment Oma came into the room. "Let go of the child. At once." She was by my side in an instant and caught his hand before it could connect with my bottom again. "There is to be no spanking in my house. If Karin has done something naughty, we'll discuss it and punish her. But not with spanking." She thrust out her chest, and Uncle Richard retreated.

By now Oma had seen the mess I'd made. There stood the ornament-free chair, its leather flapping and its fancy studs scattered all over the floor.

"Why, Karin?" Her hands flew to her temples, making me feel so very sorry for my misdeed. "Why on earth did you pull out the studs?"

"I heard the Führer say that we should collect metal." I felt tears pinch my nose so I couldn't breathe, and I slurred my words. "He needs silver and brass, just like everyone collected when Napoleon overran us."

"But Karin!"

"Please Oma . . . ? Pretty soon Otto and Horst . . ."

"Those hoodlums from the Jungvolk?"

These were some of the older neighbor boys—about ten years old. "Oma, they're just doing their duty. They're going to come around to collect metal. We'd help win the war for our country."

I couldn't stop the tears from rolling down my face, more from guilt and confusion than from the pain of the spanking. "I'm sorry, Oma. Do you want me to put the studs back in?" I put my arms around her neck and cried into her silken jabot.

"Karinchen, you never take things from anyone without permission. Even if you think it's for a good cause." She added under her breath, "This man takes everything. My sons. Now he sends children to take . . ." She shook her head and said, "We'll try to put them back again, yes? Maybe Uncle Will can help; he doesn't get as angry as your Uncle Richard."

I adored my two uncles, the paternal figures in my life. I loved Uncle Richard, despite his temper. He was three years older than my mother, and he was living with us while working on a research project at the university. Most weekends he traveled to Leipzig to be with his young wife and new-born son.

My uncles were not cowards. When the war broke out they enlisted immediately. Oma had tried to talk them out of it, but they were stubborn. At that time, they could choose their regiments. Both had doctorates: Will's in the field of art history, and Richard's in archaeology. Now a war was being fought, and although my uncles disagreed with Hitler's policies, they loved their homeland and would fight for Germany. When they enlisted they automatically qualified to be officers, but each officer was required to take an oath of fealty to the Führer. My uncles did not wish to take this oath and refused their commissions.

At suppertime Oma served one of her specialties, rouladen, a certain cut of tender beef stuffed with chopped dill pickles and hard-boiled eggs. I breathed in the aroma of the sauce, and I could hardly wait to be seated, since this was one of the few meat dishes I liked to eat. Uncle Richard's eyes still flashed red, but after a second glass of Frankfurt's apple wine—a wine tasting both sweet and tart—he became more jovial. Even I was allowed to drink a small amount mixed with water. When Uncle Will showed us how easy it was to knock the studs back in, Uncle Richard's good humor returned. In fact he told us about the cavalry regiment he'd joined. He picked me up and hoisted me onto his shoulders, and impersonating a horse, he galloped around the large oval dining room table, encouraging me to yell, "Giddy-up, giddy-up," and I used a napkin as a whip.

My uncles looked handsome in their new uniforms. Uncle Richard's was a dark shade of gray, with brass buttons, reflecting his light blond hair. Uncle Will's brown hair contrasted nicely with the light gray uniform of the *Gebirgsjäger*, a regiment consisting of mainly Austrian and Bavarian alpine skiers. He was posted to go to Finland, to guard against neighboring Russia, our ally at the time, but, as Uncle Will said, "No one can trust the Russian Bear."

The days were colder now and darkness arrived early. Every household had been ordered to black out their windows, Mother explained, to make our cities invisible to enemy planes. Oma had sewn an extra layer of black cloth onto the drapes, making sure each night that they were properly closed, with no space left where they met the wall and where a sliver of light might escape.

I imagined myself to be a bird, flying over the city in the dark. Surely there would be some light or some reflection from the River Main to guide me, letting me know that I was flying over the city rather than over open country.

We celebrated Mother's birthday in October and then Oma's a few weeks later in November. On both occasions, my favorite walnut torte was served, but it wasn't as delightful or as tasty without the topping of whipped cream. Heavy cream was rarely available and butter was rationed. We still had tea—cocoa for me—and always had a reserve of coffee for Oma, who needed it for her tired heart. When I awoke on December 6, the day of Sankt Nikolaus, I opened my bedroom door to look in my shoes for sweets, fruits, and nuts left by Old Nick. Uncle Richard made me wonder if food would become really scarce, as it had been during the Great War, when he said, "Savor your orange, Karin, who knows when you'll see another one."

CHAPTER 2

Skulls and Danzig

CHRISTMAS 1939

Oma said, "Don't be so nervous, Karin. Stop tapping your feet." I tried to keep my feet still, but it was hard. We were waiting for Uncle Will to arrive, and he was an hour late.

On that first Sunday afternoon in Advent we sat around the dining room table, with its wreath made of pine branches in the center. Four thick red candles were fastened to the green. Only one was lit, but each week an additional one would follow, until the fourth of Advent, the Sunday before Christmas, when all four candles would glow.

I sat quietly, sipping hot cocoa, passing my finger back and forth slowly through the candle's flame, while listening to the grown-ups' conversation. Uncle Richard entered the room with his lit cigarette; Oma coughed, waved at the smoke, and asked him to open the window. The aroma of strong coffee and the *Kringle*—small pastries deep fried to a crispy golden color and sprinkled with powdered sugar—filled the room. I hoped Oma would send me to fetch them from the kitchen so I could sneak one of the airy pastries.

The smoke had cleared from the room, and I went to close the window. But I longed to see Uncle Will walking down the street, coming home. I loved him and planned to marry him after I grew up. Of course I never mentioned this to anyone, least of all to my Oma, and not even to Nunu.

We wondered when Will and Richard would be sent to their regiments. Would Will be able to return to Danzig to vacate his flat? Mother and I had visited him there the previous April, just before I had turned six and entered school. That year the art museum in Danzig had hired him as curator for their department of medieval art.

Will rented his flat from an architect who had converted a fifteenth-century warehouse into three apartments. Will's was on the top floor, facing the River Mottlau. I spent hours at the window, watching ships come and go, imagining the foreign ports they had visited. Maybe they had come from Africa or, perhaps, from Guatemala, bringing coffee grown on Uncle Ossie's finca. Maybe they had come from California, where Grandmother's American relatives lived.

If I leaned out far enough to my left, I could see the famous Krantor, a medieval wooden building that housed a crane, an early method by which cargo was lifted from ships. Uncle Will had explained how this was done. The warehouses were built on the banks of the river or canals, here as well as in other Hansa League towns. The freight was lifted by cranes into the warehouses. Hundreds of years of trading had made these Hansa cities wealthy. Uncle Will said this prosperity had built Danzig's Marienkirche, a Gothic jewel made entirely of bricks, with room for twenty-five thousand citizens, more than the population of Danzig at the time of its construction. This prosperity had also financed the sixteenth-century Rathaus, or city hall, and Danzig's richly decorated merchant-guild buildings. "Open your eyes, Karin, and look at all the beauty created by shipping and trade," Uncle Will had said.

If I had to paint Danzig now, from memory, I would paint the city using the color rust, like the color of the ancient bricks of its buildings. But wherever the sun penetrated the city's dark alleys, I would use a lighter color, such as that of a claret wine. Into all of this I would blend the gold of amber found on the shores of the Baltic Sea.

Depending on the angle of the sun, the water in the canals shimmered in colors of brass and copper, due to the reflection from the brick buildings flanking the quays. The city seemed to hold secrets. I was curious to discover those secrets and to search through its dark and twisting medieval alleyways. But I was not allowed to venture out alone.

I loved Danzig not only because my uncle lived there, but because when I was visiting him, I was the center of his attention. I was six, and he considered me to be old enough to be taught my first lessons in architecture. He would take me by the hand and walk with me through the city's narrow streets until we came to a dark church or cathedral. Inside he pointed to the colors that danced on the white walls and on the wooden pews, a mysterious light created by the sun penetrating the stain glass. This light, Will said, was special to Gothic cathedrals. For the faithful in those days this magical light symbolized the presence of God. He said I was old enough to learn to recognize the difference that distinguished Romanesque, an older style with rounded windows, from Gothic, which always had pointed windows. That and flying buttresses on the exterior to help support a greater load, as these churches were now getting larger and larger. Flying buttresses, I loved that description, and it stuck in my mind. After leaving the Marienkirch, this Gothic jewel, he marched me to yet another church. Again, he held the huge creaking oak doors open for me to enter into semidarkness, lit by ever so many flickering votive lights. He didn't speak for a while, and I was pleased to think he shared my need to be still and allow the silent music of the stones to enter my being. Then he said, "Listen, you might hear the echo of ancient prayers." I strained my ears to listen but heard only the mumbled whispers of an old woman kneeling near the alcove of the Virgin Mary.

I did not consciously rationalize those lessons, or those thoughts, because I was too young. But later when remembering, I noticed how deeply they had become engraved in my mind on a simple, emotional level.

I also loved to stay at Uncle Will's apartment because I got to sleep beneath a human skull. Yes, he had a genuine human skull that sat on the bookshelf by his bed. (Will had offered his bed to Mother, but she wouldn't think of sleeping with a skull staring down at her.) The skull was a gift from Will's former girlfriend, a medical student. Mother hated it, but I liked it. He lit a candle inside the skull. Mother wanted me to blow it out. I said I liked it lit. I wanted to prove to Uncle Will that I was made of the same stuff as he.

Now I can admit that the skull was spooky. More than once when I looked at the light inside the hollowed eyes, the hairs on my arms bristled. But it was a good fear, like the tingle felt from ghost stories. At the very same time I felt safe and cozy in the bed, hearing him or Mother breathe out little snorts in their sleep.

The cold air blowing in from the open window blew away the daydream. Where was Uncle Will? I closed the window and was about to pull the drapes shut, when a taxi arrived, a rare and extravagant happening. Uncle Will jumped out and rushed around the vehicle, holding the door open, but for whom? A blonde woman emerged. Her coat opened, revealing a pair of long legs, bronzed and shiny, making me think she wore real silk stockings. Mother had only one pair left and had complained that she could not replace them now, in wartime. (Whenever she got a *Laufmasche,* a run, I had to take the stockings to an old lady who had a little machine that could repair them.)

The woman on Uncle Will's arm wore a gray fur hat that matched her coat. Her bright red saffian boots came halfway up her calves; their soft leather was molded to her legs. Who was this woman? I hated her instantly. Will paid the taxi driver and steered her toward our house.

"Uncle Will's coming," I sang out, "With a lady."

I returned to the table, straining to hear the door to the downstairs entry shut with a thud. Then two pairs of quick footsteps clicked on the stairs, and the clank of a key rattled in the door to our apartment. I shot out into the foyer.

The woman pirouetted for my uncle in her Persian lamb coat. The coat was tight at her narrow waistline and flared out into a bell shape at the bottom. Oma appeared in the door left open to the dining room. Mother greeted Will's friend, whose name was Marlene—I later discovered that Marlene was my mother's friend, and that my mother had introduced her to Will—then presented her to Oma. I hated Marlene when Will virtually peeled her out of her coat. I noticed he was trying to inhale her as well, when he bent over her shoulders and leaned over her neck, unwrapping her as if she were a precious mannequin to be placed into an expensive store display.

I had never seen anyone with features as perfect as Marlene's, and none of my friends from school had mothers who looked like her. I had met several of the young women who modeled with Mother—she did this from time to time to earn extra money—but none of them were that beautiful. Marlene had golden hair, bright blue eyes with thick black lashes, and flawless skin. Oma sucked in her breath, and I think her eyebrows lifted ever so slightly when she took note of Marlene's body, seemingly poured into a red dress made of the softest wool. I stared at her long fingernails, which were lacquered in the same shade of red. Marlene removed the gray fur toque, brushed her fingers through her perfect curls, and then stretched her arms to the upper rack to stow away the hat, looking like one of the goddess statues in the park.

We all went back into the dining room for coffee and *Kringle*. The red Advent candle, matching Marlene's dress and boots, cast a hazy golden light. Mother went to the salon to play the piano, and through the open door we soon heard the sounds of "*Leise rieselt der Schnee*," a lullabylike song about snow gently falling. Although it had rained only yesterday, Mother hoped the idea of snow would put us into a happy, pre-Christmas mood.

I studied Marlene. She seemed pleased to be in our midst, yet she looked bored, smoking one cigarette after another. Uncle Will didn't smoke, and I knew that he didn't like smokers. He always complained when Uncle Richard puffed away. Soon the ashtray overflowed. I watched Oma's eyes follow Marlene's glance as she examined her, by now, empty silver cigarette case. But Richard, the smoker, was happy to refill Marlene's case and oblige her habit. He recommended that she try his Turkish cigarettes. Although they were cheaper, they were stronger and therefore better. I hoped she would decline, but I had already learned at my young age that a smoker must smoke. She accepted his offer with a smile and again dangled a cigarette between her slender fingers, tapping her red nails on the end of a brown stick as she flicked off her ashes. It looked as if she were smoking a cinnamon stick.

Sipping my cocoa, I asked Uncle Will, "Didn't you tell me that you stopped seeing Inge because she began to smoke?"

A hush fell over the room, and not even a coffee spoon clanked against a cup. Uncle Will narrowed his already narrow eyes and shot me a drop-dead look from behind his glasses.

"Who is . . . this Inge?" Marlene asked, smiling.

"I remember she was very pretty, had thick brown hair, and she studied medicine." I said. Then I looked at Uncle Will, "Remember, she gave you the skull by your bed, where you let me sleep when Mutti and I were visiting you in Danzig?"

He tightened his lips. I shook my head and continued, "The skull! Remember? It looked so scary when you let me light the candle in it."

"A skull? Over your bed?" Marlene asked, raising her plucked eyebrows as if trying to have them meet her hairline. "A real skull?"

"From the morgue. Yes, it's real," he said.

"Isn't that rather adolescent? Something students would do?"

"Frau Heumann," Oma answered Marlene, using the formal address, "Don't forget, he was a student until just recently. He is after all . . ."

"We don't have to talk about age, Mother." Uncle Will cut in. He threw Oma a look, silencing us all.

Marlene's face changed color. Her forehead, chin, and even her nose turned the color of her dress. She shrugged and smiled, finished her cigarette and her coffee, emptied her glass of cognac, and then stood up. Uncle Will fetched her coat and carefully wrapped her up again. Then two pairs of footsteps clicked a running rhythm down the stairs. It sounded as if someone were chasing them.

A few days later Uncle Will was sent to Finland.

Käthe Kruse and the Marzipan Goose

Each morning, as soon as I jumped out of bed, I ran to my *Advents Kalender* and lifted off one of the little numbers. It was countdown time till

Christmas. This was my favorite time of year, better than Easter with its chocolate bunnies and better than my birthdays celebrated with friends, presents, and candles on a cake.

This was our first wartime Christmas. Uncle Will, stationed in Finland, was under orders to go to Bavaria on a courier run. I had hoped that he would be able to stay with us for a few days, since the train passed through Frankfurt. I would also miss Uncle Richard, who had gone back to Leipzig to celebrate Christmas with his wife and son.

Oma and Mutti had talked about soldiers who had died in Poland, and I knew that it was a sad time for some families. But snuggled in the warmth of my family's love, I was unaware of grief. The war was like a remote presence into which the siren's sound—an air-raid drill at this stage of the war—foreshadowed what would soon become reality.

Despite the cold, women stood at street corners blowing hot breath into their freezing hands, ringing little bells to draw attention to their metal boxes. They were collecting coins for the *Winterhilfe;* the money went to the families of those serving in the army. Bells chimed, coins tinkled, and the women smiled, *"Danke schön."*

Whenever the doors opened to one of the bakeries, tempting aromas of gingerbread and cinnamon stars escaped into the December air and mingled with the fresh pine scent of the Christmas trees being sold on street corners. I fantasized about the sweets and almonds that would appear on my own *Bunte Teller*—a "colorful plate" on which mandarins, nuts, gingerbread and cinnamon star cookies, and other Christmas treats are heaped. Each family member gets their own plate, and I looked forward to eating my fill. Some food-stuffs had become scarce, and I resigned myself to the fact that this year I would not get marzipan, my all-time favorite. But Oma and Mutti had saved food ration coupons and scoured farms in the country for butter, honey, and nuts, and Oma had obtained a goose just before the holiday. We would have a rich Christmas.

My grandmother did her best to create delicious sweets from the little available to her. She made quince bread, sugar burnt almonds, and caramel with walnuts. She tried to make something resembling marzipan from pota-toes, oats, sugar, ground almonds, and almond flavoring. Although it was tasty, it definitely was not marzipan.

I had seen mother hide a long white carton in the wardrobe in the hall-way. I was curious. It was just days before Christmas, and the house was quiet. Everyone had gone out on errands. I climbed onto a wing chair, but I still couldn't reach the top shelf holding the box. The box looked innocent, stashed away above towels and sheets smelling of lavender and Persil soap. I stepped on the armrest. Now if I stretched my skinny arm a little farther, I could pull the carton to the edge of the shelf. There. Yes, I got it. Then I almost fell.

The box was easy to open, and I dug into the rustling white tissue paper. That must be it. I pulled and tugged on what felt like taffeta, and wait! I stared into the face of the most beautiful doll I'd ever seen.

Mutti! She'd said that she couldn't afford much of a present this year. But she had bought me this doll, the doll of my dreams. She knew I wanted a Käthe Kruse doll more than anything in the world.

Well, there were some things I wanted even more than this doll. I wanted to have a father who would live with us, a father who would tell me that he loved me. Forget those thoughts, I said to myself. Vati is not coming back. He has remarried, and I have a three-year-old brother. Vati has the son he had wished for. And as for me? Oh well. Soon I will have this beautiful doll.

I still loved the baby doll Uncle Ossie had given me, but this new doll was special. It was the creation of Käthe Kruse, who hand sculpted the heads. She painted the faces of her dolls to resemble her own daughters' and made wigs for the dolls from human hair. Unlike the artificial-looking dolls with faces made of porcelain or celluloid, Käthe Kruse dolls looked like real girls. I had wished for a doll with hair the color of my own and with blue eyes like mine. And here she was, wearing a sky blue taffeta dress and black patent shoes, and her hair, though longer than mine, was the very same shade of ash blonde.

I could hear footsteps coming up the stairs, and I almost slid off the chair. I quickly shoved the box back in place, jumped down, and tiptoed to the piano. By the time the key sounded in the lock, I was sitting on the piano bench, innocently practicing my scales.

"Well," Mother said as she entered. "What have you been doing all afternoon?"

"I've been practicing."

"Not for very long, I just heard you start when I opened the door."

I never got away with anything. She *always* knew.

She walked straight to the wardrobe and opened it. Oh no, maybe I didn't close the carton properly? But in her carefree manner she pushed several more boxes onto my doll on the top shelf.

"You're not to look. Christmas is only two days away. You can restrain yourself that long, can't you?"

"Do you have a present for me in there?"

"But of course. And for Oma and Uncle Will and Aunt Margaret and Tante Paula."

I frowned. "Must you give *her* something too?"

I felt guilty for not liking Tante Paula, my deceased grandfather's older sister, who always picked arguments with my mother and Aunt Margaret. They were such opposites, those two. Aunt Margaret radiated pure love, while Tante Paula was a veritable "broom," a *Besen,* as we called women resembling witches. Tante Paula hated it when Oma and Aunt Margaret spoke English with one another. They never did this to exclude: they were just more comfortable speaking in the language of their youth. I felt very grown up and part of an "American" inner circle because I spoke a little English by that time and could join in their conversations.

Even though my father didn't live with us, we were a happy family. Still, I missed having a normal family, with a father and a mother. In school, I felt like someone who didn't belong. I was the only child whose parents were divorced. There were times when the girls made fun of me. They said, "No wonder your father left you. A girl with ugly glasses, and a *Kratzbürste* to boot." A *Kratzbürste* is a brush that scratches so that made me mad, and I beat them up, turning me indeed into a *Kratzbürste.*

Uncle Will arrived by train a few hours before we would all go to the church on Christmas Eve. All of us, except Oma who was busy with last minute preparations in the kitchen, went to the four o'clock service. It was dusk by that time, and it snowed.

Voices singing Silent Night, *Stille Nacht,* filled the church, and Mother, who was a warm mezzo, sang second voice to my child's soprano. The church was lit by candles, and the pastor spoke of the war and the sacrifices we must all make in these times. May God bless our soldiers and our *Vaterland.*

Our *Vaterland.* To me it seemed more a land of mothers. And I had two: Oma and Mutti.

I had a girl doll, soon to be mine. I could hardly wait to hold her and to run my fingers over the softness of her blue dress, which I knew was fancier than any I would ever own.

I shook my head at that thought. No, I wasn't being fair to Mother. She did the best she could with the little money she earned with her weaving. I had pretty clothes and she had made most of them. Mother had a talent for remembering every tuck and pleat of the dresses Shirley Temple or little Traudl Stark wore in movies. Later she sketched them, and when I needed a dress and she found the right cloth, she made me an exact duplicate of the original. My school friends envied my pretty dresses. But the process was painful, since Mother was impatient. While I was standing on a low table being fitted by her, she would suddenly jab me with a pin, drawing blood.

This for fidgeting only the slightest. After a few of these sessions, I hated anything having to do with sewing or with needles.

My father paid very little child support, only a hundred reichsmark of his three thousand reichsmark monthly salary as chief editor of the *Liegnitzer Tageblatt*. He paid no alimony. When my parents were still married, the arguments between Omi, his mother, and my mother had gotten to the point where one of the two women had to leave. Omi was from Estonia and, Father argued, he could not desert her in a foreign land. It was Mother who left.

Some time ago I had eavesdropped when Mother argued with Uncle Richard about the terms of the divorce. My grandfather, a well-respected *Regierungsrat* (government councillor), had told his only daughter that she was not to accept a penny of alimony from *that* man. She didn't. Uncle Richard had called it foolish pride.

Suddenly the crescendo of the organ, sounding the final note of the service, brought me back into the wooden pew beside my mother.

Our boots crunched us home on snow-covered streets. We carried small flashlights, tiny, yellow owls' eyes darting about in the black night. The snow continued to fall. It was fun to kick the white powdery stuff and watch it fly in swirls around my feet. Snow drifted slowly to earth, as though Frau Holle was shaking out her down-feathered pillow from the window of the sky. I opened my mouth, trying to taste the snow as it settled on my tongue, cold and wet. The night was so peaceful, it was hard to believe a war was going on, and somewhere, someone was being killed.

We shook wet snowflakes from our wooly hats and coats and smelled Christmas in the scent of pine and candle wax. The aroma of carp and caper sauce floated into the foyer. We jostled and laughed as we walked to the dining room.

The beeswax candles in the silver candelabra were lit, and the table was set with Oma's precious possessions. Silver gleamed, polished to a high sheen, and the Rosenthal china Oma always used for Christmas—white with a burgundy and gold rim—spread its luster on white damask. German sekt bubbled in Bohemian cut crystal glasses.

Grandmother stood behind her chair and bowed her head in prayer. How beautiful she looked. Her smooth skin had flushed pink from the heat of the kitchen, and her hair was wound into a French twist and shimmered like pewter with an added wider streak of silver. We bowed our heads, echoed her "Amen," and sat down to eat. Fish, usually carp bleu, was the traditional food for Christmas Eve. I was not overly fond of this meal, but Oma had a talent for making everything taste wonderful.

Long before it was brought to the table, I could smell the *Apfelstrudel* still in the oven. Oma served it with a custard-sherry sauce. After dessert, it was time to go into the salon and receive our presents. Uncle Will suddenly disappeared; then I could hear my mother play "Oh, come, little children" on the piano. When she added her voice to the music and sang, "*Oh Kinderlein kommet*," as if by magic, the tall French doors to the living room opened.

And there stood the tree, reaching from floor to ceiling. Lit by what seemed to be a thousand flickering, sparkling candles. The enchantment of it. I forgot to breathe at that moment, gazing at that wonder of light, and tears filled my eyes.

Each year the tree seemed to be a miracle. No one, except Mother and one of my uncles, who helped her light it, saw the tree before it was fully decorated and lit. A long brass wand with a small torch on one end was used to light the candles, while the other end terminated in a cone-shaped hat for snuffing them out. A big bucket of water was hidden behind the tree, just in case something caught on fire.

I greeted my favorite ornaments: angels with wax-doll faces floating above pine branches, and guitars, trumpets, drums, and tiny toy soldiers in red and blue uniforms from another time nestled in the green. There were silver foil candies, gilded walnuts, and brightly colored paper chains that I had made in school. Glass baubles glistened and stars sparkled, rocking horses rode the air, and silver *Lametta* cascaded from the branches. Below the tree was the manger, the *Krippe,* and the Holy Family, all carved from wood.

Our presents were not wrapped, that was not the custom. Two tables lined one side of the room and on them our gifts were displayed. Each person's Bunte Teller sat on his or her section of the table.

I rushed to embrace my doll. I named her Christine. She was everything I wished to be: her eyes were of the clearest blue, not mixed with gray and green like mine, and her hair was shinier and longer than my own. Tears of happiness left wet spots on Christine's blue dress.

"Have you taken a look at your plate yet?" asked Uncle Will.

I jumped up and looked.

A marzipan goose! It lay on its own platter decorated with small bits of green and red candy, looking as if it had come straight out of a miniature oven with its brown legs sticking up. It weighed perhaps half a pound and was more splendid than any I had ever seen.

"Where did you get that goose?"

"I traded it up in Finland. I think it's from Sweden."

"They still have marzipan like that?"

"Why, yes. Sweden's a neutral country. And there's more. Apples and pears for everyone." He pulled out a paper sack filled with marzipan in the shape of fruit.

"You know I love marzipan more than anything in the world."

"Yes, I remembered," he said, and when I threw my arms around him and covered his face with kisses, he colored red.

I slept with my doll in my arms, but I kept waking up, afraid I might wrinkle her dress. The next morning, after my breakfast of stollen and hot cocoa, I went back into the Christmas room and marveled at my presents. The goose remained intact within its cellophane wrapping, while I went to the kitchen to help Oma stuff the real Christmas goose with apples and chestnuts.

Mother was talking in the room next door, interrupted now and then by the scratchy voice of Tante Paula.

"To buy this expensive doll, in these times. Astrid, I call that frivolous."

"It wasn't *that* expensive," Mutti said.

"Bah. Everyone knows how much these dolls cost. A fortune. About as much as that man sends for Karin in two months, I would venture."

"You'd better not venture, Tante Paula. You're wrong, and this is Astrid's business," Uncle Will's voice cut into the off-key duet.

"You can tell her," Mother nodded to Uncle Will.

He told the tale of the doll. The doll I loved. The doll about which I would never feel the same again.

Mother had wanted to fulfill my wish, but Tante Paula was right, the doll was beyond Mother's means. Then Mother saw an ad in the newspaper, offering a Käthe Kruse doll for sale. It was brand new and still in its box. She went to see it. Yes, it was everything the ad had promised, and it cost only half of the original price. The woman wept when she handed the doll to my mother. Her husband had been killed by partisans in Poland. There would be no money coming in, and she could no longer afford to give the doll to her daughter. The girl must not know, she whispered to my mother as she tried to hide the box when the child entered the room. Mother met a little girl, about my age, with wire-rimmed glasses and blonde pigtails.

And now the doll was mine. I picked Christine up from the chair and looked at her through my own wire-rimmed glasses, which I took off to wipe my eyes.

The doorbell rang. It was Helga, one of my classmates who lived down the street. I was proud to show off my presents. When she was about to leave, I held up my Bunte Teller and offered her a piece.

She grabbed the goose.

My great big marzipan goose.

I stood gape-mouthed in the open doorway and watched her slide down the shiny banister holding the goose high in her right hand, a grin on her face.

My mouth was still open when Oma found me, staring at the disappearing girl with *my* goose in *her* hand. I must have looked like a *dumme Gans,* a stupid goose.

Oma knew. I did not have to say a word. She took the plate from my hand, pulled me into the apartment, and closed the door. "There is a difference," she said, "Between being hospitable or allowing someone to take advantage of you."

"But she was my guest. How could I tell her not to take it?"

"You could be honest. You could have put your hand over her fingers and told her, 'This is a special gift from my uncle. You may take any other sweet, but not this.'"

I felt like an idiot then and, worse, like a coward. I sobbed and sobbed and wet Oma's good silk dress.

I went to bed feeling miserable. I could not understand how this girl could have betrayed me so. And I had been weak. All of the previous night's happiness disappeared: the goose was gone. I still had my doll, my Christine, but looking at her also made me sad. I curled up beneath the big, white goose feather duvet, and read the story of the "Little Match Girl" in my Hans Christian Andersen fairy-tale book, the one my father had given me a year ago. The story made me feel grateful for my own warm bed. But then the tears came again when I thought of the little girl who did not get a doll for Christmas.

The little girl who had lost her father.

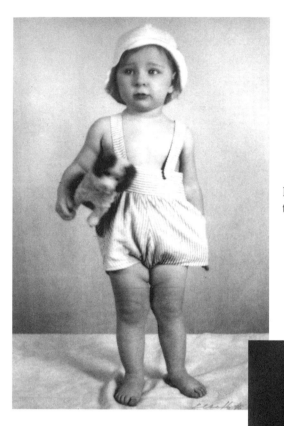

Baby Karin with
toy dog, *ca.* 1934.

Mother rescued my beloved teddy
bear from our collapsing apartment
building during a bombing raid in
Berlin in August 1943.

In the arms of polar bear at the beach, with the famous German wicker *Strandkörbe* in background, 1938.

Aunt Margaret and me in Frankfurt, *ca.* 1938.

CHAPTER 3

Aunt Margaret
and the Tapeworm

Nineteen forty brought many changes. Mother went to Berlin shortly after the New Year, where she interviewed with the head of the costume department of the Berliner Staatsoper for a position as assistant costume designer. This had been her dream. She had studied costume design in the Berliner Kunst Akademie before she married my father. If the theater hired her, she would no longer have to weave cloth for men's tweed jackets or for tapestries.

Tante Grete, whom I called Aunt Margaret most of the time, especially when we spoke English with each other, lived near my school, and from time to time I would drop by her modest flat on my way home. I visited her more often now, thinking that we would probably move to Berlin. I felt safe in the cocoon of her dark-walled living room, which smelled of camphor, peppermint, and valerian tinctures. She made me feel as if I were quite grown up. We sipped tea from her delicate black, red, and gold Minton china cups, and while seated in her overstuffed chintz chair, I would beg her to tell me stories.

She often talked about the Great War, in which she had served as a nurse. She had been a member of a Lutheran order of women known as *Johanniter Schwestern*. In the photos she showed me, she wore a habit resembling a nun's, with an impressively folded white cap. She lived the life of a chaste, unmarried woman, the life of a nun.

One afternoon Aunt Margaret pulled an old trunk from behind a screen and inserted a key into its rusty lock. I remember the trunk creaking open, the noise the hinges made, Aunt Margaret's hands dipping into yellowing tissue paper, and her swollen fingers slowly unwrapping the paper. I remember the dry rustling sound, crinkling like forgotten times. I can still smell the camphor balls. Her rounded figure, clothed in black, bent low and carefully unfolded the contents, slowly revealing an ashes-of-roses, moiré ball gown.

She held it up. I touched the cool brittle silk, using two fingers only, afraid it might disintegrate beneath my hands.

When Aunt Margaret held it against her figure, I was amazed at how the years had rearranged her shape. As a young woman, she must have been much taller. Somehow age had squashed her body, making her square.

"When you grow up, Karin, and if they have fancy balls again, your mother could alter it for you. The color would look pretty with your blonde hair. I certainly loved this dress."

"It's beautiful. Like for a princess. Mother didn't want it?"

"Flapper styles were in fashion when your mother was young. Straight, shiftlike dresses. You've seen her photos?"

"Yes." I made a face. I didn't like those shapeless dresses. "Do you think when I'm all grown up young ladies will wear gowns like this again?"

"I think they might. Fashions skip a generation or two, then they come back."

I held the dress up to me, looking into her standing oval mirror. The dress looked rather peculiar against my child's body, my skinny legs, clad in brown knee socks, protruding from the rose-colored silk. I noticed the waist, such a slender waist, and Aunt Margaret had fit into this? There was a gracefully curved neckline dipping down the shoulders. Rosettes from the same material grew on each sleeve and on the bustle. The skirt swirled like a bell.

"You must have looked so beautiful in this dress," I said.

"Well, Egon thought so. That's when he fell in love with me. The first night I wore this dress." Her face took on a dreamlike look. "Anyway, he said he did. And I fell in love with him."

"I never knew you'd been in love. Who was he? Why didn't you marry him?"

She went on to tell me about Count Egon and the first night he had waltzed her out onto the stone terrace to gaze at the moon. The setting added to the romance: it was late spring, the gardens were lush with flowering trees, and the air silken and full of the scent of lilac. "And you know," she went on, her eyes getting moist, "The moon was full and orange, hanging low above the trees and mirrored in the small lake beyond the rolling lawns. You remember, a year or so ago you played on that lawn with the rabbits?"

I remembered. We were at Schloss Prittag, the château of the Count Finkensteins, our relatives who had taken in Aunt Margaret and my grandmother when they first arrived from Utah as half-orphans. Prittag was one of several small palaces built in Pomerania and Silesia by the landed gentry in imitation of Frederick the Great's Sanssouci Palace in Potsdam.

When I visited Schloss Prittag, Uncle Reini and Tante Anna, by then an ancient couple, had received me with open hearts. Tante Anna took me to play with their pet rabbits and gave me chocolate treats. I thought it was because I had no father. Well, I had a father but my parents' divorce was still considered a disgrace by most people, who treated me as if I had a disease their own family might catch. Not so here. Uncle Reini and Tante Anna extended their hospitality and generosity down the generations, first to Oma and then to her children and now to me. I liked Prittag, where they had horses, dogs, and tame rabbits.

But I wanted to hear more of Aunt Margaret's story. "Tell me about this Count Egon," I said.

"Egon was blond, handsome, a *Dragoner*."

"What's that? A dragon slayer?"

She laughed, sounding surprisingly young. "No, *Dragoner* are part of the elite cavalry. He looked splendid in his bright blue uniform, silver buttons, white-and-gold epaulets, and the wide white-and-gold band across his chest . . ." She stopped, and a tear slid down the crease between her shiny nose and her yellowish cheek.

"We went riding through the woods of Prittag, he took me out on a little row boat, and before the summer ended he asked me to marry him."

"Then, why didn't you?"

She shook her head and for a moment hid her face in her folded arms resting on the table. When she looked up at me, she was calm and her expression had changed. Her forehead wrinkled, and she looked angry. "I loved Egon, and he had told me he loved me. When he asked Uncle Reini for my hand—yes, Uncle Reini was my guardian, your grandmother's too— he learned I had no dowry. He turned on his heel and left the house. He didn't even have the courage to talk to me and tell me what was happening. I had to hear it from Uncle Reini."

"What a rat. Uncle Reini should have ridden after him and shot him. I would have."

She stroked my hair, then she went to the kitchen to brew another pot of tea.

I swiveled around and reached for a photograph of Aunt Margaret when she was young. I tried to imagine her among the landed gentry. At Schloss Prittag, she must have seemed as exotic as a heroine out of a novel. Even now her hair was impressive. The other day she had removed some of the metal hairpins holding it up, and a long river of black shot with silver tumbled to below her waist. Her hair was so heavy she claimed it had led to a lifetime of headaches. I was not aware of any vanity in Aunt Margaret, but she must have been vain regarding her hair. She prided herself on its length and never cut it. Her eyes looked Asian, with that strange fold on the upper lid. They were not at all like the eyes of other Germans, not like Grand-mother's either, whose eyes were round and blue. I imagined Aunt Margaret stood out, while the breath of the wild and wide open spaces of the American West still clung to her. Her tales of grizzly bears and Indians and of having played with the many children of Brigham Young, and the chil-dren of her other Mormon neighbors, some of whom still had several wives, must have sounded strangely foreign and must have enlivened the boring evenings of the provincial aristocrats.

But Count Egon had looked for money; he did not want to be enter-tained by an intelligent and out of the ordinary wife. He disappeared. When I looked at the romantic rose-colored soft silk dress again, I felt very, very sad.

"You know, Karin, there were many years when I felt estranged from Germany, even though I still spoke the language. After all I was born in Berlin and . . ."

She paused, and I cut in, "How old were you when you went to America?"

"Seven. That's another story. First the ship, then the train trip across the plains, and then reaching the Rocky Mountains."

I asked, "Are they all bare, all rocky? Can one climb them?"

"They are very high," She smiled. "But not as jagged as the Alps. There are woods and lakes and they are very beautiful. In some places the earth and the hills are red, like bright copper, the loveliest sight . . ." Again her voice trailed off. "I learned so many things when I went to school there. Yes, in Salt Lake City." She nodded, answering my questioning eyes. "We had such different notions there. It was very democratic. When you're older you'll learn what that means. It's a very beautiful idea, democracy. It means the people have a voice in government, the president, the Congress, they all are of the people and for the people. You can be the son of a poor farmer and become president."

"Like our Führer. He was born poor. And now he leads our country."

She coughed. "That's not exactly what I had in mind." I could tell she struggled to regain her thought. She continued, shaking her head, "I was so naïve. I knew some women in Germany had dowries, but I didn't think that was important. The idea . . . that a man would marry for money." She stopped talking to blow her nose. "I was happy when your grandmother found a good man who fell in love with her. Your grandfather didn't look for money or a dowry. Yes." She smiled when she said this. "Your grand-parents were very happy." She took a deep breath and said, "Funny how life is. A year after Egon left, Charles arrived."

"Who's Charles?"

"Well, if I had married him, you'd have a very well-to-do auntie now. He, as they say in America, was 'sweet on me,' all those years back, in Utah. But his father was a bishop in the Mormon church, and since I was Lutheran, his family did not approve of me. Then his father died and left him silver mines in Utah and Nevada. Copper mines too. Charles came to Germany on the Grand Tour of Europe, and he proposed marriage. Ha," she giggled like a young girl, remembering. "He wanted me to introduce him to Europe's cul-ture. I said, no."

"Why? Was he ugly?"

"It wasn't that. But I had loved Egon, and he . . ." She seemed at a loss for words. Then she said, "Some people only love once in their lifetime." She shrugged her shoulders. "Silly? No?"

"I'm never going to fall in love." Then I thought about what I'd just said. It did seem rather drastic, so I added, "Only with someone who loves me. Like Opa loved Oma."

I fantasized at what might have been. I could have had this sweet and wonderful aunt in America. A rich aunt at that. Then Mother, Oma, and I could have gone to the land I longed for, to Utah, to America! But more than likely, Mother would not have wanted to go. I thought about all this a bit longer, jumped from my chair, and kissed Aunt Margaret on the cheek.

"What brings this on?" she asked.

"I'm happy that you are my aunt and live here and not in America."

Aunt Margaret had devoted her life to others. The only work acceptable for a young woman of her background was nursing or, perhaps, missionary work. When World War I broke out she was in her early forties and was the head nurse of surgery in the hospital of the University in Berlin. Germany needed nurses on the front lines, and she had volunteered. The stories she told me about the Balkans, where she had served, were more exciting to me than any of the tales in my story books.

While traveling through the mountains, she had to endure being bumped black and blue by horse carts bouncing over rough terrain. The lazarettes, or field hospitals, were primitive affairs. Toward the end of the war, after 1917, supplies had run out, and even the rats were starving. Big black rats would run over her body at night when she tried to sleep. She showed me little scars on her arm, where they had bitten her. She had crawled deep under the covers and endured suffocating heat, rather than expose any part of herself for another rat to chew on.

Then she told me that she had once had a tape worm.

"What's that?" I asked.

"Well, it's a long white worm, sort of flat and several meters long, that lives in your stomach and intestines, and you can't get rid of it. Anyway, it's not easy. It eats what you eat, so you get very thin. It can starve you to death. Sometimes parts of it come out, but if the head, which faces up toward your own head, stays in you, it grows another body."

"*Eeeh,*" was all I could say. "How awful. Couldn't you take some medicine to kill it?"

"No. Like I said, parts of it can be killed, but the head grows the worm again. But I'll tell you how I got rid of mine." She leaned closer to me and whispered, "You have to starve yourself, so the worm also starves. You get him really hungry, and then you take a bowl of hot milk and sit over it, with your mouth open, inhaling the steam."

"Why?"

"Because now, the worm is very hungry, and he smells the milk and he . . ." She stopped and made a wry smile, turning down the corners of her mouth.

"He what? Go on, go on." My fingers drummed on the wooden table.

"Well, he comes out of your mouth. The head comes out, you have to be quick and wear a pair of woolen gloves so he doesn't slip away. Then you grab the thing and quickly pull it out. And try not to throw up or you might bite off part of the worm."

"*Ooh,* that's disgusting. I think I'm going to be sick. Did you get the whole worm then?"

"Yes. He was long, over two meters, that's longer than your Uncle Will is tall. I never had another tape worm. Thank God for that."

She served me another cup of peppermint tea with honey and an almond cookie, the taste of which obliterated the image of the white and slippery worm.

But soon, I was ready for more stories. "Tell me more," I begged her.

"Another time, Karin, you should be going home now. It's getting late."

And so it was. I hurried to catch the electric tram and was home in time for supper.

There was little news from the front, and the war seemed to be on hold. I heard people call it a *Sitzkrieg,* a sitting war, where nothing much happened. I imagined soldiers sitting around, smoking, and telling stories, firing cigarette lighters instead of guns.

Mother had received notice that she had been accepted by the opera and had gone to Berlin to find an apartment for us. She wrote that apartments were hard to come by because the war had brought many government workers to Berlin.

I felt excited about moving to the capital. I had heard about the U-Bahn and the S-Bahn, the city trains speeding under and above ground. But I was also fearful. In Frankfurt I knew my way. I could take the streetcar to almost any place in town. Berlin was so large, how would I ever get around? And I had friends here, especially Nunu. She was the closest I had ever come to having a sister, and I knew I would miss her immensely. And I would miss Mother's work space beneath the roof, where she had placed her loom, which was soon to be sold. I loved to climb the many flights of stairs to this garret room and have Mother tell me stories of her student days in Berlin. All the while the loom's shuttle flew back and forth, *clink-clank, clink-clank,* again and again.

The tiny mansard was filled with this monster loom and with the carousel-like wheel on which Mother wound up skeins of wool.

On one of our last days in Frankfurt I climbed the stairs to this attic space one more time, remembering all the afternoons I had spent there. I had climbed onto the carousel wheel and Mother had spun me round and round, winding the wool while giving me a fun ride. I had squealed and laughed. Sometimes she would tickle me, and then I would hug her. Those moments were among the most perfect ones spent with Mother. But sometimes, I had gone upstairs alone, a fairy-tale book hooked under my arm. Finding the room empty spooked me. I felt too scared to read. Then I sat on the bench of the loom and imagined a witch nearby. The witch would be behind the wall or behind the doors that led to the open attic space where Oma and our cleaning woman hung out the laundry to dry. Or she might be near the space where Oma dried peas on large trays with holes, so the air could circulate. I don't know why I went up there alone, knowing full well that I'd be scared.

I thought about the move to Berlin, and I knew I would miss Hansa Allee, the wide street we lived on, which was divided in the center by a tree-lined path. I loved the rows of stately horse chestnuts. In the spring, they looked regal, with their cream-colored blossoms that stood upright like candles. In the autumn, these blossoms turned into polished stones the color of mahogany. I would miss Corpus Christi in May, when I too pretended to be Catholic. I then had run up to my room, put on a white dress, and joined Nunu when she marched in procession down the middle of the allee. Rotund priests would walk by and hand out candies to the children. I would miss all of it.

We were all crying when we embraced Aunt Margaret in a long farewell. The good-bye from Nunu made me feel like throwing up. My chest had shooting pains. Mother gave me her word that she'd send me to visit Nunu and her parents when I was a little older, but that was so far into the future that she might as well have said you'll meet Nunu on the moon. We held each other tight and mingled our tears. I said, trying to be funny, "The Indians in America make a little slit in their wrists and exchange blood. Then they are 'blood-brothers.' We're exchanging our tears, so we are 'cry-sisters.' " But Nunu didn't laugh; she just cried harder.

The Big City

Berlin was big, turbulent, and noisy. Our apartment on Bismarck Strasse in Steglitz was smaller than our Frankfurt apartment, but it was comfortable enough. My walk to school was less than a mile, an easy distance. But I was lonely, and I missed Nunu so much that I often cried myself to sleep.

In school I met Erika, whose long blonde braids I envied. She lived nearby, and we began walking to school together. Although we became friends, my friendship with Erika was different from my friendship with Nunu: Nunu was motherly and loving, whereas Erika was aloof. I could never get close to her. Erika, whose mother was English like Guggi's mother, also differed greatly from wild girl Guggi, my plum pit-spitting friend. Guggi was full of mischief and fun to be with, while Erika was a very well-behaved young lady, even at the age of eight. She smiled, showing dimples, but she seldom giggled a rib-splitting sort of giggle. I didn't like that our teachers preferred her to me.

Spring brought warmer days. Lilacs showed buds, and forsythias began to paint their branches yellow and green. Oma and I explored Berlin by subway, which seemed mysterious, traveling at high speeds underground, and by taking the S-Bahn, the train above ground. I walked around our neighborhood and became familiar with the routes of the streetcars and the buses. All of the routes were connected, and there were stops on almost every corner in Berlin. Children enjoyed a freedom in those days that is now lost. Berlin, a city of four million people, was a conglomeration of small neighborhoods, some of which were almost like villages. The River Havel connected smaller and larger lakes, one of them the Wannsee. One day Erika and I took the S-Bahn to this lake. There we bought *Brausepulver*. This sweet and bubbly powder tickled our noses as we licked it from the palms of our hands, and we sneezed while we watched the sailboats crisscross the rippling surface of the lake. The sails of these boats looked like white fairy wings.

But mostly I liked to go off by myself and read. I would pick one of my fairy-tale books and stroll a few blocks to the cemetery. I preferred this to the small park across from our apartment, where people were walking dogs or carrying on loud conversations. There was silence in the cemetery. I had made a stone bench my favorite place. There an ancient willow wept an enclosure of graceful branches around me, making me feel invisible.

At a friend's boathouse on the Wannsee, Mother had stored Uncle Will's *Faltboot,* a small foldable canoe. On some weekends Mother would take me with her to the lake. She and I would carry the boat to the water and then paddle to isolated parts near the shore. Sometimes we hid in the high brown reeds, growing there in patches, surprising the wild ducks, which took off in flight, leaving streamers of glistening drops in midair. If we found a lonely stretch of beach, we would pull the boat up onto the sand, and she and I would get out and float in the water. I'd sometimes dive under and nibble on her leg to scare her.

Our days were tranquil, and Mother was happy with her work at the theater. Since she no longer spent hours at the loom, and her hands had lost their roughness. I watched her stretch out her long fingers and admired her smooth skin and long red fingernails.

She also began taking singing lessons. Her voice teacher believed her unusual timbre—despite her being over thirty—could lead to an operatic career. He didn't charge for the lessons. But mother had stage fright. Whenever she faced an audience, her vocal cords would freeze, and she could not produce a single sound. At that time a choir was performing in the Kaiser Wilhelm Gedächtniskirche, now a famous bombed-out memorial church that has been preserved as a ruin, on Kurfürstendamm. Mother was to sing a solo, Handel's "Largo." Here, in the church's semidarkness, near the organ and partially hidden, her voice felt free to soar above the audience, rising to the vaulted ceiling. As her voice floated above me, I was filled with wonder and awe. Her voice was mellow and ethereal. I knew that my mother was singing, but it seemed as if I were listening to the otherworldly voice of a woman whom I didn't know.

At home, when Oma, Mother, and I sang silly sentences to one another in operatic style, such as "Bring me the coffee pot" or "Will you do the dishes?" I tried to make my voice sound as true and as on key as hers. When I was older I took voice lessons as well, also on a scholarship, but neither my voice nor my pitch was as perfect as hers.

Sometimes Mother would take me to Café Kranzler and spoil me with hot chocolate and cake. We usually sat outside on the sidewalk, but if we heard the sad strains of gypsy violins through the half-opened doors, she would gather up her handbag and gloves and take me by the hand to move inside. The violinists came to our table and serenaded her. They also smiled at me, which made me feel very grown up and important.

The place was stylish. The mahogany walls were shiny, and glittering crystal chandeliers hung from the ceiling. The chairs we sat on were white and gold. Small lamps wearing tiny parchment hats sat on most tables. Just as Mother always wore a hat, the only item of clothing she could purchase without ration cards. She indulged her need for fashion with these perky little things that would sit on her brown hair, slightly to one side, often with a feather whipping about or a little veil half hiding her gray eyes.

At this stage in the war, elegant restaurants and cafés were still able to purchase coffee, tea, and chocolate, items that we could no longer buy in stores.

As summer vacation neared, Mother announced, "You are going to visit your father." With a grimace, she added, "You have another brother, Karin. Kraus now has two sons. That should make him happy."

Mother had told me the story of my birth. It had been a difficult delivery, involving forty-eight hours of labor, followed by a ripping apart birth requiring a multitude of stitches. I came into the world right after midnight, and around seven, on the way to his newspaper office, my father waltzed into the room. He placed some tulips on the nightstand, flowers he had pilfered from the garden of a vacant house. He laughed at this, as if it were a joke. His excuse was that the stores were not yet open.

A nurse smiled at him and told him he was the father of a healthy little fräulein. His smile faded into a frown, and he said, "What, a girl?" That's what he said. "*Was, ein Mädchen?*"

Mother never forgave him that remark. When she told me, it hurt me too. How could Father have been so unfeeling? Didn't he like daughters, didn't he like me?

But that didn't color my feelings toward my brothers. I loved them. Wolfdieter was cute and bright, and I could play checkers with him. When I met the baby, Ebbo, I wanted to hold him and play with him as I played with my baby doll. Still, I felt like a stranger when visiting my father. I thought of him as a very old man, and I wondered why my mother had loved him. He was twenty years older than she, and he was an astonishing twenty-seven years older than my stepmother, Tante Erna.

He tried to be nice to me, and that was just what he was: nice, as in polite to a guest. During the time I spent with him, he never took me on his lap; not once did he kiss me on the cheek. Perhaps the three weeks I spent in

Liegnitz was not long enough for us to grow close. My grandmother Omi (not to be confused with Oma, Mother's mother), the old ogre who had driven my mother from the house, did not help to make me feel accepted. I was relieved when Father hung the cardboard sign with my name and address around my neck again and put me back on the train to Berlin.

Summer came to an end. There had been air raids while I was gone; the bombing had been light, but the sirens deprived Oma of her sleep. Mother often ignored the raids and slept right through them, infuriating my grandmother.

Our sleeping arrangements in Berlin were quite different than they were in Frankfurt. In Frankfurt, each of us had our own spacious bedroom. But in Berlin, Mother and I shared her room where we slept in her former "marriage bed." It was supposed to be ultramodern, but I found the gray highly polished birch wood to be cold. Oma's room could be reached only by passing through Mother's. That room was dark. Over her ornately carved bed, which was as high as the bed in the story "The Princess and the Pea," hung a large ebony cross. On the cross a silver Christ twisted in contorted agony, inspiring fear in me. I don't remember having seen that crucifix in Frankfurt, but Oma's room there had been bright, and I would not have noticed the somberness of it. A long corridor led to Mother's and Oma's bedrooms, passing the kitchen, and a spacious bathroom. Between Mother's room and the bathroom, a narrow appendix-shaped space, a "half room," became my room. It was too small for a bed, but Mother was clever. She took several wooden crates, hammered them together, covered them with felt, and fastened pillows to them and voila! I had a little sofa. There were shelves on the walls for my books, crayons, and watercolors, as well as puzzles and games. But the room was the size of a broom closet, and when my girlfriends came to visit, we had to go elsewhere to play.

The dining room was gloomy, and although we had the same furniture that we did in Frankfurt, the dark red velvet on the sofa and chairs that had reminded me earlier of Burgundy wine now looked like crusted blood to me. The paintings of my ancestors livened up the room a bit, especially the mayor's wife in blue silk with her half-bare bosoms peeping through a sheer ruffle. Our family bible, hand scripted and hand illuminated, was stored in the bottom drawer of the ornately carved walnut cabinet. There was one room in our apartment that I liked: the salon. Against the wall of this room stood Mother's upright piano. Next to the piano, near the window, grew a graceful parlor palm, whispering, no doubt—when we were all asleep—tales of the South Seas to its European plant cousins, lounging in porcelain pot caches on the windowsill. Mother's honey brown Biedermeier sofa and chairs invited guests to make themselves comfortable on the yellow-and-blue-striped satin upholstery. One wall was lined with books, and the others were decorated with watercolors and sketches by Mother's artist friends. Having house guests in this small apartment posed a problem. If Aunt Margaret visited, she would have to sleep with Oma in her large bed, and my uncles would have to sleep on the velvet sofa in the dining room.

Mother promised that after the war she would look for a more suitable apartment. But for now we had a roof over our heads and were considered lucky, compared to those few who had already lost their homes to bombs.

The summer led into a golden yellow autumn. Mother took me on long walks, and I soon saw that Berlin, a city of trees, was especially beautiful in the fall. We walked through Grunewald, a section of town in which stood grand villas from the nineteenth century, and where close by a deep forest connected the city with the exclusive suburbs ringing Berlin's many lakes. The green of Grunewald was now dotted with orange and red, and here and there glimpses of blue from one of the lakes shimmered through the foliage.

Then winter came. It snowed early, and by the time Christmas arrived, the snow lay heavy in the streets. It was the first Christmas I remember celebrating without my uncles, but Aunt Margaret came to visit us for the holidays. I was happy hugging her again.

On Christmas Eve, as the four of us trudged to a six o'clock church service, an air-raid warning made us scramble, searching for the large letters *LSR*, signifying where a *Luftschutzraum*—an air-raid shelter—could be found. There was the sign a half block away, and we entered a dank semi-darkness. I shivered. The air was suffocating, and I felt uncomfortable among strangers. But soon the all clear sounded, and we were on the street again, breathing clear winter air. In the church we found seats for only Oma and Aunt Margaret; Mutti and I stood in the last row behind them.

Again the parson prayed for victory for our country and safety for our troops. Aunt Margaret whispered into Oma's ear, but I overheard her, "Don't you think, Elsa, that just at this moment preachers in France and in England are praying for the exact same thing?" Oma lifted her shoulders in a slight shrug. I wondered, but only for the briefest of moments, whom would God protect if all these fighting nations prayed for the same thing? I leaned over and whispered to Aunt Margaret, "Of course God will protect *our* troops. I pray for us to win the war every night." And I recited in a low voice: "*Lieber Gott, bitte bitte, lass uns den Krieg gewinnen*"—Dear God, please let us win the war.

Years later I realized, it was a good thing that God had not listened to me.

On December 26, an official holiday, we visited the opulent apartment of Uncle Victor and Tante Wanda. My tante Paula was staying with Uncle Victor, her younger brother, for the holidays. We were offered Tante Wanda's specialty, a lemon cake that was dry and more tart than sweet. Oma thought it lacked sugar because Tante Wanda was stingy. But Tante Wanda explained to me—I suppose she'd seen the face I'd made while eating the sour cake—that sophisticated people didn't use much sugar. That was considered gauche. I knew the word was French and meant "left," but I did not know that it had a second meaning, doing something not quite like "educated" people would do it. When Oma heard Tante Wanda use the word *gauche,* she winced. Later she told me, Tante Wanda had been born a Freiin von Grotthus and had spent several years in Paris with her first husband, an industrialist. According to my grandmother, Tante Wanda tried to impress others with her more urbane view. This rankled Oma who had grown up in Utah, considered by many to be the Wild West. Perhaps at times she felt less worldly than Tante Wanda, and perhaps Oma was somewhat envious when she complained that Tante Wanda had sent her son Horst, then age ten, to Schule Schloss Salem, a boarding school near the Bodensee (a school later attended by Prince Phillip, Duke of Edinburgh).

Now Horst, the oldest son, was home for Christmas. He, like my uncles, had enlisted the moment the war broke out. I saw Horst for the first time and was taken by his brooding good looks. He looked like his mother, and though Tante Wanda was old now, years earlier she must have been an unusual beauty, with wild brown curls and huge dark eyes. Seeing Horst here at Christmas made Oma doubly sad, for Will had not been given leave. I could feel an unspoken rivalry going on between the two mothers, Oma and Tante Wanda. Both Will and Horst were art historians; Will, two years younger than Horst, had trumped his cousin by securing a curator's job in a museum, while Horst still looked for a position. But Horst was an officer and had risen to the rank of captain, and Will was a corporal. Uncle Victor, a general in the Great War, could not understand why Will refused to take the oath of fealty.

When the adults began to talk about the war, Oma fell silent.

I slunk away from the grown-ups and stretched out on the only part of the furnishings I liked, the large polar bear rug. Uncle Victor had shot the bear when he was in northern Russia during World War I. My chin rested on the bear's head, and as I looked around me, fuzzy bear ears framed the room. It was curious to me that I couldn't admire any of the furnishings, despite their elegance. And I was surprised that this family, our wealthy relatives, had such a scrawny tree. It was laden with silvery lametta, white candles, silver balls, and silver stars. To me it did not look like a proper Christmas tree. There was no color, and there were no angels, rocking horses, or any of the silly little toys I loved. I wasn't offered any cookies or candies, not even from the large tin box of goodies that Oma had baked (a sacrifice, made from our sparse rations) and brought as a gift. Aunt Wanda had thanked Oma and put the box on the sideboard, where it remained, unopened.

After a while, my cousin Maria joined us, smiling at Mutti and kissing Oma on the cheek while offering me her pale hand to shake. It felt cold and slightly moist. She spoke of having had tea with friends in the Hotel Adlon and rolled her eyes at her mother, letting her know she had news for her. "Later. It will keep," Tante Wanda told her.

Uncle Victor ignored Maria. Yes, I knew she was his stepdaughter, but he could have been a little more pleasant.

Maria wore a sky blue silk dress that grazed her ankles. It was much like the dress my Käthe Kruse doll wore. I admired it; the material looked so soft that I wanted to touch it. The blue complemented her light red hair. Maria's eyes were large and brown like her mother's. When she stepped away from the window into the early evening shadows, I wanted to tell her to move back into the light so her hair would look like a bright golden halo again. But it was not proper for a child to make compliments or comment on someone's looks, and I remained silent.

We did not see Victor, the youngest son. Oma asked how he was. Not well, was Tante Wanda's response. He was in great pain, and Tante Wanda was upset with the doctors. They had promised that he'd be out of the hospital before Christmas, but an infection had set in. Aunt Margaret asked about the nature of his illness. That's when I noticed everyone staring off into one of the four corners of the room. It was obvious they didn't want to talk about this subject, which only made me more curious.

I didn't quite understand why Uncle Victor's family, with all its wealth, with a father and a mother, seemed not to be a happy family at all. And what ailed young Victor? An idiot savant, Mother called him. Whatever that was. Was he an idiot? Mother sometimes would say the meanest things: he could recite entire plays by Goethe, but he could not add two and two. Mother thought the family doctor had persuaded Uncle Victor and Tante Wanda to have him castrated. Castration? What was that?

A little later I overheard Oma whisper to Aunt Margaret that Maria was having a difficult time because she was half-Jewish. Maria's father's family had converted to Christianity more than a century ago, but that did not count. It was the non-Aryan blood that mattered. Yes, Oma explained when I asked, there are new laws and they make life miserable for anyone like

Maria. Uncle Victor had to pull his former rank on a number of occasions to protect her from being sent to a labor camp. Maybe Uncle Victor felt burdened by her? I felt sorry for Maria. But it was clear that Tante Wanda loved her daughter very much. Was that enough? I had felt Maria's loneliness. She moved through the rooms as if she were only half present. I wished I had told her that she looked lovely in the blue dress, and that her hair shone like copper.

I overheard someone whisper that Tante Wanda and Maria were helping "certain" people obtain papers to leave for Sweden. That was why Maria had rolled her eyes to her mother: she had made new contacts. I was curious about why people wanted to go to Sweden, but I couldn't ask. I was not supposed to have overheard those whispers.

It was a white Christmas. The snow made Berlin look like a bed made up with fresh linen, but my memory colored that first Christmas in Berlin gray. I remember my deep feeling of isolation. I remember taking refuge in my half-room and writing, clumsily in my child's script, a fairy tale about a mermaid who fell in love with a human. In the end she was betrayed by a wicked stepmother. And the mermaid, after losing the man she loved, for whom she had taken on the body of a woman, drowned like a human when she entered the waves. She no longer belonged to the sea. She had never belonged to the land. Maybe I subconsciously copied Hans Christian Anderson. But the feeling of being alone, of being isolated, was part of the mermaid's story, and it was part of mine.

CHAPTER 4

My Father's House

WINTER–FALL 1941 *Libau*

Of all the rooms in my father's home, I loved the bathroom most. Vati had a peculiar kind of "Baltic" humor (he was born near Riga). Above the toilet hung a large sign, lifted in the dark of night from a streetcar, proclaiming, "This seat holds 14 persons." The bathtub showed an equally silly notice, "Standing Room for 20 persons only." Maybe he pilfered that from the rear of a theater. And Father was an excellent caricaturist. Every last speck of wall space was covered with his drawings, in which he spoofed himself and his days as a cavalry officer during the Great War.

In one scene, Vati is falling off a horse, and in another, he is mounting a horse from the rear. His head is turned toward the viewer, and he wears a silly expression on his face, while his officer's cap scoots down, covering one eye rakishly. In the companion drawing, he is sliding off the opposite side of the horse, and his cap lies in the mud. But my favorite showed a horse, with big grinning teeth, biting Vati on his posterior. These ridiculous scenes always made me spend far too much time in the bathroom.

I had arrived early in the year, since there had been more frequent air raids in Berlin and Mother wanted me to be safe in a small town. In early spring, when it was still too cold to go swimming in the Pahnsdorfer Lake, Vati told us to put on our bathing suits and to climb into the giant bathtub. We took umbrellas and played with the spray of the shower, as if we were enjoying a warm summer rain indoors. The water splashed onto the umbrellas. I thought this was great fun, but I caught my stepmother, Tante Erna, frowning. She, a practical soul, found it a nuisance, since more than likely she was going to have to mop up the wet tile floor. But Father would charm her and convince her that this was good fun for the children.

I loved that madcap side of my father; his other side was serious and pedantic. I don't remember him ever holding me close or kissing me, not even when I was very young. I longed to climb on his lap and to put my head on his shoulder. But I didn't dare, and he did not invite me.

Perhaps a month after I arrived, my stepmother fell as she was climbing a flight of stairs to the attic with a heavy basket of wet laundry. I heard the crash, followed by a high pitched screech. I ran toward the noise and found Tante Erna at the foot of the landing, folded together, holding her belly, wailing. Blood gushed from between her legs. I stood unable to move. Others arrived. Someone ordered me to get back into the apartment. Someone called a doctor. A stretcher arrived. Tante Erna was carried off. Father suddenly appeared in the doorway, his face white, and just as suddenly, he was gone.

Later, Vati explained, Tante Erna had missed a step, or perhaps something slippery had been on the stairs. Her fall caused her to miscarry in her sixth month of pregnancy. The doctors told Father she had miscarried a boy.

I admired my twenty-seven-year-old stepmother for being in complete control of her household, with only the help from a young Polish farm girl. I especially respected her for keeping her body changes to herself. I never knew when she had her period. I learned from my mother that when a certain time in the cycle of the moon arrived, hands would fly to foreheads and there would be groans. It was different with Tante Erna. I had not even known she was pregnant.

I should have been more observant. Father taught me to watch gestures and to remember what people wore and how they behaved. He expected me to follow in his footsteps and become a journalist. Yes, I should have seen a change in Tante Erna's slender figure, but somehow her belly had swollen unnoticed by me.

When Father returned late that night, his face had lost all color, and he acted as if part of him were absent.

I could no longer stay in my father's house, not until Tante Erna was fully recovered. She was very weak, her usually suntanned skin faded to the color of light eggshells. Every day the maid whipped up a raw egg and a spoonful of sugar in a tumbler of red wine. The doctor had said this concoction would make Erna regain her strength, but her color had not returned when I left.

Oma picked me up in Liegnitz. Where could we go to be safe from bombs? We had no close relatives living in the countryside. We took the train to Danzig and stayed in Uncle Will's apartment. He would find a solution for us.

Will was assigned to a freighter on the Baltic Sea, where he sailed between Danzig and Helsinki—back and forth, overseeing provisions for German troops. We saw him often, which delighted Oma and, of course, me too. Every so often he would bring us a carton of a particular fruit, strange and exotic, from the ship. It tasted sweet, tart, and nutty, had the consistency of a softened apple, and was orange in color. We called it Rommel fruit, since we believed it was sent to Germany from North Africa via Rommel's Africa Korps. It was a delicacy close to a heavenly confection, yet purely a fruit. (I never found out the true name of the fruit. Perhaps they were persimmons.)

Will's gift for charming women helped us find two rooms in a splendid villa, belonging to the parents of Inge Thiele, one of his many friends. The villa was in Zoppot, a seaside resort near Danzig, with a view of the Baltic Sea.

I loved Zoppot. I inhaled the smell of the saltwater, pungent with kelp, and remembered Sylt and summers spent by the seashore. Hedge roses bloomed behind the house in this untamed garden. There were gooseberry bushes and bramble berries and an orchard that promised to provide us with luscious fruit: plums, apricots, peaches, apples, and pears. The Thieles, Inge's parents, were gentle and educated people, who never treated us as if we were imposing on their hospitality. There was no financial need for them to rent us rooms, nor had the housing office mandated that they share their home, as so often happened in the latter years of the war. Yet they had opened their home to us.

The Thieles had a little dog, Krissy, a Scottish terrier who became my special friend. I had never owned a dog before, not that I owned this one, but I might as well have. She slept on my bed, and on Sundays I raced her the block down to the beach and over the sand. I only slowed down when I thought I spotted a piece of amber, but I never was lucky. Some of my schoolmates had found pieces fit to be made into jewelry. But, slow or fast, Krissy liked her walks on the beach, and she followed me wherever I went.

In the school in Zoppot, for the first time I felt like I was part of a class, and that the teachers cared.

Most of Oma's worries were concentrated on Uncle Will during this time. She had not heard from him for several weeks. Germany had opened the eastern front and invaded Russia, and ships were being torpedoed in the Baltic Sea. Oma feared that Will's boat might have been one of them. Then a letter arrived from Uncle Victor in Berlin.

A Russian submarine had torpedoed Will's ship ferrying troops from Danzig to Helsinki. Hundreds of soldiers who were on deck had been thrown into the sea and drowned. The ship remained afloat, and fortunately, Will, who was in the engine room at the time, was alive. He had suffered a deep wound and multiple fractures in his left leg. The ship put into the port of Libau, Latvia, and he was transported to a military hospital. (The town was sealed by the military and off limits to civilian visitors, even to family members.) In the hospital, the doctor planned to amputate Will's infected leg. Will had pleaded with the doctor, but the doctor refused to listen, repeating that the leg with its lacerated flesh and exposed shin bone had been stewing in a slime-soup of sea and motor oil for too many hours. There was nothing he could do to save it. "Not to worry," the doctor said, "In one week you can travel to a large rehab hospital near Berlin with your new stump, they will fit you with a prosthesis and you'll be good as new."

That night a hospital train left for Berlin. On it traveled a young nurse bearing a letter from Will that she delivered in person to Uncle Victor. He was still known in military circles as a brilliant strategist and one of the younger generals from the Great War. Uncle Victor, who normally did not engage in nepotism, came to the rescue. I suppose he thought it was a familial duty, since my grandfather—his older brother—had died long ago. The next evening, twelve hours before the leg was to come off, the doctor appeared at Will's bedside. "I've received an urgent courier message, from General Keller, obviously your uncle, who is thanking me heartily that I am trying my utmost to save your leg. Crazy, crazy, I don't have that intention at all. I told you, after four hours in the *Ostsee* broth, nothing can be done. Well, we'll see, we'll see . . ."

And from that moment on the doctor did indeed try and Will did not lose his leg.

The Thieles had gone on a trip and left us their season tickets to the local playhouse, the Kammerbühne. I saw plays that I did not understand: Shakespeare, Ibsen, Hauptmann, and Shaw. I was Oma's companion and grew to love the theater and the intimacy of darkness while sitting close to someone I loved. I learned to savor the rhythm and cadences of language, even though the meaning of words often escaped me. But after two months or so the Thieles returned. Oma decided we had been their guests long enough, and we left Zoppot to go back to Berlin.

I felt like a yo-yo when I was sent back to Liegnitz. I returned to school there, and I resigned myself to being bounced between homes and schools.

I loved my two little brothers, Wolfdieter and Ebbo (Wolf-Eberhard), the two little wolves. My father's name was Wolfgang, and he attached the "wolf" to both of his son's names. When I was born, Mother had fiercely objected to Father naming me Wolf-Linde. Imagine having to go through life with a name like Wolf-Linde.

I often took my brothers—Ebbo in a stroller—on walks to a park nearby. I headed straight for the tamarisk trees. There we sat on a bench, and I told them stories. The trees inspired me, and I made up tales of the Orient. I loved the soft pinkish gray branches of this tree, which Vati told me had come from eastern Russia. I imagined golden spires and onion towers in the distance. I loved the tiny lavender blossoms that looked like a veil thrown over the branches, where I could imagine fairies might dwell.

Yes, I loved my little brothers, but I was also jealous of them. They were part of this family whereas I felt like a guest in my father's house, tolerated because of the war. Wicked thoughts sometimes surfaced. Maybe this arrangement was welcomed by Vati because he would not have to send child support for me to Mutti?

I liked school in Liegnitz, not as much as in Zoppot, but I kept up with my class and got good marks. Until one day, when my teacher asked me how I was related to the Kraus family and I explained it to her. "So your brothers are actually your half-brothers," she said.

My schoolmates guffawed and laughed. Later during recess they began to taunt me. "Ha ha, Karin has only half a brother, ha ha," one cried out. A tall, fat girl, after laughing so hard she practically choked in a coughing fit, asked, "Which half, the right or the left?" There was more laughter, then another said, "And the youngest, is he the top half or the bottom half?" She sang, "*Ein Kind ohne Kopf bleibt ein Krüppel sein Leben.*" I had always hated this nasty song about a child without a head who remains a cripple his entire life; it is sung to the tune of the Tannhäuser overture and ridicules retarded children.

I had liked—well, tolerated—school in Liegnitz until this incident, but afterward I again hated school.

There were some happy times in Liegnitz. I remember the walks Father and I took together. We passed through fields of grain, white blond wheat wavering in the breeze, dotted with the bright blue of cornflowers and the startling red of poppies. Father would point to the short hairs of the wheat and the longer hairs on the rye, urging me to remember the difference. He showed me how cultivated oats differed from wild oats. He taught me how to identify the different types of trees by looking at the shapes of their leaves and their bark. Here in the forest, I felt as if he and I were the only two people in the world. This was a magical world of secret sounds: the hoot of an owl and the scamper of a four-footed creature as it rushed through the twigs and dry leaves. These were things heard but not seen. Father's hand was warm and his grip firm. I wanted to hold it tight, forever. His voice mellowed as he told me Russian fairy tales of Baba Yaga, the old witch who lived in the woods. I loved listening to his Baltic-German accented voice, with its softly rolling r's. He had read me some of the tales before, but it was much more mysterious to listen to them while walking together, concealed in this emerald world, with branches crackling beneath our feet and a ray of sunlight stealing through a slender pine branch, gilding a lushly growing fern or painting a fallen tree trunk with golden stripes. I expected to stumble upon Baba Yaga's hut at any moment. Once I had found her, she would wave her magic wand, and Mutti, Father, and I would live together in happiness.

Father, *ca.* 1935, showing the dueling scar of which he was so proud. Mother thought that dueling fraternities were barbaric.

One of my father's self-caricatures.

Tante Erna and my three half brothers, *ca.* 1952.

Eberhard Kraus and a young Alice
Baertels Kraus (Omi), my paternal
grandparents. My grandfather's suicide
cast a dark shadow over our family.

Omi with Peter, Tante Oda's son who was lost in Vitebsk, Russia.

Father's sister, the poet, Oda Schaefer-Lange, *ca.* 1941.

August Keller and Elsa von Hake-Keller (Oma),
my maternal grandparents, *ca.* 1904.

Family farewell party at Oma's apartment at five in the morning, *ca.* 1931. On the sofa, from left: Oda Schaefer, Mother, and Father. Oma is second from right, below her is Uncle Richard.

(Opposite)

Schloss Prittag, home of Uncle Reini and Tanta Anna, the Count and Countess von Finkenstein, godparents and guardians of Aunt Margaret and Oma. Aunt Margaret and Oma lived at Schloss Prittag upon their return from Utah.

Victor Keller (left), my grandfather's younger brother, and his wife, Wanda Keller (right), in 1946. Uncle Victor served as a general in the Kaiser's army and was a decorated hero of the Great War.

Berlin revelry during Carnival.
Mother is in the center wearing
a large-brimmed hat. On the left
is Veronika in white with the
gypsy scarf. Mother boarded with
Veronika's parents while attending the art academy in Berlin.

Mother in wheatfields
around Liegnitz, *ca*. 1932.

Mother in the fur coat my
father bought for her, 1934.

Mother wearing a new hat, the only clothing
she could buy without rations, 1944.

Päule Carlson, the love in Mother's life.

Uncle Richard during the war.

Uncle Will with Oma, Karin, and Krissy, the Scottie dog, in Zoppot, 1944.

CHAPTER 5

Hitler's Eyes

SPRING 1942

I returned to Berlin and to school in Steglitz. I was ahead a grade, and in April, the new school year, I entered the *Oberschule,* or high school, called the Bismarck Lyceum. I was automatically drafted into the Jungmädel, Hitler's youth group for girls, and Mother purchased the uniform. I proudly wore this outfit, believing the black skirt, white blouse, and black tie held by a brown leather knot would show the world that I was one of Hitler's children. Oma despised the uniform.

The weather was unusually warm that April. I had planned to go to the Wannsee after school that day with Erika, but our teacher surprised us with the news that there would be no school tomorrow. We would meet in class and then be transported to Olympia Stadium—the huge outdoor sports arena built for the 1936 Olympics—for a rally. There we would be privileged to hear our Führer, Adolf Hitler, speak.

We marched in formation into the huge stadium. We were given red armbands with swastikas on them to wear on our sleeves. Hundreds of students were already present when we arrived, and hundreds more marched in, accompanied by the deafening sound of marching bands. Drums rolled, bassoons boomed, and trumpets blared. I wanted to stuff cotton in my ears to shut out some of this noise. Hitler youth members and adults in brown or black uniforms (SA or SS) were lined up in columns, and a wide space in the center was left open so that the Führer and his marshals could drive to the podium in their open touring cars.

Everyone was standing, waiting for the Führer. Speeches were made, and we continued to wait as the sun rose higher, blasting down on us. After a long time, a rumor went through the aisles: he had arrived. Our arms and hands stretched out in the expected "Heil Hitler" salute. The sun continued to blaze yellow and round in the April sky as we waited and listened to more music, but still there was no Hitler. My arm was getting tired, but he could arrive at any moment so no arm was allowed to go limp. My arm hurt; the sun burned. Sweat poured down my face. I could not wipe my forehead, and the teachers watched to make sure that we stood rigid, at attention with our arms outstretched. I felt my body turning numb until I could not even move my legs. Sweat dripped over my eyebrows, burning my eyes. I am *not* a weakling; I am a strong German girl, I told myself, as my arm lost all feeling.

Suddenly a roar filled the stadium. It started in the rear and moved forward like the salvo of drums, growing loud and louder until it was deafening. A chorus of voices screamed, "*Sieg Heil! Sieg Heil! Sieg Heil!*" The words expressing hope for Germany's eventual *Sieg,* or victory, reverberated through the columns of people.

Our Führer had arrived.

My arm felt dead. Maybe it was kept in the air by the sheer will of thousands of people, by the electricity of the moment. The pain had stopped. There was still a light tingle, as if ants were crawling under my skin. Other than that, the limb extending from my body felt like a foreign object, not belonging to me.

A car came down the center aisle, and my heart began to race. It was followed by another car, a convertible, long and black, with the top down. Little red swastika flags decorated the fender, fluttering in a breeze generated by the automobile.

There *he* was. My breath stopped. He was standing in the slow-moving vehicle with his arm outstretched. I had heard about our Führer's bright blue eyes. I saw that they were narrow-set, deep within the face, and shaded by his thick brows. At first I could not make out their color, but then the car came closer. I craned my neck over my arm, having forgotten that it felt dead. The sun acted as a stage light, sliding over his face, eliminating shadows. His eyes caught the light, reflecting the brightness. I stood mesmerized by their blueness. I don't remember seeing or being aware of anything but those eyes. Then, at the moment when his car passed the row where I stood, maybe ten to fifteen feet from me, his head turned to the left, and his eyes, for the briefest moment in time, met mine. They were such a deep blue, the color of Mother's sapphire ring, hard, like a faceted stone and just as fiery. Never again have I encountered anyone with eyes that color, eyes that I would never forget.

I thought, "Yes, this man, our Führer Adolf Hitler, will indeed be our savior." And thinking these thoughts, in the hot sun, I melted onto the ground.

Next, I felt the tickle of cotton under my nose and smelled something strange, like ammonia. Someone tried to get me to drink water from a flask, and I found myself on a stretcher, being carried out of the stadium. They took me to a cot in a first aid station. I was given more water to drink. When I swung my legs onto the concrete floor, trying to get up, a nurse pushed me back down.

"Please," I said. "I want to go back and hear our Führer speak."

She looked at me, telling me without words, "You are not strong enough to be a worthy German girl." She said, "Lie down!" Then pointing to the water glass she said, "There, drink some more. You hardly touched it. Your body needs liquid."

I wanted to throw the water at her. They would not let me hear him speak! Then I heard a roar echoing through the tented walls of the first aid station, as thousands of voices cried out, "Sieg Heil! Sieg Heil! Sieg Heil!" I imagined our Führer mounting the podium at that moment to begin his speech. The chorus of voices kept shouting "Hail to Victory," and here I was stuck on a cot, deemed unfit to go back and hear the words of our Führer.

Exile in Marienbad

As the days grew longer, the air raids became more frequent. Most of the strikes in Berlin had been directed at the heavily populated areas in the industrial district, several miles from Steglitz where we lived. So far we had been spared.

Dr. Josef Goebbels, the minister of information and propaganda, ordered the schools in Berlin to close, and children had to leave the city. Wealthier parents sent their children to private boarding schools, mainly in Bavaria. My school, including teachers and Hitler Youth leaders, was evacuated to a KLV Lager, or *Kinder Land Verschickung*, where children were sent to the country. We left Berlin in the early summer of 1942 for Marienbad in the Sudetenland, which is now part of the Czech Republic.

Every time I watched Mother pack an item of clothing into my suitcase or stitch a name tag into a sweater or a blouse, I cried. I sometimes got so upset that I grabbed the blouse or skirt and threw it on the floor. I'd rant, "I don't want to go away. Please, don't make me. Why do I have to go to school? Can't Oma teach me here? She knows more than my teachers anyway."

"It's the law," Mother answered, stifling her own tears. "I don't want you to go, but you'll be safe from bombs. Oma will soon leave too."

"Oma?" I wheeled around to face my grandmother. "Where are you going? Can't I go with you?"

"Remember the farmhouse last year? Where the goose bit you?"

"You're going there? Ugh. I hate that place. I hope they ate that goose."

We stood at track number seventeen, waiting for the train for Dresden. I stared at the parallel shiny metal rails that would soon carry me off to a place far from home. These silvery tracks would take me to lands in the south, separating me from everyone I loved.

Hundreds of children milled about, clutching their mothers' hands. This was the first time I was in Anhalter Bahnhof, and I was amazed by the size of the railway station. A high glass dome covered the structure. The sun tried to break through an overcast sky and penetrate the glass, which was stained into a gray marbleized pattern due to accumulated soot. When I tilted my head just so and squinted, I could see the light make the dome shimmer in opaline colors.

The big black locomotive, pulling the many carriages, came to a chugging halt at our platform, breathing a large ball of slate smoke. One last exhale. Whistles shrilled. The carriage doors remained locked. The teachers counted children and marched us along as a group. My friend Erika waved at me. She shouted something in English to a woman about the same age as my mother. Oma looked up. Had she heard English? She and Mother walked over to the tall woman wiping a tear from her suntanned face. They introduced themselves, and thus Mother met Erika's sister, Lilly, and her British mother. Here, in the train station, Lilly's and Mother's long friendship began.

Mother and Oma checked my luggage for the hundredth time, and they fiddled with the large cardboard sign around my neck that had my name, address, and destination printed on it to see if it was secured tightly.

"You said when Aunt Wanda sent Horst to boarding school that you would never, ever, do such a thing." I stared at Oma accusingly. "But now you're sending me away."

"There is nothing anyone can do about this new law," Oma said, wiping away a tear and hugging me to her chest.

When the train doors opened, Mother entered the compartment with me and made sure that I would sit facing in the direction the train was traveling. Then she gave me one last kiss and left. I leaned my head out of the window as far as I could for as long as I could. The train left the station, and we all waved and cried as our mothers and loved ones grew smaller and smaller, then faded into the puffing smoke of the locomotive.

Someone told me to close the window. I tried, but it was stuck. I pushed on it. It gave way and flew up, hitting me in the chin, knocking off half of my right front tooth. The ordeal had begun.

The trip took two days: we traveled first by train, then by boat on the River Elbe, and again by train.

We reached Dresden before dark and were put up in a barnlike building with stacked bunk beds, which slept three. I was afraid of heights and begged for a lower bunk. The next morning we awoke to rain, followed by a hard summer hail. Breakfast consisted of a dark-colored gruel served with a non-descript brown beverage. At least it was hot. This was the worst food I had had since the war had begun, but hunger made me eat and drink, no matter how bad the taste.

An hour later we marched to the boat. This might have been an exciting adventure if the sun had been helpful. But no, it refused to emerge from be-hind its shield of heavy gray clouds. I was among the youngest, but I noticed a lot of older children with red eyes wiping away tears. After only one day, we were homesick already. I think few of us had ever been away from our families before.

We were marched over the gangplank onto the boat and were told we could find seats below or remain on deck. I went to the stern and watched the sailors coil the ropes that minutes ago had connected us to shore and then stow them away. The contours of Dresden were softened by drizzle. To me it looked lovely with the large round dome of the Frauenkirche, the largest church in the town, surrounded by impressive baroque buildings. I longed for Uncle Will to appear and whisk me from the boat. I wanted him to take me on a tour of Dresden, explaining the buildings to me, and then to take me back home with him.

The flat landscape of the Mark Brandenburg had long ago melted into the rolling hills and dales of Saxony, a region sprinkled with villages. Soon the slate gray river snaked through rugged yellow sandstone cliffs where we glimpsed castles and quaint churches on hillsides. Apple trees were in bloom; plum and cherry trees had already set small buds of fruit that were soon to ripen. The fields were of a rich green where horses and cattle grazed. There was no sign of war. It rained and rained, and it was cold. I was torn between wanting to stand on deck or climb down the ladderlike steps and take shel-ter from the weather. I told myself I should make an effort to get to know some of the new teachers and classmates. But in the end my hands, by then red and stiff with cold, gripped the metal rail and would not let me tear myself away from looking north toward Berlin.

We landed near Prague, and after another train ride, we arrived in Marienbad. It sounded so pretty—Ma-ri-en-bad. This is where royalty and the rich and famous, including Mozart and Chopin, had taken the baths for a variety of cures.

We settled in a small hotel. When a few days later, Erika and I, and some older girls, explored the city I saw its beauty, but my heart did not register it. Villas, buildings, and hotels, all in shades of cream and pastels, looking elegant and unharmed, lined the main thoroughfare. No bombs had fallen here. Far-reaching branches of ancient trees seemed to be protecting arms, shielding the buildings. The nineteenth-century *Kurhaus* (spa) faced the *Kurgarten* (a formal park). The *Kurhaus*'s simplicity was splendid; our teachers told us that it had been converted into a recuperation facility for soldiers from the Russian and the Balkan fronts. And there, in the *Kurgarten*, I saw the first amputees. Young men on crutches, many with their empty pant legs pinned up. I wept.

Small coffee houses lined the main street. One time after Erika and I had received some money from home, we decided to indulge ourselves in a café. Delicious-looking cakes were on display in the coffee house, but we had no ration coupons. We settled for a cup of *Malzkaffee* with milk and sugar.

Our teachers sometimes took us on walks through the huge park in the heart of the city. The varied shades of green were intense. Trees and shrubs looked mysterious and prettier than the ones in the Grunewald. Even so, I missed the forest back home with its familiar pines and wild growth of underbrush. Everything looked arranged here, like an exquisite bouquet of flowers, and I found it too perfect.

The hotel where we were quartered was luxurious, like something out of a nineteenth-century novel, but its red velvet elegance could not make up for the hostility I felt from the teachers and youth leaders.

Even though I slept in a large room with three other girls, I was suffocating from loneliness. Loneliness was a sack without holes that someone had pulled over my head. I could barely breathe, and I felt invisible. I could keep in touch with Mother and Oma by letter only. But I longed to hear their voices, an impossibility since telephones were not available.

In addition to our schooling, we were taught to sweep our rooms and to make up our beds. We had to keep our issue of sheets and towels and our personal clothing, underwear, and nightclothes in perfect order. Everything was to be folded and put away in wardrobes, as well as in something called a *Spind,* which had lots of shelves. We had to place our clothes *Kante auf Kante*—edge on edge—so that not even a fraction of an inch of an undershirt or a nightgown protruded from the garment above or below. I could manage quite well with the straight lines of towels and bed sheets, but the clothes presented a problem. If anything displeased the youth leader inspecting our personal belongings, she would pull at the stack making all of the clothes tumble to the floor. Then we had to pick them up and refold each and every item. Even though some of my classmates learned to be orderly to the extreme from these drills, I learned only to rebel and to play tricks on the youth leader.

We slept in beds made up of three mattress sections. After one of my *Kante auf Kante* fiascoes, and after having spent most of the evening refolding clothes, I recruited one of my fellow sufferers to remove the middle part of the mattress of the youth leader harassing us most. We hid the mattress part in the closet, and in its place we put a bowl of ice-cold water. After we had remade the bed, we didn't have to wait long for the expected scream. We watched through a crack in the door as the woman ran down the corridor, dripping water and yelling and cursing at the top of her lungs. Several of the teachers appeared in the hall, and one of them shouted, "Oh, keep quiet. Change into dry clothes and get a hold of yourself." We giggled behind our door and were never found out.

Otherwise, our schooling proceeded as it would have in Berlin. Nazi indoctrination sessions with our Hitler Youth leaders were held in the afternoon. We learned about our Führer's struggle, his *Kampf,* and we were told of his strong vision and spirit. He was our great Father; he would take care of us. We children had nothing to fear. We were meant to grow up into strong and healthy German women who would bear our Führer and our Vaterland many blond, blue-eyed children. I wondered about the blond part; after all, the Führer himself had almost black hair. If all Aryans had blond hair, was the Führer not fully Aryan? I found the courage to ask this question of one of our more likable youth leaders. She stared at me and blushed, then her mouth opened wide in a silent protest, but she did not answer me.

On many afternoons we sat in a circle and sang songs (this part I liked), or we learned folk dances. Great emphasis was put on physical fitness. Every day, including Saturday, when we had to attend school for half a day, started with calisthenics. In the afternoon we played handball, ran hurdles and relay races (which I was good at), did broad jumps, and shimmied up poles in the gym of a local boys' school.

Food was scarce, and none of us ever got enough to eat. I have always been a slow eater, and with this horde of hungry girls, I never got to the buffet in time for a second helping, which was necessary because we were doled out small helpings the first time. By the time I reached the trays, they were empty. That's when I resorted to telling icky stories. I discovered a way to get more food: I would make my classmates nauseous by telling them stories of festering wounds, of the cook's snot running into our food in the kitchen, and of my aunt Margaret's tapeworm, all the while watching the girls' faces to anticipate when anyone would get sick and run from the table. Then I swooped down on their food.

I ate. But I did not win popularity contests.

Advent came, and I knew that Christmas was just a few short weeks away. I missed my family's closeness during that time and the sight of the candlelit tree. There was no Christmas tree in the boardinghouse. Our youth leaders made sure no mention was made of Christmas; the emphasis was placed on Germanic pagan ritual instead. On Christmas Eve, which had always been a night of magic for me, they marched us through heavy snow into the forest. We stomped up one of the hills surrounding the city. On the summit, noble firs—the "Oh Tannenbaum" trees—stood as dark silhouettes, like paper cutouts against the white. A full moon hung like a huge yellow disk in the sky, and I watched snow crystals sparkle on needled branches. We sang songs celebrating Germanic heroes and sang about the *"Hohe Nacht der klaren Sterne"*—Night of Stars—as we celebrated solstice. I thought our youth leaders were stupid. The solstice had been December 21, three days earlier. Why not celebrate it on the actual day? Why this silly pretense of having us march up here on Christmas Eve?

Then came the surprise. The wise youth leaders presented us with a Christmas tree substitute. High on that snowy hill they lit the four points of a cross made of tree branches, equal in length and thickness. I believe they had put tar on it and lit it. After the fire caught, they rolled the cross down the hill, just as Germanic tribes had done in earlier times. The rolling, flaming cross became a wheel. I was surprised as to how pretty it looked, and I understood the reason for making us adore this flaming wheel: it resembled a slightly bent swastika.

To celebrate the New Year, our school put on a holiday talent show. I played a clown and was proud of my solo number. Our least popular teacher was the math teacher, Fräulein Käte Pfeiffer, an obese woman with mottled grayish pink skin that resembled undercooked pork. She was the embodiment of the ugly *Blaustrumpf*, bluestocking teacher, and we wondered how she came by her triple chin and bulging belly in this time of food scarcity.

With the talent show approaching, I hoped this would be the moment when I would gain the forgiveness of my classmates for my icky stories. My costume was ready: a painted clown face, wig, hat, and false nose. I dressed in baggy black pants and jacket, and I carried a little black cardboard box resembling a camera.

One of the girls played the accordion, and I sang a song one of the older schoolmates had picked for me. "*So wie mein blondes Kätchen, so küsst kein anderes Mädchen*"—So as my blonde Katie, so kisses no other girlie. I did not understand half of the words I sang. At the end of the song, I sank to my knees and gazed at teacher Käte with lovesick clown eyes and asked if I could please take her photograph. She nodded yes, a happy gleam in her eye. Click! My "camera" spritzed a stream of cold water right into her pasty face.

Applause and wild laughter.

Teacher Käte rose from her seat, pulled off my clown nose and my hat, and slapped me—hard. Then she left the room. I rubbed my flaming cheek. I didn't like the sound of laughter coming from the girls, for now, they were laughing at me.

After almost eight unbearable months of exile in Marienbad, Oma came to my rescue. But only after the school had made a terrible mistake.

Oma arrived in mid-January. The school had put me into a provisionary hospital in a small hotel. I shared a room with Erika and two other schoolmates; all of us were ill with either scarlet fever or diphtheria. The wise personnel reasoned that if you were ill with one disease, you were immune to the other. I had a fever, but I felt quite well. I was bored, though, and thought of escape. Perhaps I could slither down sheets tied to the wrought iron railing of the balcony—a maneuver I had seen in a film. After all, I did well in climbing and sliding down the pole in gym, but all I had with me were nightgowns. I couldn't very well run through town barefoot in rosebud-flowered flannel.

I should have liked it there: for once I got enough to eat. Erika never ate her cream-of-wheat, and I finished her bowl and licked her spoon clean.

One day Oma marched into my room, accompanied by Aunt Margaret. My mouth must have stood open for the longest time, the surprise was so complete.

When they received the telegram that I had scarlet fever, Oma, who was with her sister in Upper Silesia at the time, traveled to Marienbad the fastest way they could. (Mother's papers were stamped *unabkömmlich* [indispensable] for the war effort. A daughter ill with a life threatening disease did not qualify for travel.)

Oma took one look at me and at the other girls, then turned toward her sister. Their eyes met and both nodded in agreement. Oma had been a nurse for a short time before her marriage and was familiar with diphtheria and scarlet fever. But Aunt Margaret had more experience, having nursed dozens of cases of both in the Great War. They stood by my side, each putting their cool hands on my forehead. Then they yanked me out of bed and hauled me down the stairs to see the woman responsible for this makeshift hospital.

In the former breakfast room, their voices grew louder and louder. They concluded that I suffered only from a common cold; I had run a fever but did not have scarlet fever or diphtheria. Why did these so-called nurses not recognize this? A day later Renate, a girl who had shared my room, died of diphtheria.

Oma and Aunt Margaret packed up my belongings and moved me to the small hotel where they were staying. It was heaven, sleeping beneath a fluffy feather bed and in the same room with two of my favorite people. At night, Oma snored in a deep gurgle and Aunt Margaret kept up the tempo in a higher register; they sounded as if they were snoring a duet. It felt so cozy, so warm to be with them. But I trembled at the thought of having to go back to that dreadful KLV Lager. Fortunately, Oma was able to obtain my release, using the school's mistake as a bargaining tool.

SECOND SIGHT
JANUARY 1943

The train pulled into Anhalter station. How different Berlin looked to me now, on my return. I gulped mouthfuls of Berlin air, this air celebrated in song as invigorating and often compared to champagne. Now I inhaled as if during the last eight months I had been deprived of the simple act of breathing.

I spotted Mother on the platform. She was wearing one of her perky hats with a veil covering half her face. I ran up to kiss her, but she grabbed my shoulders and held me back. "Don't come near my face," she held up her hands. "I don't know what I have. It might be contagious."

Then I noticed her eyes; they were red and half stuck together by something crusty, sticky, and yellowish. I stepped back. Again I looked at Mother. Aunt Margaret went closer and lifted Mother's little veil to have a better look. Oma frowned and put her arms around Mother. Everyone talked at once. "What's wrong with your eyes, Astrid? Have you seen an eye doctor?"

"I don't have time. I work over twelve hours a day."

We boarded the S-Bahn, with me helping Mother lug my heavy suitcase.

Oma and Aunt Margaret carried their own smaller ones. Mother stopped for a moment, took a breath, and said, almost as if apologizing, "Sometimes everything swims in front of me, I can't make out the individual characters in a word. It interferes with my work. I'm afraid my eyes are failing."

"Astrid, foolish Astrid. This looks serious," said Aunt Margaret. "You'll have to see a doctor tomorrow. This can't wait."

In addition to her regular job as a costume designer for the Berlin theaters, Mother, fluent in English and French, had been drafted by the army to translate letters from POWs six hours a day. She hated this job. She said she felt as if the square brick building she worked in was filled with fear. Still, it was better than working in a munitions factory where several of Mother's friends had been ordered to work.

At that time, many of the letters came from British soldiers who had been taken prisoner by General Rommel's Afrika Korps during the North Africa campaign. Mother hated having to cross out sentences about life in the camps with her big black opaque writing stick. After her "editing" job, the letters would be sent to Switzerland, and from there, they would be forwarded by the Red Cross to their destination. She wouldn't talk about what was in the letters. Only once did she tell Oma and me that she was touched by a letter from a soldier from Bournemouth, England, whose wife had died in childbirth. The soldier worried about his infant daughter. Reading these letters brought the simple lives of these soldiers into focus. These soldiers wore a different uniform and obeyed a different command, but like Germany's young soldiers, they too suffered in this war. Mother had to remind herself that *they* were the enemy and that *their* planes bombed our cities. She was connected to the soldiers through their letters, and they had simply become young men with children, wives, and sweethearts.

The following day, Aunt Margaret dragged Mother to the university *charité,* where a specialist diagnosed Mother's problem as Egyptian eye disease, a disease that if not treated would lead to blindness. She had seen the ophthalmologist just in time. The professor concluded that she had picked up the disease from a letter that came from a POW camp in North Africa.

The professor cauterized her eyes in the clinic, then Mother had to undergo a cure at home. The drops burned her eyes. Mother, who never flinched when in pain, screamed when Oma administered the drops. She ran in circles, shrieking, "My eyes are on fire," clutching at her eyes as if she wanted to tear them from their sockets. Blinded by pain she ran into the furniture. But then one day, the world appeared as clear as before. No, she said the colors looked more vibrant, the world more beautiful, since she had been given the gift of sight a second time.

Oma and Aunt Margaret had saved me in Marienbad from diphtheria and scarlet fever, and we had come back just in time to save Mother from going blind.

We prepared for a visit with Tante Wanda and Uncle Victor. Oma changed into a black dress, and she told me to put on my dark blue and black plaid skirt and to match it with my navy sweater.

The creaky cage of an elevator took us up to my uncle and aunt's apartment. Young Victor answered the doorbell. He was barefoot. He tossed his stringy blond hair from his forehead and grinned at us. That's what put me off: his ear-to-ear grimace. The last time I was here he was in a hospital. I remembered something about castration, and that still puzzled me. Now I wondered why he didn't cut his hair, put on some shoes, and enlist in the army like the rest of the young men.

Cousin Maria appeared, swollen eyed and pale. She barely reached Victor's shoulder but ordered him to go to his room, as if she were filling in for her stepfather, the general. Shadowlike, she moved into the salon. Her dark gray woolen dress made her almost invisible in the dim light of the apartment; only her flaming red hair made her stand out against the darkened backdrop. Her legs were two flesh-colored commas—thin and slightly bowed, clad in rayon stockings. She motioned for us to follow her. The heavy drapes were drawn, as if to keep errant rays of sun from stealing into the room, preventing even a sliver of hope to brighten the gloom. Swathed in black, Tante Wanda sat on the sofa, too weak to get up and greet Oma.

I already knew why everyone was so sad.

Horst, the eldest son, had been killed at Leningrad.

Uncle Victor had left the house hours ago, right after the message had been delivered. He still had not come back from his walk. The three women sat alone, mourning the dead soldier. The old soldier, Uncle Victor—a hero from the Russian campaign in the Great War—could not cope with the death of this young soldier, his son.

Uncle Will had always spoken of Horst as a sensitive young man who wrote poetry; he was not at all like his warrior father. I glanced up and met Horst's eyes looking at me out of a silver frame. Again I was struck by how handsome he was, with wavy brown hair and large dark eyes like his mother's. And now he was dead.

The siege of Leningrad began on September 1, 1941; Horst had lain in the trenches outside the city ever since. The message the officer had left informing my aunt and uncle of Horst's death, this piece of yellow paper, lay on the sideboard. I read it. A hand grenade had hit him straight on. It said there was nothing left of him to bury.

I thought of that. Nothing left of him to bury. Nothing? He had been a tall man, wearing a uniform and boots, but there was nothing? I imagined little bits of flesh and pulverized bones flying through the air. What happened to the blood? Did it sink into the earth? And while my thoughts revolved around this death over and over again, Oma sat by Wanda, who by now had put her head in Oma's lap, and stroked her hair while she wept out loud.

Maria brought a clean handkerchief to the women. At one point young Victor put his head through the door, still grinning, but Maria sprang to her feet and closed the door in his face.

I was happy to be in the S Bahn again on our way home. Oma was still crying. Maybe her thoughts were with her own two sons.

Who would live and who would die?

We arrived home at the same time as Mutti, who had just returned from work. She and Aunt Margaret wanted to hear about our visit. Oma said, "Poor Wanda," reaching for Mother's arm to help support herself. Aunt Margaret rushed to her, asking her if she needed some water.

"No, thank you. I just felt weak." She sat down by the dining room table and her face looked as gray as Tanta Wanda's had. "The terrible irony," she said. "Young Victor, who can't function on his own is alive. And Horst is dead." Oma seemed to have trouble breathing, and by now Mutti arrived with a cup of strong coffee. Oma smiled a thank you, took a sip, and went on, "And Maria is in constant danger of being taken to a labor camp. Only because she's half-Jewish." She nodded in answer to Aunt Margaret, "Poor girl. She now wears a golden amulet with a cyanide capsule around her neck. In case she gets arrested. And to top it all off, she's been diagnosed with leukemia."

What was cyanide? I'd heard that it was a poison to kill rats. Why did she wear it around her neck?

"But . . . but what would she do?" Mother asked.

"She'd bite down on the pill. Painless. It's over within seconds. Elisabeth wears the same thing."

Mother frowned. "I stopped by Elisabeth's to invite her to a recital. She declined, very politely. Said she doesn't go out these days. She intimated it's because of her looks. People stare, and sometimes say things. Different from Maria. With her red hair and fair skin she's more or less safe. Elisabeth should at least pluck her heavy eyebrows."

"That shows how absurd those Nazi ideas are," Oma said. "Elisabeth looks exactly like her great-grandmother Keller. Yes." She nodded toward my mother. "The one in the ancestor portrait in Uncle Victor's house. The one with the little white cap on her dark hair and the prominent nose. She's your great-grandmother too. Elisabeth looks nothing like her Jewish father."

I tried my best to understand what they were talking about. To me it sounded as if they were speaking in code: castration, cyanide, great-grandmothers, Jewish fathers.

"Why doesn't Tante Elisabeth want to go out?" I asked.

"*Kind,* it is dangerous in this time to look Jewish. You never know what someone might do for that matter. If a person were to attack her, or call her names, the police would do nothing," Oma said. "I know that only her husband's good standing with Goebbels has protected her. So far." (Her husband, Walter Schultze-Mittendorf, had attained fame with the design of the movie *Metropolis* and was now the premier set and costume designer of the Ufa film studios, which were under the direction of the propaganda minister, Dr. Josef Goebbels.)

"But Maria. You said Uncle Victor protects her. What would happen if he can't?" I asked.

"They'd cut her ration cards even more. Then she'd be on a starvation diet. Tante Wanda would share food with her, but it would be hard for all of them. Young Victor gets reduced rations."

"Why? Is he half-Jewish too?"

"No," Oma looked annoyed by all my questions. "He's Uncle Victor's son, you know that. He's a little . . . they say he fell from the diapering table. On his head. That's what they say."

"And Maria. You said they'd do other things to her. Like what?"

"They'd put her to work. Clearing rubble after an air raid or working in a labor camp. With her frail health, that would kill her. God knows . . ." Oma looked at me, her expression changed from annoyed to compassionate and then to angry. "We have to thank Herr Hitler for that. I knew it from the beginning, didn't I?" She turned to Aunt Margaret for confirmation.

Aunt Margaret nodded. "Yes, Elsa. You foretold a lot of things. When they first burned the synagogues, smashed the store windows, smeared the mannequins in the Jewish department stores with red paint . . . ," she shook her head. She looked at me and asked, "They never taught you about *Kristallnacht* in school, did they? Part of our shameful recent history." Then she turned to Oma. "Elsa, you've always been able to predict things, but with Herr Hitler in power it didn't take a clairvoyant to foretell what would happen in Germany."

"This tyrant," Oma said.

Mother poked her in the ribs. As if I didn't see that and know exactly what it meant. I disagreed with them, but I wouldn't snitch on them.

"Oma," I said, "The Führer is not to blame. It's those people under him, they're at fault. He can't know everything that goes on."

"If he doesn't know what goes on, then he should not be leading the nation." She grew tired of our argument and said, "Karin, you'd better go to your room."

I moved toward the door. Then I heard Oma say, "Poor Wanda. Horst, so intelligent, with a great future ahead of him. Dead. Died for the fatherland at Leningrad. There is something wrong here." Her voice rose, "How could God permit such a thing?"

Aunt Margaret looked shocked. "Elsa," she said. "Don't blame God. Leave Him out of this."

Mother left the room and squeezed by me in the corridor. No one had answered Oma's question. I too wondered, why would God permit such a wrong?

The blockade of Leningrad lasted from September 9, 1941, until January 24, 1944, nine hundred days. Reportedly, during this siege, one million of the city's inhabitants either died of starvation or were killed during the German bombardment. There were no numbers made public for the high German casualties.

CHAPTER 6

Of Stalingrad and Vitebsk

WINTER 1943

In late January 1943, I went to Liegnitz to visit my father. His household was busier than ever, and I was thrown into a hurly-burly family circle, where people were coming and going, and life was an ever-whirling flow. Omi, my paternal grandmother, had died some time ago, and Tante Erna had free rein. Many of her friends and relatives visited. There were two beggars, regulars, who appeared at their appointed time each week for their allotted handout. Vati was generous; he even tipped the streetcar conductor. When I reported this later to Mutti, she wondered, if this could be the same man who had pleaded with her to be decent and not insist on alimony, the same man who paid the court-ordered child support only grudgingly?

This time I noticed Tante Erna's swollen stomach. She wore loose fitting dresses, and the maid whispered that a new baby was expected in March.

Except for shortages of food, Liegnitz was a peaceful place and seemed to be removed from the direct winds of war. Of course, news of the war reached us through the Deutscher Rundfunk, the official airwaves under Goebbels's control. On January 31, 1943, Field Marshal Fredrich von Paulus surrendered the last of his troops to the Russians. This perhaps was the turning point. For the first time in this war, German troops were forced to surrender and retreat. Goebbels sugarcoated the defeat and explained to the people in his radio address that these retreats were necessary to gain a strategic advantage.

Goebbels had lied to us, and by now the rumors were spreading: Germany was losing ground. Some even mentioned the unmentionable, that Germany might lose the war. The earlier euphoria that had accompanied Germany's taking of France, Germany's victory in North Africa, and

Germany's storming through the Balkans into Greece and into Russia had changed to doubts. I argued with Vati and Tante Erna that our Führer would find a solution, that he had a secret weapon he would unleash and let us win the war. They tightened their lips, afraid that I might repeat their words in school.

This defeat at Stalingrad cast a deep shadow over the people. It was as if the glory of all the earlier victories had been wiped out by this one, horrific loss. I overheard Father say to Aunt Erna that the defeat would herald the defeat of Germany.

The front page of Vati's paper printed Dr. Goebbels's speech given on February 18th, in the Sportspalast, that proclaimed the necessity for *totaler Krieg*—total war. We had listened to the long-winded diatribe on the radio, but I had become bored and gone into the kitchen to see what was bubbling in the pots. Through the open door I could hear the thunderous applause and the fanatical "*Ja, Ja, Ja!*" of the audience, interrupting his speech numerous times. Fifteen thousand people were reportedly present, and Vati said the audience was made up mainly of party members. Goebbels exhorted the German people to give up certain comforts with a willing spirit. The same hysterical "Ja, Ja, Ja!" was heard again. Luxury restaurants, fashion shops, cabarets, and dance halls as well as beauty parlors were to be closed; women were to greet their homecoming soldiers with natural-looking hair. "Ja, Ja, Ja!" None of these places were needed at this stage of the war, he said, when terror must be fought with terror. Cinemas, music halls, and theaters would remain open to uplift the crowds. But the German people must make these sacrifices when sacrifices are called for. Judging by the roar, the people in the crowd sounded more than willing to make sacrifices.

I overheard Vati whisper to Tante Erna that it was a brilliant speech, but he said that it distorted the truth and that it was a masterful manipulation of the masses. Tante Erna, whose brother was fighting on the front lines, said, "Aren't we making sacrifices enough, sending the men in our families to war?"

Father's sister, Tante Oda, came to Liegnitz to visit Vati shortly after I arrived. I wondered why we had not taken the train together since we both lived in Berlin. There must have been little communication between the adults.

I admired her; she was a poet, a writer of novellas, and an essayist who had won several literary prizes. I had visited her from time to time in her bohemian apartment in Berlin, and I had been impressed with her many books, with the drawings on her walls by her artist friends, and with the wonderful terracotta statue of her, nude, with arms raised, that had been sculpted by Fritz Klimsch. I was most impressed that she, a poet and writer, could allow her home to just *be*. She did not clean. Mother used to say, "She lets *Sieben grade sein*," meaning that Oda regarded seven as an even number: the saying describes someone who doesn't care about minutiae. Once a week a cleaning woman came to do the housework. Between those days, though, the dishes piled up, plate by plate, cup by cup, and by the end of the week there was no room in the sink and not a clean dish in the cupboard. Sometimes I began to wash a few cups or plates, but Tante Oda always told me to stop that nonsense. Time was to be used for more important things, like having a conversation or reading to me from her own or another poet's writings.

I loved her graceful beauty, her slanted eyes the color of the sea, her silver blonde hair. Poets had written about her, and painters had painted her. When Mother first met my father and Oda at the same party, she was so taken with Oda that she fell in love with my father. A strange transfer of attraction.

Aunt Oda had one child, Peter, whom she adored. I had met him in Liegnitz a few times, but he was nine years older and we had shared no interests. I have only the faint memory of a wheat blond male spirit, wafting about Vati's household.

At barely eighteen, Peter had been drafted and had served in the Sixth Army under General von Paulus in Russia. A short while before Paulus surrendered, Peter had been flown out of Stalingrad to a different post. Tante Oda did not know where he was.

Her green eyes were perpetually rimmed in red. Her thoughts were of her only son in Russia. She moved from room to room as if she had lost something important, something she could not find. Her fears had spun her into the state of a sleepwalker. The great love of her life, her second husband, Horst Lange, a novelist who was younger than she, had also fought in Russia. Shrapnel had lodged in his brain, and he had lost one eye and was in a hospital, fighting to retain the sight in the other. Both husband and son created a double anxiety for my Tante Oda.

Tante Oda had brought a few of Peter's letters with her to Liegnitz, and when she read from them, I sat very still, fascinated by what our soldiers encountered in Russia. Peter wrote of this vast land that I had become acquainted with through the *Wochenschau,* the weekly newsreels, that were shown before feature films. Peter complained about the unending rain in October and of roads having turned into rivers of mud. The letters brought to life what I had seen in the newsreel clips: artillery and tanks getting stuck in mire, and soldiers sinking up to their ankles in sludge.

Father then reminisced about when he, as a youth, had visited a relative's estate in the south of Russia before World War I. The land had not changed, and neither had the roads. Father spoke of the vastness of Russia, a land Napoleon's army had not been able to conquer.

"But our Führer can still win in Russia," I said, stomping my foot. "They are primitives, Slavs. We Germans are brave and our soldiers can win."

"Karin," he said, shaking his head, " There's Slavic blood in us too. Look at your cheekbones, look at your Aunt Oda's tilted eyes. After all, why shouldn't there be, our family has been in the Baltics for centuries." Father frowned and shook his head. I sensed that he didn't want to argue with me about Hitler and his winning or losing the war, but that he felt he had to call me on the Slavic issue.

Father went on about Russia's unlimited manpower and the passion of the simple Russian peasant for his Mother Russia, a passion much like a religious fervor, making the common man capable of the most astonishing feats while defending his land.

I kept silent.

Then, when the reading resumed, I listened with fascination as Peter vividly described his life. The soldiers were plagued by lice. The first time Peter squashed two, then, a short while later, twenty. After a while there were too many, and the continuous crawling he and his comrades felt on their skin drove them crazy. Peter knew that his mother would worry about the soldiers in the cauldron not having enough to eat, and he wrote, "Mutti, don't worry about our going hungry, we have horses and when they get wounded, they wind up in the stew."

Winter set in around Stalingrad, and already in November the temperature sank to minus twenty degrees Celsius. The bunkers were covered with thick earth. Each soldier had an issue of several blankets, and a little iron stove kept them from freezing.

Peter wrote of loneliness, of fallen comrades whom he'd seen dying. When Oda read these heart-wrenching parts, she choked on her tears, and Father took the letter from her shaky hands.

Peter tried to write daily—his letters substituting for keeping a daily journal—but often he could only manage to write a few times a week. The letters were airlifted from the trenches and reached their destination in a relatively short period of time.

Vati remarked that maybe by writing Peter could stay the horrors of war. Maybe by writing he could hold on to the connection to his mother; by writing, he could remain sane in an insane world.

In early December, the letters stopped.

After Tante Oda returned to Berlin, she heard from Peter again. His ability to speak Russian had delivered him from Stalingrad. I don't know where he learned Russian; could it be that Omi, who would not teach me, had taught him? Requisitioned by a unit that had lost its interpreter, Peter was airlifted out of the cauldron.

Tante Oda sent some of Peter's letters of the westward retreat to my father, knowing they would interest the journalist-uncle. Peter's descriptions of leaving scorched earth behind were extremely visual, and Father said Peter would some day become a fine writer. It had pained this sensitive young soldier to have to follow orders to burn down the few farmhouses and barns that had withstood the earlier German conquest of these lands. Father, Oda, and Peter had a love for Russia's wide skies, for Russian music and literature, and, by extension, for the Russian peasant who had been exploited for centuries.

Long after the war, I heard of Peter's last letters. He had arrived in the ancient Belarus city of Vitebsk, which lay on a strategic route on the river Dwina, leading to Riga and Ostpreussen (East Prussia). By June of 1944 this basin was completely encircled by the Soviets, and Vitebsk fell. Peter was declared *vermisst*—missing in action—a fate that Oda had so dreaded when she thought him still to be at Stalingrad.

For years Oda lived with the hope he might still be alive or lost somewhere in the vast spaces of Russia. His language ability would have helped him survive. But as the years passed, her hope dwindled.

His words on crumbling paper were all that was left of him.

Zugzwang in the Lair of Wolves

Tante Erna was due to give birth at any time, but she felt strong and happy, and she assured me that I was not a burden to her. I hoped for a little sister, and when I walked by a church steeple where storks had built a nest, I sang to them, "*Storch, Storch, Bester, bring mir eine Schwester . . .*" But the storks didn't listen to me, and within a week Aunt Erna went into labor and came home from the clinic with another baby brother. Father named him Wolf Hubertus; we called him Hubsi. I suppose my father was proud that he was still virile at his age, and that he had fathered so many boys.

I now slept in Omi's spacious room. I should have been content, but when I lay in bed, images of her intruded. I had felt rejected by her and had never received the slightest sign of her love. Try as I might I could not think of her in loving terms. Revere your elders, I was told. Respect the dead. But I could not. She too was my grandmother but different from my Oma. I could not help but compare the two. I thought of the white swan princess Odette from *Swan Lake* and her opposite, the evil, black Odile. Although my grandmothers were old women and certainly not fairy princesses, they seemed to me to be mirror images of one another.

There was a difference even in their use of their respective first languages. When Oma spoke English with Aunt Margaret, they always included me in their conversation, translating certain words, in hopes I would learn their language. But this was not so with Omi. She was born in Dorpat, Estonia, which was part of the Russian Empire at the time, and spoke Russian and German. She conversed with my father in that softly rolling and beautiful tongue, but only when she didn't want anyone else to understand her. I learned English from Oma but only one word of Russian from Omi: nyet.

Oma was a happy woman, given to singing. She would often grab a broom, or a Biedermeier chair, and waltz around the rooms. Omi was dour: she had a turned down mouth and yellowing skin, and she always dressed in black. Her long skirts swept the floor as if she had forgotten time and still lived in the century of her birth. She used to crown her thin, slate gray top-knot with a black lace kerchief, folded to resemble a bird's nest.

I was too young to know (and only learned this years later) that Omi had valid reasons to be melancholy, or rather, depressed. Before her marriage she had been a much admired, beautiful young woman. She grew up in a wealthy merchant's household, and her marriage at age sixteen to a much older man had disappointed her. My grandfather was an idealistic man who spun himself into his fantasies; he was an unsuccessful novelist who earned his income as a journalist. After Bismarck unified the country, many foreign-born Germans had felt drawn to the center of the new, strong Germany and had flocked to its capital, Berlin. My grandfather left his highly regarded editing position at a newspaper in Riga, in exchange for an inferior one in Berlin. My grandmother did not like Berlin, nor Germany; she considered it foreign and hostile and came to feign the helpless stranger in the big city. Then my grandfather lost his job at the paper, because his writing style was considered to be archaic. My father was getting promoted at the *Berliner Zeitung* and received offers from several small town papers. (One of these offers would take him to Liegnitz where he became the chief editor of the *Liegnitzer Tageblatt*.) My grandfather's depression grew, knowing he could not return to Riga. After the Versailles Treaty, the Baltic lands were lost to Baltic Germans. There was no return.

My father's family had not been wealthy, but what little they had in currency or real estate had been lost during World War I. Father continued to live with his parents, helping with their expenses. He also rented a small flat in a dubious neighborhood, to which he would take women he could not take home to his mother. On December 28, a cold and drizzly night, Father returned to his little flat long after midnight, a giggling and half-tipsy girl on his arm. His key entered the lock, but strangely it was already unlocked. The door squeaked open. In the dark apartment, semilit by the sulfurous green-yellow beam of a street light, he found his father. The big man lay sprawled on the bed. The top of his head had been blown off by a single gunshot.

I have always wondered how my father was able to break the news of his father's grisly suicide to his mother. How could he admit to this prim Victorian woman that he kept an apartment for trysts with loose females? And how could he explain his father's access to his apartment?

The suicide left my father with feelings of guilt. The suicide made him give in to his mother's demands. Suicide, like venereal disease, was something no one talked about or acknowledged. My father felt that Omi had to be protected like a beloved stranger in a strange land. This duty fell to him, and he promised he would never desert her.

When Father married my mother, it was agreed that his mother would live with them. Their apartment was large, and there were numerous bedrooms; counting the living room, the library, and the formal dining room, there were nine rooms in all. The arrangement might have worked, but Omi was insanely jealous of every little thing my father did for my mother. If he brought a fancy bonboniere of chocolates home to his young wife, he had to bring the identical gift to Omi and to my Aunt Oda, who, recently divorced, also lived, along with her son Peter, with my father and my mother. When Vati bought Mother a fur coat, Omi ordered him to buy one for his poor, divorced sister. He could not afford this and refused. But on everything else, he gave in.

Oda returned to Berlin, with Peter in tow. Oda's presence had been the one ray of light in this gloomy household. Two more years of suffering with Omi passed before Mother found the courage to give Father an ultimatum.

"Please, Woga, find an apartment close by for your mother, or I will leave."

He made his choice: he allowed Mother to take me, his daughter, and leave.

After Father remarried, Wolfdieter was born. As a boy he was a *Stammhalter,* a keeper of the lineage. Omi began to tolerate my stepmother, but it had not been easy for Tante Erna in the beginning. Intent on improving my stepmother's education, Omi would sit in an upholstered easy chair in the kitchen and read Emanuel Kant or Friedrich Nietzsche to her. While Erna's eyes teared up from chopping onions, and her face flushed from bending over steaming pots, she had to listen to the words of philosophers. How much of these lectures would she remember?

In those early years, during one of my summer visits, I had opened the door to the nursery and caught Omi kissing my one-year-old brother's penis. I was maybe four years old, but the sight of this old woman in black bending over a little naked baby on the diapering table, hovering over his sweet pink skin like a giant malevolent crow, paying homage to his little *Schniepel,* haunted me. To me, this act proclaimed that girls are worthless and that only boys count.

Thoughts about the dead woman in whose bed I lay would scramble through my mind, keeping me awake, feeling guilty because I detested her.

On a gray afternoon, the doorbell rang. Tante Erna was diapering Hubsi, and she sent me to see who was at the door. Two men in brown SA uniforms stood in the doorway. They asked for my father.

"Who is it?" she called.

"There are two men here."

"Our business is with Herr Doctor Kraus. May we come in?"

Tante Erna came to the door, holding Hubsi in her arms. I saw by the look on her face that she did not welcome these visitors.

"My husband is at the paper. He'll be home in about an hour."

Just then Vati appeared from his study.

"He's at the paper, eh?" said the shorter of the men.

"What . . . , what's this all about?" Father asked, first looking at the men, then at Tante Erna. "I came home a while ago, didn't you hear me when I came in?" He turned to the men again and waved them into the apartment. "What can I do for you?"

The three disappeared into the library. Tante Erna and I went back to the children's room. I noticed she was trembling.

"I think I know what this is all about," she said. "Your father has held out this long, but now, I'm afraid he'll have to join."

"Join what?

"The NSDAP, the Nazi party. They have been putting a lot of pressure on him lately; Goebbels gave new directives. Every man or woman working in the press or in radio has to be a member of the NSDAP. We were always surprised that your father was able to withhold this long. We thought maybe they didn't pay much attention to provincial newspapers. Liegnitz is such a small town."

"But what if he doesn't want to?"

"He'd lose his job. No one would hire him at any other paper. No one would publish anything he wrote ever again."

"I don't like the book he wrote about Rudolf Diesel anyway. It's boring," I said.

"I'm afraid he thinks it's boring too." She leaned toward me and whispered, "The publisher didn't let him go on with the book he was writing. A new look at Machiavelli. Too controversial. The publisher suggested the Diesel project."

I didn't know who Machiavelli was and didn't want to ask. Maybe he was someone I should know. My tante Erna looked so unhappy, I wanted to cheer her up. I said, "I like the Baltic humor book he wrote. That made me laugh."

"Yes. He had fun writing that book. In those days we laughed a lot."

Just then Father walked into the room. He closed the door behind him and leaned against it. His face had lost all color, the folds in his cheeks seemed deeper, blending into the dueling scar on his right side. He said, "Zugzwang," and indicated with his head that I should leave the room.

Later I learned that Tante Erna had been right: Father was told he would have to join the party or lose his job. He joined the NSDAP. I asked about the strange word Father had mentioned—*Zugzwang*—and was told it was a word used in chess, when one player forces another to make an undesirable move.

A few days later on my way home from school, I dashed to catch the streetcar running down the center of the Goldberger Strasse. I caught it by jumping onto the step, and I found a seat and began reading my book. After about two stops a lot more people crowded onto the tram. An old man stood near me, looking out of the windows as if he were staring into space. He held onto the leather straps dangling from the roof of the tram and swayed with the streetcar. The man looked frail, and he wore a large yellow star on the right side of his shabby black coat. I stared at the writing on it, *JUDE*. I had been taught to be polite to older people and got up, offering him my seat. For a brief moment, his haggard face lit up. He nodded to me and maneuvered to sit down. A fortyish man grabbed my shoulder and pushed me back into my seat.

"A German girl does not get up for a Jew," he said, spitting out the words.

I was back in my seat but not for long. The old man's face flushed red, and he averted his eyes and stared at the floor. I didn't know what to do. I felt so sorry for him. I knew I could not get up and offer my seat again, but I felt uncomfortable in it, watching the old man's humiliation.

I pushed through the crowd and hopped off at the next station.

My hands dug through my pockets, looking for coins, but they came up empty. I had no money for another tram, and I walked home. When I got there everyone was angry with me because I was late for supper.

Later that night, when Tante Erna came into my room to say goodnight, I told her what had happened. "But Karin," she said. "The conductors all know your father. He always tips them. You could have told them who you are and you'd pay tomorrow."

I shook my head. "It's done. But why was that old man wearing a star?"

"That's another law Goebbels issued. All Jewish people have to wear a yellow star. To let everyone know they are Jews. I've heard they cut their rations again. I don't know how they can exist. I thought by now most Jews had left Germany. That poor old man. He's probably quite alone."

The baby was crying, and Tante Erna left the room, kissing me on the forehead. She had treated me like an adult, like someone she could talk to. I still felt sorry for the old man wearing the yellow star, but I no longer felt alone.

Fire from Above

I returned to Berlin in August. Happy to be back home in our apartment, I snuggled in the wide sofa with its many pillows. Mother always made everything look beautiful. Even now, with long hours spent at work, she found time to go to the flower market. Through the half-open door I admired the sunflowers in the copper pitcher in the entry; they were bright and burnished as if they were still in a garden, bathed in sunlight.

The flowers brought me back to the fisherman's cottage on the island of Sylt; the old house had been surrounded by sunflowers. I longed for that summer of four years ago. I longed for the sea and for my dreams of mermaids. I longed for peace.

Mother dangled a cigarette from her hand, her elbow resting on the table. I watched the smoke curl in graceful spirals, framing the oval of her face in whispers, and thought that even the smoke wished to caress her. She lifted her slender hand, her long fingers tipped with scarlet connected the cigarette to her color matched lips, and when she exhaled and blew smoke in ringlets toward me, my ten-year-old heart felt ready to crack wide open, loving her so much. I loved her beauty and her large gray eyes as they gazed at me half-hidden by a curtain of lashes. I wanted to slide the smoke rings onto my finger and pledge myself to her; I wanted her to be mine forever. But she was as ephemeral as the smoke veiling her.

It was August 23, 1943. For me to have returned to Berlin was against the orders of the Third Reich, which mandated that all children be in a safe place in the countryside. But it was summer, and the schools that kept records of us children were closed, so no one would know where I was. I had my ration card from Liegnitz, which Mother was able to register in the same grocery store with hers and Oma's. It would last until I returned to my father's place in September, when I would receive a new one for the next month.

There had been air raids. Now the siren sounded again. It was an hour earlier than the customary time for a bombing. (People said they could set their clocks by the arrival of British planes.) We had finished dinner, and Oma and Mutti were lingering over *mucke-fuck,* our ersatz coffee made from hickory nuts and some kind of grain, which tasted offensively bitter. Mother sipped cognac, real French cognac, and blew smoke rings. I don't think she inhaled, and I believe Oma was glad to be summoned into the cellar by the siren, since she disliked Mother's smoking. Smoking was verboten in the cellar.

Mother always took her time when the alarm sounded; the bombs were meant for others. The house warden banged a reprimanding rhythm on our front door, shouting, "You have to come down, now!" Mother, who had recently studied "La Habanera," from *Carmen,* trilled that aria at him: "*Ja die Lieb hat bunte Flügel*"—Love has colorful wings, such a bird you can not catch. I heard him grumble as he hobbled back down the stairs.

Oma threw Mother a chastising look. She grabbed our coats, and we followed the house warden and reached the vestibule. I was curious about what was going on outside. Mother pushed at the heavy oak door. It creaked as it opened, and we stepped onto the sidewalk.

There!

We saw them.

In the darkening sky phosphorous lights slowly floated earthward, marking the way for British bombers, leading the pilots to tonight's target. Like gigantic triangular snowflakes, they floated above our section of Berlin. As in a game, they signaled that "You Are It!" Someone with a Berliner's mordant wit had named these flares, which brought destruction and death, *Weihnachtsbäume,* which is German for "Christmas tree." There was a strange beauty in all of this. My heart pounded faster, and I reached for Mother's hand and pressed close to her. Then we too went down into the cellar.

The other tenants in our building were already in their customary seats. The cellar had been fortified a few years earlier. Heavy beams were placed to withstand collapsing walls and ceilings; a small opening was dug to connect us to the neighboring cellar, leaving an alternate route of escape in case the building collapsed and the way out to the street was blocked—*verschüt-tet*. This loosely closed hole in the cellar wall could be opened with a shovel or a pick axe. The cellar was outfitted with cots along the walls, and we had a kerosene lamp. There were a few chairs, candles, shovels, flashlights, and some food provisions and water. Some people kept pillows and blankets in the shelter; others carried small suitcases up and down the stairs each time the alarm sounded.

Mother never expected to be in the cellar for any length of time. She carried only her handbag. Oma had packed photo albums and some necessities for all of us in a suitcase she kept in the cellar stall where potatoes and apples were stored in winter.

When we entered the cellar, faces with skin the color of watery oatmeal stared at my flamboyant mother and me. I worried that someone would give my presence away to the authorities. I was self-conscious about my looks: I was skinny, with scrawny legs, wire-rimmed glasses, and dirty blonde pigtails. I kept looking at Mother, the only lovely sight amid the colorless faces in this dank basement.

People in the cellar joked about "fat Emma" and how this Emma had brought us air raids and possible death. "Damn fat Emma, for bringing us the Tommy's revenge." They were referring to Reichsmarschall Hermann Göring, the commander of the German Air Force, who had boasted after his Luftwaffe started to blitz London that our air defenses were so strong that no British plane could penetrate German airspace. He had declared, "If even one of the British planes manages to drop a single bomb on a German town, *dann will ich Emma heissen*"—then you can call me Emma. Emma was his wife's name. Even the house warden, a member of the Nazi Party, cursed Göring and shook his head.

Soon we heard the whistles, the zinging sound of bombs, the high-pitched hum that sounded like gigantic metallic insects, the roar of airplane motors, and then the explosions that followed.

The bombing had started.

We heard a few *Sprengbomben,* or blockbusters, detonate near us; our house convulsed as the explosions reverberated in the building. These bombs were followed by the *Brandbomben,* the incendiary bombs. Again there was a high-pitched zing, then the *wham* and the shaking. Time and time again we heard the whistle, coming closer—followed by the bomb's impact. I buried my face in my grandmother's shoulder, my right arm stretched out to hold on to my mother.

When I opened my eyes, I saw us all as ghosts—strange ghosts, with large eyes surrounded by white eyelashes, hovered above bodies coated grayish white with the dust of fallen plaster and pulverized concrete.

"The building is on fire. Out! Everybody out," shouted the house warden. We scrambled to our feet. Oma grabbed the suitcase from the potato bin, and we ran to the exit, coughing, tying handkerchiefs across our mouths. It was nighttime, but it was so bright outside on the street that it could have been daytime. The street was lit up with a ghostly, stage-set light, red and orange from the fires mixed with the white, bluish green reflection from the floating Christmas trees. All was veiled in billows of smoke through which I could see probing searchlights crisscrossing the dark sky above the brightness. Suddenly a plane was caught in the cross beam of the lights, looking like a moth trying to escape, and when the flak hit the plane, it was as if a star exploded in a jagged flame above the smoke. An eerie stillness hung above us in the sky, while bombs rained all around us, bursting with horrendous noise.

"I need help to put the fire out under the roof," the warden's voice coughed through the dust. Mother rushed to his side, and they, and several others, climbed the five flights of stairs to the attic. Mother told us later what happened. Sand lay heaped in large containers, and there was water. Water was useless in fighting phosphorous bombs, but the sand would smother the flames. There was another rain of bombs—one crashed through the roof near them—but there was no more sand. Everyone had to run for their lives.

Mother stopped by our apartment on the second floor. The door had been blown wide open. Mother's eyes lit upon the antique chest in the entrance. She grabbed the dozen sunflowers from the pitcher and an armful of hats and umbrellas. When she emerged from the burning house, she was a strange sight: tall and slender, framed by the blazing building, in her arm a large bouquet of sunflowers.

I stared at her, wondering if she had lost her mind.

Grandmother took the load from her arms. "Astrid, flowers. . . ?" Oma shook her head. "Hats? Umbrellas?" Was that a reproach? She did not say, why not the ancient family bible, the ancestors' portraits, why not the silver? Mother stood mute.

"Mutti, my dolls, and my teddy bear?"

Mother cast a long look at me, turned and ran back toward the burning building. I ran after her, shouting, "No, I don't need them, no, don't go, no!" I tried to catch her, and when I caught up with her, I tried to hold her, as did my grandmother. The house warden grabbed Mother's jacket. She shook us all loose and disappeared from sight.

I do not remember how much time passed before I heard the awful noise: crunching, crashing, exploding walls, beams, and wood. My heart felt as if it would stop beating and drop to my feet. I bit my lips, something bitter rose from my stomach. Oma locked her arms around me and squeezed. When I opened my eyes, I could not see a thing; the smoke was biting, thick, and acrid. My eyes burned. Soot, dust, ashes, and rubble were all around me, and heat blasted as if from a furnace.

A voice screamed, "My God, the staircase is collapsing." I choked and looked up. An incandescent light sliced the gray, as if a giant torch were spitting fire up, and at the same time, the fire licked down the blackened spinal column of the stairwell. Part of the house imploded in a shower of sparks, like giant fireflies. I looked away, held my breath, and bit my lip until it bled.

And then a spectral figure emerged from swirls of orange and gray, stepped out of the smoke toward me, and became my mother.

My mother, bearing a silver teapot and my toy bear.

We had now joined the thousands of people who were homeless, *ausgebombt,* the bombed out. The gray hordes walking in limbo. Everything of value was gone: our sixteenth-century hand-illuminated bible and our early eighteenth-century ancestors' portraits. I liked the portrait of the woman in blue silk, with glowing skin tones and wide-set blue eyes, more than I liked any of the others. She wore a fancifully coiffed silver wig. Now her portrait and her husband's—he was also bewigged, wearing his scarlet mayoral costume replete with golden chains and medals—were gone, reduced to ashes. My Käthe Kruse doll, my baby doll, my toys, my books, the silver, the china, Mother's piano and costume sketches, my father's drawings, and the Christmas ornaments, all were ashes.

HIMMEL UND ERDE

After the air raids in August, Goebbels ordered mass evacuations, and all nonworking women and preschool-age children had to leave Berlin. That included Oma, who went to stay with her friend in Upper Silesia again. The housing authorities had secured a room for Mother in an apartment in the district of Halensee, and I went back to my father's house.

I hoped to forget the night of bombs, but I worried about Mother. I knew there were nightly air raids in Berlin, though little was told of their destructive terror in the newspapers. All of the newspapers were heavily censored. My father complained that some of his front page articles were cancelled just before the paper went to press. When this happened, he was forced to quickly come up with another lead article, telling a different story. There were many who listened to the BBC to find out the truth of what was happening in the war, but this was illegal. If anyone spread the news to others, he or she risked jail or even death.

I often thought of that night when we had been bombed. I mourned for the things I had lost, most of all, for my Käthe Kruse doll.

"Karin, come on, you're usually so cheerful. Let me see you laugh again," Tante Erna coaxed.

But I could not laugh. My forced smile looked like a grimace. Nor could I make the silly faces that had amused my little brothers. Even their playful antics and the cute new baby did not cheer me up. When people spoke to me, I sometimes mustered a tight lipped grin but usually kept a sullen silence.

I think Father felt sorry for me. This time he tried to make me feel like I was a part of his family and of his life. When he had to write a review for a new theatrical production, he would take me with him if I did not have school the next morning (Tante Erna preferred to stay at home with the boys). After the play he would take me to the Ratskeller, the restaurant where he normally drank wine and played skat with his friends. His *Stammtisch,* or permanent table, would be waiting for him. Attached to the table was a bronze plaque with his name engraved on it. When he ordered his favorite—a pork cutlet—he would order *Himmel und Erde* for me, since I didn't like fatty meat. This dish called "heaven and earth" was also served as a side dish to Father. It was a simple meal of mashed potatoes and apple sauce, and I loved it. He ordered red wine for himself and *Himbeersaft* for me. This delicious drink, tasting of raspberries and summer, reminded me of the times when Oma had taken me into the woods to harvest wild raspberries. But sometimes there were little white worms in the lush fruit, and when I found one, I would squeal and drop my berries.

Father expected me to keep quiet while he wrote his review, but later he would read it to me. Because I was allowed to stay up—on Saturday nights only—until after midnight, I felt grown up and was honored to be treated as Father's assistant.

After he finished his critique, I would accompany him to the *Redaktion,* the press room, where he gave last-minute instructions to the typesetters and the printers. I inhaled the smell—acid mixed with motor oil and ink—of the printing process. On those nights I wanted to grow up to be a journalist. I was impressed by these magical black beasts, the huge presses that clanked, growled, and spat out the early morning edition that would be delivered to thousands of homes in and around Liegnitz.

For those few hours I forgot the bombing.

Then there were times when Vati, sensing my continued sadness, took me on long walks. I felt a harmony and closeness to him when we walked far across rich brown earth showing the stubble of the recent barley crop, or when he pointed out fields of potatoes being harvested by big women in heavy skirts and kerchiefs tightly tied around multiple chins.

The scent of autumn, musty and smelling of mushrooms and decaying leaves, hung in the air. It smelled of acrid smoke and of chaff burning in the fields, so different from the odor of burning houses. There was the rich scent of fertile, turned-over earth. We walked alongside reedy lakes where wild ducks quacked and often lifted into the air in a sudden swoosh, leaving a V-trail of silver drops. And sometimes we saw swans. I had read they mated for life. Why couldn't humans be like swans? Then my father and my mother would still be together.

I loved the swans. At night, I thought, they must turn back into enchanted maidens; they were too perfect in their grace to be animals forever. My father and I also explored deep woods. The birch trees shimmered in silvery gold; the beech and maple trees were turning orange and red. Vati would again tell me tales of Baba Yaga, and as we walked, I expected to come across her little block house sitting on chicken legs deep within a dark forest. I imagined her forest to look exactly like the one we were in. The little house would turn with the wind and would either conceal the entrance or show an open door to whoever approached, wind and house divining the stranger's intentions. I grew to love Baba Yaga, and I imagined her as a benign witch who would provide refuge for me if I were ever lost among her trees, and then no war could touch me.

The Double Countess

In the winter of 1943, arrangements had been made for Oma and me to stay with a close friend of Oma's—I called her Tante Mietze—in Eisenstadt, Austria, near the Hungarian border. We had arrived here in late November. It had snowed, and the town, with its eighteenth-century yellow sandstone buildings and red-tiled roofs, was covered in white. I walked through the narrow curving streets, and as I turned a corner, I came upon a quaint onion-shaped church tower near the former city wall. It felt as if I had stepped into one of my father's Russian fairy-tale books. I stomped through the snow, kicking up white powder with my boots. I spread my arms and swirled around, feeling free in all this white, far away from the gray soot of bombed Berlin.

Christmas was only a few weeks away, but Oma was not in the holiday spirit. The loss of our possessions weighed on her. The memory of the fire and the collapsing building would surface at odd moments, making her weep. I too had these flashbacks; I often dreamed of flames chasing me through blackened and deserted streets, and I would wake up sobbing. Mother was also having trouble letting go of the memory. Tante Mietze showed us one of Mother's letters, written in September. "Dear Mietze," it read,

> this may sound absurd, but when I took a last look at our apartment, it was as if I had been intoxicated, or crazy, as I was struck by the beauty amid the horror. There was the large vase filled with sunflowers, yellow-orange, sitting on the chest in the entry, behind it, the wall to the living room collapsed, the silk curtains blazed the same color as the sunflowers and the ancestors began melting in their gilt frames. The beautiful face of the woman in blue—the one you always admired—shriveled. It didn't burn, but the heat made it all crumble and shrink and detach from the frame. I could not think. I loaded up with hats and umbrellas and grabbed the sunflowers. I had a hard time to tear myself away from the fire, the heat, the terrifying beauty.

The letter reminded Oma that Mother had not saved the ancient family bible. I later wondered, why hadn't the adults—knowing Berlin was being bombed—stored certain irreplaceable family heirlooms in a safe place in the countryside? But we did not know anyone with a farmhouse or a place in the country. And as the war enveloped more of Germany, there was no safe place.

At night, when I thought of my dolls and my fairy-tale books, I wept. But I had my teddy bear with me, which still smelled of smoke, and I would cuddle between his fuzzy ears.

Oma worried about her two sons who were stationed on two different fronts: Uncle Richard was in Greece, and Will had been dispatched to Finland after his leg had healed. She worried about my mother braving the air raids. Poor Mother, she never got enough sleep because she had two jobs, worked twelve hours a day, and had to spend part of her nights in shelters.

I received my one and only Christmas present early, a pair of bright red Hungarian leather boots. This was a practical gift as well as a beautiful one. The boots kept my feet dry in the grim weather. Ever since meeting Marlene, Uncle Will's friend in Frankfurt, I had dreamed of owning a pair of red boots. The boots came almost up to my knees and made me want to dance and twirl as I had seen Hungarian dancers do. I had bright red boots to dance the czardas in and to crunch the snow beneath my feet.

Oma also received a present—a huge side of bacon—from our host, Tante Mietze. It had been smuggled in from Hungary with my boots. The bacon had the shape of buttocks clearly marked in it. When I pointed this out to Oma, she told me that the peasant woman who'd smuggled the bacon had probably sat on it for many hours during the train ride. The woman had been traveling with our bacon and her load of food stuff, all hidden beneath her many layers of skirts. Hungry as I was, my imagination ran away with me, and I could not force myself to eat of the bacon. I thought of the woman making a *Pumps* (passing gas) on the bacon. It made me queasy, just as I had made the girls in Marienbad feel when I told them icky stories. Maybe this was my punishment.

There would be no other presents, and since paper was in short supply and few books were being printed, I did not get a book from my father.

Sugar and butter were scarce, and baking required powers of invention. Luckily, Oma was gifted with a sensitive tongue and a great imagination. She made the artificial marzipan she had tried earlier in the war, but now, when there was nothing else to rival it, the persipan, as it was called, tasted delicious. Oma used wartime margarine, a nasty tasting fat, to make cakes, but then she buttered the bottom and sides of the cake pan, so the taste of butter would dominate.

A Christmas tree lit by wax candles stood in the corner of the living room. Oma and I had our own bedroom but shared the other rooms with Tante Mietze and her son, Wolfgang. He was sixteen, tall, and handsome, and he wore the gray Luftwaffenhelfer uniform. His friend Herbert was in the same antiaircraft troop. He was blond and equally handsome, and even though I was only ten years old, I dreamt of these defenders of our skies, rather than dreaming of sugarplums and nutcrackers.

Christmas Eve arrived, and the four of us were invited to a gathering at the Esterhazy's château. This was the social event of the year, and I felt overwhelmed mingling with members of Austrian-Hungarian aristocracy. Oma had briefed me: I would meet the countess, a close relative to the actual owner, Fürst (Prince) Esterhazy, who was living in Hungary or abroad somewhere. I was to curtsy, smile, and speak only when spoken to. I learned that Haydn had lived at the court for more than seven years and was conductor of the Esterhazy's orchestra. He had composed some of his most memorable music in this château. I was prepared to be awed.

We crossed the threshold and walked into a fairyland. When the doorman in blue livery opened the wide double doors to this rococo palace, we entered—for a few scant hours—a place of long ago, where war did not exist. We ascended the large, curving stone staircase and passed through another set of double doors before being escorted into the great salon. Music floated toward us as we entered the room where a string quartet played Haydn. And there stood the tree, perfectly proportioned and reaching up to the high ceiling. The tree was decorated with hundreds of candles that were reflected in Venetian glass mirrors, on the gleaming amber parquet floors, on the highly polished furniture, on the golden frames of the paintings, in the sparkle of window glass and, most of all, in Oma's eyes.

How beautiful she looked that night in her prewar dress of navy blue *peau-de-soie.* The room smelled of pine and of beeswax candles. An unknown scent overwhelmed the candle wax, encircling the Countess Esterhazy whom we now approached. She smelled as I imagined the heroine of a love story would, seductive and overpoweringly exotic. Oma told me later that the countess wore one of Guerlain's perfumes, Shalimar, I believe. I took the fingertips of the hand she extended, a white and bejeweled hand, and made a deep *Knix* (curtsy). I felt faint from her heavy perfume. When I looked up, I almost fell backward: there were two countesses. One of them stood before us smiling benignly, dressed in burgundy moiré, wearing a ruby necklace and matching chandelier earrings, her thick silver hair swept up in a French twist with small tendrils curling onto the curve of her long neck. The other one stared out at us from a portrait on the wall.

Who was more beautiful? I had to look twice, but then I realized that they were one and the same: the portrait was of the countess standing before us. She was much younger and *stark naked,* painted in hyperrealism. Her pose imitating Botticelli's *Birth of Venus.* (I loved this painting and had looked at it often in our Renaissance art book that was now ashes.) The countess's portrait appeared to be somewhat larger than life-size, blonde wisps of hair meeting mother-of-pearl thighs, rosy nipples pointing upward from dome-shaped breasts.

I stared. Oma pulled me away, whispering to me and chiding me for staring. Much as I wished, I could not take my eyes off the painting, nor could I look away from the live woman.

She didn't seem to mind my stares; for when she looked back, I saw a twinkle in her eyes, almost as if she were winking at me.

I watched Wolfgang. He blushed purple like our boiled red cabbage. His ears lit up like little round flashlights do when covered by a red kerchief. And the countess's lips were still curled in a smile as he bent to kiss her hand.

The string quartet continued to play Haydn's compositions; Christmas carols followed later. Glasses of *Glühwein*—a hot mulled wine flavored with honey, cinnamon, and cloves—were passed on silver trays (even to me). *Kringle* were served, deep fried crescents of airy pastry, white with powdered sugar, that would melt in your mouth. A variety of delicacies sat on the tables, but I remember only the sweets. Just as the night was beginning to get a little boring, long after my bedtime, a horde of Hungarian musicians burst into the room and made their violins vibrate, alternating between wild and joyous gypsy melodies and haunting sounds of sadness. Were they *real* gypsies? Mother had bemoaned the fact that gypsies had disappeared from German cafés some time ago. She'd wondered where they had all gone? I would write to her, letting her know that the gypsies were here in Eisenstadt and doing well.

Tokay wine was passed to the guests and it lit fires in their blood and reddened their cheeks. But Oma would not let me have even a small glass of this sweet golden wine, the pride of Hungary. But I stole a sip from her glass when she wasn't looking. It was delicious.

The Countess Esterhazy danced a mazurka. Swirling her burgundy skirts, her eyes sparkled, and she laughed, tossing her head and loosening up strands of silver curls. Age had been kind to her. I admired her, thinking how wonderful it would be to grow old and still be able to dance, to grow old and still be beautiful and full of life.

Reflecting after all these years on that night, I realize it was my last Christmas in a still genteel era. Without knowing it, I stood with one foot in a soon to be forgotten age, and with the other in a coarser, and decidedly bleaker, world.

CHAPTER 7

Swimming in Amber

SPRING–SUMMER 1944

The Russians were far from Eisenstadt, and the skies above us had been quiet. No sirens awakened us at night; no droning of bombers was heard, and there were no air raids.

Why then did Oma move us from Eisenstadt? I felt sad to leave Tante Mietze, Wolfgang, and his friend Herbert. If we had to leave at all, I wanted to go back to Father's house. I argued that I was older now and could help with my little half-brothers. But I hadn't heard from Father since I left last autumn, and Oma wanted me to stay with her. I felt doomed to grow up without a father.

In the spring of 1944, we moved back to Zoppot, near Danzig, to live again with Uncle Will's hospitable friends. But the wind blew cold through the spacious house by the sea. The only consolation was that I got to be with Krissy, the first dog I had ever loved. I went back to my previous school, with the helpful math teacher, and made friends with merry, brown-eyed Elke, a new girl next door.

In early June, Elke and I conspired to watch the sun rise from the sea. We got up before dawn, crossed the cool, white sand at twilight, and took off every last stitch of clothing, certain that we were alone. We left our clothes strewn on the red-and-white-striped seat of a big *Strandkorb,* one of many on the beach. (These large basketlike shelters had seats that lifted for storage, and the high-backed shell shielded beachgoers from wind, rain, or sun.)

We watched the horizon for the first tinge of red, then we ran into the surf. The water assaulted us with an icy shock. But we splashed and swam, pretending we were sea creatures.

The waves washing over me felt wonderful, and the briny water made me feel sleek as I dove and swam, and I opened my eyes underwater. The sun tinged the world surrounding me in colors of early morning, pastel apricot mixed with the blue green of the sea. I loved it when the waves broke the light underwater into a prism. But I had to come up when the saltwater burned my eyes too much.

"You have mermaid eyes," Elke said, "The exact color of the sea." Then she giggled, "But now the whites are all red. Like a monster."

I wanted to dive down and bite her leg to scare her, to show her I really was a red-eyed sea monster. But when I ducked under, something scraped my toe. I groped deep in the water, into the sand, and grabbed a hard object. Amber. I surfaced and held it high against the light. It was the same shade of honey gold as the sun.

I felt a pang of longing for my father. The Baltic Sea and the amber reminded me of him. His eyes so often seemed to gaze toward an imagined, far off horizon. He was aware of this and said it was from having grown up in Riga, where he took long daily walks along the strand looking far out to the sea. "Karin, you and I will always long for what lies beyond the horizon," he said once, making me feel grown up and included.

I looked at the amber in my hand—an oval ending in a point, no longer rough but rubbed smooth by moving sands. I knew from geography class that amber was fossilized pine sap, and that this area had once been a vast conifer forest before the last ice age. As it got colder, ice rolled over the land and white covered the green. Later, when the earth warmed again and melted the ice, the Baltic Sea was born. To me, it seemed the forests that died so long ago had left us their amber tears.

Suddenly I was overcome with sadness, and I resolved to write to Father as soon as I got home.

I dove once more, wanting to savor the peace and quiet of the sea. When I came up for air, I noticed that the sun hung suspended, a yellow disk gilding every wave. It was as if we were swimming in liquid amber.

The water felt even colder now. Goose bumps covered our arms, and our teeth were chattering.

That's when we saw them: two sailors sat on the beach, watching us and waiting for us to come out of the water. From a distance we probably looked much older to them; they could not have guessed that I was eleven and Elke twelve. Shouting at them didn't help, they wouldn't budge. We couldn't get out stark naked, so we kept cowering in the cold until I spotted an elderly couple walking along the beach. They, too, must have come to observe the sunrise. My waving became frantic, and the woman drew closer. I stayed low, the water covering me, and shouted out our predicament. All the while I clutched the amber in my hand. She laughed and brought us our towels and clothes. Her husband walked on a discreet distance, while she shooed the sailors away. As soon as she motioned that it was safe for us to come out, we dashed for the towels, draped them around us, grabbed our clothes, and raced for the *Strandkorb* to get dressed.

We were both so cold we could barely say "*Danke schön*" to the helpful woman. I slipped the amber in my pocket and in my head began to write the letter to my father on the way home.

I knew exactly what I'd tell him: it was true, I was just like him—always looking at what lies beyond the horizon.

When I got home, Inge Thiele told me that Oma had been furious with me for sneaking out before dawn. I was afraid to go to our rooms. Oma heard us talking, though, and called me from the upper floor. I climbed the stairs taking two steps at a time. I fingered the amber in my pocket and gave it to her. I spoke of my father and of his youth in Riga, walking the beach and often finding amber. Her anger evaporated with my tears; I did not have to explain, she understood.

She was no longer angry with me, and when I cried, she folded her arms around me.

COUP DE GRÂCE

On June 6, 1944, the Allies landed on the coast of France. Perhaps that was the reason Oma decided a few weeks later that we would cross Germany from the Baltic Sea resort of Zoppot and move west to stay with Tante Paula in Wiesbaden.

Or perhaps Oma was doing one of her good deeds again. She never could refuse a favor to Uncle Victor, especially since he had indirectly saved Will's leg.

The years had not been kind to Tante Paula: she had become more forgetful and crankier. Uncle Victor was desperate to find a reliable person to share his sister's apartment and keep an eye on her. Oma was that person.

We moved into her spacious late nineteenth-century apartment. It was on a street lined with linden trees, near a gushing fountain. Wiesbaden had so far been spared from heavy bombing, though pilots would occasionally drop their surplus bombs here before returning to their base in England. Wiesbaden, like Marienbad, was a famous spa city; people had flocked here to take the baths since Roman times. Connected to the healing waters were

gambling casinos. These were all closed now, during the height of war. Because the city had been spared, concerts sometimes took place in the Kur-
park, people still sat in sidewalk cafés and drank ersatz coffee, and little shops
continued to sell elegant hats, the only clothing items not rationed. But our
lives were strained, living with Tante Paula, the "old dragon," as Oma and I
secretly called her. We now belonged to the underclass of the bombed out
and could not be choosy.

Tante Paula upset Oma daily with her greed. There were constant arguments about food. "Paula, I just bought Karin's milk, where is it?"

"The milk was for Karin? I drank it. Why can't I have it, I want milk, too,"
she said, slamming the door as she walked out of the room.

Oma ran after her. "Paula, you know that children need milk to build
bones. That's why Karin has milk rations. They're not for you, not for me. If
you ever do this again, I guarantee . . ."

"You guarantee what? I'm hungry. I want some milk. You live in my apartment, it's only fair I eat and drink what is there. Including Karin's milk."

Those words left Oma with her mouth wide open. Later she whispered
to me that from now on I was to come with her when she bought my milk
and drink it right then and there. I didn't like that idea. I wanted it to be
made into cream-of-wheat or into some kind of pudding. But Oma insisted. She treated milk as if it were a medicine I must take.

Again I had to adjust to a new school. I don't remember much about the
school in Wiesbaden, except for my two new girlfriends, Irmi and Lilo. They
lived kitty-corner across the street from us, and we walked to school together. Irmi was wheat blonde and very shy, and Lilo was a brunette with a
vivacious temperament. I walked between them, feeling an affinity to parts
of each of them.

It was summer, and only a few weeks of school were left before vacations
began in the latter half of July. I also was taking fencing lessons, which were
a lot of fun.

Perhaps Father's university years and his having been a member of a dueling fraternity influenced me in choosing fencing. Father was proud of the
scars cutting across his cheek as well as the ones on his head. Mother thought
it barbaric for grown men to cut themselves with sabers. I fenced with what
we called a *Florett;* I believe it's also called a foil, a thin and lightweight fencing sword. I loved the sport, wearing a mask and white clothing and, most of
all, being able to show aggression under control. There were times when Irmi
came to watch me, and I liked that she was paying attention to me. I was told
I was good at the sport, and I was proud of my ability, until Mother obtained
a rare traveling permit and came to visit us.

Oma took her to the sports hall where I fenced. Oma was pleased with my progress, but Mother turned down her mouth. During a pause, when I went to her and took down my mask, she asked, "Must you pick such a masculine sport? Couldn't you be doing something more ladylike?"

"Like what? Ballroom dancing? Prepare for a cotillion, now, in wartime?"

"I didn't mean dancing." She shrugged—she, an excellent dancer. "You're not all that graceful. But surely you could pick something else. Fencing . . . just look at your thighs. It's going to make your legs muscular and ugly."

I looked down at my skinny legs and knobby knees, a kid's legs. "I hope they *do* get muscular," I shouted at her.

"Astrid." Oma fluttered her hands as if they were peacemaking wings. "Karin's doing well with her fencing. I'm proud of her. You might as well say that bicycling would give her big legs. Silly. Karin found a sport she likes, and I am glad for her."

I hung my head and *poof,* all the joy of showing off for my mother had evaporated like water splashed onto hot asphalt in summer. Why couldn't Mother approve of something I did? I had longed for her, longed to be with her so much, but now I wished her gone and back in Berlin.

I met Helmut at the fencing school. I was flattered that this nice looking thirteen-year-old boy was paying attention to me, a scrawny eleven-year-old. At times when we left at twilight, he walked me home. One day he presented me with a fountain pen; another time he gave me a small bottle of perfume that smelled like violets. The perfume reminded me of the scent the maid at my father's house had worn, not at all like the French perfume Mother still used on occasion. But I was happy with the gifts and that a boy had taken the trouble to buy me a present.

When I told Irmi, she showed me her ring. It was a sweet ring with forget-me-nots in their distinctive light blue enameled on silver. "It's beautiful," I said.

"Udo gave me it," she said. "But keep it a secret. He said when we are all grown up he will marry me."

"You mean . . . ? You're much too young to think of that. But *mein Gott,* that is so romantic."

When Helmut and I reached Tante Paula's house a week after the perfume gift, he leaned down to kiss me. What an idea? I pushed at him. Was he crazy? A kiss signified something important, like an engagement. It might be all right for Irmi—she was twelve going on thirteen—but I was only eleven.

And also, I was afraid I might get pregnant from a kiss or get syphilis, like the last maid in Father's house had.

Helmut pinned me to the wall, grabbed my shoulders, and forced his mouth onto mine. I clenched my lips and tried to push him away. "You took my gifts. At least you can let me kiss you."

It wasn't easy, but I managed to draw my leg back to gain more leverage, then, a strong upward jerk with my bony knee, and he let go of me and howled, holding himself.

"You bitch," he cried out.

I was still mad. He thought he could buy me with his stupid fountain pen and his perfume? Luckily I carried both with me. I dug them out of my satchel and threw the pen at him. The perfume followed, splattering and drenching his clothes. I imagined him going home to his mother, or worse, meeting his fencing friends, smelling like violets. I ran into the house, slamming the heavy mahogany door so hard that the colored glass rattled.

I knew I would see Helmut in fencing school. He was a very good fencer. He was also a lot taller than I, and he had long arms. There was no chance I could out fence him, besides he had advanced to fence with an épée. I worried about how he would treat me when we met again. Mother had done her bit to take the joy out of my fencing, and now this boy had given that sport the final coup de grâce and not a gracious one either.

SIPPENHAFT

It was Thursday, July 20, 1944, and the clock showed 6:55 p.m. It was the middle of the summer, so the sun was still bright, sending long rays through the lacy curtains. Mother turned on the radio to listen to the Deutschlandsender's evening news. The usual fanfare and martial music blared from the brown box. We were seated around the oval dining table; Oma poured peppermint tea, and Tante Paula reached across the table to have the first go at the liverwurst Oma had cajoled from the butcher that afternoon. I didn't eat very much these days. Most of the food was bland or made with half-rancid fat, and the black bread tasted bitter and coarse. Bassoon and trumpet sounds filled the room and were soon joined by rolling drums. Oma left the table and shortly after returned with a bowl of fresh *Quark* and finely chopped chives. I smiled. She knew she could get me to eat if she brought out this cream cheese–like spread and a freshly baked *Schrippe,* a crisp French bread bun. She said she'd saved it especially for me.

The music stopped. An announcer told us that a special broadcast of our propaganda minister, Dr. Josef Goebbels, would follow, preempting the regular news.

We sat in silence. Something important had happened. Oma put down the teapot, I stopped scooping the *Quark* onto my plate, and Mutti sat with her fork poised to attack a tomato. Even Tante Paula's knife halted in front of the liverwurst, stabbing the air.

Then Goebbels's voice sounded over the radio. He could charm people with his silvery voice, and he knew how to use his "instrument" to persuade. But this time he sounded gruff and angry.

There had been an attempt to kill the Führer at the Führerhauptquartier at Wolfschanze, he said. My breath stopped when I heard those words. He continued. The nation must not worry, our beloved Führer, Adolf Hitler, has been protected by the Greater Forces governing the fate of Germany. This Protecting Force, his Destiny, knew our country needed Adolf Hitler in these trying times. And he, Josef Goebbels, was happy to report that the coup had failed. Our Führer was safe and well. I sighed a loud breath of relief. Oma and Mutti rolled eyes and looked at each other, then at me.

Oma said, "Idiot. Destiny, greater forces, stupid. Goebbels studied to be a Jesuit priest and now he doesn't dare use the word *God*. These Nazis make me sick."

The propaganda minister continued, telling us that despite a bomb exploding near the Führer, he was not wounded or injured. But the traitors to our nation, all of them Wehrmacht officers in whom the Führer had placed his trust, were now in the state's custody and would have to pay for this despicable act with their lives.

As Goebbels went on, I sat with my mouth wide open. Tears rolled down my cheeks. "Those traitors, devils, why would anyone want to do this to our Führer?" I broke down sobbing.

"Karin. *Shh,* I want to hear what Goebbels has to say," Mother said.

His speech continued. After he finished, the martial music played again, then news commentators with bland voices filled the void. One of the announcers told us that as soon as the radio van could be brought from Königsberg to Rastenburg, the place where Hitler was staying, our Führer would address the nation.

We sat around the table as if someone had hypnotized us. I wanted to speak, but the stern eyes from the adults kept me quiet. Mother and Oma exchanged glances; Tante Paula sat quietly, chewing on her bread and liverwurst. The music blared. Mother and Oma didn't like marches, and I knew this music would be torture to their ears. Mutti turned the volume down.

Everyone waited for the Führer to speak. Oma looked at her watch and at me.

"Go to bed, *Kind,* it's getting late."

"I want to hear what the Führer has to say. I'm old enough, I want to hear him. Maybe they just say he's alive, I'm scared."

"He's alive. *Unkraut vergeht nicht*"—weeds do not perish—Mother said under her breath, making me angry again, especially now, after someone had tried to kill him. How could she call our Führer a weed? How awful. This from my own mother.

The setting sun tinted the curtains orange, then red, and then it was dark. The music changed to something Wagnerian. It was better than the marches but still not anything I liked. Then the station broadcast the *Eroica* from Beethoven. I drank my tea, hoping to be allowed to stay up. The clock ticked. I dozed off. When my head dropped onto the table, Mutti touched my shoulders and whispered, "Go to bed. Now, Karin. I'll be in later to kiss you goodnight." It was after eleven o'clock. My ears perked up when the announcer told us to be patient, Hitler was expected to come on the air at any moment. I shook my head and told her I didn't want to go to bed. Not yet.

"All right. Then at least brush your teeth and put on your pajamas. I'll call you when Hitler comes on," Mother said.

I had fallen asleep at the table again when Mother led me off to bed. I slept soundly, when Hitler, at 1:00 a.m., came on the air and assured the nation with his inimitable gravelly voice that he was alive and well.

I read his speech the next day in the noon edition of the newspaper. He accused a tiny clique of officers of treason. He called them ambitious, stupid, and criminal. He told the nation that he did not fear the fate they had planned for him, but that Providence had spared him for the good of the nation. Had the traitors been successful, terrible consequences for the German nation would have followed.

The paper named some of the generals who were part of the putsch and said that the collapse of the coup was total.

I was happy.

Mother was reading the next page when her eyes widened and the color drained from her face. "Look, *Mutter,*" she showed Oma the paper, "Just look. Witzleben is one of them."

"No. It can't be, let me see."

"Here. Field Marshal Erwin von Witzleben has been arrested . . . and . . . he is one of the traitors . . . then it names several others."

Oma shook her head. "What will happen to his family?"

Mother shrugged. She shook her head, and with tears spilling from her eyes, she spoke through a stopped up nose, "You know the Nazis reinstated the old Teutonic law, *Sippenhaft* (*Sippe,* meaning kinship or consanguinity, and *Haft,* meaning arrest or detention). It doesn't look good for Edelgard, or her mother."

"I know what that means," I said. "We learned that in school. It's from the German sagas. When a man is a traitor, his blood is bad and all in the family have to be killed."

Oma and Mother turned toward me and threw me looks as if I were a monster. I didn't utter another word. Then the two embraced, crying. I felt like an outsider.

"Poor Edelgard," Mother said. "What will become of her?"

"Who is Edelgard?" I asked.

Oma turned and told me she was the general's daughter and one of Mother's childhood friends from Liegnitz. They had each gone their own way, but Mother remembered her fondly. She had liked the father, the old General von Witzleben—a stern and aristocratic man from an old Silesian family—whom she had met on several visits to their country estate not far from Liegnitz.

That evening I heard the adults whisper far into the night. They discussed what had happened and what had gone wrong. The way I understood it, Mother and Grandmother were sorry the putsch had not succeeded. This confused me. I knew they didn't admire the Führer the way I did, but to wish him dead? And to wonder what had gone wrong, hoping that it had gone right? Right for the traitors? Then we would be without our great Führer. Who then would lead us to victory?

Mother went back to Berlin, and a little while later the trial began. It said in the paper that the conspirators had confessed readily. "Good," Oma said. "Then they will treat them with decency."

There was a brief trial, presided over by Dr. Freisler. Oma said this "doctor" was considered to be a cruel man who lacked education. She wondered where he had received his Ph.D. The executions were carried out in Plötzensee on August 9. The daily newspapers published photos of the executions the following day. They showed Field Marshal von Witzleben and five others hanging, strung up with piano wire, from six meat hooks in a sparse, rough-walled room. Their uniforms were no longer those of proud German officers but had been reduced to blood-and-urine-stained, filthy rags.

Oma kept swallowing hard, trying to keep down an upwelling of pain. "They've been tortured. This decent general has been tortured."

I asked, "Why?"

She waved me away, too upset to talk. Then she grabbed the newspaper from me and said, "Karin, don't ask. Don't look." But then she opened the paper again and commented on what she saw. "They wouldn't even let him wear his dentures. To degrade him further."

I leaned over Oma's shoulders staring at the signs pinned to the dead men, proclaiming them to be traitors. I tried to see them closer up, but Oma covered the pictures with her hands.

A documentary film about the putsch and the executions was being shown in a local movie theater. Oma had passed that theater and told Tante Paula there were quite a few people going to see this movie. She asked, "How could they record these tortures? Who has such a demented personality to enjoy filming, and now the audience, watching these horror scenes?" What disgusted Oma most was that she had also seen women waiting in line to get in. Lower ranking SS men in black and SA men in brown uniforms composed most of the queue. She said she saw no soldiers or officers in military gray, though many were in town recuperating from war wounds.

"I think the soldiers are as revolted about this film as we are," Oma said.

Even during the war Oma and Aunt Margaret spoke English when together, the language of the enemy, the language of their youth. They spoke it on the streets and, later, in the hospital where Aunt Margaret lay with a broken hip. The hospital was a one hour train ride from Wiesbaden, and when Mother was still in town, we had all gone to visit her. That afternoon I felt as if I might never see her again. She looked so forlorn. Her long steel gray hair was disheveled, and I asked if I could comb it. She smiled a response. I combed it out, which was not easy with her lying in bed, and plaited it into braids, which I arranged on her head like a dark pewter crown. Her skin was pale yellow, and her eyes had sunk deep within puffed folds and were mere slits now. I held her hands and kissed her cheek, and then we said good-bye.

Oma visited her as often as she could, while I stayed home with Tante Paula, since she complained when we left her alone.

Why did the sisters speak English? Did they do this to provoke or to be secret? Were they oblivious to any danger when they spoke their own mother's tongue in a public place during the height of war? Were they not aware that they caused suspicion? Were the looming and ever-present placards, *Feind hört mit*–the enemy is listening–showing the silhouette of a man or a woman touching his or her lips in a silencing gesture, not making them aware that every man, woman, and child was being solicited to watch for traitors and spies?

Then, on a sunny day in late August, a telegram informed Oma that Aunt Margaret had been moved from the hospital she was in, which had an excellent orthopedic facility, to an unheard of hospital in the countryside. There was no forwarding address or telephone number given so that Oma could make inquiries. Another day passed, when a second telegram told us the sad news: Aunt Margaret had suffered a heart attack and had died.

Two days after that, Oma received a box wrapped in plain brown paper. She opened it hesitantly. I watched her shaking fingers. Her normally rosy skin paled to the color of bleached bone, even her fingernails faded. Then she caught her breath, lowered her chin, and resolutely ripped into the brown paper. A rectangular wooden box was inside. I looked on with curiosity as she worked open the box. She fumbled with the small brass catch, trying to open it. The picture of Aunt Margaret sprang into my mind, as I had seen her grope with a brass lock—so many years ago—when she had shown me her rose-colored ball gown. Then Oma jerked her hand back, as if the box might contain vipers. She held the box for a moment or two, then lifted the lid and stared at its contents.

She sat down in her chair, motionless.

I went over to see what Grandmother was looking at. She still sat immobile as tears began to roll down her cheeks. When I saw the grainy gray stuff—ashes it looked like—in the box, I wondered why she was crying. Was she upset that someone had played a joke on her after they emptied out their fireplace?

I picked up the small white card that had escaped the box and fallen onto the floor. Now my breath caught, lumping in my throat. The card informed Oma that these were the remains of her sister, Margaret von Hake, who had died of cardiac arrest two days earlier.

Oma closed the box. Slowly and deliberately, she picked it up and took it to her bedroom. She carried it with her hands extended before her as though she were a priest, holding the monstrance.

It was hard for me to hold back, to not run after her and cradle in the comfort of my grandmother's arms. But I sensed she needed to be alone.

I held on to the image of my aunt Margaret. I pictured her long thick hair and her wire glasses that were always sliding down her nose. Where were those glasses now?

Oma's stifled crying could be heard throughout the apartment. Tante Paula swept into the room a little while later, accusing me of making Oma cry. Then she found the brown wrapping paper still lying on the floor and asked who had sent a package, adding, "I hope they sent something good to eat."

I did not want to tell Tante Paula, but I had to. She sat silent for a moment or two, which was unusual for her. Then she went into a tirade about Oma speaking English with her sister. Yes, it had to come to this. And hadn't she been a member of the Johanniter order? She probably had boasted about that in the hospital. Everyone knew that the Nazis hated these ancient Christian orders and had tried to eliminate them. They had probably killed her as a traitor. After all, didn't she have connections to America?

On she went, and I was getting angry, but I knew I had to keep my mouth shut and not provoke her. Through the door I could still hear Oma's muffled weeping.

Would explaining to Tante Paula help? I tried. "Tante Paula, please try to understand," I said. "Oma was not even three years old when her mother died in Salt Lake City. Aunt Margaret was more than an older sister, she was a mother to her. You must have heard the stories, their father was always gone, working for the Union Pacific Railroad. Aunt Margaret was all she had and English is their native language. It was natural to speak it when they were together. Please, don't even mention this traitor idea to Oma, please. You'll make her feel at fault."

Tante Paula nodded but looked at me sideways.

I looked at my silver watch, not aware of the time. The watch was a treasured gift from my aunt Margaret. I wept and could not understand why my heart felt so heavy. I had never lost anyone I loved before. I loved Aunt Margaret deeply and now she was dead. And Oma's suffering added to my pain.

There had been rumors about extermination hospitals, though we knew no particulars about them at the time. Oma suspected that Aunt Margaret had been killed. She had no sons fighting in the war and no other close relatives, except my grandmother. After the war we heard that the Nazi regime had killed the old, the mentally retarded, and the chronically ill. All of them were considered expendable as Germany tried to conserve food for the military and the workforce. Oma's suspicions of Aunt Margaret's death were confirmed after the war, during the second Nuremberg trials, when the name of the particular hospital and its personnel where she had died was revealed in the newspaper.

In later years I often wondered if she had been aware, my sweet aunt, of what was going to happen to her when they transferred her from the orthopedic hospital to the other one? Did they load her directly from the ambulance into the large structure meant for killing, along with other "patients"? Did she panic when she heard the poison gas hiss as it flowed into the room?

I hoped that her strong faith allowed her to face her fate with courage and with calm. Maybe she did indeed die—then and there—of a heart attack. Or was there a special room in that "hospital," where a doctor gave her an injection, quick and merciful, to bring about her death? I still wonder if her life would have been spared had she not conversed with her sister in the tongue of the enemy?

The knowledge of Aunt Margaret's death adds to my struggle with my background: born German, under the "hooked cross," the swastika. Aunt Margaret's volunteering for service during World War I had not been enough. She had been born to an impoverished but noble family, and as a nurse, she had offered her fatherland her robust health. The young Nazis did not look that far back; they did not see the German heroine from the Great War when they looked upon the old woman with black and gray streaked braids wound around her head and oval steel-framed spectacles habitually sliding down her shiny nose. They saw an old woman who was dispensable, and so they exterminated her. My beloved Aunt Margaret.

FALL–WINTER 1944

They did not come with wings. There had been no air-raid warning when they struck. There had been no droning of planes flying above.

I will never forget the sound. The abrupt awakening from a deep sleep, from absolute silence, hearing the *ziiiiiing . . . ziiiiiing,* then *zoom-whoom-CRASH.*

I swung the feather bed from where it rested on my feet to my head. Then part of the wardrobe-sized, green *Kachelofen* (tiled stove) fell on me. Feathers flew in all directions, but the thick feather bed protected me. I noticed something wet drip down my face and wiped at it with my hand. In the eerie green light streaming through the curtained windows, the stain on my hand looked brown. My forehead was oozing blood. I wound a cotton kerchief around my head, trying to stop the flow.

Oma rushed into the room, shrieking, "Come, come . . . , to the cellar. Bombs."

"But there's been no siren."

"Never mind. They're bombing us, hurry."

Oma saw my scarf and moved it aside to look at my wound. "Ouch, Karinchen, the cut is right next to your large vein." She tied the scarf tighter and told me she would tend to the wound once we were in the cellar.

I must have looked like a bandaged chicken; feathers from the down cover were everywhere, in my hair, stuck to the blood on my face and all over my pajamas.

Old Tante Paula appeared like the ghost from Dickens's *A Christmas Carol.* Her long white hair hung in loose wisps down her back, her white cotton nightgown was dusted with white plaster, and her thin white legs looked like sticks, stuck into oversized brown shoes. She complained, "This is all your fault. We had a peaceful city until you came. It's you! You brought the bombs from Berlin."

Oma kept her calm, pointed to the wardrobe in the foyer, and directed Tante Paula to put on her coat. The old woman kept shaking her head, looking dazed. Oma then guided her to the closet. She opened the double doors and helped Paula into her coat. I couldn't understand why Oma was so nice to the old dragon. Then the three of us, dressed in heavy coats—though the weather was warm now, in early September—made our way to the cellar, down the wide, curving staircase.

One of the windows in the stairwell allowed me a view of the house diagonally opposite our own much smaller building, at the intersection of our two streets. The apartment building, six stories high—counting the attic apartment—was lit up in a ghostly blue and green light. The façade of the building had been sheared off, neat and clean as with a giant saw. The people looked like actors on a multileveled stage. I could see men and women scurrying in their rooms, as if they were trying to find an exit. I found myself in a bizarre theater, looking into the different apartments, bedrooms, living rooms, watching people rattling on doors that wouldn't open and seeing others run out and just as quickly dash back in again. But this was not a stage. Why are people running in and running out? I wondered if the stairs had collapsed. And while all this frantic activity went on, in this half-standing building, not a sound was heard. Maybe my fear had made me deaf, but I don't remember hearing anyone scream, or even cry, for help.

"Those poor, poor people," Oma said, tugging on my sleeve, urging me to get away from the window and to keep walking down to the cellar.

We had almost reached the entry to the cellar, now a bomb shelter, when we heard another whistling zing and then another blast. We were thrown against the wall opposite the entrance door, and more plaster added yet another coating of white to my feathered appearance. A horrendous crash followed the blast. The stained glass of the entry door blew out, raining multihued splinters. Sharp pointed shards framed a clear view of the building across the street. The building caved in on itself—in slow motion—turning floors and ceilings into rubble. A single door stood upright atop the ruin, a bed and a table were still visible. This was the tiny rooftop apartment where Lilo, my vivacious friend, lived with her mother. Its fall had been cushioned by the floors pancaked beneath it. No one was moving. I shuddered and choked when I looked at the space where my shy little friend Irmi had lived. It had been an elegant apartment on the second floor. Now only rubble could be seen through the clouds of dust. Grandmother peeled me off the wall and practically pushed me down the cellar stairs.

One of Wiesbaden's leading actresses rushed past us. She lived on the floor above us. I stared. Wait . . . no hair, she was bald. I had always admired her rich chestnut hair. No, that couldn't be. A moment ago I had felt fear, then sorrow, then fear again, but now I had to stifle a nasty urge to laugh. I bit the inside of my cheeks raw. What had happened to the poor woman? Had the blast blown off her hair? She looked so weird, and she was wearing no makeup, only a flannel robe and felt slippers similar to my grandmother's. Oma looked discreetly at the floor and whispered, "She always wears wigs, it must have blown into some corner."

People crowded into the cellar, and I could feel their fear. Some prayed, others talked in whispers. Grandmother and I had been through the bombing raid when our house burned down in Berlin, and now our earlier fear was rekindled. Our fear was as great as theirs. Oma gripped me tight to stop my trembling and whispered, "*Shh, hab keine Angst, Karinchen.* God will protect us. Don't give in to your fear."

Suddenly we were plunged into darkness: the electricity had been cut. Someone lit a candle. Somebody else said this would have to be blown out if we were hit; we might have to survive for days in the cellar before someone would dig us out. The candle would use up too much oxygen. I leaned closer to my Oma, shaking more than before.

When I looked down at her feet, I saw that her felt slippers showed dark stains, a wet ooze. "Oma, what's wrong with your feet?" She looked down and took them off. Shards of window pane were lodged inside, and her feet were badly cut. The rush of adrenalin had spared her the pain.

Another blast shook our house and more plaster fell, adding more dust to our specterlike shapes. Then the house calmed down and became still once more.

People prayed. "Our Father, Who art in Heaven . . ." I said my child's prayer in a small voice, "*Lieber Gott, mach mich fromm, dass ich in den Himmel komm*"—Dear Lord, make me devout, so I can enter heaven. But I did not want to enter heaven, not yet. I had my whole life ahead of me; I wanted to see my mother in Berlin and had yet to meet my count from Spain, who would come to me on a white horse, romance me with guitars, and take me away from the gray of Germany.

We sat in the dark and waited. A man began to sing "Ave Maria" in a sonorous baritone. It was calming to hear this voice. This man will protect us; God will protect us.

I was the only child in the cellar, most of the others were old women. After a long period of calm, one of the women left the cellar. When she came back, she reported that the last blast we had felt was another bomb that had fallen into the exact same apartment house across the street: one building, three hits.

Again I thought of my two friends who lived in that house. Now there was nothing left, not even the attic apartment.

We left the cellar in the early morning light. All we saw was gray. Even the orange disk of the rising sun hid behind slate-colored roofs. The dust from the blasted apartment house and the smoldering fire fed by exploded gas lines made the scene look like something out of the Wochenschau. But no, not quite. The black-and-white newsreel carried more authenticity than this; the color of this scene made it surreal. It was as if I were looking through a curtain of dust and smoke at a painting of an inferno.

Tante Paula's apartment was in shambles. She wailed. Oma began cleaning up, and Tante Paula was getting in her way. Oma's feet hurt, even though I had helped her to remove some of the splinters with tweezers and she had bandaged them. Every step was torture for her. But she went about her task, smiling at me and even humming a tune. I got a second broom and swept up shards and fallen plaster.

The cut on my forehead was deeper than Oma had first thought. She had cleaned it and put on a *Leukoplast,* a sort of Band-Aid, but blood kept seeping through. Later we went to a Red Cross center to have Oma's feet looked after and my wound stitched.

When we came back, Tante Paula asked Oma to buy her a refill of her medicine. The pharmacy across from us was heavily damaged and now served to hold the dead from the building across the street. Aunt Paula knew this, so why had she not asked earlier, when we left to go to town? Oma, without a word, took the empty prescription bottle and went back out to get it filled.

I stood numbed at the corner of our street, viewing the destruction of the large building that had housed about 340 people. Not even the skeleton of the building was standing, only a huge heap of rubble. Every one of its occupants was dead. Had they been in the cellar, many of them would have survived. I looked on as they brought bodies into the pharmacy. They laid them on sheets on the floor. A man in uniform came up to me and asked if I knew anyone who had lived in the bombed building. I said yes, two of my school friends. "Would you please come with me, perhaps you can identify them if they are here?" I didn't want to go. But at the same time it made me feel important to be asked to help this official, and I followed him.

The dust of the place made me sneeze. It smelled icky-sweet like a strange medicinal powder and, at the same time, like insecticide. Then I saw the mangled bodies close up. I looked away. There was a hand, the fingers full of ink stains. I thought I recognized that hand. Irmi's fountain pen had always leaked. My eyes were drawn to the ring on the person's middle finger; it had forget-me-nots of blue enamel on silver. Irmi's ring. Blackness welled up and I couldn't see any more.

When I came to, I found myself staring into my grandmother's blue eyes. "*Kind,* you shouldn't be here. This man had no right asking a child to identify the dead."

I was told that I had fainted onto the corpses, and that just at that time Oma had come back from her errand and given the man in uniform a tongue-lashing that he would remember. My sweet and gentle grandmother was always a lady, but when it came to protecting me, she could be a terror.

The city condemned Tante Paula's apartment building after the bombing because it was unsound. They gave us two weeks to move out. I tossed and turned in my bed beneath the partially collapsed tile stove at night, worrying that the apartment house would bury us, like my friends had been buried across the street.

We would return to Berlin, but first Oma had to find a place for Tante Paula. After a week, Oma found a place for her in an *Altersheim,* a home for the aged, in the small Hessian town where Tante Paula and her brothers were born. Even the family's cemetery plot, holding generations of Kellers, was there. Maybe the proximity to the graves was the reason Tante Paula became obstinate and refused to go. It was difficult for Oma to convince her that this was the best, and only, solution.

When we came back to Wiesbaden, Oma and I celebrated Tante Paula's absence by making caramel candies as a surprise for Mother in Berlin. The ingredients used up more food coupons than we could spare, but it was fun to cook with Oma. We used equal parts of milk and sugar and took turns in stirring and boiling and boiling and stirring until the mixture thickened and turned to a rich caramel shade. I felt my arm go numb from all the stirring before it was done. We poured the batter onto wax paper, and before it cooled entirely, we rolled it into candy-shaped confections that we decorated with walnuts. Then Oma and I got ready to board the train for Berlin.

Some had thought the bombs were torpedoes shot off by British Mosquitoes. Years after the war, another rumor suggested they had been our own stray V-1 or V-2 rockets, fired from the Harz Mountains, a new location for much of the rocket industry formerly based in Peenemünde.

Unfriendly Fire

We were fortunate to find two seats on the train from Wiesbaden to Berlin. Oma and I crowded into a third-class compartment with wood-slatted benches. Others, not that lucky, had to sit on their suitcases or stand up in the corridors. The train chugged along at a slow pace and was a far cry from the efficient trains that had been Germany's pride not so long ago.

After a few hours of travel we heard planes overhead. My body reacted in a visceral way to the drone of the engines, expecting to hear the bombs *zing* and explode. I know I must have scrunched and ducked, for Oma sheltered me in her arms. The train stopped. Whistles blew, shrill and persistent. The train-master shouted through his megaphone that all passengers must exit and take shelter in the ditch along the tracks. "This train is filled with civilians. We must show ourselves to the enemy planes," he said.

The people in our compartment filed out, one after the other, pushing, eager. Oma and I and a young soldier, not more than eighteen, were the last ones. When Oma and I turned to exit the train, he stopped us. "Don't go," he said. "They'll shoot. Machine gun you down. You're safer in here." He pointed to the space beneath the benches. I took his advice and slid underneath.

Oma was more hesitant. "They'll see it's a civilian train. They're Americans, they won't shoot," she said.

"*Neh,*" he shook his head. "They're fighter planes, probably British. Whatever they are, Tommies or Yanks, it's war. They'll shoot at anything moving, anybody. Believe me, you're safer in here."

Oma reluctantly got on her knees and crawled next to me underneath the bench. The soldier spurred her on. It seemed as if he wanted to shove at her to make her move faster. When we were both under the wooden slats, he threw suitcases on top of the bench above us. He pushed my head back under when I tried to see what he was doing. He said the baggage would provide cover from ricocheting bullets or flying shrapnel. Then he also dove to take cover under the bench opposite us.

The planes buzzed lower now, flying directly above. *Zoom . . . zing . . .* an ugly noise, coming close, then closer. We heard the *da-da-da-da-dack* of machine guns. I heard screams. Loud screams, piercing-the-air screams. I was shaking. I pushed my middle fingers into my ears to block out the sound and pressed my face into my grandmother's soft breast.

There was another sound. The planes were coming closer, but they sounded different, as if they were diving at us. A flash of a bright light like a jolt of lightening lit the interior of the train car for a second. The shooting stopped, then there was an explosion. The train shook, and my ears hurt. Oma and I were trembling. The train's whistle sounded again. Its pitch was higher, more insistent, as if trying to drown out the shrillness of screams. The train began to move. All I could see of the soldier were his boots and legs by

the window. He stood there oblivious of the danger to himself and commented on what he saw outside. "I wonder if they are going to make it. All
these people running alongside, some of them covered with blood. My
God! They're trying to jump aboard. They're hanging on in clusters. *Ach,*
there's a few falling off. Damn, one of the planes is banking, making another
run . . . they're shooting them down while they're running." He shouted,
"Can't they see they're all civilians? My God, there's a woman who's stuck
and is being dragged by the train. Goddamn."

When the train began to move, it first felt as if a shiver went through it,
then it caught itself and began to *chug-chug-chug,* gaining motion. It sounded
like the hooves of horses, coming into a full run now, hooves grabbing the
ground, clanking with front legs in unison, pulling the big black iron body
along, gaining speed.

The train gained momentum.

"They're still shooting. You better get back down again," the soldier said.
The low flying planes were still overhead, and the machine gun fire kept up
its rhythmic beat, mowing people down. The train left them behind in the
ditch, the soldier said.

A man burst into our compartment, out of breath, his coat in tatters and
drenched with blood. He told us of the scores of people killed and the many
that lay wounded. "One of our fighter planes intervened. Got one of them.
Came down right near the running people. . . . Oh my God," He choked.
"If they don't get help soon many more will die."

Oma dug through my suitcase and pulled out one of my undershirts. She
ripped it into strips and bandaged the man's arm, which had been lacerated
by shrapnel. Then Oma rummaged through her traveling bag, searching for
the caramel candies we had made two days ago as a present for Mother. She
offered the candies to the men. The young soldier took only one, knowing
how scarce everything was. The older man took several. I looked at the
young soldier and was surprised to see tears rolling down his face. Oma
changed seats with me and put her arms around him. I felt jealous. *He's a
grown man, a soldier. Why is he crying?*

He shook more and more, and he put his head on Oma's shoulder.
Between sobs he told us his story. "I live in Frankfurt . . . was on two-week
furlough. Took me four days to get home from the East, and when I arrived,
they'd just had one of the biggest bombing raids ever. Our house . . . gone.
My mother, sister . . . underneath the rubble. I dug and dug with my bare
hands, but there was just broken concrete and bricks. God, they had to drag
me away. They're dead. Mother. Little Hanni." I caught my breath and felt a
stab in my chest, hearing his story. Then he said, "Father is stationed in Norway, how do I write this to him?" He shook his head. "I don't know . . ."

Oma didn't speak. She held him a little tighter and kept stroking his back. Soon he stopped shaking, and his sobs quieted. He wiped the last tear from his face and then made a loud explosive sound, blowing his nose into a gray-and-blue-checkered handkerchief. "Thank you," his words sounded muffled. "I needed to tell somebody about it. Thank you." Oma squeezed his hand and moved back to sit by me.

When hours later we pulled into Bahnhof Zoo Station in Berlin and said good-bye to the soldier. I asked if he had wings hidden beneath his gray army coat. "Why?" he asked. "I think you are our guardian angel." He laughed, shaking his head. I added, in a more somber voice, "You're going back to the Russian front. You need your own angel now."

He no longer laughed.

Oma said, "We'll always remember you." She gave him a little peck on the cheek and whispered, "And we'll pray for your safety."

We wrote down our address, and he promised to write, but we never heard from him. Maybe he did have wings and they carried him far away from this terrible war.

PILFERING APPLES

We arrived in Berlin, Oma and I, on a clear October day, and I was again taken by the beauty of Berlin. Its many trees were already dressed in reds and golds, the gaudy colors of autumn. This was the first time we were given housing in a stranger's apartment. The housing authorities had issued Mother an additional room for the two of us, leaving one less for Frau Kuhnert in her own apartment. The sour look on her horse face turned even more lemony as she watched Oma and me maneuvering our suitcases through the door. Frau Kuhnert also had to share her large kitchen and luxurious bath with us. The location was ideal, half a block from the fabled boulevard, the Kurfürstendamm, and near the Halensee S-Bahn station.

Mother tried to make me forget the bombing in Wiesbaden by taking me cycling or walking through the woods, where the trees, rather than the buildings, were on fire. The leaves floated to earth and made swishing sounds when rustled by our feet. There was no school, and I had time on my hands. Mother still worked twelve hours, six days a week at her two jobs and could only spend time with me on Sunday. I sometimes borrowed her bicycle, and Erich, a thirteen-year-old neighbor boy, and I explored the Grunewald or cycled all the way to one of the many lakes. I told Erich about Uncle Will's little *Faltboot,* which Mother kept for him in a boathouse in Wannsee. That gave him the idea of pilfering apples.

Erich knew of a large estate bordering the River Havel that was close to the largest lake in the vicinity, the Wannsee. He seemed to know the layout pretty well, describing the weeping willows where we could tie up our boat, climb over a wall into the orchard, and steal apples. I was all for it. Of course I didn't mention any of this to Mother.

"This is it," whispered Erich. "Use only your right paddle, we turn here."

There were the willows. We tied up the little boat and grabbed two net bags. Erich gave me a leg up onto the top of the wall. He was first to jump off.

I knelt on the wall, looked into the garden, and saw that the trees were full of ripe red apples. The trees winked at us, smiling and beckoning us to come and unburden them from their load of fruit.

Erich waved me on, "Come on down, come on," he called.

Then I saw them. Two German shepherd dogs on leashes, pulling two black-clad guards. Were they SS?

"Erich," I yelled. "No! There are guards. Come back. Eric! I'm leaving. Come." I shouted and jumped down.

I untied the boat and waited a moment as Erich leapt from the wall. We were off, just in time.

The men appeared on top of the wall, standing with their feet apart as if they were planted there, looking through binoculars in our direction. We waved at them. They noticed we were children. "No more pranks. The dogs don't have a sense of humor. They'd eat you for supper next time," one shouted.

"The dogs don't have a sense of humor," repeated Erich, raising an eyebrow. Then he added in a low voice, "Ha. Nazi dogs. No humor. Like their masters."

I was out of breath and felt a jangle of nerves. "I thought you knew who owned the place," I said. "I wouldn't have come if I'd known it was guarded like this."

"I know who owns it."

"Who?"

"Goebbels. That's who."

"Goebbels? Are you crazy? We could have been shot."

"Naw. We're kids, remember? He's got six kids himself. He likes kids."

"Silly, he's Catholic. *And* a Nazi. They always have a lot of kids. Doesn't mean he likes them. He only likes young actresses. Did you hear that he wanted to . . . ?"

"No." Erich cut me off. "I don't care who the old goat shacks up with.

The papers said he was in the Eagles Nest, with the Führer. It's usually not guarded like this when he's out of town. I'm sorry. I so wanted to come home to Mother and bring her some apples from Goebbels's garden."

A month or more went by, and late in November, I volunteered to look after a neighbor's four young children while she ran errands.

I found balloons on the desk. What luck! I blew them up to entertain the kids. We had fun, floating them out of the window, pretending they were large white snowflakes. I wished they had been red, yellow, or green, but white was better than nothing.

When the woman returned home and saw what we were playing with, she grabbed me by the collar and dragged me back to my mother, shouting the entire time. I had no idea why she was so upset. I thought she'd be grateful that I found something to entertain her brood with. Those children were crybabies and impossible. Hitler wanted women to have many children, and she had produced four in as many years. This had earned her the *Mutterkreuz,* an honor or a cross of valor for mothers. I thought the children themselves were the cross, a heavy one to bear.

I had no idea this woman attached such value to those silly things.

Mother sent me off to the other room, but I pressed my ear to the keyhole and overheard the woman's complaints. "My last prophylactics, and Hans is coming home on furlough for Christmas. What am I going to do? I can't get pregnant again. I'll go crazy. Your daughter, your daughter is to blame. No, make no excuse. I don't ever want to see your girl ever in my house again."

What were prophylactics? Mother didn't tell me.

A few days later our doorbell rang. I opened the door. A woman, identifying herself as a representative of the Halensee school district stood in the entry, firing questions at me.

"What are you doing here?"

"I live here."

"Yes, I can see that. Why are you not in school?"

"There is no school in Berlin . . ."

She coughed, "Of course there's no school in Berlin, but there are schools outside of Berlin. Where is your mother?"

Oma appeared and asked the woman to come in. She sent me to my room. I always had to leave. Through the door I could hear an agitated back and forth of voices, with Oma pleading that at this time of the war our family wanted to stay united in Berlin. She was told that the *Oberschule* I would normally have attended had been evacuated to Mistroy, and that's where I would have to go.

The evening before I was to leave, the air-raid sirens went off earlier than usual. On our way down to the cellar, Oma and I stepped out onto the street, hoping to see Mother coming home from work, sprinting toward our house from the corner of Ku'damm where the streetcar would let her off. No mother. "Look Oma," I pointed to the Christmas trees in the sky. "Will we be the target tonight? Like when we were bombed out?"

Slowly they floated down from the dark tent of the night. Oma took my arm, "No, they're going down over the Tiergarten, over Charlottenburg. But come into the cellar, *Kind,* we could get hurt by the shrapnel, or a stray bomb. One never knows."

To a degree we had become blasé about the threat of bombs. The luminous phosphorescent flares, marking the targeted area the bombers were to hit a few minutes later, looked beautiful, in a sinister sort of way. This was the season of Advent and soon candles on our pine trees would be lit, but these "Christmas trees," signals of death and destruction, would be the only Christmas trees I'd see that season.

A large section of the elegant Tiergarten district was hit that night and razed to the ground. Oma said she was glad that her friend Frau Winterfeld, who lived in that part of town, was safe in her country estate in Pomerania. The zoo was bombed again and heavily damaged; many animals were killed. I worried about my special love, Knautschke, a hippo baby born more than a year ago, during the time when we were bombed out. We had visited him then, before I left Berlin, marveling that new life survived amid bombs, life from as far away as Africa.

The day I left Berlin, the newspapers printed the news: "Knautschke lives!" Even total strangers were laughing and talking to each other, happy that this little hippo's life had been spared. He had become a symbol—maybe because of his name, Knautschke, the suffix "ke," indicated it was a typical Berliner name—and as such he was a representative for all of us ordinary citizens in our suffering city.

Knautschke survived, and so would we.

ACTING LESSONS

I arrived in Mistroy two weeks before Christmas. The train ride had been rather pleasant. With no planes shooting at us, the trip took only about three hours. Mistroy, with its white-as-sugar sand beaches by the Baltic Sea, was a pretty Victorian, fin de siècle resort town, and I would have loved it under different circumstances. The small hotels had the look of stylish gingerbread houses, with fancily carved woodwork around doors and balconies. Dense forests stretched to the edge of high chalk cliffs that dropped abruptly to the gray-blue sea. Farther inland, small villages slept near lakes where reeds and water lilies grew. The girls who had been here for more than a year described Mistroy as a magical place.

But I was miserable. We were housed in a formerly fashionable boarding-house, which in prewar days had been centrally heated. In December 1944, there was no fuel for the radiators. I had to cut firewood, which I was not strong enough to do properly, and start a fire in the makeshift cast-iron stove in our bedroom. I had to perform this chore every fourth day, taking turns with my three roommates. The black exhaust pipe pushed through wooden boards that replaced the glass in the window and sent out sparks. Watching the sparks swirl about like fireflies, I feared that the room would catch on fire.

I knew no one when I arrived: not the teachers, not the girls, and not the youth leaders. But I liked telling stories and soon made friends. After dark, while the fire crackled in the stove, and the black of night was intermittently lit by an errant spark, the four of us crowded together on one bed. My roommates kept urging me to tell them stories. Girls from other rooms soon crept through our door and huddled down on the beds with us. I made up ghost stories, but most of all I liked to show off and to tell them of child-birth. There was the birth of Hubsi, which I embellished, and my step-mother's stillbirth in the sixth month of her pregnancy. When the girls spoke of wanting to have six or seven children, I told them about morning sickness and suffering and blood, which I had seen gushing from Tante Erna. These stories were gory, and the girls liked them better than ghost stories. Perhaps reality provided more of a thrill than made-up tales.

After a few nights of stories, I was called before the principal. "German girls are strong and made to have lots of children," she lectured me. *Ja, ja,* I thought, I've heard all this before from my Hitler Youth leader. "Karin, you are sabotaging the ideal of the Third Reich. I don't want you to ever talk about this subject with your classmates again. Understood?"

I understood. And I stood—sullen and silent—before this woman with the steel gray bun and the steel gray eyes behind thick lenses on her broad nose.

I felt a strong urge to escape, to get out of Mistroy, to get back to Berlin, but I had no idea of how I was going to accomplish this.

When Christmas came—much as in Marienbad—we celebrated in non-Christian style. Our youth leaders decided it would be fun if we had a cos-tume party. Yes, it would have been a lot of fun—on any other date. On New

Year's Eve, or *Fasching,* but on Christmas? We made costumes from crepe paper during our crafts class. I chose to be a *Pfefferkuchen* heart. My costume was made of brown crepe paper. I glued pink curled paper to the edges of the brown paper to make it look like sugar icing on the brown gingerbread heart. The paper costumes covered our thin undershirts and panties. We were all bare-legged and wore canvas *Turnschuhe,* a cross between a gym shoe and a ballet slipper. We rushed down to the boardwalk wearing our flimsy outfits in the cold winter night, slipping and sliding on the thin coating of ice, which crackled beneath our feet like breaking glass. Once at the edge of the sand, the youth leaders lit a Yule log, and we danced around this fire and sang songs about the wonders of oak trees and nature, all things connected to old Germanic customs and far removed from *Weihnachten,* the Holy Night.

Following this excursion into a Teutonic past, its roots and imagined customs, half of the girls got sick with the flu. Our youth leader chided us, calling us weaklings and saying that we were not fit to be called "hearty German girls." She, of course, had been dressed warmly during the celebration in a *Trainings-anzug,* a sort of sweat suit athletes wore.

Hot with fever, I fainted in gym class. That got me a lot of attention. I could have come alert sooner, but I liked it when the teachers hovered around me as I lay on the wooden floor with my eyes closed. The next day I fainted again, but this time I faked it. And the next day, and the next. In fact, I fainted several times a day, whenever I knew a teacher was around. After a few days of this, the gym teacher took me to the local doctor. He found nothing wrong, but he suggested that they send for my mother. He said that she should have me checked out by a neurologist in Berlin. He wrote down a name and gave the paper to the teacher.

I had found a way out.

Mother arrived, worried that I might have a brain tumor. The train ride to Berlin was a nightmare. There were no empty seats, so both of us stood—or sat intermittently on my suitcase—the entire way to Berlin. The train knocked us about, and passengers pushed at us in the narrow corridor running alongside the compartments. The train was overcrowded with refugees from East Prussia, who were carrying their possessions in trunks, suitcases, and sacks.

I had to step over people and belongings to get to the water closet. The toilet was clogged and the floor around it wet with the overflow of excrement. When I opened the door to it, my stomach did a flip-flop. The stench hit me right where my breakfast was digesting, bringing it up. While the train jostled and jerked, I performed a balancing act: I tried to hover above the toilet as I had been taught (so as not to pick up any germs from the seat) and tried not to vomit onto the already filthy floor. It was disgusting, having to swallow my breakfast a second time, but it was also thrilling to perfectly aim the last bit of it into the grubby sink.

It was such a different ride now, in January, than it had been last September when Oma and I traveled from Wiesbaden to Berlin. Then, we had been shot at and had almost lost our lives, but the trains were clean and we had found seats. In only three and a half months German trains had lost all of their former appearance. It had taken Mother only a few hours on the train from Berlin to Mistroy, traveling northeast, when now, traveling in the opposite direction, it took a full day and part of the evening.

The refugees from Pomerania and East Prussia crowding the train told us tales of horror, of what the Russians did to women and to men: how they raped, plundered, and sometimes mutilated, how they cut off women's breasts and men's "parts," and how they massacred. I listened. My ears heard the words, but my brain did not know how to interpret them. I knew that the Russians spread horror and that they were on the move west, and I was frightened.

Fear of the Russians had driven these people to leave their homes and their farms with the richest earth in Germany to seek refuge by going west. Mother hugged me. She sometimes put her hands over my ears when a particularly grisly tale was told and said it was a good thing I was coming home.

I was so happy to be away from Mistroy that I cried—sporadically—all the way back to Berlin. Mother didn't understand why I was crying when I said I was happy, and she didn't believe me when I told her that I had faked the fainting spells because I hated Mistroy.

After lengthy examinations, the eminent professor from the Humboldt Universität confirmed that I was well and that nothing was wrong with me. "Your daughter should go on stage," he joked, "Become an actress. She certainly played her part well."

His words became my inspiration.

By chance I met one of the older girls from Mistroy more than a year later. At first I did not recognize her. A gray haired woman was with her, a nurse companion. The girl had a glazed look, and though she smiled at me with broken teeth, I knew that she didn't know who I was. The nurse told me that she and several other girls from Mistroy were staying at a home for war-injured women. I learned that Mistroy had been taken by the Russians a few months after I left. The girls were then shipped off in traveling trailers—moving brothels—where they were forced to service Russian soldiers, as many as forty to sixty soldiers a day. Many of the younger girls did not return.

CHAPTER 9

Quiet before the Storm

We were always cold. Newspapers reported that January 1945 was one of the coldest on record. People said this would freeze the Russians in place, slow down their speedy advance toward Berlin. Oma sneered. Hadn't Napoleon's invasion of Russia proven that just the opposite would happen?

In Frau Kuhnert's luxury apartment, the central heating had not worked for more than a year. Oma and I shared one room without heat. The three of us used Mother's larger room during the day as a living room. Here we depended on a tiny electrical heater and a small iron stove, where again, as in Mistroy, the flue went through a wooden board that had replaced the window glass. People were better off living in less modern apartments. There they would have tiled stoves (like the one that fell on me in Wiesbaden) and could make a fire safely. There were intermittent blackouts, and our teeth chattered from the cold when that happened. But during these blackouts, we would still have gas for cooking. Thus we would spend most of our time in Frau Kuhnert's kitchen trying to get warm, huddling near a big iron pot on the range where one of Oma's watery soups would be simmering.

Electricity and gas were rationed, and hot water for taking a bath was a luxury that we would indulge in only on special occasions. Most of the time we went to the public baths, but the water there was lukewarm and the time allowed behind the locked door was ten minutes. Then the door would unlock by means of some strange device so that the next person could enter. Ten minutes was not long enough to enjoy a bath.

To bathe in our own tub without time limits, to feel cleansed of the dust, smut, and odor of smoke was an enormous pleasure that is hard to imagine in normal times. During those moments in the bathtub, the war disappeared: every fear, and even my hunger, floated off in the warm water, along with the dirt.

To save water, Mother and I took baths together. She often sang in the bathtub. Sometimes she would entertain me with one of the *Lieder* she had studied, and sometimes she would make up words and melodies, trying to match them to the moment. I liked it when she sang, "*Des Meeres und der Liebe Wellen . . .* " to me, something about the waves of the sea and the waves of love. While the steam obscured the peeling oil paint on the walls, I squinted to blur my vision, imagining the cracks to be veins in marble. And Mother shampooed my hair and acted as if I were still a small child.

I had conflicting thoughts about my mother during these baths. There was envy: I'll never be as pretty as she, I thought. I have knobs for breasts, and they'll never get fuller. She had long and slender legs and the most beautiful feet, ankles, and knees, which I had been told my father had compared to those of an Egyptian queen. I snuggled against her firm bosom in the warm water and wished that she could take me back into her womb, that she could have hopes for me again. A handsome boy would emerge from her body, not an unwanted daughter. Why does she always let me know that my father wanted a son? She gave birth not only to a daughter, but to a daughter who couldn't do anything right. Why am I so stupid, so bad in math? Pröpenine, my little *Maus,* my mother would say, don't cry about the math grade. You're doing well in German, in history, and in music. You're a girl, and you don't need math. Come little Karin, let's take a bath. Mother's going to sing you a lullaby. *Aah* yes. Mother sings, Mother scolds, Mother punishes, Mother kisses, Mother believes she's the best mother when she cuddles. But then she changes, abruptly, and let's me know where I stand.

All these thoughts crisscrossed my brain in the warm water, while leaning against her warm body, loving her, hating her, and feeling alone and sad.

She was lonely too. The man she loved, Päule Carlson, was far from her. He was a leading physicist and worked on one of Hitler's defense schemes. But early that year, despite restrictions on travel, Uncle Päule managed to visit us. He and mother had known each other since before the war. They had skied together, and he'd taken her up high into the sky in his glider plane. I liked him; he was ruggedly handsome, with suntanned skin even in the midst of winter, and he always had a pipe in the right corner of his mouth. He wore tweed coats with leather patches on his elbows and looked like an English country squire. Päule Carlson was Swedish—therefore he had not been drafted—and had studied in Germany. He was thirty-six years old, the same age as my mother, and a respected physicist. On this visit he looked especially grave. "Soon our world is going to change," he said.

"Can't you leave? Go back to Sweden? Your mother must be terribly worried about you. There you're safe, Päule, go back."

"No, I can't. Impossible. Let's not discuss it." He broke off the conversation.

I knew something was wrong and he was troubled by it to a great extent. But I forgot my worries when he gave me his personal edition of St. Exupery's *Little Prince*. His love of flying and space and the freedom he felt in the air were something I could relate to. Maybe in a few years he would teach me to fly in his glider plane. I liked this man and hoped that he and Mother would get married after the war. Always there was this qualification, *after the war*.

At the Briefzensur, the office where Mother censored POW letters, she had become friends with Margrit Hagen, a woman who was more than ten years younger than she. Margrit and Mother exchanged books of poetry, and Mother invited her to our house for tea—chamomile or peppermint—on several Sundays. Here Margrit practiced English with my grandmother. Oma liked her and perhaps entertained hopes that this vivacious young woman, with the thick dark curls who liked poetry and art, might be a possible match for Uncle Will when he returned from the war.

One day Mother came home in tears: the SS had arrested Margrit. Oma sat down in shock. Why? Mother didn't know, but she would find out. She planned to visit the prison where Margrit was being held. Oma warned Mother, "You don't know why she's in prison. Maybe she's involved with an underground group. They might suspect you and arrest you as well." But Mother would hear none of it. Margrit was her friend, and she would visit her.

After Mother came home from her visit to the Charlottenburg Women's Prison, she told Oma the astounding facts. A nurse, who had been present at Margrit's birth, had denounced her. The nurse knew that Margrit's biological mother was Jewish and that the Hagens had adopted her. All this had come as a shocking surprise to Margrit. She thought this was a mistake, a colossal mistake, and showed her *Ahnenspiegel,* her Aryan pass, to the SS man. He tore it up as counterfeit. She was told that her birth mother, Hanna Schwartzschild-Ox, an unmarried society member of Frankfurt's Jewish elite, had become pregnant. Wishing to avoid a scandal, Hanna had given her child up for adoption. Everyone who heard the story was puzzled: why, after all these years, had the nurse denounced her and reported the Hagens to the authorities.

"This is insane," Mother shouted.

"No," said Oma, "It is evil." She kept silent for a while, then went on,

"Yes, evil. So many denunciations, *ach Gott,* people turning others in. What a country we've become."

They cast a sideways glance at me. I felt insulted. Did they think I would talk about what I heard and get them arrested? "You know I don't repeat what I hear at home. Never. You can trust me," I said.

Oma put her arms around me. "Karin, I know, but sometimes a word escapes and then we'd be in trouble. Be careful."

"I don't go to school, there aren't any youth meetings, there isn't anyone I talk to. Besides, you know I'm always careful with what I say."

"Ha. Often you get carried away and talk too much," Mother said.

"Thanks a lot," I said and banged the door shut when I left the room.

But I was curious. I put my ear to the crack in the door and listened, when a little while later Mother went to the foyer, picked up the phone, and dialed the number Margrit had given her. The number connected to the house warden of the Hagens' apartment house. I heard Mother repeat what someone told her at the other end. She kept repeating, "They're on vacation? Where?" over and over again, as if she were partially deaf.

Mother hung up. She stood, not moving, shaking her head. "On vacation. Now, with Germany crumbling?" She turned to Oma in the doorway, saying, "Can you believe that? There are no trains other than for refugees and the military, and if they had a car, there'd be no gasoline. The roads are crowded with refugees crisscrossing the land. On vacation, with nowhere to go and the country in a state of collapse?"

Oma said, "Maybe they've been arrested. Like Margrit."

Oma's words proved to be prophetic.

After Mother's next visit to Margrit, Mother told Oma that the authorities could not prove Margrit had a Jewish father. That turned out to be her salvation, for the time. The family of her birth mother had disappeared. The bureaucrats needed proof of both sides of Margrit's parentage. The file listing her as Jewish had to state both *her father's* and *her mother's* names. Margrit would remain in prison as long as her full parentage was not known. And Mother kept visiting her, bringing her poems by Rilke, apples, and occasionally some of Oma's baked goods.

I was a year ahead in school and normally would have entered the *Untertertia* in the lyceum, but all the schools were closed and Oma decided to teach me at home. I could keep up with my lessons in history and in English and German literature and composition, but Oma was not prepared to teach geometry and algebra or physics, chemistry, and biology. That year without formal schooling left a big gap in my education that I could never fill.

When I heard Mother and Oma discuss my school situation, I was afraid they'd send me back to live with my father. But by late January 1945, the Russians were advancing toward Liegnitz in Lower Silesia. They had already taken Upper Silesia. We heard that people were fleeing, adding Silesia's population to the stream of refugees from Pomerania and East Prussia crowding trains and roads leading to Berlin and Dresden.

While we huddled in the cellar during the air raids, I often thought of my little brothers, somewhere on the road to the western lands. The weather had turned warm in those last few days of January, and the snows melted. A small blessing.

How could my father endure these hardships? He was not a well man, and he looked ten years older than Hitler, who was the same age as my father. Perhaps Father had decided to stay? No, that would be unlike him. He would want to protect his young wife from the Russians and would escort his family west.

Mother's work at the state theaters slowed to a few hours a week. Hitler had insisted that the theaters perform as usual—in these unusual times—and had kept them open. In 1943, after some of the worst bombing raids, Mother had memorized Hitler's edict that was posted backstage: "Theatrical performances are needed because the morale of the people must be maintained." When one of the Staatstheater was bombed, it was hastily rebuilt, keeping Mother employed.

But the incessant bombing of the city center and its theaters had been too much. The opera, bombed to the ground for the third time, was temporarily installed in a former revue theater, the Admiralspalast, near the Friedrichstrasse railway station. Now, in February, even those theaters that had escaped being bombed closed their doors.

When Mother came home on a Friday evening, she pulled a blue feather headdress and a *Walküre* helmet from a bag, as well as a black tulle skirt, a black sequined top with the thinnest straps, and several other odds and ends, mementoes of her costume-designing career. I fingered the cloth, ran the feathers across my face, and fantasized about wearing them on stage.

Later that night Mother sat on the sofa, her arms hung and her head fell to her chest. The closing of the theaters had thrown her into a depression.

Private theaters and cabarets, as well as chic restaurants such as Horcher's, had closed in February 1943, when Goebbels had declared *totaler Krieg*.

I had never been to Horcher's, but I had heard Mother talk effusively about its elegance and its famous kitchen. Mother had dined there last with her friends Karl and Veronika Wolfram in January 1943. Karl was the principal bass-baritone at the Staatsoper and that came with some privileges. They had feasted on venison, lobster, and caviar at the height of war. (Beef and pork were rationed, but lobster and venison were available—for the right price. The average citizen was hard-pressed to find German beer in one of the famous *Berliner Kneipen*. In these cozy smoke-filled corner pubs, professors rubbed elbows with truck drivers. But French champagne flowed freely up to the end of the war for those who had the money.) Horcher's closed after Goebbels's declaration. But it was Göring's favorite restaurant, and he managed to change Goebbels's mind. It was reopened as a Luftwehr officers club. Göring would be able to continue dining on lobster in this rarified atmosphere.

After the war, Mother promised, I would experience Horcher's myself. Mutti would take Oma and me to celebrate my confirmation in the Lutheran Church. That would be next year, when I would turn thirteen. The war was certain to be over by then. Since the theaters had closed, Mother censored POW letters eight hours a day. Most nights we spent more hours in the cellar than we did in our bedrooms. A constant up and down from bed to cot. For Berliners, sleep was as scarce as food. Yet everyone went on with the business of living as if this were the norm.

The Berliner Philharmonie, under the direction of Wilhelm Furtwängler and occasionally under the baton of Herbert von Karajan, was still giving concerts. Every able- or not-so-able-bodied man in the city was called to defend Berlin, but for these musicians, Goebbels made an exception. They kept on performing, for Goebbels believed that music was a necessary balm for the terror-stricken population. I heard Oma say that Goebbels regarded music as a sedative, as social control, but whatever his reason, she was happy that we still were able to attend concerts. I heard Furtwängler conduct Beethoven's Fourth, and a week later the Fifth. The Fifth, with its heralding opening bars became a symbol of survival to me, and it has been my favorite symphony ever since.

Normally we lived in scrappy clothes, but when we went to the Philharmonie we dressed in our best. Oma wore her standby, the navy blue silk dress, and I slipped into a dress of burgundy taffeta with a white lace collar. We checked our galoshes and heavy winter coats in the cloakroom, and later, sitting on the velvet upholstery, we felt as if there was no war going on. The touch of my crisp taffeta made me feel as if I were a different person. I appeared as a well-dressed girl, no longer a skin-and-bones child walking over rubble in scuffed ski boots and spending nights in a shelter. I would let myself sink deep into the softness of the seat, then I would close my eyes and enter the mysterious world of images, which the music painted onto my inner eyelids.

During the time Mother visited Margrit in jail, I was pressed into another kind of undertaking by my friend Erich, the boy I had tried to steal apples with. Erich was almost fourteen and feared being drafted by the *Volksturm,* the German Home Guard. He listened to the BBC with a growing desperation, mapping in his mind each mile the Allied troops advanced toward Berlin. An Allied invasion of Berlin would keep him out of the dreaded uniform and the last battle.

He raised *Kaninchen,* little fuzzy rabbits, in a hutch in the attic, where he also hid a shortwave radio. The rabbits were the lure that made me follow him up the stairs and into the cold. We took them out of the cages and cuddled them, warming our hands in their fur.

One day he had gone upstairs a half hour ahead of me. I was mounting the last step, when suddenly I heard music, jazz music and trumpets and what Erich later explained was big band music. A song came on, in English, "Boogie-woogie . . ." And there stood Erich, holding a radio and looking like a thief caught in the act.

"Erich! You're listening to the BBC again. You can get arrested for that."

"Right. That's why you're going to the doorway and listen for footsteps. Let me know if anyone's coming up the stairs." I stood undecided, my mouth hanging open.

"Go. It's important. The news comes on any moment now."

I stood by the door, holding it open, and tried to listen to the music and for footsteps. I heard footsteps. They were running down the stairs. Good. Then I heard two pairs of boots clonking up.

"Erich, quick, hide the radio!" I slammed the door shut, and I ran toward the rabbit hutch, when the door ripped open again and two policemen entered.

"What are you two doing up here, eh?"

I probably looked guilty, and I admired Erich's calm. He stood feeding a carrot to the rabbit and raised his shoulders slightly, as if he had been asked the most stupid question ever. "Na, what does it look like? They have to eat first if we're going to eat them."

"Ha ha," the fatter of the two laughed. "Eat or be eaten, huh?"

I looked at Hannibal, the rabbit in my arm. He was going to be eaten? The two men left. I stood shaking.

Erich said, "Stupid idiots. Why would they come up here?"

"The music was pretty loud. Anyone would know it's not the music the Deutschlandsender plays. Maybe someone heard it and called them. It's too dangerous Erich. Don't do it, please."

"What could they do to me? Put me in jail or something?"

"They'd put you in a place for delinquent children. That's what they'd do."

"My father would get me out. He works for Speer."

"Hitler's architect?"

"That's right." Erich took the rabbit from my arm and put it back into its hutch. "Karin, I heard only snatches . . . then they came. The BBC said something about Dresden. Go, Karin, go to the door. Maybe they repeat the news."

I went back to the door, reluctantly listening for footsteps, while at the same time I tried to hear what was being said on the radio. But by now Erich had turned the volume down.

I watched as Eric sank onto a crate and wondered why he cradled his head in his arms. When he looked up at me, his eyes were red and wet. He choked on his words, "Dresden is in ruins. The entire inner city, the *Alt Stadt* gone. Nothing left." He looked as if someone close to him had died. "Have you been to Dresden?"

"No. I went through it once, but I didn't see much."

"It's the most beautiful city in all of Germany. Why did they do that? There's no industry there, nothing . . . just people and all those Baroque buildings . . . and now it's gone."

He looked as if he himself had been hit by a bomb. I knew he wanted to be an architect, like his father. Hearing that this great jewel of German cities was in ruin, left him with tears streaming down his face.

"Maybe it's not true," I said, putting my hand on his shoulder. "The papers said nothing about it."

He shook my hand off. "Damn them. Damn all of them. I was hoping this nightmare would be over with and there would soon be peace. Damn! Now I hope Hitler gets his wonder weapon finished and uses it on England. Wiping that little island from the face of the earth." He broke down crying again, which made him sound less angry. "Dresden. That was so unnecessary."

"Erich, please. We don't know how much damage was done."

"Maybe the newspapers will print a watered-down version tomorrow. You know that Goebbels keeps all the really bad news out of the papers. The Allies *want* us to know. They want Hitler to give up. To capitulate. But he won't. He's mad." He waved his hand as if he were swatting a fly. "Come Karin, let's give Hannibal his dinner."

"You're not going to eat him, are you?"

"I don't want to. Depends on Mother. We haven't had any meat in a long time."

"The Führer eats only grains and vegetables. He's a vegetarian. We should all be vegetarians, then we wouldn't have to kill animals."

"We'd just kill all the young men in Germany, and the young men from America, Russia, England, *ja,* kill the people and leave the animals alive." Erich pulled the radio out from under the rabbits' straw again. "Go stand by the door, Karin. A few more minutes. Please, it's important."

Toward the end of February we received news from my father and his family. They were among the last to leave Liegnitz, on Friday, February 9th, and they had been lucky that space was made for them in an already crowded and overloaded truck. It was a newspaper delivery truck, filled with the driver's family and his relatives. The driver did this last favor for his former editor-in-chief, my father.

Erna's sister-in-law lived in Dresden, their destination. They were only able to take two suitcases, and Erna had to make a last minute choice: she could take practical items, the photo albums, or the silver. My father had to be torn from his collection of more than four thousand books, many of them first editions.

The truck rumbled on through the night, then ran out of gasoline near the Silesian border. The driver siphoned off fuel from an abandoned truck. Then they stopped again. The driver lifted the hood, trying to find out what was wrong, while other overloaded trucks passed them. Later these trucks also ran out of fuel and sat on the shoulder of the road. Some people jumped off the trucks and began walking. But to flee the advancing Russians on foot was an impossibility for Father and his family. Hubsi, the youngest, was not yet two, and Father was in poor physical condition.

Luckily, the driver of the truck my father and his family were on was resourceful. He had reconnected a loose wire and the truck was able to move again. The truck made it to Goerlitz, and the driver dropped my father and his family off at the railroad station. They were able to prove that they were refugees from Silesia and were allowed to buy tickets to Dresden. People from Goerlitz itself, who could not get tickets, pushed and shoved, creating chaos and fear. But no one stormed the train, and Vati, Tante Erna, and their three sons made it into a compartment. They arrived in Dresden at the main station, where they stored their suitcases and boarded a tram to Erna's sister-in-law's apartment. The family had been on the road with little food and no milk for the children for three days.

They had arrived.

When they got to the apartment, they found a note tacked to the door, informing them of a change in plan. The sister-in-law wanted them to come to her mother's more spacious house located on the outskirts of town, where Father's large family could be better accommodated. There she was preparing a "Welcome to Dresden" dinner for them. Father, Tante Erna, and the three children summoned their last strength and again boarded a streetcar.

It was Tuesday, the evening of February 13th, when they arrived at their destination. That night the RAF (the Royal Air Force) saturation-bombed the inner city. Moving to the suburbs had saved Father's family from the firestorm that destroyed Dresden that very night.

Wolfdieter, eight years old at the time, later told me of the fires he saw burning in the distance that colored the entire sky blood red. They feared further bombing and left for the moors not far from Dresden. My father's family spent a week there beneath open skies, without proper clothes or blankets and with a toddler to take care of. I don't know how my step-mother managed. Saint Peter must have smiled on them, for the weather was dry and unusually warm for February.

The Dresden firebombing lasted two long days and nights. Some people tried to save themselves and ran, their bodies aflame, into the River Elbe, only to suffocate when the oxygen was sucked from the air. Others made it to the other shore, but when they emerged from the water, they began burning again as soon as the air hit the phosphorous gumlike substance on their bodies. These human torches ran on until they collapsed and died.

The fire burned so hot that skeletons melted into the sandstone founda-tions of the cellars. It was so hot that the color of the sandstone changed from yellow-beige to a deep orange. Estimates of the dead numbered any-where between thirty thousand and three hundred thousand. With vast numbers of unregistered refugees from the eastern provinces crowding Dresden, only an approximate tally of the dead could be made.

DREAMS OF FARAWAY

Oma's cooking lessons were lost on me, especially since our meals were limited to potatoes and rutabaga, potatoes and beets, potatoes and cabbage, or white cabbage made into sauerkraut. She insisted I watch her make soup, which consisted mainly of water with some vegetables and—if we were lucky—a bone to give it flavor. Sometimes a few grains of barley floated in the broth.

Oma believed that learning to cook was a necessary preparation in order to become a wife and mother. I did not tell her that I had given up my dream of becoming a farmer's wife in the former German African colonies. I no longer wanted to be a wife or a mother, anywhere; I was going to be an actress. That new fantasy had taken hold after the doctor had told my mother I had performed "my part"—the fainting—well.

Until recently, influenced by Hitler Youth leaders, many of my school friends and I had planned to be farmers' wives in Africa. Hitler promised that after the war we would reclaim the African colonies we had lost after the shameful Treaty of Versailles. I'd envisioned myself sitting on a veranda, sipping tea and planning the menu with a native cook, while my husband, a big white hunter, stalked an impala in the bush—food for tomorrow's dinner. It was a nice dinner to dream of, so different from our watery soup. But by now I knew that we would never regain the colonies.

I had always longed for faraway places. I suppose I'd inherited my great-grandfather's wanderlust, which first led him to America and then to Africa. I had heard the stories of his surveying new routes for Union Pacific to connect Salt Lake City to New Mexico and the Santa Fe railroad. He later pioneered railroad building in German East Africa.

But I dreamed of America.

Oma and I would go to Utah after the war. I mentioned it to her, and she agreed. They did not have birds of strange plumage in Utah—I was still mad at my mother for not taking us to Guatemala—but in Utah they had grizzly bears and Indians. And Oma had spoken of the most beautiful mountains and landscapes with bizarre red rock formations. She still dreamt of Utah's big skies and the brilliance of stars at night.

Dreaming became rather difficult, as it was interrupted by the many nightly trips into the shelter. During the day, I cluttered the kitchen table with my sketchpad and watercolors and wrote fairy tales. On paper I was free to escape from my gray world into underwater palaces made of coral and seashells, or into castles in which lovely maidens married handsome princes, dined on venison, and were never cold. But in our real world we were freezing and never had enough to eat. Because of the air raids, we never had enough sleep. This was especially hard on Mother who still worked long hours and had to spend much of her time commuting back and forth from home to work.

Good Friday fell on March 30th. Oma and I went to a large church to hear Bach's St. Matthew's Passion. The music filled me with wonder and an aching sadness, but after the Crucifixion, there was the promise of the Resurrection.

Church bells rang when we left the house of worship. When would they ring for peace?

The air raids were constant. American bombers by day, British attacks by night. People no longer said "good-bye" to each other when they parted but wished each other luck in surviving, shouting, "*Überleb's!*" We all tried to do just that, *überleben,* surviving the bombs, the shrapnel, the hunger, and deprivation.

Mother's job censoring POW letters slowed down, since few letters were able to leave Germany via neutral Switzerland. I think Mother's work consisted mainly of showing up at the dreaded place. This was preferable to being conscripted into the FLAK, Flieger Abwehr Kommando, to man anti-aircraft guns.

Mother waited each day for news from Päule Carlson. But each day she returned from the mail slot empty-handed, and each day her eyes grew sadder.

During Päule's last visit Mother's face had acquired a glow, like an inner light. She had looked beautiful. When I mentioned this to her, she smiled a shy little smile and put on the record of Zarah Leander, singing, "*Eine Frau wird erst schön durch die Liebe . . .*" In a low and sultry voice, this Swedish singer—so popular in wartime Germany—sang, "A woman only becomes beautiful when in love," and Mother nodded. That was Mother: happy, glowing, and in love. But all of that had vanished now. She no longer played the record, but sometimes she put on another song by Zarah Leander, a sad one telling of the wind whispering tales of love and happy endings. "*Der Wind hat mir ein Lied erzählt . . .*" Mother hoped against hope.

I wondered why she threw up so much. She seemed to take Päule's silence so much to heart that it made her physically ill. Oma tried to cheer her up. "Astrid, hardly any mail gets through now. Päule would write if he could. He loves you. You will see each other again when the war is over."

Mother shook her head. "No, I'm afraid he's in Russia by now. Foolish man. I begged him to go back to Sweden. He told me he didn't believe in turning his back on the country that had paid for his studies and had offered him an excellent career. He said he was not a rat leaving a sinking ship."

"He's Swedish. If the Russians arrested him, they'll let him go back to Sweden."

"Mother, don't be so naïve. They'll inter the scientists, and if they need any of them, they'll ship them to Russia. They won't let him go back to Sweden. No, not the Russians."

Mother's illness grew worse, and she had to be hospitalized. On a sunny April morning, Oma and I visited her in a clinic in Grunewald. I pilfered hyacinths for her, tender white symbols of spring growing in the wilderness of a garden, surrounding a bombed-out villa.

The room in the clinic was sunny, but Mother was not. She looked as if she were underneath a black cloud and needed Päule to bring back the color to her face. The red sparks had vanished from her brown hair as it fell in dull strands to her shoulders. I became aware of how very thin she was, noticing the outline of her hip bones poking through the thin white blanket. "You look as white as your sheets," I said.

I asked Oma what was wrong with Mother, but she shook her head and said she didn't know. Mother whispered she had to have a small operation, an *Eingriff,* whatever that meant. "Don't worry Karin," she said, "I'll be home in two or three days. Meanwhile, behave yourself and help Oma."

I smiled and kissed her, telling her to get well and to come home soon. I even joked, "Come home to greet the Russians. They'll be here soon." This earned me a box on the ears, stinging me, even though she was weak now, and a stern look from the nurse.

A month later Mother told me that she'd had a miscarriage. I was sworn to secrecy, but I suspected my grandmother knew, though she had chosen to act blind to the actual cause of Mother's illness. The child was Uncle Päule's child, a love child. Abortions were strictly prohibited by the Nazis—interested in creating as many children of the master race as possible. But Mother had been bleeding, and in these last weeks of war she'd found a doctor who helped "clean out her uterus." The doctor risked much by placing her in his clinic.

She spoke of how gifted this love child would have been. This made me jealous and deep down I was glad this future rival was gone. But later I felt guilty.

HITLER'S BIRTHDAY
CELEBRATE THE FEASTS WHERE THEY MAY FALL

It was Friday, and Mother would come home early from work. I was always happy when I saw more than a fleeting glimpse of her. I walked half a block to the corner of Kurfürstendamm, hoping to spot her jumping off the trolley car. The streets smelled of pulverized concrete. Added to this was an all pervasive metallic odor from the explosives. This spring no flowers brightened the drab, shelled buildings and no pink of early petunias or purple of pansies shouted happiness. Nor could I spot the yellow of daffodils in the window boxes that in prior years had cheered up passersby. Many of these boxes hung half off their hinges. Trees came into leaf late that year, as if afraid to expose their tender growth to the ravages of war. Most branches were bare and brown, though a few valiantly tried on a soft veil of green. Perhaps a few birds still sang, but I don't remember hearing any. Maybe they had taken shelter in the countryside to get away from the exploding sounds of bombs. By now the Russians had advanced to the outskirts of Berlin, and the birds in the country would have to put up with artillery and machine gun fire. That spring, there was no tranquil place to be found in or around Berlin.

The once elegant Ku'damm looked bleak. Some buildings were left standing, while others had been reduced to facades and heaps of piled rubble. In the few buildings still standing, most of the windows were shattered. Occasional rays of sun found the many shards of glass littering the sidewalk and transformed them into sparkling precious stones. Beauty amidst the ruins. Only the crunch of my ski boots stepping on this glass reminded me of the source. In the center of the wide sidewalk, small steel and glass showcases had in former days displayed samples of the elegant merchandise available in the stores nearby; these cases had been empty for sometime. Now they showed hostile glass fragments, jutting like the bared teeth of a watchdog ready to snap.

And not a flag fluttered in the breeze.

That was the most amazing thing of all. It was April 20, 1945, Adolf Hitler's fifty-sixth birthday. In past years on this day, every major thoroughfare had been decorated with huge banners; from every building had flown an oversized flag, the black swastika on the round of white centered in red, blood red.

Many apartment dwellers had formerly vied with their neighbors in paying homage to the Führer by flying their own flags from their windows. But not today. My eyes wandered up and down the street, and there were no flags.

For the first time since he took power, Hitler did not make an appearance on his birthday, even though the weather was sunny, as would be expected for the 20th of April. Through the clouds of dust from bombs and artillery, patches of blue sky spoke of the typical "Führer weather." This was a strange phenomenon. It was said that if the Führer stepped out onto his balcony to make an appearance or left the chancellery to review a parade in his honor on an overcast or rainy day, the skies would lighten and the sun would emerge from behind clouds. Some trusting souls believed that Hitler even had dominion over the weather, as he did not allow Saint Peter to rain on his parade. But on that April 20, he remained hunkered down in the bunker of his heavily fortified chancellery.

I remembered those former years so vividly, since my birthday is close to Hitler's. When I was very young (with an apparently overly developed ego) and first noticed the multitude of flags decorating the Hansa Allee in Frankfurt, I believed they were put up for me. "How pretty," I'd cried out, "For my birthday party."

"Don't be silly," Mother had said, "The flags are for Adolf Hitler."

It was chilly this April afternoon. But so far, no bombs. No Mother coming down the street. But wait, I saw something bright. There she was! I'd forgotten that she'd taken the bicycle. The orange silk scarf she'd tied beneath her chin fluttered in the breeze created by her furious pedaling. Mother always did everything as if she were in a hurry. She never walked to the trolley or S-Bahn, she ran. She didn't leisurely pedal her bicycle, she raced as if someone were chasing her. She had seen me and came to a stop, almost running me down, braking by scraping the pavement with the soles of her shoes. How stupid, treating her good leather walking shoes that way. Who knew when she'd be able to get another pair. Then she jumped off and greeted me with a big hug.

"Follow me, I'm in a hurry," she said swinging onto the bicycle seat again and pedaling home.

"Why? What's happening?" I asked, running behind her, trying to keep up. "I'm going to a party . . . have to change, eat a bite . . ."

"You're going out?" I asked. "At night? With the air raids?"

Mother sang an old German saying, "*Wir müssen die Feste feiern wie sie fallen*"—We have to celebrate the feasts where and when they occur.

Mother locked up her bicycle in the entryway and ran up the stairs, skipping a step each time. I followed, out of breath. I begged her not to go out that night. "Please, please, Mutti!"

She closed the door behind me and took off her scarf and coat.

"What's gotten into you, acting this way? You're not a baby. Oma will be here with you. God, I'm only going to Gertie's; you know where she lives. Don't worry, *mein kleiner Hase.*"

I hated her when she called me her little hare. All those stupid animal names: a *Gans,* a goose, when she thought I did something stupid; a *kleine Maus,* or little mouse, when she was loving; or a *Hase,* when I was scared. I was not; I was brave. After all I had survived the bombing in Wiesbaden, the attack on the train on our way to Berlin, and the terrible children's evacuation camp in Mistroy. I could handle any situation. But now I worried about Mother's safety, going out at night to a strange building with an unknown bomb shelter.

Oma appeared from the kitchen calling, "Soup's served!"

I was hungry and forgot about Mother and the animal names.

We were having turnip soup again. Oh well. After a few bites Mother disappeared, and within a very brief time she reappeared, forcing me take a deep breath. Even at thirty-seven she looked glamorous. Her hair had regained its luster and fell in waves to her shoulders, "like ripe chestnuts," I'd heard Päule Carlson say. He was right. It was brown with a touch of golden red. She had applied mascara and thick black lashes now fanned her large gray eyes. She wore her favorite black silk dress. It had been made just for her, but now that she had lost weight, it hung loose on her figure. As if she were modeling, she quick stepped a pirouette, and the dress with its fluted hem twirled around her, rising to show off her shapely legs. "That's because it's cut on the bias," she said. "Remember Karin, it's the mark of a good dress to be cut on the bias. Very few seamstresses know how to cut this style." Why did she always teach me silly things like that? A bias cut! I thought of needles and pins and her pricking me while fitting clothes on me. Now it had become my job to wield a needle and to darn socks. And that was difficult enough, to remember how to put a wooden egg in a scratchy woolen sock and mend the hole in the weaving, crisscross method. Bias cut indeed.

Oma asked, "Why are you all dressed up? What's the occasion?"

"The occasion?" echoed Mother. "Oh . . . remember, it's the 20th of April. Our great Führer's birthday. More than likely his last."

Oma shot her a look that said, keep your voice down. Frau Kuhnert might hear. Even I knew that Frau Kuhnert had a golden party pin, meaning she had joined the NSDAP, the Nazi Party, years before Hitler came to power.

"Yes, yes," Mother waved her off with her hand, lowering her voice. "Gertie invited some doctors from the university clinic. They're providing the alcohol. And food. And then there's Peter and Heinrich and . . . you know . . . people of like minds."

Oma shook her head. "You've not been well, Astrid. It's only been ten days since you left the clinic."

Mother swirled around the room again. "I feel great. Strong as an ox."

I wanted to say stupid as a cow, but of course I dared not.

"It's gallows humor, what you're doing. It's not right. All of you might get into trouble. You know what that means." Oma made a gesture of slicing her right hand across her throat. Her eyes filled with tears. "Don't go, Astrid. Germany is dying. This is not the time for frivolities. Berlin is in ruin. And you go off, dressing fancy." She shook her head. "Don't go."

Mother repeated the silly slogan about feasts. "Besides," she went on, "The

Russians are at the gate, who knows what will happen then. I'm still young. I have to live and have fun now and again."

Mother sprayed Chanel N° 5 behind her ears, the French perfume I was not allowed to touch. She returned the crystal bottle with the rubber squeeze ball and its silken tassel to her dresser, and grabbing her nutria jacket, she breezed out of the apartment, leaving us in the trail of her perfume.

I sighed. Mother, she was so beautiful but so headstrong. I patted Oma's hand and put my arms around her. With my eyes closed I inhaled Mother's lingering scent, wishing it would contain magic that would make me as beautiful as she was.

We had just gone to sleep when the air-raid alarm sounded—*Ouiiii ouiiii*—the sound rising and falling in its infernal tonality, jarring us out of sleep. In the dark I stepped into my ski pants that were lying next to my bed. I slept wearing socks and heavy underwear, as well as a sweater. I grabbed my thick jacket and slid into my ski boots. A dim flashlight lit our way as we walked down the three flights of stairs to the cellar. The drone of planes echoed nearer and nearer, then the bombs hit. They were close, quite close. Oma and I huddled on the narrow cot and prayed for Mother's safety. Then the high, one-note of the all clear sounded. Back in our room, we stayed awake for a little while, hoping Mother would come home.

A few hours later, the siren wailed again. Another air raid, another visit to the cellar. After the all clear had allowed us back upstairs, I slid my boots off, collapsed on my bed, and immediately fell asleep.

The morning dawned with low clouds and drizzle. I went to the window to look for Mother. When I opened it, the early morning air choked me. Dust from plaster and concrete hung thick after last night's raids. I leaned out of the window and saw the rubble of collapsed buildings close to our house. The air smelled coldly electric. Farther off buildings were on fire.

Footsteps on the stairs made me close the window. I rushed to the door and listened as the steps came closer, and then I knew they were not the *clickety-clack* of Mother's high-heeled shoes. I went back to bed, burrowing deep into my feather pillow, hoping to sleep for another hour. Then I heard footsteps again, heavy footsteps coming closer. It sounded as if two or three men were carrying or dragging something up the stairs, making *thump-thump* noises. My heart was pounding so hard that I could feel it in my throat.

Someone tried to fit a key into the keyhole but missed. Something thumped against the front door, and the key made a scratching sound. Oma and I both jumped out of bed and ran to the door to open it.

There was Mother, with two men. Her arms were slung over their shoulders, and she hung like a corpse between them. Her skin was yellow and her hair matted and wet from sweat or rain. Her mascara had smeared making her eyes look like the hollow black eyes of Käthe Kollwitz's starving women, whom I had seen in Mother's art books. The emaciated bodies of two tall men dragged her into the apartment. Oma looked as if she were about to scream, but she covered her mouth with her hand, swallowing any sound that might be trying to escape. She indicated that I should be quiet so as not to arouse the curiosity of Frau Kuhnert. The men followed us through the open door into the bedroom. They deposited Mother onto her bed. Her right arm moved as if trying to fend off an annoying animal, and I thanked God that she was still alive. Then she threw up, something green and slimy that spread like an evil witch's pond over the gold damask of the quilt. I ran for a towel and wiped her mouth, holding my nose against the sour smell as I cleaned up the vomit.

Oma escorted the men back to the entry. They stopped and whispered to her, apparently not wanting me to know what had happened. They did not realize that I was the only one who could get our family doctor to come and help Mother.

The trip to the doctor on my bicycle was like a ride into a nightmare. Last night we had only heard the explosions of a few bombs, but the closer I got to the Gedächtniskirche and the Tauentzin Strasse, the more I saw the scope of the destruction. Maybe this air raid had been the Allies' birthday present to Adolf Hitler.

Several of the many bombed houses I passed were smoldering gray, orange, and red; billowing clouds of slate smoke rained particles that tasted acidic on my tongue. Other dwellings lay in complete ruin. I held my nose when I passed buildings where the sickeningly sweet smell of gas was escaping from broken lines. Debris covered the sidewalks and scattered into the streets. At times I had to carry my bicycle over shards of broken glass and sharp pieces of concrete. A skinny black cat with one white paw limped across my path, perhaps in pain, then disappeared into a ruin. Acrid dust got into my lungs, provoking a coughing fit. After a little more than an hour, on a trip that should have taken less than twenty minutes, I reached the doctor.

He looked at me in a befuddled way, this old man, scratching his grizzled head. I felt safe now in his presence and was certain that he would help Mother. He told me he thought it brave of me to come for him under the circumstances, but he was sorry. He couldn't leave his family at this time.

I told him I wasn't brave. I had to come. I had no choice. I repeated what the two men had told Oma was the cause, "wood alcohol," and that Oma had turned to me and said, "Quick, child. Lose no time, go get the doctor." I told him I was angry with Mother for having put herself into this mess. I also told him Mother had been at a party, and the young doctors from the charité clinic had provided the alcohol. Even though I often hated her, I also loved her, and now she needed help. I blurted out all of my feelings to this man, hoping he would understand.

"Why didn't one of the doctors help when everyone got sick?" Dr. Schulz asked.

"I don't know. I think they got sick too."

Old Dr. Schulz shook his head and raised his bushy eyebrows.

Then I sobbed, "Maybe she'll die. You *have* to come with me."

I think that outburst made him change his mind. He unlocked his bicycle from the railing in his entryway, and we began to pedal. When we encountered the impassable sections of the street, we carried our bicycles. I offered to carry his medical bag, but he wouldn't let me.

After examining Mother, he told Oma and me that Mother suffered from an acute case of alcohol poisoning. During peacetime this might have been marginally serious, but now, with everyone undernourished and wearing their bones close to the skin, it could be fatal. It was fortunate Mother had vomited so much, she had rid her body of most of the poison, but her life was still in danger. The doctor gave her a potion to drink—which also brought on spasms of violent heaving—and left medicines for us to administer. He prescribed bed rest, lots of bed rest, and plenty of fluids. He also prescribed chicken soup, black tea, and applesauce. She was to eat white bread only.

Chicken soup? An impossibility. And tea? White bread? We felt lucky when we had a loaf of sour-tasting black bread. Only the applesauce was a feasibility.

Mother had been exceedingly lucky to have survived that episode. She told us later that someone had added apple cider to the wood alcohol to improve the taste. This encouraged more drinking. The mood grew boisterous, and the party was loud. One of the women got very sick, then passed out. Mother had joined the men in bellowing satiric verses, ridiculing Hitler, sung to the tunes of popular students' songs. We had so much fun, she said, weakly, laughing at this recollection. Oma chided her, saying she behaved like a naughty child. Mother went on, telling us that they ignored the sirens. The house warden had knocked on the door repeatedly, but they ignored him. (This was a mistake. These little dictators were not to be ignored; most were card-carrying Nazis. Formerly these wardens were lowly concierges, but now as appointed "officials," they were in a position of authority over the apartment residents.) Toward morning the house warden summoned the police, who were synonymous with the SS in those days. The men who brought Mother home had barely made it out of the servants' rear door when the police barged in through the front door.

When Mother finished her story, Oma stood shaking her head, silent, not reprimanding. I think she knew Mutti had punished herself enough.

And so Mother took to her bed. For one week she could barely move. When the air-raid sirens summoned us into the cellar, she was too weak to get dressed. The house warden came to look after Mother and talked to us as if we were errant children. Wagging his index finger at Oma, he told her this was against the rules and that Mother was obliged to come into the cellar. What ailed her anyway? he asked. Oma, whom I remember as being incapable of lying, fabricated some weird story. I remember her saying, Mother could not be moved because she was too ill. Oma told him that Mother suffered from an inflamed appendix, a piece of her anatomy that had been removed when she was sixteen.

APRIL WALTZ
APRIL 27, 1945

Oma struggled with her shoes, tying frayed laces.

"Where are you going?" I asked.

"*Ach,* Karin. The butcher is the only place still open, and he too is closing shop today. Frau Bauman said he's selling everything out." She hefted herself from the chair and grabbed her string shopping bag.

"But Oma, they're shooting from the church tower."

"I have to go. Who knows when we'll be able to buy meat again. It's our last chance."

I slid on my stocking feet across the wooden floor and landed on her, throwing her back onto the chair. "I'll go," I said, getting up and putting on my boots. "You'll do no such thing," Oma said, but I cut her short and put my hand over her mouth. Not very respectful but effective.

"No, Karin," she cried, freeing herself from my hand, trying to hold me back. But I'd already snatched the net bag and torn the ration cards and the *Geldbörse* with the crumpled paper money and coins from her hand, and before she could argue any further, I was out the door, straddling the banister, and sliding down each section of the mahogany railing.

I heard her shouting after me. "Come back, come back right now," and a few moments later, in a meeker tone, "Be careful, child."

I was the only one in physical shape to go. Grandmother suffered from angina pectoris and mother was still recovering from her escapade on Hitler's last birthday. There was no food in the house. There was no choice.

The heavy door closed behind me with a thud. My heart raced. I had to pee, but I didn't want to go back to the apartment. I can hold it. I'm scared, that's all, I tried to convince myself.

There were valid reasons for my fear. The nightly air-raid warnings had stopped. Now Russian planes attacked without warning. They also flew low and fired machine guns at people moving in the streets. But, worst of all, one of the Soviet tanks surrounding Berlin had broken through the German lines, and three or four Russian soldiers were holed up in the tower of the half-bombed Hochmeister Church half a block from us, shooting at any human target.

Once on the street, I looked over my shoulder at the church behind me. All seemed to be quiet, and seeing no one else about, I crept along, hugging the walls of apartment buildings, keeping my eyes to the ground. Then I reached the intersection of Johann Georg Strasse and Kurfürstendamm.

What?

I barely missed running into a pair of dirty military boots dangling at eye level. My eyes traveled upward, and I quickly looked away. But then my eyes were drawn as if by a magnet to the figure swinging from the lamppost. A *Schutzwehr* soldier of our home defense, probably no more than fourteen years old, hung from the old-fashioned streetlight. His face was red and blotched, his features bloated into a grotesque mask. I backed up slowly. His blackened tongue protruded from cracked lips, and his dead eyes stared at nothingness, glazed and bulging. I felt vomit welling up. I swallowed hard, sucking in my lips, trying not to look, and yet, I couldn't stop staring at this figure that made me weep and sick to my stomach, all at the same time.

A huge wave of sadness mixed with anger swept over me. I read the crude cardboard sign pinned to the boy's narrow chest. It looked as if it had been scribbled on the spot: *Ich bin zu feige Berlin zu verteidigen, deshalb hänge ich hier*—I am too cowardly to defend Berlin, that's why I'm hanging here.

Something smelled like excrement. I held my nose. There were dark, wet stains between his legs. Was this what death smelled like? How could this be? He was still a boy, a few years older than I, but just a boy, hanging from the lamppost. *Unter der Laterne* were part of the opening lyrics of the war-time song "Lilli Marlen," but like everything else in our surreal world, this lilting song had been turned upside down. "Underneath the Lamppost" was no longer a lover's promise to meet again after the war, but the future lament of a mother for her dead son.

I trudged on, down the Kurfürstendamm, then across the Hallensee

Brücke, a wide railroad bridge. Soon the elegant Ku'damm with its shops changed into the Koenigsallee, an urban street lined with elms. This was the beginning of Grunewald—the untamed forest. I passed stately apartment buildings, riddled with shrapnel, their windows broken and patched with cardboard or wood. In front of some half-bombed villas early lilacs bloomed purple amid the yellow and orange of isolated tulips, mingling their spring-time perfumes with the acrid odor of war, fires, and explosives.

I felt sick to my stomach again. The boy soldier's image stirred behind my eyelids. I tried to make it go away by running faster, but the specter of his body swinging in the wind kept pace, moving just as fast as my legs would carry me.

I reached the butcher.

The shop, with its white tiles smeared with red animal blood, felt stifling. The blood sausage lying behind glass counters gave off a peculiar metallic odor mixed with salt, garlic, and other spices. Frau Baumann, from our apartment building, was standing in line with some other women who lived on our street. They nodded hello. I probably sounded as if I had a cold, talking through a willfully blocked up nose so I would not have to inhale the smell of blood and meat while trying to forget the dead soldier.

The drone of low flying Russian planes and the explosions of intermittent bombs could be heard. Some of the women made fun of the clumsy Soviet planes. I did not think those planes were anything to laugh at. The Russian planes did not saturation bomb like the American or the British planes, but they still caused enough damage.

I watched as the last of my neighbors paid. I was terrified by the idea of having to go home by myself with bombs exploding nearby and hopped from foot to foot, as if that would make the butcher sell his sausages faster.

Frau Baumann received her wrapped package, and having observed my tapping feet and drumming fingers, she asked, "Are you nervous, Karin? Scared?"

"Me? Scared? No way!" I lied.

"Good. You're a *deutsches Mädel!* German girls are not afraid."

I asked, "Please, would you wait for me? I'll be right along, and we can all walk together."

"We'll walk slowly. You can catch up with us."

They left. Through the glass door I saw them walking away at a normal pace. How could I possibly catch up to them? When it was my turn, I stuffed the sausages, meat, and soup bones into my net bag and ran after them. I ran as fast as I could. Ran until I ran out of breath. Damn, my side stitches again. I had to stop. I doubled over and held my breath. Then I ran again, hunched over now, the pain making it impossible for me to straighten up. I was gaining on the women and hollered, "Wait!"

I heard my cry fade. My mouth was wide open, but there was no sound. My legs were moving, but it felt as if I were running in place. The distance between the women and myself was not lessening.

Above me the drone of a plane had grown louder and louder and LOUDER. Now directly overhead, the plane was one enormous hum. Then a huge *BANG* exploded the air. A great yellow-orange light leapt up. My mouth, still open, opened ever wider into a scream, keeping the noise from tearing my eardrums. The blast threw me to the ground. After what seemed a long time I dared to open my eyes. The bomb had struck the bridge. Iron girders, like the blackened ribs of a carcass, struck the smoking sky, and concrete lay heaped in a pile of rubble. Clothing was strewn about, along bits of human debris and parts of bodies. An arm with a hand still clutching a patent leather purse had been hurled near to where I crouched.

My neighbors. A moment ago they had been alive, walking, and chattering. Now they were torn pieces of flesh.

I held my mouth. But this time I couldn't stop it. I vomited, again and again. It ran through my fingers. My stomach kept convulsing long after it was empty. Then I rose and wiped my hands on the yellow-green of a forsythia bush. My hands smelled putrid and my mouth tasted foul.

I ran. The bridge was impassable. I knew there was another, smaller footbridge not far off to the right. I found it, but it had no railings. I looked down from the height of a two-story building to the network of train tracks below. I have always been afraid of heights. But I had to cross this four-footwide bridge with nothing to hold on to. I slung the string bag over my shoulder, gripping the loop handles with my teeth, and lowered myself onto hands and knees. Slowly, I crawled across.

I made it to the other side. Then I took in a full breath. Exhaled. Relief. The Hochmeister Church, where the Russians hid in the steeple, lay a block ahead of me. I crept along the buildings. Suddenly there were shots, machine gun fire—*da-da-da-da-dack*. Bullets hit the pavement—*ping-ping-ping.* Bits of cement from the sidewalk left small whirls of gray dust, and bullets carved neat round holes into the stone facade of an apartment building to my left. I crouched, taking shelter in the arch of an entrance door. I tried to hide, ducking my head between my knees—like an ostrich—but my front was fully exposed. The bullets kept flying, ricocheting as they hit the street, and like pebbles thrown onto a lake, they skipped across the pavement.

Then suddenly, there was silence. The shooting stopped. I took another deep breath. Had they realized they were shooting at a child?

Our apartment building was half a block away. I ran home, running faster than I had ever run before. Halfway through the door I threw the shopping bag full of meat onto the kitchen table. It hit the table with a hard, dead thud. On my bed I buried my head in a pillow. For a long time I did not speak to anyone about what I had witnessed.

I tried to make sense out of what I had seen, but I could not. My head sizzled and buzzed as if my brain had been overloaded with electricity.

Was everything Hitler had told us a lie?

It came quite suddenly, this feeling of clarity, as if someone had ripped a dark veil that had been clouding my vision from my head.

Yes, the Führer had lied. He had lied all along. There would be no *Wunderwaffe:* the "miracle weapon" that was supposed to save us at the last minute didn't exist. That too had been a lie. Berlin *would* fall to the Russians. The Führer could not protect us. He was hiding somewhere in his bunker, and he and all of us were doomed.

That afternoon, I lost my hope. While living within a world of fantasy, I could handle the bombs, the lack of food, and the uncertainty of tomorrow. But it was as if I had awakened from a long sleep. I realized that I had been blind and deaf to what I had seen or heard from my family and from others around me. I had refused to see the truth. Like a draft horse trudging his course pulling a wagon, I had worn blinders. How did that happen? I shook my head. Hitler had been able to put blinders on so many of us, but these past few hours had torn mine off.

Illusions and hope lay at my feet like the shriveled pieces of rubber from a burst balloon. Nothing made sense. I had seen women alive and chattering, then torn to bits, all within seconds. But even worse, I had seen a murdered boy close to my own age. "Underneath the Lantern," this sweet plaintive song had for me turned into a *Klagelied,* a song of woe, to the tune of which a child soldier swung in a dance of death in the April wind.

And Horses When They Cry
April 27–April 30, 1945

Thick smoke and clouds of dust, black and sulfurous, crowded out the last patches of blue in the darkening sky.

I tried to appear calm. But below my skin, deep below my muscles and my bones, I shivered, my thoughts running amok with fear of what the Russians might do. Would they kill us? Would they rape the women, my beautiful mother? I remembered some of the horror stories I'd heard from eastern refugees.

We rarely stepped out onto the street during these days. And if we did, we covered our mouths with handkerchiefs to keep out the sickening stench of corpses decomposing beneath collapsed buildings and the stink of uncollected garbage turning squishy and smelling rotten-sweet. Even breathing through cloth was noxious.

Berlin lay under siege. The constant clamor of battle was deafening. The heavy doors to our cellar merely muffled the din of the Russian artillery, which kept up a barrage of fire day and night. Russian planes strafed and bombed intermittently. We didn't know how far the enemy was from our side of town. The lone tank that had broken through the lines last week made us think that the Russians were close. The same soldiers who'd shot at me when I returned from the butcher were still holed up in the church tower. They had not yet exhausted their ammunition, for we could hear the intermittent *da-da-da-da-dack* of their machine guns. The dull thunder of the artillery moved closer and closer. Our building shook as if there were ongoing earthquake tremors.

Then came a new sound: a horrendous grinding and swishing roar, followed by a screeching that threatened to split our eardrums. This was the high-pitched "song" of the *Stalinorgel,* which the Russians called *Katyusha,* or Little Kate, a strangely affectionate name for this infernal weapon. The *Stalinorgel* was a multibarreled rocket launcher that could shoot rockets simultaneously out of many pipes—hence the ending of the name, *Orgel,* meaning "organ." Its projectiles angled low over the rooftops, hitting the buildings broadside. The combination of bombs, artillery, *Stalinorgel,* and machine gun fire made Oma declare that "this is the *Götterdämmerung*"—the end of the world.

And it was the end of our known world.

Many of our neighbors had moved into the cellar weeks ago. It offered relative safety, since it was fortified with added wooden beams and sandbags that would protect from stray shrapnel. This cellar, like the earlier ones we had sheltered in, also had openings to adjoining buildings. If our building was hit by a *Sprengbombe,* or by a *Stalinorgel,* we could escape from under the rubble through a neighboring cellar.

I don't remember when we moved into the shelter. Mother had held out as long as possible, saying she did not want to live like a rat in a hole beneath the earth. But Grandmother's logic had won out.

We each occupied a narrow cot under which we placed our suitcases.

Every so often we went upstairs to get some food, to use the bathroom, and to have a *Katzenwäsche,* a little cat's wash. We probably stank, but everyone else stank as well, so it mattered little. During those times when the bombing was intense, and we could not go upstairs to the bathroom, we used a bucket concealed behind a screen.

The atmosphere in the cellar depressed me. It felt as if something heavy were sitting on my chest, and as time passed it became more and more difficult for me to breathe. Although the streets were dangerous, I snuck out one day, hoping to find a sign of spring, a glimpse of blue sky, or a flicker of hope in all the gray.

As I stepped out onto the street, a crowd of women armed with large butcher knives ran past me. My God, whom are they going to kill? I thought. One of them looked over her shoulder at a young boy, maybe her son, and shouted, "Go get a knife, there's meat down the street." What did she mean? I dashed up the three flights of stairs to our apartment, found a butcher knife in the kitchen drawer, grabbed the ever-present string bag, and ran, following the women.

Around the corner on Nestor Strasse, but still obliquely in view of the church tower from which the Russians shot, atop rubble and covering part of the sidewalk, lay something big, something dead. A horde of women crawled over this dead thing, some of them climbing astride, wielding blades and cutting. I slowed my run. Crept closer. Tried to see more clearly. Afraid to see more clearly.

It was a horse. Its head was laying twisted to one side, and there was a small pool of moisture below it on the pavement. I also noticed wet spots on the side of its nose, darkening the brown fur. The eyes looked as if they were alive, staring at me. They were large and framed by black bristle lashes, and the pupil amid the brown iris was black. The eyes looked wet and seemed to be filled with a bottomless sadness. Were those tears? Had the horse been crying? Did horses ever cry?

The women were cutting into the brown fur, ripping open the skin, cutting into flesh, and exposing red meat, sinew, and bones. The animal was bleeding, though someone said the horse had been dead for a while. How long was a while? Could one still eat the meat? I had brought home the last rations from the butcher a few days ago. But it wasn't much, and soon it would be gone.

Could I cut into a horse? I, who loved horses. I was quite close now and saw one of the women tear off a large chunk and triumphantly carry off the bleeding trophy, carrying it high, like a flag. The women wore drab clothes that were now soaked with blood. They looked like crows ripping into roadkill.

The knife bobbed on my arm, and its blade reflected an errant beam of sun through the holes in the net bag, as if it were reminding me why I was here. Go get your share of the meat, it said. I slung the bag over my shoulder, getting the knife with its message out of my sight, fighting my rebellious stomach.

I was still swallowing hard when I saw something else. One woman had hacked into the flesh with a cleaver. Suddenly she stopped, looking at what she held in her hand: the bloodied shreds of a uniform, covering part of the white of a soldier's lower leg, which was still wearing a boot. She screamed when she saw what was in her hand, dropped the leg, and ran. The women—their gray faces spattered with red—stopped their frenzy. They had all seen it by then. Below the mutilated carcass of the horse lay the dead body of a German soldier.

I turned and ran home.

CHAPTER 10

The Russians

MAY 1–MAY 2, 1945

Silence. An eerie quiet had descended upon the streets. No bombs exploded, the thunder of artillery had stopped, and no machine guns were heard.

"Hitler is dead, Hitler is dead." The rumor raced through Berlin. What? Where? *Hitler has committed suicide.* Was this another crazy rumor? Would there be peace now? Who would now be our *Reichskanzler*?

Eleven days had passed since the Führer's birthday.

Amid the new quiet, along with rumors and uncertainty, our cellar door blew wide open, and in strode the first Russians.

My pulse beat so fast I thought I'd faint. I felt very cold. Mother looked deadly white. I stared at these Russians. I kept very still, holding my breath, hanging on to the arm of my mother. The Russians had taken Berlin.

They were tall, these first Russians, and wearing neat uniforms, with their guns slung across their shoulders. They were officers. One of them spoke in fractured German with rolling *r*'s.

"No fear, everything *gut*, we no hurt. Attention. We order. You no let German soldier in, no people no live in house. *Alles gut* then. You take in soldier, we shoot all in this house. *Alle.* Understand?" As if to underline what he meant, he made the gesture with his rifle in his arm pointing to a wall and mouthing, "*Da-da-da-da-dack . . .*"

He asked who the house warden was, and when the old man appeared, he put him in charge to carry out his command. What irony. The house warden was *still* in command, even though, until a week ago, he'd worn his Nazi Party membership pin on his lapel. Oma raised her eyebrows in disbelief.

And then there was Myron, a young Ukrainian, who had come to study architecture in Berlin with the permission from the Soviet Union before Germany declared war on Russia. He lived in our apartment building and felt at home in Germany. Above all he did not want to be repatriated to Russia. Revealing his origins by speaking Russian with the soldiers would put him in jeopardy. But he was a kind young man and when a group of up to twenty or so Russian soldiers tried to invade our cellar, he sent them to a warehouse, far down the street, where they could find an ample supply of alcohol.

A short while after they had gone, three more officers entered and pushed past Myron. They gesticulated, pointing their rifles, and charging through the cellar.

"*Deutsche Soldaten, habt ihr Soldaten hier?*" The voice of the elder officer was harsh as he demanded to know if we had any soldiers in our cellar.

"No, there are no soldiers here, I give you my word," Myron answered them in German and then in Russian. The handsome one—yes, one of them looked as if he had stepped out of an Ufa film—gestured for the others to be done with the search. His lake blue eyes had fastened onto a woman in her early twenties, and he gestured for her to follow him out of the cellar. He removed his cap for a moment, tossed his deep black hair out of his face, only to capture it again under the cap.

The girl hesitated. He promised they would treat her with respect. He explained they were hungry and asked her to cook them a meal upstairs in a regular kitchen.

They chose our apartment for this. Later, Mother questioned the girl, asking her what had happened to the rubber tree that was in our apartment. Why was it looking so sick? Mutti had rescued this plant from a bombed building and nursed it back to health, and it had again displayed glossy fat leaves. That's when the girl told her story.

The officers themselves prepared the meal; some sort of goulash, she told us. This was the first meat she'd eaten in months. She, like all of us, was undernourished and devoured her food. At the same time the men plied her with vodka. Whenever they were busy getting more food or opening another bottle, she poured her full glass into Mother's plant. Drunk, the handsome one began fondling her. Then he got rough and tore at her clothes. This was no game. She realized that the others were looking on, waiting their turn. She screamed and fought with him, as he wrestled her to the floor. At that moment his superior marched through the door. The major pistol-whipped the offending lieutenant out of the apartment, down the stairs, and ordered the others to follow. He later came back to the shaken girl and apologized, said he had given orders that no one was to rape any of the women. The girl was safe for now, but the plant died.

At that time a woman from our building told us, "Hey, the Ivan isn't that bad. They're cooking something delicious down the street. Go, you'll need some bowls though."

The Ivan, as the Russians were called by many Berliners, had set up a large kettle in a provisory field kitchen at the corner of our street and the Ku'damm. Soldiers ladled out the stew to children and to old people. Oma and I were curious and hungry, and armed with bowls and spoons, we went to investigate. There was indeed a yellowish mass bubbling in a black iron kettle, smelling like sugary confections from long forgotten times. A soldier smiled at us with black-stained, crooked teeth and doled out generous portions.

I never learned what was in the pot. Someone said it was a Russian Easter food. I knew the Russian Easter came after ours, but a whole month later?

Whatever the soldiers were doling out at the Kurfürstendamm corner tasted of butter, cream, sugar, egg yolks, and vanilla, like a promise of new beginnings, a promise of peace and plenty. I had to restrain myself to leave something in my bowl for Mother.

Later that day, some tenants from our building returned to the cellar with net bags filled with bottles of oil, hard Polish sausages, wines, and assorted canned foods. They came from the corner house, which up to a few days ago had been an undercover SS house. The Russians occupied it now and opened it to plunder.

Oma and I went. Oma was still concerned about the Russians raping anyone from age ten on up. I was a five-foot-four twelve-year-old. To make me look younger she braided my hair, which usually fell loose below my shoulders, and tied pink bows onto each of my pigtails. I detested these babyish bows.

We entered the cellar, passing a Russian soldier standing guard at the entrance. The cellar gave me goose bumps. It smelled musty and of unknown disinfectants. Near where we had entered, bottles were stacked in racks in one of the open side stalls. Lots of bottles. Oma shivered. Was she cold or did she also feel that something menacing was going on? We heard sounds coming from the end of the corridor. Muffled cries.

We filled our net bags in no time at all. We dashed toward the door leading to the street. The same soldier who had allowed us to enter barred our exit by placing his rifle from wall to wall. He motioned for us to move down the hallway in the direction of the barely audible moans.

I squeezed Oma's arm so hard that it must have hurt—later her arm turned black and blue. My heart pounded so crazily that I could feel it in my throat. Just at that moment a man appeared in the entrance. The Russian was focused so intently on us, he didn't hear him approach. The man startled the soldier, who then shifted the position of his rifle enough to allow Oma and me to push past him with a speed I could not have believed possible from my grandmother.

Shots rang out. We ran as fast as we could, and by the time we reached the center of the street, shots whizzed by very close, too close. I felt something on my leg.

"I've been shot, I've been shot," I cried, feeling something wet running down my calf. I saw my white kneesock turn brownish red, "Oma, I'm bleeding. I've been shot."

"Keep running."

We reached our building, and I collapsed against the inside of the heavy cellar door, safe—for the moment.

Oma trembled, and I cried. Mother rushed to our sides, wrapping her arms around us both. Then she saw my leg.

"Karin, stay off the leg. Come, lie down."

I fell onto the cot, and Mother looked at the leg. She saw no entry wound, not even a scratch. I had *not* been shot: a bullet had broken one of the bottles, and the contents had stained my sock. It was Worcestershire sauce. I laughed. I couldn't stop laughing. Our mission had netted us twelve bottles of Worcestershire sauce, a condiment to accompany steaks, which we hadn't eaten in years. This was what we had risked our lives for.

"Stop that hysterical laughing. Pull yourself together," Mother said.

"I can't." My laughing spasm turned into a cough. "I was so scared." I crossed my arms, hugging my chest. "It's freezing, I need a sweater. Mutti, what will the Russians do now?"

I had stopped laughing. By then tears streamed down my face. Oma put her arms around me, rocking me. "*Shh,* child," she said, "*Shh,* we're safe now. *Shh,* things will be all right."

Our neighbors who had returned with bottles of oil and tins of meat from the SS building's cellar had been the lucky ones. The women who had entered the cellar later, like my grandmother and I, were herded into the former interrogation and torture chambers and serially raped.

The Face of Our Conqueror

A few days later the second wave of conquerors arrived in Berlin. These troops—Mongolian regiments—no longer wore neat uniforms: they appeared in tattered, mud-caked brown tunics and baggy pants, tucked into short boots. They rode down Kurfürstendamm on what we called *Panje-wagen*—primitive horse-drawn wagons—hauling small artillery and supplies. Their horses were small, short legged, shaggy, and of an unknown, perhaps Mongolian, breed.

After seeing these new troops ride down the Ku'damm, our fears multiplied. They talked about it in the cellar, and people could not believe what they'd seen. *This* ratty horde had given the death blow to Berlin?

We had to face the truth. We were the conquered. And yes, these men in their horse-drawn wagons were our conquerors. We were the spoils.

After Mother saw the Mongolians, she dragged me from the cellar. "You are coming upstairs with me," she declared, hauling me to our apartment. She had decided to hide me in the *Hängeboden,* a sort of hanging closet in the foyer. The *Hängeboden* was a large shelf about four feet wide, six feet long, and perhaps four feet high. It had a hanging lid and was usually placed above a doorway. When closed, it was almost undetectable to those who did not know of its existence. Mother climbed a short ladder, opened the lid, and threw out the odd cartons and suitcases that had been stored there. Then she stuffed it with blankets, a pillow, and a chamber pot. "In case nature calls," she said.

I did not like hiding in here. No, not at all. What if a Russian or one of those Mongolians discovered this hideaway? Mother and Oma would be in the cellar. What would I do? When Mother closed the door, I was left in total darkness. I felt as if I were entombed. I remembered seeing the opera *Aida* with my grandmother. I had nightmares for weeks after seeing Aida sealed up alive behind a wall. I switched on the flashlight Mother had left me with, scribbled something into my diary, and tried to calm myself. But rather than getting used to the situation, I got more and more panicky.

I think Oma felt my telepathic message: "Please get me out." I heard her footsteps and the ladder being dragged over the wooden floor. Then I saw my grandmother's pink face appear in the opening.

"Oma, I can't stand it here. Get me out. Please. I'll die in here . . ."

"*Kindchen,* the Russians will do unspeakable things to you. It's not safe for you in the cellar. I'll come up often. Here, I brought you something to eat." She handed me a piece of dark bread with a thin coating of lard sprinkled with coarse salt and a thermos of chamomile tea.

"Just let me out. I'll think of something. I'll disguise myself."

"Disguise yourself? As what? A boy?"

"No," I snickered, knowing by then that she'd let me out. "You'll see."

I sorted through old clothes in a trunk and a little while later showed myself to Oma. She stepped back a pace, shaking her head. Gone were the braids, the ribbons, and the childish look. I'd put on an old, baggy pair of Mother's ski pants, a pair of ski boots so old the leather had cracked into fissures, and a bulky sweater full of holes. Then I stuffed a narrow pillow between my shoulder blades—my undershirt held it in place—creating the effect of a hunched back. Over these clothes I slipped on a tattered jacket that had been left by a former tenant. And to hide my hair, I tied Mother's orange and gray plaid scarf around my head, securing the knot on my forehead so that some of the fringes hung in my eyes. As a final touch, I rubbed my fingers in a pail of coal dust, added some flour, and streaked this over my face. When I looked into the mirror, I grinned. A stranger looked out at me, a seemingly daft one at that.

Oma escorted this new Karin into the cellar. I could see I had done a good job by the look on the tenants' faces and by Mother's opened mouth.

It wasn't long before another group of soldiers arrived. They demanded watches. "*Uri, Uri,*" they cried, pointing to their arms already fully decorated with wristwatches.

Oma, ever honest and accommodating, took off her watch and handed it to the first soldier in line. He grinned, showing a gap between big front teeth, his slanted eyes crinkling to invisible slits, while he strapped the delicate gold watch onto his left wrist. Above this, his brown, hairless arm displayed seven or eight watches, as did his right arm. Mother whispered, "Oma is too agreeable. I'm not giving him mine, and don't you give him yours, Karin." My silver watch, my prize possession connecting me to Aunt Margaret, was hidden away in a suitcase below the cot. The soldiers left.

A single soldier entered the cellar. This particular one looked for women. "Frau komm," he said to a woman near me. I got up and ambled toward him. Mother tried to grab my sleeve, but she was too late. I walked pigeon-toed, crossed my eyes, and let my tongue loll out and spit dribble down my chin. I let my head droop low, cocking it toward one shoulder, while my arms drooped askew from my shoulders. When I approached the soldier, muttering unintelligible sounds, a strange thing happened. The soldier's eyes opened wide, and he stepped back. He turned on his heel and fled our cellar.

My disguise had worked! Mother and Oma embraced me. The woman thanked me. But I worried, would I be able to keep up this charade?

A little later, several Russians stormed into the cellar. These were the same soldiers who had demanded the watches. They gesticulated and shouted, wanting to know who lived in apartment 2b. A trembling old woman got up and said that she did. They dragged her upstairs to her apartment, demanding she return their potatoes. The poor woman stared at them dumbfounded. Their potatoes? Then they yanked her up the stairs to the floor right above hers and showed her the lavatory, where they had washed their potatoes in the toilet bowl when suddenly the potatoes had disappeared. She had performed a trick; she was an old Baba Yaga, a witch. They wanted their potatoes or they would shoot her. The woman trembled, blabbering through tears.

Oma was in our apartment at the time, fetching a change of clothes. She overheard part of the argument taking place next door, and it became obvious to her that the Russians didn't understand a word the old woman was saying in her defense. Oma went over and tried to help, knowing that mere words could not explain things to the Russians who'd apparently never encountered a flushing toilet before. She went over to the bowl, threw in a piece of cardboard the length of a small potato, and pulled the chain. Voila! The cardboard flushed down the large drain. That's what it is, she tried to clarify. It's a toilet. They still didn't understand. However, one of the men ran downstairs and found that the cardboard did not reappear in apartment 2b.

The soldiers warmed to my grandmother and asked her to cook for them. These Russians seemed to see the world in two colors: white and black. Grandmother was "white" because she was an honest woman who understood them. They called her their little old Baba, their little old Mother. They asked her to boil potatoes and to fry up bacon and eggs. They still painted the other old woman as "black" and kicked her down the stairs. Oma cooked for the soldiers. They liked the taste of her food, and later they came down to the cellar to bring her potatoes and bacon as a gift.

There were other soldiers, one of them chasing after my mother, trying to grab her sleeve, saying, "Frau komm." She lay down behind the back of the old house warden on his narrow cot, pointing to him, "This is my father."

"*Vater nix gut.* Vater go," the Russian said.

I don't know how Mother managed to grab the bottle of reddish cough syrup; perhaps it was lying under the cot. Shielded from full view by the house warden, she took a swig, coughed, a racking, nonending cough, and spit red stuff onto a white handkerchief. The soldier recoiled, turned, and ran.

Another young woman in the cellar was not so lucky. She kept telling the soldiers that she had syphilis. Several left her alone, but one soldier dragged her up to a bakery at street level and raped her savagely. Weeks later she discovered that the soldier had infected her with syphilis.

One of the oldest inhabitants of the apartment house, a woman of about eighty, came screaming down the cellar stairs.

"Seven Russians raped me. Seven Russians raped me," she wailed over and over. At first it struck me as unreal, almost funny. I soon sobered to the fact that something terrible had happened to the poor woman. Her hair was a scramble, like a grayish brown bird's nest that had fallen out of a tree. Her hollow eyes darted in every direction, looking for enemies or a place to hide. She wore no skirt, only a light pink rayon slip and a torn, dark silk blouse patterned with dainty rosebuds.

Someone gave her a swig of brandy, but this made her cough and spit. Still, it revived her, for some color returned to her face.

I was curious about what went on above the cellar and slipped out against Mother's orders. On the street I ran into my friend Erich, for whom, only two months ago, I had stood guard in the attic while he listened to the BBC.

"Hey, Karin, is that you?"

"Yes, it's me." I felt my face get hot. I shrugged off my embarrassment as to my disguise, hoping he wouldn't see that I was blushing underneath the soot. "What are you doing out on the street?" I said.

"It's pretty bad over there." He indicated his building with a nod, "They dragged off my father. The Russians . . . , Mother . . ." He shook his head. "I couldn't protect her. There were too many of them. Beasts. I can't stand to be around . . . , all those Russians." He balled his fists. "I want to kill them, but there's shit I can do." He sobbed.

"I'm sorry," I said, stroking his arm.

He jerked it away, saying, "Karin, you shouldn't be here. What if they catch you?"

"Look at me, Erich," I took a few demented-looking dance steps, "I'm the village idiot. They're afraid of me."

"I wouldn't count on it. Not now. Maybe in a few days things will be safer. Rumor has it that Marshal Zhukov promised his troops a week of plunder and rape if they gave him Berlin. *Vogelfrei.* You know? Free as a bird. Only birds don't behave like these swine. The week is almost over." He looked over his shoulder at some Russians strolling down the street with their arms linked, singing sad songs with hoarse voices, and intermittently taking swigs from vodka bottles. Erich went on, "Know what? Admiral Dönitz surrendered the German forces to the Allies. They'll sign a peace treaty. Then this . . . ," he choked on the word *rape,* "will stop."

"So you still listen to your radio?"

"Yeah, I still have the radio. But Hannibal, you know my favorite rabbit?"

"The little white fuzzy one?"

"Right. Mutti didn't butcher it. She knew I loved him too much. I hid the radio in the hutch, remember? The Russians didn't find the radio, but they ate Hannibal."

He turned to go home. I worried about him, even though he was short for a fourteen-year-old, the Russians might still suspect him as a former *Schutzwehr* soldier.

"What are you going to do now? Go back into the cellar?"

"Yeah. I've cooled off a bit *Is' ja alles Scheisse*. It's all shit," he said.

He was right.

My disguise made me feel invisible. I crept along the shadows of the archway leading from the street to the *Hinterhof,* or courtyard. A beech tree grew in the center of this paved square, and several Russians were circling the tree on bicycles. I squinted to see if one of the bikes was mine. No, thank God. It looked as if they were new to this mode of transportation. One of them mastered riding quickly, but I shall never forget the sight of another, wearing a flamingo pink, quilted satin house robe. The robe caught in the spokes of the rear wheel, and he tumbled down. But he jumped back on the bicycle. Up and down, up and down, he kept falling off over and over again, like those little toy men you knocked down in an amusement park only to have them bounce straight up again. Meanwhile, the dressing gown became dirtier and dirtier, and its hemline soon hung in shreds.

They acted like children, and it looked like fun. I was tempted to drop my disguise and ask for a chance to ride the bicycles with them. But even though I looked like an idiot, my brain was still functioning. I returned to the cellar to a scolding from both Mother and Oma.

Frau Schlosser, the widow of a well-known concert pianist, came running into the cellar, weeping and screaming something about pigs, swine, and apes. She had found her apartment in shambles. The strings of the Bechstein grand piano had been smeared with excrement. Apes? Every piece of her fine upholstered furniture had been soiled. Even her crystal chandelier was covered with it. How were they able to get up to the twelve-foot ceiling to defecate on the chandelier? I envisioned chimpanzees clad in Russian uniforms swinging from the drapery rods on the windows to the chandelier to do their business. The thought made me want to giggle. I often got these ridiculous images that spurred me on to laugh during the most serious of occasions. It even happened once during a funeral. I knew this was not the time to laugh, and I tried to stifle the urge by biting the inside of my lip.

But when I looked into the eyes of Frau Schlosser, I was overcome with compassion for this old woman. I impulsively said, "I'll help you clean up the mess." She smiled, but Oma said no. It was not safe for anyone to go to an apartment for more than a few minutes because the Russian vandals might come back at any time and do worse.

Why had they chosen that apartment and left the others alone? Myron believed the Schlossers' possessions indicated wealth, and the Russians associated elegant furnishings with the ruling Nazi class, hence their rampage of hatred, their befouling the enemy.

On the day of the German surrender, three men in tattered clothing asked us for shelter. They still wore remnants of their former uniforms, and the house warden would not let them enter. He told them that if the Russians found them, we would all be shot. They hovered on the cellar steps, while several of the women gathered pieces of their absent husbands' civilian clothing to give to these men. Frau Schlosser handed a suit to one of them, saying, "Go. Change clothes in the empty bakery and then burn the uniforms." We didn't have any men's clothing to give them, but Oma handed them a paper sack with bacon fried potatoes.

Then they were sent off.

This scene played out over and over again throughout the city, pitting German against German in an ethical dilemma. It would have been humane to give shelter to these fellow Germans, but then our lives would have been at risk. We had helped the men with a few pieces of clothing, but no one took up the real issue, to save their lives by hiding them. I remembered the boy soldier swinging from the lamppost less than a week ago, killed by fanatical Nazis. If these men were caught by a straggler of the SS, they would certainly be shot or hung. And if caught by the Russians, they would be sent to Siberia.

I thought about the men—my fellow Germans, two old men and one still a boy—for a long, long time. Hitler had drafted them to defend the doomed city in its last hours, and by turning them away, we were, perhaps, condemning them to death. That was one of the cruel lessons of war: it was them or us.

My cot felt hard that night. I tossed on the lumpy mattress, trying to find comfort, wondering if those men had found a safe place. I wept for a long time until I fell asleep.

The weeklong battle for Berlin took a huge toll in human lives: the German and the Russian armies each lost an estimated one hundred thousand men. One hundred and thirty six thousand German soldiers were taken prisoner; most of them were old men and boys who had been drafted during the last weeks of combat. These German POWs were transported to Siberia, and the few who did survive would not return for at least three years. It was estimated that more than one hundred thousand German civilians, mainly women, died in those last days of fighting in Berlin. About one hundred thousand women and young girls were raped; some of them were forcibly taken from their homes and dragged off to places where soldiers queued up to rape them. An estimated ten thousand Berlin women committed suicide because they had been raped.

PART II

Sometimes even to live is an act of courage.

Lucius Annaeus Seneca, writer and philosopher (3 BCE–65 CE)

Children playing in the rubble
created by the Allied bombing
of Berlin, 1945. (The Granger
Collection, New York.)

Adolf Hitler (1889-1945). Hitler's eyes
were of a cutting, piercing blue, eyes
that I shall never forget. (The Granger
Collection, New York.)

Adolf Hitler, riding in a convertible. (The Granger Collection, New York.)

Trial of Field Marshal Erwin von Witzleben (center, standing). Witzleben was the father of Mother's childhood friend. He was tried and executed for treason in 1944. (The Granger Collection, New York.)

Ruins of the Kaiser Wilhelm
Gedaechtniskirche, January
1945. (The Granger Collection,
New York.)

Soviet Red Army at Brandenburg Gate, May
2, 1945. (The Granger Collection, New York.)

Red Army soldiers patrol the streets of Berlin,
May 1945. (The Granger Collection, New York.)

Berlin in ruins, 1945. Berlin received by far more
shelling and bombs than any other German city.
(The Granger Collection, New York.)

Photos taken by the author of the ruins of Berlin in 1946
on a return visit to her old neighborhood in Halensee.

CHAPTER 11

Frau Komm!

EARLY MAY 1945

A rifle butt slammed against the cellar door and a Russian soldier burst in. Cold air blasted at us from the draft. The women in the cellar pulled their heads a little lower between their shoulders, as if trying to disappear. I clenched my teeth to keep them from chattering with cold and tugged my headscarf down onto my face.

Myron sat by the cellar door, his self-selected post. He seemed to be dozing but sprang into action when at least five other Russians followed the first. Myron and the soldiers gesticulated; their rapid fire of Russian sounded harsh and angry. Myron's arm swept across the cellar. He shook his head, and we understood: these were not soldiers he could send off to the storage building down the street to pilfer alcohol. These were soldiers on a mission, determined to find what they were looking for.

The soldiers went about their search in silence. The skin on their faces stretched taut, their lips formed tight lines, and their foreheads furrowed as they plunged bayonets into bedding. I caught my breath when they speared my down pillow and the feathers flew out. The Russian soldiers laughed, but I felt like exploding. I wanted to strangle them as they turned our cots over with their rifles. Russian boots kicked at wooden crates; one kick split open someone else's wooden chest. One soldier spiked my suitcase onto his bayonet. He dropped it and then kicked it till it opened, spilling my clothes and, what embarrassed me most, my underwear out onto the floor.

Mother and I stood stock-still, as if we were concrete statues. Mother, clutching her cough syrup bottle, again clung to the old house warden. I stood behind Oma with my head hanging to my chest, not daring to approach any of the soldiers with my "idiot's" walk.

My heart drummed a crazy rhythm as the Russian who seemed to be in charge walked up to the house warden. I was afraid he'd select my mother for a "Frau komm." He put his face close to the old man's and demanded, "*Wo Soldaten?*" The warden answered in a barely audible voice, "Officer Ruski, there are no German soldiers here. Please, believe me." Then he confessed, his palsied shaking distorting his voice, "two old men and a young soldier, still a boy, all from the home front asked for sanctuary last night. But we sent them away."

Mother, relieved the Russian had paid no attention to her, transformed from a concrete statue into a woman of flesh and blood. The Russian officer grunted, walked from corner to corner, looking here, looking there, and then turned on his heels to leave. His men followed him out of the cellar.

The people exhaled one communal sigh of relief, and it was as if that single sigh of a dozen or more breaths swooshed out the open door behind the soldiers.

Myron walked back to the cellar entrance and stood listening. He probably heard the same faint boot steps audible to me, then he ventured farther, up the cellar stairs and into the foyer. As he stood there, he reported later, he'd heard the Russians ransacking one apartment after another. With the cellar door open, we could hear boot steps running up the stairs and stomping across the parquet floors and crashing sounds.

The Russians left the building. The half-charred uniforms they had found earlier in the bakery next door had made them think that the men were still hiding nearby. Again, I felt sorry for those men and hoped they would be far away by now, safe, wearing Herr Schlosser's civilian clothes. Myron later told us that someone had seen the German soldiers at our cellar door last night and reported this to the Russians. Neighbors still informed on neighbors, even now, after the collapse of the Third Reich.

Frau Schlosser was no longer the only one with a vandalized apartment. The Russian soldiers, angry at not finding German soldiers hiding in the building, had wrecked other apartments in the building, ours included. Luckily, even though they had torn up our rooms, the Russians had not smeared excrement anywhere. Upholstered chairs had been sliced open with bayonets, vases lay broken, and beds were upended. In another apartment, they had overturned an aquarium, soaking the carpet and leaving the fish to die, gasping for air.

We continued living in the cellar, feeling a certain safety in the proximity of so many people. Oma and Mother would not let me help them clean our rooms; it would be too dangerous for a girl to be caught by a Russian in an apartment. Oma had started to cook upstairs again, but by now we had next to nothing to put into the pot. We had a few potatoes, a few lentils, and some turnips left. We were lucky because we also had salt and pepper, which some of the others didn't have. This at least flavored the soup. And we had running water but no electricity. Oma or Mutti made fires in the iron stove in the kitchen so they could cook our meals. I was allowed to go up only when the soup was ready, and I looked forward to the half hour I spent upstairs, slurping my watery soup as slowly as possible.

A few days passed, and Myron, sitting as usual by the cellar door, motioned to Mother. When she didn't respond, he shouted, "Frau Kraus, there's someone here to see you!" I trudged behind her to see who it was.

In the doorway stood a disheveled stranger that I did not recognize. Mother cried out, "Cecilia," and quickened her pace toward her.

I was shocked. Mother's old friend looked like a ghost, not dead, yet not alive. She was only twenty-eight years old, but something had happened to her so she no longer was of a specific age. Her red hair had lost all color and was caked with mud, her once translucent skin showed black and brown bruises. I remembered her eyes as small and watery blue, but now they were red-rimmed, and sacks of loose skin drooped beneath them. She stretched out her arms to Mother, her palms open, as if in supplication. "I walked here from Potsdam," she whispered. I averted my gaze from her face and stared at a dirt-caked toe protruding through a hole in her sock and shoe. Her clothes hung in shreds, and I wondered how she could have walked all that way in shoes that were mere flaps of torn leather.

Mother embraced her. I had never liked Cecilia, but seeing her in that state, I couldn't help but feel sorry for her. Mother put Cecilia's arms around her shoulders and helped her up the stairs. I followed.

"Astrid, my apartment's gone. In the last week of fighting. Gone." Her eyes had a faraway look, as if she didn't understand where her apartment had disappeared to.

"You can stay with us," Mother said and led her to the torn sofa with protruding springs. "Karin, would you make us some tea, please?"

As I came back, balancing the tray with cups and peppermint tea, Oma entered from the hallway. Cecilia limped to my grandmother, embraced her feebly, then fell back onto the sofa. Mother unlocked the cupboard and came back with the sugar bowl. She poured tea for all of us, and then she put two pieces of brown candied sugar into Cecilia's tea. (Where did she get the sugar from? She must have been hoarding it for a special occasion.) Mother slapped my hand when I reached for the sugar. Dislike for Cecilia again replaced my pity. Mother always placed her friends first. Now it was

Cecilia receiving these special favors. I moved to a corner of the room, teacup in hand, sipped, and listened. Cecilia twisted the cup in both of her hands as if warming them on the hot liquid, and slowly her story came forth, sentence by sentence, in a raspy voice that sounded as if she were spitting out rotten food.

"You were right, Astrid," she said. "I should have stayed here. It was a mistake to try and make it to the West. But now I'm back . . . till I can get to my parents."

"But there's no transportation to the West."

She waved a tired hand. "I know, I know."

"How far did you get?" Mother asked.

"I made it almost to the Elbe. I could see the river when I was coming out of the forest. That's when they caught me." She broke off, sniffling.

"The Russians caught you?"

"Ha," she made a hoarse laughing sound, but there was no humor in it. Then she buried her face in a pillow, pummeling the upholstery with her fists.

Mother touched her shoulders, but Cecilia jerked away. "Cecilia, what happened?"

"Ha," she made that same sound again. "I saved myself for this? To think that I wanted to be married, to have children . . . I'll never be able to look at a man again," she broke off weeping. Oma and Mother sat mute, looking at each other and shaking their heads.

I remembered that Mother always spoke of Cecilia as a devout Catholic, praising her as a good girl, even at the age of twenty-eight. I'd wondered then, what did it mean to be a good girl at age twenty-eight. What did that make me, who had often misbehaved since age five? Now it dawned on me that Mother had meant something altogether different.

Cecilia had heard the same gruesome tales of Russians raping refugee women coming from the east. This had motivated her to try to reach the western side of the River Elbe where the Americans were already entrenched. Cecilia had been near hysteria when she had planned her escape. Not heeding Mother's warning, she'd set off, hoping to swim across the river and then make her way to her parents' home near Düsseldorf.

Cecilia composed herself enough to tell us her story, and the room fell silent.

She had walked and walked. Occasionally she caught rides from people going in the same direction. She made her way through a dense forest to reach the open fields surrounding the river.

While talking, Cecilia fished a rag of a handkerchief from her pocket and swiped at the tears running down her cheeks. "I saw the river," she said. "A band of gray through the trees. That's it. I'm safe, I thought. Then suddenly there were soldiers . . ."

Mother cut in, "Then there *were* Russians."

"No," Cecilia screamed. "They were Germans. German soldiers! They saw me and their eyes changed to something . . . , like beasts. Like they had suddenly sighted their prey. They fell upon me . . ." At this point, she hid her face, shaking.

Oma stroked her hair, but Cecilia shook her head and Oma withdrew her hand. Oma and Mutti sat mesmerized and had forgotten that I was in the room. I tried not to make any noise, hoping I could stay.

Mother said, "Did they all . . . weren't there any who defended you?"

"Yes. Two of them. Officers. They ordered the men to stop. They threatened to shoot them. The soldiers only laughed. They said . . . ," her voice trailed off.

"It's all right," Oma said. You don't have to talk about it now."

"Let her talk," Mother said.

Cecilia blew her nose and went on. "They said it was their last chance to be with . . . to have . . . a woman. 'Go ahead, shoot us. We don't care,' they taunted the officers. 'Soon we'll be dead or in Siberia.' "

I remembered the way Cecilia used to look. When she appeared out of the dense green forest, a lone woman with flaming hair, she must have seemed like an apparition to the soldiers.

These were German soldiers. How could they hurt a German woman? It sounded as if most in that troop had done the same unspeakable thing to her that the Russian soldiers had done to women in Berlin. I sat quiet, frightened and confused.

"How many did this?" Mother asked. "Ten? Twenty?"

"I don't know. It blurred . . . I think I passed out."

Oma gave Mother one of her chiding looks. "Astrid, ten soldiers? Twenty? Would a hundred be worse?" Oma looked sickened, and she breathed noisily. After she'd composed herself she said, "This country . . . chivalry, decent behavior, everything we believed in is gone. One soldier would have been too many." Oma took another deep breath. Then she said in a gentle voice, "I think it was lucky you passed out. It was your body's way of protecting you."

Cecilia nodded and shook her head: a *yes* and a *no* in the same gesture. "When I came to, the soldiers were gone. It was all a haze. I didn't remember much at first. Then I felt a knifelike pain, a burning between my legs. Slowly I began to remember."

She told us how she had staggered in her torn and bloodstained clothing through the forest. Whenever she heard anyone approaching, Russians or Germans, she hid in the dense underbrush. A kindhearted old farmer found her and was so moved by her sorry state that he gave her a ride in his horse-drawn cart and shared his meager food with her. He told her about his only daughter who was a FLAK helper—many of these helpers manned anti-aircraft guns. She'd been killed by shrapnel at age twenty-one, only a month ago. He wrapped Cecilia in his coat and took her as far as Potsdam. From there, Cecilia had walked to our place.

Now Cecilia had become a stranger to herself and to us. In one afternoon she had turned into an old woman, with gray skin, drab hair, and an absent mind.

Oma went to her, and this time Cecilia let Oma clasp her in her arms. They both wept. Cecilia stayed with us for a little while, then she was hospitalized by the Red Cross. Later, after the Western Allies occupied Berlin, she found transportation to Düsseldorf to join her parents.

Mother insisted I still wear my disguise wherever I went. It became bothersome since I had to walk pigeon-toed and slouch whenever we saw Russian soldiers on the street.

One day Oma sent me to a food distribution site on the opposite side of our street to get a ration of bread. As I passed an apartment building, I heard loud moaning coming through a half-opened window. This was the house where Siegrid, a girl from school, lived with her widowed father. I had barely met her when I was sent to Mistroy, whereas she had returned to Berlin because of the sudden death of her mother. I remembered her as a pretty girl, two years older than I, who wore her thick, copper-colored hair coiled around her head as if it were a crown. The groans grew louder, as if someone were in terrible pain. Should I go in and ring her doorbell? Or would I be intruding? What if she was alone and needed help? I rang the bell.

A woman, in a nurse's uniform, let me into the apartment. Siegrid lay on the floor writhing. Had she fallen? "What's wrong?" I asked, afraid to get too close.

Siegrid looked up at me as if she didn't recognize me. She still wore her hair wound in braids, but some strands had come loose. The copper looked unpolished and was darkened with sweat and dirt. She lifted a hand from the floor, and I could see it cost her great effort to wave me into the room.

Meanwhile, the woman packed up the syringes and the injection paraphernalia, stashing it all into her medical bag. She explained, "Siegrid has to have a series of sulfa injections. It's a good thing you came to see your friend. She needs someone with her." She nodded toward the kitchen, "Perhaps you can make some tea. Hot chamomile would be good for her," she said. "I have to go now, hope to see you again." And with these last words still hovering in the room, she ran out of the apartment.

"Where is your father?" I asked.

"Karin? Is that you?"

I nodded, realizing my disguise must have fooled her. I still stood by the door not knowing whether to come in or to leave.

Siegrid said, "Father always goes out when the nurse comes. He can't stand to see me in . . ." and again she doubled over and cried out in a high-pitched scream, like a young cat I had seen once, trapped in a bombed building.

I stood cracking my knuckles. Oma had felt weak that day and had told me to go and get bread and come straight home. They would worry about me. The Russians were all about, and I could still be raped, even though I felt relatively safe wearing my "armor."

Still, I decided to make myself useful. I made a pot of tea and took it and two cups into the living room. I put it all onto the table in front of the sofa, kneeled by the crouching Siegrid, and tried to pry her loose from the Oriental rug. She put her weight on me and we slowly stood up, then I guided her to the sofa.

"You scared me half to death. What's going on, what kind of injection?"

"I have syphilis. These sulfa injections are killing me," she went on, "I feel like I'm burning up."

"I heard of syphilis, but what is it?"

"It's a disease. It can kill you. You get it from being raped."

"The Russians?" After I asked this, I immediately thought, what a stupid question. But after what happened to Cecilia, who knew?

She nodded and wept. "There were so many. Maybe twenty," she whispered. "They came in, looked around. At first they didn't even look at me, then they saw a photo of Father with some men in Nazi uniforms. *Au, Karin,*" she interrupted herself, groaning.

"You don't have to tell me now. Here, drink your tea."

"I can't talk when Father is here. They must have thought he was a Nazi. He'd never even joined the party. To teach him a lesson, they forced him to watch. They stuck a bayonet at his temple, and every time he tried to close his eyes, they pushed. He had to keep his eyes open, but he told me later, he kept them open but willed himself not to see." She shook her head. "I don't know how he did it. I heard them laugh and taunt him, and then I passed out. Thank God."

Siegrid put her head on a pillow and closed her eyes. After a while she lifted her head and reached for the teacup. She blew on the hot drink and took small sips. "If we had only been in the cellar," she said. "But Father hated to be stuck down there." She paused and looked at me. In a changed voice she asked, "Why are you dressed like that?"

Apparently she was feeling a little better, since she had noticed my weird clothes. Early on, I told her, my mother had not wanted to move into the cellar, but Oma had convinced her that it was the safest place for us. "And that's why I'm wearing this. To make me look scary to the Russians. It's uncomfortable, and sometimes the little pillow that's supposed to make me look like a hunchback, slips. But so far it worked."

She shook her head.

"Father is almost sixty, you know," she said. "I feel so sorry for him. I'm all he has. He feels guilty, every time the nurse comes . . . but I told you that already." Then she added, taking another sip of tea, "I'm so happy you came. You will come again, won't you?"

I did. I visited her as often as I could.

On my way home I thought about Cecilia and about Siegrid and her father, and I wondered where the mind went, when it willed itself away.

REVELATIONS

When I returned home, I opened the cellar door and bumped into Myron. He saw my red eyes and asked what had happened. I sat down on a rickety stool near the entrance, not wanting to go inside and have the neighbors see me and ask why I was crying. I could not stop the tears. Myron asked me again, and I told him what had happened to Siegrid.

"The Russians are pigs. Monsters," I said, wiping my nose with an old, torn handkerchief. "Why do they hurt people so much?"

"Karin, yes, but if you'd seen some of the concentration camps they liberated . . ."

"Oh, I know about those," I waved my hand, dismissing his words. "Where they hold political people. That's where we were afraid they'd put Mother. Because she always runs off her mouth. Oma's always warning her. Well, before, when Hitler was still alive, that if she wasn't careful, she'd wind up behind a barbed wire fence."

Myron shook his head. "No. I'm talking about something entirely different. Camps where they put Jews and Gypsies. Were they political?" He looked down at his scruffy boots, still shaking his head. "These troops came through Poland where they found villages and sites with thousands and thousands of dead. And thousands of Russian soldiers had been starved to death, they were Slavs and not considered worth a piece of bread. After seeing that, they came to hate Germans more than ever. They saw things so horrible they are beyond understanding."

"How do *you* know these things then. How?"

"You saw that officer I was talking to the other day? He was from near my village. Near Kiev." Myron lowered his voice, not wanting to be overheard. "He's been through camps built for the purpose of *killing*. He wouldn't give me details. I could see he was getting sick to his stomach remembering what he'd seen. Germans had done that. The officer told me that Marshal Zhukov himself, you know, the general who took Berlin, became even more ruthless after seeing such atrocities."

"That's not true! I know there were places for people who were traitors. I told you, I know all about those. That officer made those things up, so he and his soldiers would have an excuse to behave like beasts."

"The officer had no reason to lie. I'm sure that once newspapers are printed again, you will hear of it."

"I have to ask Oma if she knows about this." I started to weep and pulled out the torn handkerchief. I rocked on the rickety chair for a moment and frowned. "You believe they rape out of hate?" I asked, looking Myron in the eye.

"That . . . ," He looked lost in thought for a moment, "And other reasons. You know the motto, 'To the victor go the spoils.' Many of these soldiers had not been home on leave, for all these years. Nothing to go home on leave for, their own villages were more than likely burned to the ground by the Germans. Families were scattered. Rape and pillage. That's always been the case in wars with Russia. Karin, Russia is a poor country. In the cities, people live in run-down apartments, and in the countryside, in dilapidated shacks. The soldiers believed that Germans were also poor, downtrodden, and deprived. They conquer Berlin and what do they find? In some of the apartments, like Frau Schlosser's, Persian rugs, crystal chandeliers, silver. They've never seen such luxuries. And they find this here, in Berlin, which is mostly in ruins. They endured immense hardships in this long war while their families lived in hovels. Now they see the defeated enemy still has more than they'll ever have. So they vandalize, they destroy, they rape. It's part of human nature. Ugly. But that's what it is."

"You don't want to go back to Russia, do you?"

"No. I'm trying to get my papers in order so I can stay. I love the Ukraine, but most of my family has been deported to the Gulag. I don't want to live under Stalin. In some ways he's worse than Hitler."

"No one is worse than Hitler. He lied to his own people."

"Maybe they're equal. Go ask your grandmother about concentration camps, I'd be curious to know what she will tell you."

I had stopped crying and pushed my wet handkerchief back in my pocket. I shook my head, quick jerking movements, trying to rid myself of the imagined skeletons whirling behind my eyelids. I didn't want to think about death camps. I had seen enough suffering in the past year to last me for the rest of my life.

Besides, Germans would never do such things. Camps for killing people? I remembered Margrit Hagen. She had been jailed because of something Jewish. I didn't remember exactly what it was. Then I thought of Cecilia and her rape by German soldiers. This puzzled me. Out came the handkerchief again.

I walked to Oma's cot and found her resting. I was hesitant to wake her, but if I kept any of this in me any longer, I would burst. "Oma, I have to talk to you." She opened her eyes. I repeated Myron's horror tales. Her brows drew into one bushy slate line, then she looked at me with her round blue eyes that never told a lie, saying, "Yes. There were concentration camps, for dissenters and communists. Death camps for Jews and Gypsies?" She shook her head no. "Hitler wanted the Jews to leave Germany. Most left early, like the Ladenburgs, our relatives in Frankfurt. After *Kristallnacht,* they left for France. Your little girlfriend who lived on the corner, Esther?" I nodded, I had been angry with her for leaving without saying good-bye, "Well, she left with her parents for England. And Gypsies? Most were musicians. Remember them playing for the Esterhazy in Eisenstadt that Christmas? No, Karin, perhaps there were some labor camps for Jews and for others, but death camps? No." She paused for a moment, then said, "He's got all this from a Russian? You can't believe everything you hear."

It was clear to me, Myron didn't know what he was talking about. He was Russian. Obviously, he'd fallen for Russian propaganda.

Toilet Paper, *Mein Kampf,* and Portraits

The longer hours of sunlight brought us a little more warmth, and my disguise weighed on me. The cellar was still cold and damp, and so far I had not suffocated in the heavy sweater, the ski pants, and jacket. But day after day this costume, an erstwhile "good idea," was becoming a plague.

There were rumors that the Allies were going to arrive in Berlin and divide the city into four sectors: American, British, French, and, of course, Russian. But none of us knew which part of Berlin would go to whom. Every day we prayed for the Americans to hurry up and free us from the Russians.

Meanwhile, we went on living our ratlike existence in the basement, and day by day our putrid smell increased. I don't know what I longed for more: a bath or a full stomach. Each was an impossible dream. Another simple wish was to be able to go to the toilet in peace, without Mother standing guard and urging me to hurry up, fearing Russian boot steps on the stairs, or some other real or imagined danger.

We were among the few lucky ones who still had running water and flushable toilets. But we were running out of usable paper. Each time I went, Mother would repeat, "Don't use more than two sheets." The texture of the paper we used—square-cut pieces of old newspaper pages—was awful. In the top corner of each square, Mother had punched a hole and tied the sheets together with a piece of frayed string. She fastened this bundle onto a hook by the toilet. There were not many pages left. What would we use next? Some people used old romance or detective novels. But we cherished the few books we had acquired in antiquarian shops after the bombing.

Those were the little comforts we wished for: a bath, privacy in the bathroom, toilet paper, and food to fill our bellies.

People began to bargain and trade possessions. Trees sprouted cardboard signs that were tacked to the trunk and lower limbs with thumbnails: Will trade cooking pot for warm socks or Will trade man's boots for woman's sweater. One sign proclaimed in rhyme, "*Tausche 'Mein Kampf,' noch ungelesen, für einen Toilettenbesen*"—Will trade *Mein Kampf,* still unread, for a toilet brush. Was this an example of Berlin humor, I wondered, or did the person really want a toilet brush?

Mother would have welcomed *Mein Kampf,* for toilet paper. It was poorly written, and no one I knew would confess to having read it. Frau Schlosser, who was not a Nazi, said that was a mistake. Had more people read it, she felt, they would have known Hitler's plans and perhaps been more vigilant and able to prevent his seizure of power.

In the midst of our meager existence, Oma took me to Fräulein von Fournier's apartment several times a week to have our portraits painted. Petite Fräulein von Fournier lived only two blocks from us and had persuaded my grandmother to sit for her. She promised to capture us in pastels. She had no other income and needed to earn a few marks, and there was little else we could spend money on. The painter's apartment was an oasis amid the rubble of our gray lives. The ever-present danger of the Russians was forgotten for those few hours spent amid old-fashioned velvet pillows and lace curtains. Having our portraits painted seemed an idiotic undertaking, given our circumstances. Perhaps Oma hoped she could forget our troubles for a few hours and lend some semblance of normalcy to our lives. But what was normal? Having your portrait painted was something out of the ordinary in any event.

On one particular day, Oma and I trudged the two blocks, carrying a bag containing my blue, gray, and peach plaid organdy dress. In Fräulein von Fournier's frilly bedroom, I changed from my idiot's garb into a dress and was transformed into something resembling a young girl. Ironically, I could breathe more freely in the dress with its tight waist than I could in the baggy ski pants. I fastened the small pearl-shaped buttons up to the flat rounded collar, and within a moment, I felt pretty again. The ugly scarf had come off earlier. I brushed out my hair, shaking it, fluffing it out. I rinsed off the flour and coal-dust mixture that was part of my disguise, then scrubbed my face hard with Fräulein von Fournier's nailbrush, until my skin was red and almost raw. I then dusted my face lightly with the big pink puff resting within the gilded porcelain case containing scented face powder—something French no doubt—from better times. As a final touch I applied a hint of rouge from the painter's cosmetic box. After finishing with those vanities, I enjoyed looking in the mirror, feeling like a presentable young girl again.

Oma was first. While waiting, I paged through a heavy book of Spanish art. Then it was my turn. I sat stiff and bored until I could no longer stand it and squirmed. "Sit still!" I was told. While I itched to move around, I forced myself to become as immobile as a statue. I imagined myself to be a princess in a palace in Spain, wearing a huge hoop skirt and pink ribbons on a strange hairdo and holding a lace fan, just like the young princess in Velasquez's *Infanta Margarita*. Imagining that I was this young girl helped pass the time. Then, while I was still in Spain, Fräulein von Fournier put the pastels back into their lacquered wooden box, wiped her hands on a color-stained towel, and told me I was free to get dressed.

This thought did not appeal to me. "Oma, I like wearing a dress again. Can't I keep it on? It's so good to feel like me." She shook her head. I pleaded, "Do I have to change back into an idiot again?"

"I'm afraid so, *Kind*. Go, look out on the street? There are probably still some Russians about."

I went to the window. The street was empty. Then two soldiers swerved around the corner, cradling rifles as if they were babies, swaying from side to side. Russians. Worse, *drunk* Russians. Much as I hated to change back into my disguise, I conceded. I had to. Then Oma and I crept back to our house.

Resurrection and Death

During the third week in May, Margrit Hagen came to visit. This was the first time we'd seen her since her arrest by the Gestapo in January. Before that we had spent many a pleasant Sunday afternoon with her. I liked her; she had read poetry to me and always treated me as if I were someone to be taken seriously, not a silly child.

Now she stood in the front hall, a thinner version of herself, but her skin color was healthy. She was nicely dressed in a woolen skirt and tweed jacket. Mother took her by the shoulders and held her at arm's length, looking her over. "Margrit, you look wonderful! No longer with an ashen face like out of a graveyard."

Margrit managed a small smile. "It's good to see everyone." She handed me a round object wrapped in brown, grease-stained paper. "I'm living in a Russian barracks now, run by the Red Cross. And I've eaten well during the last few weeks." She pointed to the package I held and the longer one she carried. "Here," she said, "I brought you a Russian cake and a loaf of bread. I hope you like it."

"Like it?" I ripped into the brown wrapping. Inside was a golden cake with raisins protruding from the crust. "*Hmm,* smells so good. I can hardly wait . . ."

"You're a young lady now. Restrain yourself," Mother said. Then turning to Margrit, she asked, "So what happened to you? Tell us. Sit down, please. I'll make some tea."

Margrit made herself comfortable on the sofa. I sat down next to her and could not stop looking at her. She had soft brown eyes with long lashes and thick brown hair falling in waves to her shoulders, and she had a gentle way about her.

"What happened?" She avoided Mother's questions, her eyes wide. "You know what happened. The Russians took Berlin, entered the prison, and freed us. That's what happened. What a feeling! Suddenly the doors to the outside world opened, and there we were. I'd forgotten how sweet the air can smell. Even with all the smoke and the fires still burning. I felt like singing. The Russians gave us a change of clothes . . ."

Mother stared at Margrit's tweed jacket.

"No," Margrit shook her head, "These clothes are from the Red Cross. They're donations from Switzerland. But the first thing the Russians did was feed us from a soup canteen. Some sort of goulash. Delicious. I'd been starved since last January. I'd lived on a few crusts of bread and water soup for more than three months. I ate so much goulash I got sick." She laughed, a tinkling laugh.

"And the Russians . . . ?" Mother squeezed her face into a strange grimace. "I mean, they didn't rape, they . . . ?"

"No. Why? They were our liberators. We were Nazi prisoners."

"Yes. Of course. How stupid of me. Only, I've seen a lot of normal be-havior turned upside down lately."

Suddenly Margrit's expression changed. Her large eyes filled with tears. Mother took her hand and said gently, "So the Russians did do something?"

"No Astrid." She shook her head as if caught in a slow motion film. "My parents are dead." She pulled a handkerchief from her handbag and wiped her face. "They had been arrested and sent to a camp."

"What kind of a camp? For dissenters?" I asked

"No. A death camp," she said. "The Russians told us what they found in the camps. I can't talk about it. I'm very lucky I didn't wind up in one of them." The blood had drained from her face, and she looked ashen. Through her tears she whispered, "Imagine. My parents. They were hung as traitors to the Third Reich." Almost inaudibly she continued through her stopped up nose, "Hung, in a courtyard while people watched."

Mother's face contorted into folds I had never seen before. "Margrit! Then . . . when I tried to phone them for you, they'd already been arrested? That's what we thought, when the concierge said they'd gone on vacation. Remember?"

Margrit nodded. She swallowed hard. "The Red Cross established that my parents had been transported to a camp at Sachsenhausen. The Gestapo in-terrogated them, over and over. They called them traitors because they had lied on my Aryan pass, they had sworn I was their biological child. The Nazis knew my birth mother was Jewish, now they wanted to know who my 'real' father was. Either my parents didn't know or they didn't want to tell. I think it may have been the latter. Father knew how the German bureau-cracy worked. As long as the Nazis didn't know if my father was Jewish or Aryan, they couldn't close my file. That kept me safe from being shipped off to one of the camps. My poor parents. God, they didn't tell! Why couldn't the Allies have come sooner? To think they were killed just before the war ended." Again she wept.

The cake remained on its plate, uneaten.

Bread and Shoes

The never-ending rain added to our misery. Mother's mood was as gray as the sky. Would things ever get better? It seemed as if the Allies were never going to enter Berlin, never going to free us from the Russians. Had the West abandoned us? If those things I'd heard from Myron and Margrit were true, maybe we deserved to be abandoned? I thought about the death camp rumors for a while. No, they couldn't be true. Margrit must have also heard about them from the Russians. It surely was all part of a hate campaign to justify the Soviets' behavior.

We were starved not only for food but also for news. The only newspaper in Berlin was the *Tägliche Rundschau,* a paper sponsored by the Russians that we didn't read. We were hungry for news from the West. When we had electricity, we listened to the BBC, but we still felt cut off from the world.

Many times when I was sent to buy bread, I returned empty-handed. Bread was distributed on street corners, but we never knew when or where. One day I was out looking for bread again, walking up and down the streets, using up the precious leather soles of my only pair of boots. I had walked a few kilometers down the Kurfürstendamm and concluded that today would be one of those bleak days without bread. I gave up and turned for home. But there on the corner of Kurfürstendamm and our street I encountered a man who sold hand-tooled, wooden shoe soles. I thought of Mother, and how only a few days ago she had been fantasizing nonstop about buying new shoes. She wanted open-toed sandals for the summer. I sympathized with her, because my own ski boots, hot and bothersome, grew heavier each day.

I picked up one of these wooden soles and stroked the smoothly polished wood. The instep curved to a high heel, all made from a single piece of wood. It looked almost like a sculpture, one fluid sweep of what might become a graceful, though cloglike, shoe. I had an idea. Oh yes, Mother would like these, once I attached uppers to them. I fingered the coins and paper in my pocket, the bread money, and bought a pair of the highest heels the man sold.

Oma was disappointed when I returned without the bread, and she did not notice the wooden soles I carried. Mother was not home yet. I rummaged through an old trunk containing bits of fabric and discards. I found the sleeve of an old red suede jacket. I searched through drawers and came up with a few decorative nails, the kind used on leather chairs—the same type of nails I had removed from Oma's armchair so many years ago. The nails I found were smaller and made of brass. I cut the suede into four wide strips and nailed these crisscross onto the tip where the toes would go, taking the measurement from my own feet, which were only slightly smaller than Mother's. Then I cut four long, slender straps, which fastened onto the instep. These straps would cross in back and tie in front, making sort of an ankle-strap sandal.

When Mother came home, we sat down for supper. We had the same watery cabbage soup that we always had, peppermint tea, and, in place of bread, a slice of air.

After we finished our meal, I left the room. When I returned, I surprised her with the sandals. I held them high and let them dangle on red straps from my hand, offering them to Mother, and she could not believe that I was giving her these shoes. Her eyes sparkled when she tried them on. She hugged and kissed me and then ran to retrieve an old bottle of nail polish. Minutes later she coquettishly displayed her newly pedicured feet, her red toes dazzling from red sandals. I had not seen Mother this happy in a very long time.

Happiness on an almost empty stomach.

RUBBLE WOMEN AND THE STARS AND STRIPES
SUMMER–WINTER 1945

Just as we became desperate with hunger and thought things would never change, the news came that soon, very soon, the Western Allied forces would arrive in Berlin.

But for now, the Russians continued to give orders.

Along with the other tenants in our apartment building, we continued to sleep in the cellar for safety reasons; occasional forays by Russian soldiers still led to rape and pillage. When we were all gathered together, the house warden announced that our building was to fly the four flags of the conquering nations on the day the Allies entered Berlin. People grumbled, "Damn this flag business. Aren't we done with that?"

Our block had to be cleared of rubble, and everyone in the building had to shovel debris. Oma and Mother tied large cotton scarves over their hair, while I still wore the ugly orange scarf. We wore aprons over our bulky jackets and pulled on ski gloves, and we began clearing broken concrete and bricks. I giggled when I looked at my formerly elegant mother, looking like a peasant woman working in a potato field. We shoveled the wreckage into piles at the edge of a collapsed building that had been hit by the rockets of a *Stalinorgel* during the last days of battle.

We were lucky; our block was not as badly bombed as some of the other nearby streets. I hoped I would not encounter bodies in the rubble, but when I began shoveling, fat black rats, huge, almost as large as rabbits, scurried from the ruins. I had never seen rats before. Oma called these creatures audacious because they had the nerve to appear in broad daylight, showing off their well-nourished bodies that had fed on whatever was buried within the ruins. My gloves soon hung in shreds, but I kept shoveling even after my hands began to bleed. Concrete dust hung in the air, choking us and obscuring the blue of the sky.

I hated being a *Trümmerfrau* or, in my case, *Trümmermädchen,* rubble girl. I stacked brick and cleared away broken concrete fragments. I worked fast because I wanted to get back to the business of making a flag. I shoveled some more. A woman from our building screeched. She had seen something that made her jump back. I looked over her shoulder, and within the mass of stone debris, a mop of thick brown hair, now coated with bits of gray concrete, had become visible. It had to be part of a woman. The head hung to one side onto her shoulder, and the upper body was clad in a torn dark coat. I stared. Where there should have been a face, fat white maggots wiggled on what looked like crusts of dried blood. Empty eye sockets surrounded what would have been a nose. I turned away, and my stomach flipped. Out of the corner of my eye I saw a big glossy rat staring straight at me. Then it turned and disappeared in a crack between the chunks of rubble.

I vomited, and Oma came to me. She had seen what I had seen. By now I couldn't stop shaking. I sobbed and hid my face on her shoulder. She too shook as tears rolled down her cheeks. Oma took me by the hand and marched me home. She told the house warden I was too young to be shoveling among corpses. We did not tell mother, who was shoveling farther down the street. And we never talked about what we had seen.

In the cellar, the house warden gave us the choice of which country's flag to create. Mother's hand shot up, "We want to sew the French flag," she said, speaking for the three of us. Her motive was suspect to me, since the French flag was the easiest one to make, requiring only three bands of red, white, and blue cloth. But Mother insisted that she loved everything French, not only her gloves and perfumes but also Baudelaire and Proust, and she defended her position with conviction.

"Nonsense, Astrid," Oma said. "I grew up in America. We are going to make the Stars and Stripes."

"Mutter, that's crazy! With forty-eight little stars and all those stripes? And where do we get the cloth for the blue, the red . . ."

"And the white." Oma finished her sentence. "The same colors and the same cloth we'd use for the French flag. I insist, Astrid. We are making the American flag. Right, Karin? You're going to help."

"Of course, Oma," I kissed her on the cheek. "I can make one of the stars, then we'll fold it and put it on layers of cloth, and we can cut out several at a time."

We hoped Frau Kuhnert would help us with our huge task. After all, the flag would go between the windows of the apartment we shared. But she didn't want to have anything to do with flags or with welcoming the conquerors. Other residents chose to make the French flag and the British Union Jack (not an easy one either), but one family had to be forced to make the Russian flag, since there were no volunteers.

I knew the history of the Stars and Stripes, which Oma had told me many times. I thought how much easier it would have been to make the first flag, since it had only thirteen stars. But I was happy to help Oma, whose mood soared in anticipation of the arrival of the Americans. She sang, "Yankee Doodle comes to town, . . ." while pressing us into service to do Betsy Ross one better, to create an American flag out of odd bits of material.

Months ago I had seen a large red Nazi flag in Frau Kuhnert's part of the hall closet. I asked her if we could use it? I glowered at her, making it clear if she said no, she would be suspected of being a Nazi, which she most likely still was. She let me have the flag. I saw her flinch when I cut out the white circle with the black swastika and threw it in the trash. Rummaging through old suitcases and shelves, we found a cornflower blue tablecloth with a soft floral pattern. This would have to do, and from the street, no one would know that it was not solid blue. We ripped the red flag apart and cut it into strips, but the tough part came when I had to cut the white sheet into equal-sized small stars. The scissors were blunt and frayed the edges of the little stars.

We sewed the red stripes onto the plain white background of a sheet, and the stars onto the blue. The application of all those little stars into neat rows was dizzying. Then we hung the flag from a rod between two of our third-floor windows.

The three of us stood on the street, looking up at our flag, high above the others. Oma smiled, "We'll fly it again on the Fourth of July." She gave me a big hug. "Oh, Karin, if only you could have seen the parades and the fun we had on that day back in the States."

More weeks passed, and it was not until a sunny Saturday, July 8, that we welcomed the first Americans. We stood in a crowd on the Potsdamer Chaussee, clutching the small Stars and Stripes paper flags an American soldier had passed out earlier. People jostled and pushed. Everyone wanted to be close up to have a good look at the Yankees, or *Amis,* as Berliners soon called American soldiers. Tanks rolled by and armored trucks motored down the highway, showing us fresh young faces. I wished I were older when I saw how handsome those Americans were. The soldiers looked tanned and smiled with big white teeth. I thought it strange that many of them were chewing and laughing with their mouths open. I couldn't figure out why so many seemed to be eating, yet I saw no food in their hands.

Troops marched in rank and file. I waved my little flag wildly, jumping up and down. Some waved back at me, and one soldier threw candies toward me from an armored car. Children scrambled for the treats. Some kids stuffed pink strips of a strange hard candy into their mouths but then spat them out again. I ripped into the glossy brown paper of a Hershey bar and bit into the soft sweet taste of chocolate, my first in years.

The Americans brought me my first taste of a little bit of heaven.

Why couldn't they have come earlier? So much bloodshed and suffering could have been prevented. But Oma was happy. "Why think of what's behind us?" she said. "The main thing is, the Americans are here. *Now.*"

We lived in Halensee and still didn't know which of the four sectors we would be in. Soon we found out we were in the British sector, which was not our choice, but I said, "Thank you, *Lieber Gott*," that it was not the Russian sector.

It was as if we had all awakened from a bad dream when the Russians left and the British occupation troops appeared on our streets. After all those months in the cellar, we moved back into our apartment.

It was unbelievably wonderful to go out onto the street, without my disguise, to enjoy the sun's warm rays on my skin. It was unbelievably wonderful to go to the park unafraid and watch birds hop from branch to branch or read a book on a bench, all things we had not been able to do for such a long time.

I no longer had to sleep on a lumpy cot in the cellar but could snuggle into my pillow in my own cozy bed. I still shared the room with Oma, and even listening to her snores was bliss. My clothes—short-sleeved blouses, skirts, and an old pair of sandals—felt light and comfortable after wearing ski boots, pants, and jackets for so long. Summer was here, bringing sunshine and warmth. It brought forth dandelions, which I picked to give a taste of fresh green to a slice of bread, and young nettles, which added a taste variety to Oma's soups. In spite of a gnawing hunger and not knowing where our next loaf of bread would come from, the three of us were happy again.

A RUSSIAN AFTERMATH

I stopped by Siegrid's apartment and again found her in pain. She was lying on the sofa, a down quilt drawn up to her ears. She shivered despite the warm day.

"Is it still the injections?" I asked.

"I have cramps. Terrible cramps."

"Is it your monthly . . . ?"

"No. But it's . . . I'm bleeding. As if all of me is running out." I stood looking at her, frowning, again I was at a loss as to what was happening. She guessed by my puzzled expression that she needed to explain. "You know, those swine, those Russians, they got me pregnant when they raped me. Pregnant and syphilis. As if one thing wasn't enough."

I shook my head and stared at her, my questions written on my face.

"I had an abortion. I couldn't have a baby, not a Russian baby and not with syphilis. I'm still not cured. The doctor did it yesterday. He didn't have an anesthesia. He put me on the kitchen table, while the nurse held me down. Then he gave me an aspirin."

I wanted to ask her if it had hurt a lot, but I was afraid. I wanted to know, yet, at the same time, I didn't want to know. In the end I asked, "Did it hurt?"

"What do you think? You sit with your legs splayed apart and he goes in and scrapes out your inside. It hurts like . . . it feels as if someone is scooping out everything that's inside of you."

I felt sick to my stomach again. "Is there something I can do? I mean, would you like some chamomile tea or . . . ?"

"No, thanks. *Shh.* I hear Father."

The key sounded in the lock, and a few moments later, her father appeared. He was a handsome man, who looked a bit like an elderly statesmen. His hair had gone pure white, but he had a shock of it. I said hello to him and good-bye to Siegrid, and I told her I would visit her again soon.

I visited Siegrid a week later and found her up and busily packing boxes and suitcases.

"Are you going somewhere? Has your bleeding stopped?"

"Not entirely. But Father told me to get ready. We're leaving soon. I think he was able to get us onto a Red Cross transport to the West."

"Where are you going?"

"Vati wants us to move to Stuttgart. My aunt lives there. His sister."

"How about your treatments?"

"There are doctors in Stuttgart." There wasn't anything to laugh at, yet she laughed, making a high, tinkling sound. I realized that was the first time I'd ever heard her laugh. It was an eerie sound, as if she were about to cry or to scream. Then she sucked in her lips and grinned. "They have more medicines in the West than here. I'm sure I'll get well. I agree with Father, it's best for me to leave Berlin. All those memories. I can't sleep . . . , have nightmares. Sometimes I think I'm going crazy. That's all Father needs. A dead wife and a crazy daughter."

I went to her and put my arms around her. "You're not crazy. I hope you can forget. I hate to see you leave. Promise you'll write. Please let me know how you're doing."

"Sure. I'll write," she said. Then she pointed to a box sitting on the table. "Karin? I have a box packed for you and your mother. We weren't bombed out, so I have enough clothes. Maybe your mother can use some of my mother's clothes?"

I went to her and hugged her. "I'm sure she can. Thank you."

I returned to Siegrid's house later that afternoon, and she showed me several books she wanted me to have, including an entire set of late nineteenth-century Courts-Mahler romances. I longed for them, but I knew Mother would not allow me to read them. Once a neighbor had given me a Courts-Mahler novel, and after Mother found it, she threw it in the trash. She claimed reading this type of book would spoil my taste for good literature. Siegrid was generous and I didn't want to offend her, so I told her I already had this set of books. Then she turned over the leaves of several illustrated volumes lying on the dining room table: *One Thousand and One Nights,* books on Greek and Norse mythology, Hans Christian Andersen's tales, and Grimm's fairy tales. I opened them to the flame-stitch lining and leafed through gold-edged pages, admiring the colorful illustrations. I felt my eyes get wider, my lips quiver, making me lick them. And then I laughed, imagining myself as a salivating dog staring at a bone. Here I was, as hungry as a starving dog, but my appetite had been wetted by the printed page.

"Do you like these, Karin?"

"Like them? You're so lucky. I owned some beautiful books once, but they all burned. I miss them. Mother said it'll be years before nice books will be published again."

Siegrid scratched the nape of her neck. She looked at me, then at the books, and then back at me again. She tossed her head, shaking loose a strand of copper, which spiraled onto her forehead. She squinted and grimaced. Then she surprised me. "Take all the fairy-tale books," she said. "I think you'll appreciate them more than I do. I read them when I was your age, but now I like adult books, *Anna Karenina,* that sort of thing."

I pressed my eyes shut, tight. Then I opened them quickly, hoping that the books would still be on the table and that I had not been dreaming.

Secrets

No sooner had I made a friend than I lost her. With Siegrid I had redis-covered a friendship reminiscent of the one I had formed with Nunu in Frankfurt so long ago.

But I brooded about her illness—syphilis. I had heard that word often, yet I didn't understand fully what the illness was or what it meant. What were those diseases—syphilis, gonorrhea, tuberculosis—that could be serious and passed on from one to another? I was afraid to talk to my grandmother about this subject, but I had to know. After all, Oma had been a nurse.

Oma sat peeling potatoes when I entered the kitchen. My question must have sounded like an attack, as it came without a prelude. "Oma," I asked, "What is syphilis? How do you get it?"

The knife in her hand quivered, a long brown peel spiraled toward the enamel bowl. Oma's face flushed. "It's a terrible disease. You can get it by sit-ting on the toilet. That's why I taught you to never sit down but to hover when you're in strange places. Remember?"

"And gonorrhea?"

"The same thing."

"Well, the maid in Vati's house had syphilis and they let her go. Maybe they were afraid they'd get it from using the same toilet. But the Russians gave it to Siegrid. And they raped her. Oma, please. I don't understand any of this. Can't you explain?"

Oma took a deep breath, annoyed with my questions. "The Russians were infected, and when they raped Siegrid, they passed the sickness on. Now will you please get yourself a knife and help me peel the potatoes?"

End of conversation.

I could not ask Mutti because she was out scrounging for food for us. Then I remembered the medical dictionary in Frau Kuhnert's bookshelf in the hallway. I took the heavy book, carried it to my room, and looked up the word *syphilis.* Anatomical illustrations in vivid colors accompanied the text. The detailed parts showing female genitalia shocked me and caught me in a web of interest. How did my parts compare to those pictures, I wondered? I tucked the book under my arm, grabbed my mother's magnifying mirror—

the one she used when plucking her eyebrows—and locked myself into the bathroom. I opened the book to the embarrassing pages. Then I laid down, wiggled out of my panties, and maneuvered the mirror between my legs, trying to get a close look at a part of me I had never seen before.

What I saw was pink and glistening and not at all like the skin on my face or the rest of my body. I saw a few hairs sprouting. Worse, I believed what I saw resembled the illustrations. I was horrified. I had syphilis. I quickly pulled up my panties, smoothed down my skirt, and rushed out of the bathroom sobbing.

Oma caught me in the hallway. "What's the matter, Karin?"

"I'm ill, like Siegrid. I have syphilis."

"That's absurd," Oma said. "What makes you think that?"

"I looked at . . . , at myself, there," I indicated where with a gesture, "in the mirror." Oma said nothing but just glowered at me. "You wouldn't explain anything to me." I never raised my voice to my grandmother, but then I yelled, "I took Frau Kuhnert's book from the hall closet. There are those hideous pictures of sick people in that book. They look all pink down there. I must have picked it up from a toilet seat. Maybe our own, maybe some sick Russian had used it."

A kaleidoscope of expressions—shock, embarrassment, and sadness, topped by a certain bemusement—swept over Oma's face. "Karin, now, now," she said, shaking her head. "It is perfectly normal for a girl—a woman—to be pink there. You're not sick. No, not at all. You would have to have been . . ." Oma interrupted herself with coughing.

"You said you can get it from a toilet seat."

"That's true but extremely rare. People get it from . . . Well, women get it from being raped."

"Then why did Vati's maid have it? She wasn't raped."

"Maybe your mother can explain this better than I can. We'll wait until she gets home, shall we?"

Mother did not come home until after I was asleep.

I went to bed thinking of everything Oma had said. I was angry that she wouldn't explain the mysteries to me more thoroughly. I was old enough to know. All this fear of rape, my disguise, yet no one had ever told me what it was all about. I knew it had something to do with sex, but how did that happen? I couldn't make sense of it.

When I was in bed, I was afraid I'd get caught in a nightmare. I closed my eyes and forced myself to think of something pleasant. I often did this at night, making myself think of butterflies, flowers, or something I had seen in the park earlier that day. Today there had been a skinny little dog dragging its leash—the first dog I had seen in months. I had laughed when it lifted up its patchy-furred little leg to pee on a package someone had leaned against a bench. The owner of the package had not found this funny. I concentrated on those images, and they helped me chase away the darker visions.

A RUSSIAN AND A YANK

That summer, Sergei, Myron's friend, became a steady visitor to our apartment, bringing us bread, salami, bacon, and other needed food items. Like Myron, he had come to Berlin from the Ukraine to study architecture a year before the war broke out. Although he was twenty-nine years old, I found him attractive. His eyes were slanted like Aunt Oda's and were just as green. His dark blond hair was wavy and thick and fell into his face when he laughed. Sometimes Myron joined us for tea, which Oma brewed. We had delicious black Russian tea—with compliments from Sergei. The men poured vodka into their cups, and Oma and I sweetened ours with a tea-spoonful of honey. Myron often brought his guitar, and the two men sang mournful Russian melodies. Sometimes Sergei got up and danced, crouch-ing on the floor with his legs shooting out in rapid succession, while his arms remained folded over his chest. His body had the right balance be-tween athleticism and grace, like a ballet dancer's. I loved watching his movements. When he finished, all out of breath, I applauded, then he would pick me up and whirl me about. He joked with me and called me his little sister. But his eyes twinkled, and he'd say silly things like, "When you're six-teen I'll spirit you away and marry you."

"Should you not ask me first?"

"No, my little princess. I'll come on a white horse and pick you up and away we'll ride."

How did he know my fantasies of white horses? I reminded myself that my fantasies also included a Spanish count, and that he was Russian. But he caused me to shiver a little when he looked at me in a certain way.

The food he brought came from the black market. Little by little, Mother and Oma traded whatever we could spare—opera glasses, magnifying glasses, clocks, and jewelry—for food. Sometimes Sergei brought cigarettes, and these were kept in lieu of currency in a carved box, to be traded in the future for labor, to pay someone to chop firewood for our little black stove. Cigarettes were slowly replacing the German reichsmark as currency, since the mark was practically worthless. Oma introduced Sergei to Frau Schlos-ser and to other women, and he sold their jewelry as well. Sergei would reward Oma for making these introductions by bringing us an extra Polish sausage or loaf of bread.

Had it not been for Sergei, we would have starved.

The Americans had introduced new ration cards, but the food allowed us was just above starvation level. It was estimated that a person needed about twenty-three hundred calories a day to maintain their muscles and to go on living. Now rations were classified in categories related to the work a person performed. I suppose it was a fair system, based on the calories expended daily by the body and the type and amount of work a person did. Coalminers received the highest rations—of course, we didn't know any coalminers in Berlin—then the *Schwerarbeiter,* or heavy laborers. Included in this group were university professors and mathematicians, people who used their minds. Next were office workers and so forth, who were issued light workers rations. Nonworkers, such as Mother and Oma, received the lowest rations, based on about nine hundred calories a day. Since I was a child, my rations were a little bit higher. The difference was in the milk and extra butter rations I received.

Soon after the first electric trams rolled down our streets and the S-Bahn and U-Bahn were running again, we visited Tante Wanda and Uncle Victor. They had been our wealthy relatives, but they were now hungrier than we. They did not know a Sergei, and their family consisted of four adults who all drew minimum ration cards. Tante Wanda had never greeted Oma more warmly than she did that day, when we arrived with a large loaf of bread.

The farms surrounding Berlin were now in the Russian zone, and farmers were obliged to supply the Russian army with the food they grew, which made it difficult for us to trade with the farmers as we had earlier. In the fall, Oma and I still took the train to a little outlying village where we knew a farmer who would exchange cigarettes for potatoes and carrots. But by trading, we all risked arrest.

But soon after the Americans entered Berlin, Mother, because of her fluency in English—not because of her homemaking skills—got a job working as a housekeeper for an American colonel. Oma and I had snickered behind her back. Oma could not believe she found this particular work. Of course, it was not her "choice," but Mother was willing to scrub floors so Oma and I could eat. We should not have laughed.

Mother now moved into a higher category of ration cards, and since she lived at the American's house and ate most of her meals there, Oma and I were able to use her rations as well.

Oma doubted Mother would last any time at all doing this kind of work. When I was little, we'd had a nanny for me and a maid for the household.

Then when I was older, we had cleaning women who did the heavy work. After we were bombed out, it was Oma who had cooked and ironed with my help. It was I who threw our Persian runner onto the long metal rod in the courtyard and beat the dirt out of it with a wicker whisk; and it was I who hung our laundry up to dry, making a game by color matching it in patterns as I went along the clothesline with the wooden pins stuck in my mouth. I had cooked simple meals and made jams and caramel candies with Oma, and I felt qualified to work as a housekeeper. But Mother? I believed I could do the work, but I was too young.

At first, Mother complained about her situation. She felt déclassé—she used this word often—cleaning the home of one of our conquerors. She was usually tired and depressed, and on her day off, she would complain that her job was demeaning. Oma would gently tell her, "Astrid, honest work is never demeaning. I would work as a toilet woman if I had to."

Weeks went by, and Mother kept working in Dahlem for the colonel. He occupied an elegant one-story villa we called a "bungalow"; its design was an imitation of American one-storied homes. The villa was requisitioned from its owners, Max Schmeling, the former world heavy-weight boxing champion, and Anny Ondra, his film star wife. Mother had allowed me to visit on a day when the colonel was out of town.

Every child knew who Max Schmeling was: a superstar boxer who had once defeated Joe Louis in America. He later lost to Louis in a rematch. People reported that Hitler had been extremely angry when his German "superhero" lost to a Negro.

Standing in the house Max Schmeling had built, I felt in awe. The house was all very grand, but also strange because it was made up of two separate halves that mirrored each other. In the center were the main living room and the kitchen, but off to the side was a dainty salon that had been Anny Ondra's. Otherwise, the house had two wings: a his and a hers. The colonel occupied Max Schmeling's rooms, which were furnished with leather sofas and carved woods. His bedroom was decorated in warm brown colors and led to an adjoining brown marble bathroom. Then there was Anny Ondra's bedroom, the feminine opposite of Max's. Her room was all frills in pink and peach, like ever so much whipped cream over strawberries. Dainty Meissen figurines danced on the peach-colored marble mantle of the fireplace, and the gilt-edged mirrors reflected the room's satin and lace. I tried to imagine the massive figure of the boxer visiting his blonde beauty in her bedroom, and I giggled when I pictured him stretched out among the many fluffy pillows beneath the draped silken curtains cascading from the bed's canopy. Maybe that's what he liked, dainty frills for a brief while, and then back again to the unadorned comforts of his own rooms.

Now Anny Ondra's rooms were left unused. In the large living room, I leafed through the photo albums still lying on the coffee table, as if the Schmelings would come through the door at any moment. There were photos of Max's trips to the United States and scribbled notes about how he loved America and all things American. Maybe that's where he got the idea for his American-style home. I admired Anny Ondra's fragile and piquant beauty, and I wondered where she was living now. She was probably in Bavaria, where most prominent citizens had spent the last years of the war. And where was he, the great boxer? I wondered what he would think of an American colonel living in his house?

Much later I learned more about Max Schmeling's life. He was born on September 28, 1905, and died on February 2, 2005. He was awarded the highest German medal in 1971, the Grosse Bundesverdienstkreuz. In 1991, he became the first German to be inducted into the Boxing Hall of Fame in the United States.

In the late 1930s, the Nazis had ordered him to divorce his Czechoslovakian wife, but he refused. The Nazis also tried to have him fire his Jewish manager, Joe Jacobs, but again he refused. In fact, because of his fame, he was able to help several of his Jewish friends escape from Germany. On November 8–9, 1938, *Kristallnacht,* he hid two Jewish youths in his house. In 1941, as a soldier, he was seriously wounded while parachuting into Crete, which was then occupied by the British. After two years in hospitals, he was discharged from the army in 1943 and spent the last two years of the war as a civilian liaison in prisoner of war camps. From 1946 until his death at almost one hundred, he lived in Hamburg.

Many of Mother's friends had still not returned from the West where they had fled from the bombs and the advancing Russians. Mother made new friends, one of whom was Ursula, a woman twelve years younger than she, who came to visit us on Sundays, Mother's day off. Ursula had long, light blonde hair, which she wore tied in a ponytail. She was tall and statuesque. One day she seemed nervous and eager for Oma and me to leave the room so she could talk to Mother about her boyfriend. We left, but I pressed my ear to the door to eavesdrop.

"He told me he loves me, but he said he could never marry me or take me back to the States," Ursula sniffled, blowing her nose.

"Of course not. There is supposed to be no fraternization. But this won't last. Things will change, maybe he will be able to in another year?"

"No. Never. He told me he is Jewish. When he said that, he watched me, expecting me to say something. I said, 'So? I could marry you. Germany is no longer a Nazi state.' That's when he said, 'But *you* are German. Germans did such awful things to Jews. I could never take you home to my parents. They'd disown me.' "

" 'But Harry', I said, 'Wouldn't they understand, I had nothing to do with all of that. I'm not a Nazi. We love each other. That's what's important.' "

I listened at the door, wondering what Mother would say. I would have told Ursula that Harry's parents were foolish. Ursula didn't hurt anyone. But his parents were far away in America. They didn't know. They thought all Germans were monsters. It gave me chills to think that so many people in other countries would now think we Germans were all guilty of Hitler's crimes.

I went on listening. Mother was quiet, not her usual talkative self. Then she said, "Ursula, are you so sure you want to marry this Harry? Aren't you a bit more infatuated with the captain's uniform than with the man?"

"I love him, even though he is a little odd. He spends more time with his Böcklin train set than he does with me."

Aha, I thought—loving electric trains myself—and made a mental note to ask Ursula to take me along some day to meet her boyfriend and his trains.

Then Ursula contracted typhoid fever and had to be hospitalized in a quarantine ward. But Mother visited her, against regulations and without regard to her own health or ours or anyone else's.

"Imagine," Mother announced, when she got home from the hospital, "Ursula has lost all of her hair. Her long beautiful hair. She said it came out in bushels." Mother shuddered. "She'd run a comb through it and find herself with a handful of hair in her palm. Ursula wept. She looked like a little bald child. Pathetic. Karin," Mother turned to me, "do you know where my orange scarf is, the one you wore during the Russian weeks? I promised to bring it to her."

"I'll get it," I said, rushing off to find it.

A few days later Mother went to inform Harry about Ursula's illness and took me along. His apartment was in Zehlendorf, which had for the most part been spared from the bombs. A tall, muscular man in his midtwenties opened the door. His hair was short and of a deep brown. He smiled and asked us to come in. The news about Ursula's illness shocked him, for a moment he had no words, and the smile left his face.

I liked this man, who said, "Call me Harry."

When we entered, I found his apartment spacious but dark. I almost stumbled over the tracks of a train set. Then I saw them: trains, trains everywhere. The doors to other rooms were left open, and train tracks ran from the entry hall to the living room, to the dining room, and to the kitchen. They made a circle in the kitchen and then ran into what must have been a bedroom. It boggled my mind to find so many tracks and trains and all of the accessories one would find in a Böcklin store. There was an entire town set up within the crisscrossing of tracks. There were miniature houses with red slanted roofs, looking as if someone had put little triangular hats onto their square shapes, round balls of trees pretending to shade houses, and long elliptical trees, looking like poplars, framing imaginary streets. There was a tiny train station and an entire town center with a city hall, a fountain, and a perfectly proportioned little red brick church with a gray steeple crowned by a silvery cross. My mouth must have dropped open as my eyes tried to take it all in.

The captain asked us to wait in the living room, while he went into the kitchen to pack up oranges, cookies, and chocolate bars for Mother to take to Ursula. He said we could keep some of the oranges and candies for ourselves.

I pointed out to Mother that several tracks allowed trains to pass each other from different directions. I was in awe. When the captain returned with the gifts for Ursula, I was on my knees, examining a locomotive. He smiled. "Would you like to see them run?" he asked. Would I? Was he joking, or kidding, as Americans would say?

Soon locomotives chugged along, puffing clouds of smoke; an engine tooted as another train came from the opposite direction and gathered speed. I held my breath, afraid they would crash. Harry smiled again and said, "Not to worry, it's all under control." And indeed, in the last moment, the first train switched to another track and the trains passed each other. It was all so real, I half expected to see tiny people walk out of miniature doors.

After more than thirty minutes had passed, Mother motioned for me to get up and say good-bye. I stood up slowly and thanked the captain for the fun I'd had, and he told Mother to bring me again, for another run with the trains.

When we boarded the U-Bahn for home, Mother said, "Amazing what Americans can get for their cigarettes."

"You mean Harry? You think he bought those Böcklin trains with cigarettes?"

"He doesn't smoke. That makes him a rich man. No one I ever knew, even the wealthy Finkensteins in Prittag, owned sets like those. And now, an overgrown boy like Harry is able to buy them with his cigarette rations. To the victor . . ."

After Ursula was released from the hospital, she moved in with us during her convalescing stage. Oma had volunteered to take care of her. The captain contacted Mother, asking if he could visit Ursula at our house. No one knew how to tell him that she was bald and didn't want to see him. The poor guy, he probably thought she had met another man. I wanted to tell him the truth and have him be patient until her hair grew back, but more than anything else, I would have liked to visit him to play with the trains. But Mother thought it was better if he didn't know about the hair. Ursula's hair had been one of her major assets.

Ursula, in a hurry to regrow her treasure, resorted to the most disgusting methods. She caught her urine in a bowl and poured it over her scalp. She also asked Oma for onions, which she diced and massaged onto her baldness. The smell left much to be desired, but the unctions worked. Her hair grew back fast, thick and glossy.

A little more than a month went by, then the captain came to pick up Ursula. I could see the surprise in his eyes when he saw her, with hair shorter than a boy's, but thick and white blonde as a wheat field in summer and just as shiny. She took his hand and a smile returned to his face when he ran his fingers over her peltlike hair. He caressed her face. She leaned against his chest, whispering, "I'd lost it all. I was bald. Bald. I didn't want you to see me like that."

He gently lifted up her chin and brushed her lips with his. "I told you I love you. Long hair is nice, but . . . ," then he laughed. "Mother would appreciate you bald. We're Orthodox. Mom doesn't have any hair, she shaves it and wears wigs."

"What?" said Ursula.

"Yes, we're Orthodox Jews. Once a woman is married, she shaves her hair."

Later, I was delighted when Ursula invited me to Harry's place to play with the trains. But the following week, her eyes were red and I could see she'd been crying. "Harry has orders to ship back to the States," she said. "Once he's home, he'll forget me." She looked over her shoulder to make sure we were alone. "He's very attached to his mother," she whispered. "If his mother won't allow this marriage, then he'll forget me. You know what he's looking forward to? To his first night home. That night he gets to sleep in the same bed with his mother. Isn't that strange?"

Yes, it did seem a bit strange. I couldn't quite picture this tall, masculine-looking U.S. captain crawling into the same bed with his mother. Wasn't that something little boys did? Maybe he was just a little boy in uniform. That's why I had so much fun with him, playing with his trains.

After Harry went home, he wrote to Ursula a few times and had a buddy deliver the letters to her. But then the letters stopped. Soon Harry's "friend" began taking Ursula sailing on the Wannsee, to restaurants, and to his apartment. Harry and his trains were forgotten by Ursula but not by me. I missed them both.

A ROOM OF MY OWN

I now had a room of my own. It was one of the small attic rooms on the third floor that formerly had been maids' quarters. From my window I could look out into the garden and have my eyes bathe in the green of shrubs. I enjoyed looking at the yellow and orange of the dahlias, piercing the fog of early autumn like small flames, and the cream and crimson of the chrysanthemums, and I reveled in the last of the deep pink peonies.

But I am getting ahead of myself. Toward the end of summer we had moved from the two rooms in Frau Kuhnert's apartments to a three-story villa in the suburb of Nikolassee, near the Schlachtensee, one of the many lakes surrounding Berlin. The house belonged to a distant relative, Sabine von Schmidt, on my grandmother's side of the family, the von Hakes. The family had fled the bombing of Berlin and moved to a chalet they owned in Bavaria. Our move was to the Schmidts' advantage and a stroke of good luck for us. The housing authority had partially filled the villa with refugee families from East Prussia and, with Oma's pleading, had allowed us to move from the British sector to this villa in the American sector. Here we could look after our relatives' property.

It was a hot summer, but here in the suburbs, among the many trees, the temperature was pleasant and the flies did not pester. The inner-city flies were huge that year. If they had been fewer, I might have thought of them as exotic insects or even found beauty in them. They were of an iridescent green, picking up golden sparks in the sunlight. But they buzzed close to our faces like Stuka bombers and tried to get into any food left uncovered. Oma said they had bred from maggots. I remembered the woman's head without a face and knew what maggots fed on.

Mutti had fastened fly catchers everywhere, those long dangling yellow snakes of gummy paper. But Mutti was often not home when the yellow turned black from dead flies and looked like a lasso an evil magician might whirl above his head. I did not like touching them, and I left them hanging until Mother came home. But sometimes I was in a hurry and, flitting about the room, got my hair caught on the sticky stuff. Oma rescued me, but I could see the flies repulsed her as much as they did me.

There was no need for fly catchers in our new home.

I loved the house, the garden, and the space, and I loved being near woods and lakes.

The drawback was the bathroom situation: the people sharing the second floor had bathrooms with bathtubs, but we only had the guest toilet for our use on the ground floor. There was a small toilet near my room, but during the winter, the pipes froze and I had to go all the way downstairs.

Four tenants, one married couple and two spinsters—refugees from the East—had occupied the second floor since late 1944. They were decent people, and they had taken care of the house. We had use of the entire ground floor. The kitchen was large and had several pantries that remained pitifully empty of food. It had the most up-to-date electric stainless steel stove and oven. But we couldn't use any of them, since the electricity was on only at certain hours, and even then it was rationed.

The house had a large foyer with a wide staircase. On the upper floor, bedrooms and one sitting room circled a wide landing. The children's rooms were located far from the stairs and the master bedroom. Above this floor were the dormer rooms where I had found my cherished haven.

The staircase led to the upper floor from the left side of the foyer. Its steps were made of a golden wood, and it had a gleaming banister that Oma forbade me to use as a slide. Between the kitchen and living room was a formal dining room with walls covered by a green-gray silk upon which were painted murals depicting flowers and fruit. Oma had a key to this room, and she kept it locked, since it contained silver, china, and table linens. To the right of the entry was a narrow hall leading to the guest toilet. Tall, mirrored guests' closets lined this corridor. Two forgotten lambs hung on satin hangers. Actually, they were Persian lamb fur coats, one gray and one black, waiting for their owners to return.

This former guest toilet, with its hand-tooled leather-and-gold-imprinted wall coverings and dark brown marble floor and matching basin with gilded spigots, was now our elegant bathroom. Rather it was our elegant toilet, because there was no shower or bathtub. One of the spinsters, Fräulein Hemet, quartered in one of the Schmidts' children's rooms, was kind and let us use her bathtub. But in the winter the water from the faucet was ice cold, and I would have to augment it with scalding water I carried up in a black cauldron.

Directly across the foyer was the living room. When we first visited the house and Mother had opened the doors to the living room, she had clapped her hands as if she were Carmen and whirled around with a renewed sparkle in her eyes when she saw the ebony Bechstein concert grand. Soon she would have Veronika and Karl Wolfram and other singers and musician friends gather for a musical evening.

The room's French doors opened onto a terrace with a stone balustrade. One side of the living room adjoined a conservatory with three walls of glass overlooking the garden. Mother slept here on a daybed, soft with cushioned chintz echoing the flowers outside her windows. In the winter, when it was cold, she would move inside and sleep on a sofa in an alcove, next to the huge stone fireplace. The fireplace shared a wall to Oma's room, the former library. It was cozy to climb into bed with Oma surrounded by the many leather-bound books. When I gazed out of her window, I looked straight into the branches of a weeping willow tree, where I watched a thrush hop from limb to limb as I listened to its song.

Wide steps led from the stone terrace into the garden. Now in late summer, the garden was a riot of color. Our drab world of gray had been transformed as if by magic into a fairy tale with colored illustrations.

I entered school again. It was high time for me because I had missed almost an entire year of classes. I was twelve years old, and even though I had lost schooling, I was now in the *Untertertia,* the right class for my age. The lyceum was a short walk from home, and I soon made friends. But almost immediately I had a run-in with one of my teachers. We were studying the Reformation in my history class, when the Dominican monk Johann Tetzel came up. Tetzel was infamous for his methods of selling indulgences and had coined the phrase "When the coin in the coffer rings, the soul from purgatory springs"—*Wenn das Geld im Kaestchen klingt, die Seele in den Himmel springt.* Tetzel was tricked by a poor robber knight named Hans Stulpe von Hake, who, when he encountered the monk on a narrow country path, asked, "How much will it cost to buy an indulgence for a crime not yet committed?" "Why," the monk said, scratching his beard, "that would cost double, sir." So done. The knight bought his indulgence and off he rode around the bend. When the monk came around a rocky outcropping, the knight clubbed him over the head and stole the entire box containing all of the indulgence money Tetzel had so far collected. He then pinned the indulgence for "a crime not yet committed" to the black cassock of the monk.

When the teacher read us this story—one of our favorite family stories—I could not restrain myself, and I blurted out, "Hans Stulpe von Hake is my ancestor."

The teacher's face grew red, then purple, making me think she'd explode. She chided me for being an outrageous liar and sent me home.

Oma came to my rescue. To the school she trudged to confront the teacher. She straightened her spine, growing an inch or two, and said, "My granddaughter does not lie. I am Elsa von Hake Keller, and Hans Stulpe von Hake is indeed my direct ancestor. You owe Karin an apology. And please apologize in front of the class."

The teacher stared at the worn wooden boards of the floor as if she were looking for a dropped coin, apologized first to my grandmother, then went back into the classroom with me and apologized to me in front of my class-mates. All the while she glowered at me, and from that day on, I never could do anything right. She almost succeeded in making me hate history, which had been one of my favorite subjects.

The Lumina Theater was about a fifteen-minute walk from our house. I loved to go to the movies, to go into a dark place and be transported into a different world. Oma often told me I shouldn't spend my allowance on such foolish pleasures. She thought I should rather rent more books from the pri-vately operated library. I managed to do both, read voraciously and go to the movies. I was surprised therefore when I came home from school and Oma told me to get ready, we were all going to the Lumina to see a movie.

I should have known something was wrong. When we arrived at the the-ater, Mother was waiting for us, waving our tickets. She had come home early from work. Women and a few men crowded around the entrance. I said hello to a few of my classmates milling about with their mothers. What was going on? Official-looking women sat at tables and scribbled on paper forms.

We entered the theater and found three seats together. The Lumina filled to capacity in no time. I had argued with Mother, who was nearsighted and wanted to sit close, that she knew I was farsighted and had to sit in the back. She had glasses to correct her vision, I didn't. "You might not want to see this film that clearly," Oma said. This puzzled me even more, since I had no idea of what we were going to see. The theater's marquee had been a blank slate of white.

Then came the shock.

The film was a documentary about concentration camps, about the sights the Allies had encountered when they liberated Auschwitz, Bergen Belsen, Dachau, and Birkenau. The film showed horrors more frightening than any horror movie could produce: the living skeletons of Dachau and the heaped skeletons of the dead at Auschwitz, the interior of barracks where the inmates had lived, and the extermination ovens. There was footage of rooms filled with shoes and rooms filled with women's hair. All of this—the shoes and the hair—was to be used at a later date; we Germans practicing utility among the horror. I covered my eyes most of the time, but curiosity made me peek through spread fingers. But then the horror overwhelmed me again and I squeezed my eyes shut. I fought to keep my stomach from turning and wanted desperately to relieve myself in the toilet, but I could not push through the many people seated in our row. There was no escape.

When the film finally ended and we left the theater, our reason for being there became clear to me. Mother went first, then Oma and me, to the table where the female officials exchanged our theater stubs for next month's ration cards.

"They certainly know how to punish us," Mother said.

"And to think that we had no idea," said Oma, sighing. "But you are wrong, Astrid. The film was shown to have the truth made known. Not to punish. We've all denied the death camps. I too could not imagine those horrors," Oma said. She blew her nose and wiped her cheeks. She went on, "Tell me, how many would see this movie of their own free will? It was clever to force it on us with the ration cards."

Soon winter came, and it began to rain. Cold and damp penetrated the thick stone walls of the house, hung to the inside of the walls, and clung to my bed sheets. Even my woolen sweaters felt clammy and refused to keep me warm. Despite Mother's additional rations, we still had little food or wood for the fire. On Mother's day off, she and I stole into partially bombed buildings at night, carrying a saw, and cut down mahogany banisters from stairwells that had remained standing. The wood didn't burn very well, but it was better than nothing. We also cut down a few small trees, but that wood was much too green, and its acrid smoke made us cough. Our rations allowed us a small allotment of coal, which we used in the iron kitchen stove. There we heated water, cooked, and gathered in the evening. Oma had bought a galvanized tub, like the ones people had used in earlier times to wash clothes before washing machines. She heated water on the stove for my weekly bath. While I bathed, Oma splashed water over me, laughing and singing "Yankee Doodle Dandy" and other American songs, since she said it reminded her of her days in Utah. Modern conveniences were of no use now. In contrast, items we discovered in the poorer areas of Berlin were now worth their weight in—no, not gold—cigarettes. A fifty-year-old iron, into which one had to insert red-hot coals, cost a few cigarettes and enabled me to iron my clothes during the blackouts.

My room remained cold, but as an extra treat Oma sometimes came up with the hot iron and passed it over my sheets—to take away the clamminess—just before I crawled under my two featherbeds that kept me warm.

The blackouts added to our depression, scheduled as they were during the early evening, when people needed light. But the hours were posted in the newspaper, and I often set my alarm clock to wake me up at three in the morning when I knew the power would be on for two hours so I could iron my clothes, without burning myself, using an electric iron and do my homework for school.

The days got shorter and colder. Soon it would be Christmas. Oma still welcomed Sergei and his gifts of sausages and other foods. He kept ogling me in a strange way, and though when I first met him I had thought him attractive, I developed a dislike for him. Maybe I was influenced by what I'd heard eavesdropping. Some time ago, before we moved, a neighbor had said to Mother, "You should not associate with this Sergei. He's a 'one hundred and seventy-fiver.'"

I wondered what that meant and asked Oma. She shook her head and in turn asked Mother. Mother explained that it was a paragraph in the German penal code. Oma wanted to know what that paragraph dealt with. Mother dismissed Oma's question, saying that the woman was confused and that it was a paragraph punishable under Hitler, and after all, Hitler was now history. It had to do with perversions and homosexuality. "What's that, Astrid?" Oma asked. Mother blushed and said it was related to men loving men. "Oh, bah, it's always been that way," said Oma. "Even Alexander the Great and Hephaiston were inseparable. Many great men have had close friendships with men."

Mother rolled her eyes and patted Oma on the arm. "You're such an innocent."

I also rolled my eyes but only in imitation of Mother, since I had no idea what they were talking about. But something in the way Sergei looked at me made me feel uncomfortable. He was handsome and turned women's heads. Why did he like me? I was practically still a child. When he tried to kiss me, edging his moist lips along my cheek toward my mouth, I pushed him away.

Sergei brought us a Christmas tree, some Russian cookies, and pirogue, a potato dumpling filled with meat. He brought me a blue and gray plaid woolen dress, not new. It was bought on the black market, but it was a good dress and exactly my size. He gave Oma a pair of woolen brown stockings and Mutti a warm scarf. Sergei loved horses and Oma gave him a framed copper etching of a hussar on a rearing horse. The day after Christmas he arrived feverish. Oma took his temperature and shook her head: the thermometer read 103. She told him he couldn't go out in the cold wind but had to spend the night with us. Mother left late for work, braving the icy wind to get back to the colonel's house. Oma made up a bed for Sergei on the sofa in front of the large fireplace. He seemed content and smiled at me.

Sergei cooled down the hot peppermint tea Oma had brewed for him by diluting it with a large amount of vodka. He picked the cup up between his thumb and his index finger, spreading the other three fingers like a fan. I thought he looked silly. *Affektiert.* Then Oma brought in a glass of water and two aspirins, which she made Sergei swallow. He looked comfortable when I left him to brush my teeth. Oma went to bed, but then I heard Sergei moan. I went back into his room to see if he needed anything.

"Come here, my princess," he whispered. He didn't look sick to me, though his skin was flushed, maybe from the fever. "Do you want me to get well?" he asked.

"Yes. Of course."

"Then you come here and kiss me."

I bent down and gave him a quick kiss on the forehead. "Goodnight," I said.

He grabbed my arm. "That's not a proper kiss. Here." By now he'd thrown off the blanket and I saw what I had only seen on my baby brother, but here it looked like a pink-skinned rat, small, wiggling, changing shape, getting larger. I closed my eyes as he pulled me closer. He pushed my head down and said, "There, kiss me there, go ahead, it won't bite you."

I jerked myself free and ran from the room, slamming the door behind me, not caring who heard it.

No one heard it. I heard only loud snoring noises coming from Oma's bed.

The next morning Oma wondered why I refused to bring breakfast to Sergei. I didn't tell her why. She put the teapot, cup, and plate with bread and jam on a small tray. When she knocked on the door, Sergei did not answer. Oma turned to me with a puzzled expression on her face. "I wonder if he's all right?" Then she opened the door a crack, calling out, "Sergei? Are you awake?" No answer. She opened the door a little wider. "Sergei?"

All the while I shifted from foot to foot, afraid of what Sergei would say.

Oma pushed the door fully open and entered the room. The blankets were folded, and the pillows were fluffed and placed at the head of the sofa. Sergei was gone.

When Mother came home I told her what had happened. She hugged me and said she was proud of me. I had handled the situation the proper way. Then she berated herself for not having paid heed to the woman's gossip, but the more she talked, the more she got all worked up, calling Sergei a pervert and a child molester.

I felt guilty somehow. I should have woken Oma up. But what could Oma have done? We had no telephone. The police station was kilometers away. Mutti and I realized how little we knew about Sergei. He had been a good friend, but it had never occurred to us to ask personal questions. We realized that we didn't know where he lived, not even his last name. We only knew that he was Myron's friend.

"Oma is such an innocent," Mother said, "Don't tell her."

"But when he doesn't come back, she'll wonder what happened."

"She'll think he was arrested for dealing on the black market. Let's leave it at that."

CHAPTER 12

Black Bread and Song,
White Bread and Tears

WINTER–SPRING 1946

In January 1946, icy winds from the Russian steppes brought even colder weather, and now, without Sergei, we really suffered from hunger. I hated getting out of bed to go to school and stayed in the warmth as long as I could, until Oma, still huffing from having mounted two flights of stairs, would drag me out of the feathers by force. There was nothing in the day to look forward to, certainly not breakfast, which consisted of a slice of dry black bread, often burnt on the stove, and a cup of *mucke-fuck*. Sometimes Oma made oatmeal just for me. I wanted her to have some too, but she'd used my milk rations in the making and refused to eat even a bite.

But today was not a day for oatmeal because Mother was giving her first musical party tonight. I was excited. Oma was already busy with food preparations in the kitchen. She was making small cakes baked in half-moon shapes and filled with bits of black market cheese and a savory mush made from rutabaga and potatoes. Mother had bought a small black stove to aid the fireplace in heating the large living room, and we had purchased extra coal and some wood. Guests would bring along vodka. The house would be filled with singers and musicians, toting violins and wind instruments. And Mother had invited the Wolframs.

Veronika Wolfram—Mother's friend since her student days in Berlin—and her husband, Karl, formed the core of what would grow into a group. I looked forward to seeing them in our house, since Mutti and Oma had recently taken me to hear *Peleas and Melisande,* the fairy-tale opera by Ravel, which had not been performed during the Hitler years. By now I had learned that "our" Führer had a limited taste in music, favoring heroic Wagnerian operas.

That night the Wolframs arrived by car, a vehicle made available to them during Karl's engagement singing Peleas. My young eyes stared in admiration at Veronika when she swept into the house. She had golden hair (her hairdresser had discovered a tint that made her hair look as if it were spun of the glistening metal), a narrow patrician nose, and large blue eyes fanned by what I believe were thick false lashes. She wore a velvet gown of a rich emerald color, complete with a trailing train. The slim, long sleeves formed little points on her white hands. I noticed her high cleavage and ample bosom that she quickly concealed by tossing a silver fox stole around her shoulders. I wondered if she wore the fur so high on her neck because she wanted to keep her throat warm or because she wanted to cover up her décolleté. She kept herself wrapped in the fur when she entered the living room and later when she sang. I stared in fascination at the bouncing fox tails, dangling from the hem of the stole, dancing on her derriere in rhythm to the music.

At six feet four Karl Wolfram towered above the other guests, and his sonorous voice filled not only the room but also the house. His voice could even be heard far down the street, as it had when he "sang" the *Fliegeralarm,* the air-raid warning, when we still lived in Steglitz. There he had fooled the tenants, sending them into the cellar in the middle of the night. This had awakened Oma, and she had chided the adults for their infantile behavior and forced Karl Wolfram to give the all clear signal in his huge voice that carried into the basement. Footsteps could again be heard as neighbors scurried back upstairs to get some much needed sleep. We were lucky, because no one ever found out that the "alarm" had come from our apartment. Mother would certainly have been punished by the authorities for that sort of mischief.

Veronika was not the only one who looked theatrical. Karl Wolfram wore a long, black coat that made him look like an illustration of a vampire. The coat had a capelike collar, and around his neck, he'd tossed a fringed, cream-colored silk scarf. I knew singers had to keep their necks warm, but a simple woolen scarf would have done the job. Still, I liked Wolfram. His size, his coat, and his scarf all reinforced my idea of what an opera singer should look like.

And I appreciated Veronika for dressing like a diva, even when only performing in our home. Oma said that by dressing up, Veronika was paying her respect to the Muse; Mother said Veronika thought of herself as a diva, though that status had sadly eluded her. She found engagements in minor opera houses and small town concert halls, while her husband had risen to fame mainly in Wagnerian roles. His booming bass-baritone, his "instrument," was in high demand.

Mother had given parties when the Wolframs had no car available to them, and like everyone else, they had to take the S-Bahn. Veronika then simply tucked the train of her gown into her belt, took off her high-heeled satin pumps, and pulled on thick socks and rubber boots. This impressed me to no end. There were times when she was the embodiment of elegance, but she could also be both practical and down-to-earth.

During those evenings, when the musical troupe assembled in the Schopenhauer Strasse, I asked Oma if I could sleep with her in the library. I liked to listen to the music making and the singing as I drifted off to sleep.

Most of the songs sounded sad, but I also heard laughter through the wall. But for some reason I didn't think it was happiness that brought forth the music. It seemed more like a banding together or a seeking of comfort that brought these artists to our house, the same type of comfort I sought in Oma's bed.

Mother kept repeating that she had a sense of disconnection from the real world. Maybe the others felt the same way. No one knew what the "real world" was in those postwar days. A few theaters had opened, and the philharmonic and the opera gave limited performances, presenting the people with a degree of normalcy, but most did not feel "normal." Berliners walked as if they were the disembodied spirits of their former selves, floating in gray.

It was most apparent on the streets. Recently I had gone to Halensee, our old neighborhood, on an errand. I noticed men and women ambling about with no regard to vehicles on the street. Traffic was light, since Germans had no private cars, but there were occasional trucks and military vehicles one had to watch out for. On that particular day, I saw a small British truck hit a man. The man fell and the driver cursed at him. Then the man got up and limped off, and I was relieved that he didn't appear seriously injured. But I hoped that he'd learned his lesson and would look before crossing a street.

Berliners were all ambling through life without looking. Mother and her friends needed these parties to keep their eyes open, to keep sane.

It was not easy to feed the guests. When there were only a few people, Oma sometimes served a thin potato and onion soup with toasted black bread (we held the slices into the fire, practically burning the bread). At other times, she cut the toasted black bread into small squares to make it resemble cake and topped it with the only jam available to us, *Vierfrucht Marmelade*. The jam, as the name implied, was to have been made of four fruits, but I suspect it had red beets and other horrible edibles mixed in with a hint of perhaps semirotten apples and pears. The reddish brown jam tasted bitter, but the guests didn't mind. They poured great amounts of vodka into their tea, immunizing their taste buds to the flavor of the bread and jam.

Meanwhile fingers pounded the black and white keys on the Bechstein more vehemently, voices grew louder, and the songs more boisterous. I wondered why no one in the house complained about the noise. Was it because they regarded these occasional musical orgies as something strange and wonderful, as I did, or was it because we were related to the owners of the villa?

Then one day, Lilly Penske came to one of the parties. Mother had become friends with her when they first met at the Anhalter Bahnhof, when her much younger sister, Erika, and I were sent to school in Marienbad. Mother and Lilly had much in common and both were aspiring singers.

Lilly embraced me, as she sang out in her booming alto voice, "I am so very happy to see you!" When she saw Oma, she dashed to her, lifted her up, and swirled her around the room. Oma screeched, half hating this demonstrative behavior, half loving it. Mutti smiled, as she nodded toward Oma, and said, "Yes, this is our old Lilly. Right? She never changes."

"Are you back in Berlin now?" I asked.

"Yes, my sweet. And so is Erika. The whole family is together again. You must visit us soon, promise? Erika would be happy to see you."

The Penskes' apartment in Steglitz, the heavily bombed section of town where we had lost everything, had miraculously survived the war. After our miserable stay in Marienbad, Erika had refused to be evacuated with the school again. Frau Penske, Lilly, and Erika—all but Herr Penske—had found a safe haven in Bavaria. Now they were back in Berlin.

I went to visit Erika. Lilly was not home, but Erika and her parents were happy to see me. Their kitchen was welcoming and cozy, and Frau Penske brewed a fragrant black tea, which she served with my favorite, amber-colored rock sugar. She opened the cupboard and the tantalizing aroma of fresh white bread wafted through the room. I had almost forgotten the sweet and fragrant scent of bread. The light golden crust invited me to sink my teeth into it, and I had to swallow the saliva gathering in my mouth. Frau Penske took a slice and held it over the flame above the round ring in the grate of the black iron stove. I was afraid she'd burn it, but no, it toasted just slightly, which released more of the aroma of golden wheat and of heaven. The scent of the bread triggered the memory of pent-up hunger. It had been so long. I could hardly wait for the bread to reach my mouth. I again inhaled deeply, and then I couldn't help myself, tears ran down my cheeks as Frau Penske buttered this thick, now slightly toasted, bread. I wept even more when she took a spoon and spread orange marmalade onto the butter. She offered me the slice on a small china plate.

"Karin, why are you crying, dear?" she asked.

"I'm so happy. So happy to be getting something this good," I said.

"Then eat. And drink your tea."

My hand flew toward the plate, then I stopped, not wanting to seem too eager.

"Eat, go ahead, eat," she repeated.

I watched as she toasted slices for Erika, Herr Penske, and herself. I was overwhelmed by the bread, the sumptuous butter, and the extravagance of the orange marmalade. Tears kept running into the corner of my mouth making me taste salt while I chewed.

Frau Penske turned, seemingly embarrassed by my display of emotion at the sight of food. She told me, almost apologetically, that her sister sent English money to her from London, and she had permission to buy a certain amount of food in the British commissary, since she was still a British citizen.

When I left, Frau Penske handed me a brown paper bag. The bag smelled so good that I didn't need to open it to know that a loaf of bread was inside. Once again moved by Frau Penske's kindness, I wept.

"For all of you," she said. "*Auf Wiedersehn.*"

ZIGARETTEN

Oma untied the satin bowknot on her little black velvet pouch, opening the flaps to reveal what was left of her jewelry. There was her pearl necklace and the gold brooch given to her by friends in Salt Lake City as a memento of America. She would never part with the latter. There were some other small pieces and my favorite pair of earrings. These dangling earrings were intricately wrought jewels my grandfather had bought in Budapest, while Oma and he attended a cousin's wedding. Oma wore them only once, to complement a dark rose-colored satin gown, because she thought that they were too flamboyant for Germany and for her age. She was thirty-five at the time and felt old, even though her flirtatious Hungarian cousins told her she was a magnificent woman. Even my grandfather had admitted that she had never looked more beautiful, though his jealousy rose in proportion to his pride in his lovely wife.

To me the earrings looked like something Scheherazade of *One Thousand and One Nights* might wear. Within the filigree of gold, rubies nestled and tiny pearls grew. The earrings were chandeliers that were designed to hang down low from the earlobes. Oma said they were too showy for Germany, where people wore understated jewelry. In Oma's youth, even furs, such as wild mink or sable, were worn on the inside of velvet cloaks to keep the wearer warm without appearing ostentatious.

Oma's pierced ears had grown shut, since she had rarely worn her pearl studs, even before they were sold. Mother and I did not have pierced ears. I loved these fairy-tale earrings and hoped they'd be mine one day. But then I would have to have my ears pierced. That was a torturous idea, but to wear those earrings, I would do it.

That spring Oma decided to trade them on the black market, but I begged her not to. I held them up against my face and looked into the mirror, trying to imagine myself all grown up. I would toss my head and have them swing, allowing the rubies to catch the light. Oma took them out of my hand, wrapped them in a white handkerchief, and put them into the bottom of her handbag. Their destination: the black market at Potsdamer Platz.

Sergei had traded for us before, and now Oma was hesitant about performing this chore herself. Even though I wanted the earrings for myself, I encouraged her, "Of course you can bargain yourself. We don't need Sergei."

We had taken a few other things to trade with Sergei, an old camera and one of Mother's watches, but the earrings were more valuable. As much as I wanted them for myself, I had to be practical and admit that we had little choice. We were hungry and had to eat them, so to speak.

The Potsdamer Platz buzzed with soldiers from the occupying armies. It looked like a circus or a strange medieval market festival in one of Breughel the Elder's paintings. The peasants from yore were now transformed into American GIs, milling about, bargaining with Camels or Chesterfields for Oriental carpets, oil paintings, cameras, jewelry, and electric trains. The Russians traded their food, butter, potatoes, lard, and chunks of beef or pork for cigarettes (they had cigarettes of their own but preferred American brands). Or they traded food for watches or typewriters. I wondered if the Russians had wives or girlfriends in Russia, since they rarely traded for women's jewelry, like the Americans and the British. American soldiers with their American cigarettes were the most successful in this business, and they always beat the Russians in obtaining cameras, especially the highly sought after Leicas.

We had to trade twice: we had to trade the jewelry for cigarettes, and then we had to trade the cigarettes for butter and other foods from the Russians. To preserve the butter we would melt it and save the liquid in a glazed ceramic pot. This way the *Butterschmalz,* the butter lard, would last for a few months in the pantry.

American soldiers who did not smoke held large future bank accounts in their hands. Cigarettes were the path to wealth in the postwar days. One carton of cigarettes, representing one week's ration, would trade for a one-carat diamond; one pack of cigarettes would buy us one pound of butter.

Oma began chatting with a young GI who was eager to see the earrings. She shyly withdrew the handkerchief from her purse. The soldier leaned over her shoulder trying to peer into her bag. I thought he was most improper, sidling up to Oma like that and breathing onto her. I pushed him away, and he laughed. Oma unfolded the white cloth with great care, and there sparkled the rubies within the gold.

The soldier seized an earring, examined it, then he held it up next to my ear. "Will you try it on so I can see how it looks?" he asked.

"My ears aren't pierced," I said. "That's why we're selling them. Otherwise Oma would give them to me." As I said this, I wondered why I lied.

He was in a good mood and still laughed. "Okay, I'll hold it here for a moment. All right? My fiancée back home has more or less your coloring. She'll have to pierce her ears when I bring them things home. But they sure are pretty. My, they are so pretty," he kept repeating while I struggled to untangle the earring caught in my hair.

Oma got seven packs of cigarettes for her earrings. We would be able to trade for butter and other edibles for a long time.

When we took the S–Bahn home, I watched as three elderly men, dressed in well-tailored, black, prewar overcoats now somewhat shabby, stalked the platform. Round and round they went, these professorial types, throwing furtive glances at two smoking GIs. Their eyes kept shifting from the GIs to the concrete slab of the platform. My eyes followed theirs, and when I looked down, I saw the men wore excellent shoes—slightly scruffy, but not yet shabby like mine were, showing an earlier good quality. I tried to inch closer to watch. Oma knew what was going to happen next and pulled me away, trying to spare the men the embarrassment of being observed.

A train pulled up to the platform, and as the GIs were about to board, one of them tossed down his cigarette. The three men converged on the discarded butt, two of them bumping heads. The man who was the quickest flicked off the glowing end with his thumbnail and shoved the stub into his coat pocket. The other GI dropped his cigarette and let it roll slowly onto the platform. When one of the elderly men reached for the butt, the soldier's foot shot out and ground what was left of the cigarette into tobacco grime. Round and round, the soldier's heel demolished the butt. Then his buddy dragged him into the train as the doors were closing. I hoped he'd be squished. Oma turned her head; she could no longer bear to be a witness to the humiliation of the old men.

Everything could be bought with cigarettes. Women sold themselves for cigarettes, some because they were smokers, and others to save their families from starvation.

Veronika spoke in whispers to my mother about a woman she knew in Halensee whose husband was a violinist in the Berliner Staatsoper. The violinist had come back from a camp in Russia, where he been taken as a prisoner while performing with a group of musicians for German soldiers. He came back with tuberculosis and weighing a hundred pounds to his former 170 pounds. The woman hid her husband in a small back room and received GI visitors in the bedroom. The GIs supplied her with cigarettes, which she traded for butter, milk, and other foods to help her husband regain his health. It made me wonder, was this woman a martyr? Or was she a prostitute?

Then there were women who'd sell their children's rations for cigarettes. One of Mother's close friends had tried to persuade Oma to sell her a pack of cigarettes for a week of milk rations, but Oma refused. The woman trembled and wept, and she almost went down on her knees to beg for the trade. But Oma refused again, chastising her for taking milk from her children so that she could smoke. When the woman turned to leave, Oma took pity on her and put six of the little white cylinders into the woman's purse. She fell upon Oma's neck, thanking her over and over again. I swore that day, I would never smoke.

House of Ice

I liked school better after I met Brixie, and she and I soon became close friends. Brixie was also born in Silesia, and like me, she considered herself a true Berliner. In fact there was a saying, "A true Berliner is born in Silesia."

Brixie had black-brown hair and large almond-shaped green eyes. She was tall and slim and had a perky nose and full lips. I was still flat chested, while Brixie had begun to round out. I envied her looks and tried to copy the way she walked, swinging her hips like a model on a runway. We had few clothes, most of our skirts had gotten too short, and there were no stores where we could buy new dresses. Mutti's sewing machine was ashes, but she knew a dressmaker in Potsdam, outside Berlin in the Russian zone.

Potsdam, a beautiful leafy historical city by the lakes, has been associated with Frederick the Great and his Sanssouci. It is renowned for the Potsdam Conference where Truman, Stalin, and Churchill met in 1945. Measured in kilometers, Potsdam is not far from Berlin, but in postwar Berlin, getting there was difficult, since it was not part of the city's four sectors. The S-Bahn did not connect directly. No matter the complications, off to Potsdam we went.

Brixie and I each took down a chintz curtain from our respective homes—hers was in shades of blue, and mine was orange and red with flowers. Mother designed a different dress for each of us. She found that she had enough material to create skirts with a bias cut, her famous bias cut. Since we wore the same size, Brixie and I exchanged dresses, and even our schoolmates did not notice. Later, we dyed sheets—one a dark pink, another one blue-green—and had those made into dresses as well. With my blonde hair and Brixie's dark mane, the dresses looked different on us, and we managed to double our wardrobes.

This was also the year I turned thirteen. One morning, close to my birthday, I woke up and found my white sheets stained red. I shrieked and galloped down the stairs to Oma.

"What is it child, what happened?" She needn't have asked, for when I turned around she saw the backside of my pajamas blooming with something like the shape and color of poppies. "Oh, Karin," she smiled, "You are a little woman now."

I did not want to be a "little woman," if it meant bleeding every month. I knew about these events from my mother, and I had anticipated that I also would be visited by this dreaded event one day. Now that day had come.

What would I use to protect myself? We didn't even have decent toilet paper? Oma looked through Mother's drawers and found a string thing with two flaps hanging down, front and back. Onto those I had to fasten hand-crocheted *Binden* with safety pins. After use, these napkins had to be soaked in a pail of cold water and bleach—when we had it—then they were washed, rinsed, and wrung out. But the most embarrassing aspect was that these napkins, which looked like limp white rats killed during a lab experiment, had to be dried. But where? I didn't want anyone to see them. Oma suggested drying them in the basement. I clipped them on the line with wooden clothespins, but the air in the cellar was damp, so "they" stayed damp. When it was summer and hot outside, I waited until the other tenants had left the house, then I'd sneak these little horrors out into the garden and hang them low behind shrubs. The minute I heard someone come home, I'd rush outside to bring them back in.

It was September, and we huddled around the radio in the kitchen to listen to the proceedings of the Nuremberg trials. We also bought copies of the

Der Tagesspiegel, the newspaper founded by the American forces, where more and more facts were made public on a daily basis. The names of those Nazi leaders who had been involved in planning the extermination camps and who had come up with the Final Solution, which led to the slaughter of millions of human beings, were headlined in the paper. The stories detailed the methods used by the Nazis to enable this plan to grow to such unimaginable proportions.

Göring was found guilty of his crimes and was sentenced to death by hanging. He pleaded to be shot, befitting his status as a former aviator and ace in World War I, but this was denied. He escaped execution by committing suicide in prison. Someone had smuggled cyanide into his cell. Rather than face death by a hangman, he took the pill. At least he had stood up at his trial: Hitler, Goebbels, and many others had killed themselves before they could be tried. Goebbels had even killed his wife and their six children. I asked Oma questions regarding the suicides, and she said, "All these leaders, *diese Übermenschen,* believed they represented the 'master race,' and in the end every last one of them turned out to be a coward. I should think that if they'd believed in what they were doing, they would be defiant and stand up to a military court. But no, they proved to be *Untermenschen.*"

I tried to make sense out of this jumble of senselessness. The Nazis had tried to dismantle the concentration camps before the Russians or the Americans reached them. They weren't successful, but they had tried. To me, it proved they felt guilty. They had tried to keep their evil a secret. Rather than face retribution, they killed themselves. Henrich Himmler, disguised as an ordinary soldier, had been arrested by the British toward the end of May 1945. He also bit down on a pill of cyanide. It was rumored that several Nazi leaders escaped to South America. They tortured, they slaughtered, and then they ran off or killed themselves.

There were many nights when I tossed in my bed, but sleep would not come. The past was incomprehensible to me. The vast numbers of slaughtered Jews, Gypsies, and "undesirables" was overwhelming. How could such a thing have happened? How could we Germans face the future? How could anyone believe in a decent German ever again?

Autumn leaves, only yesterday yellow and orange, had turned brown. They blew from the branches and began to crumble. I liked the trees, especially after they had been deprived of their leaves, because then their true structure was revealed. When I ran home from school, I made the leaves rustle beneath my feet, and every so often I bent down to pick up one of the shiny horse chestnuts. During the night, frost painted delicate fernlike patterns on my window. By November, winter had set in fully, and this would turn out to be the coldest winter of the century.

The colonel gave Mother an army blanket. We dyed it dark brown and had the seamstress in Potsdam make it into a suitable winter coat for me. Thinking about this some years later made me wonder, why did I not use one of the two wearable fur coats hanging in the guest closet? Well, for one, I was too young to wear fur. But Mother and Oma's coats were old and threadbare, and neither of them would touch the Persian lamb coats. They belonged to Oma's relatives, and they were taboo.

When the snow piled high in the streets, I pulled my old ski boots from the closet and wore the hated things again. The temperature fell to minus four degrees Fahrenheit. A polar wind blew from Siberia's tundra straight to Berlin. It was so horribly cold that while walking to school, I froze the part of my legs just above the boots. When I peeled off the multiple layers of socks worn over woolen stockings, my shins had turned blue and the skin cracked and bled. I froze the fingers of my right hand as well, when I removed my mitten to open a door. My hand nearly froze to the doorknob, but I was able to pry it loose from the cold metal by breathing on it. For many years the frostbite in my fingers and shins was reactivated during severe cold weather.

It was so cold that the water in my pitcher in the wash basin froze. Even in the tiny insulated room where my breath added some warmth, the temperature never rose above the freezing point. To brush my teeth and wash my face—forget anything else—I had to crack the ice on top of the pitcher. I began to thoroughly detest this Victorian-looking cheap china, on which garlands of roses and angels encircled my very own iceberg. Sometimes the ice was so thick that I couldn't have cracked it without cracking the pitcher as well. I felt tempted to do just that, but it was the only one we had. (Oh, there was also a matching chamber pot with the same kitsch roses on it, but no angels, neatly tucked away under my bed.) When the ice was unbreakable, I took my toothbrush downstairs, so that I could perform this little bit of civilized hygiene in the semiwarm kitchen. This was more practical, since the baking soda, a substitute for the Clorodont toothpaste, which we had run out of long ago, was handier there.

Sometimes the ice was thin and I could wash my face. I recoiled when the artic water touched my neck, but Oma would pull me over by the collar and inspect it. She'd also look into my ears and send me back up to wash again if she didn't think they were clean enough. I had to contend not only with icy water but also with harsh, gritty soap, which had gotten even grittier after the war, if that were possible. This soap didn't foam, and I thought it should be called a bar of sand rather than a bar of soap. Using this brown cake on my skin directly, without a washcloth, would raise small red blisters. I tried to keep away from the soap and the ice water as much as possible.

While visiting Mother at work one afternoon, I chatted with the colonel's secretary, an American WAC. She asked, "Would you like an . . . ," but I did not fully understand the rest of the sentence; it sounded as if she had said something about "skin cream." But I knew it had to do with an American cosmetic, so I smiled "yes." She went into another room and returned with a jar of Arid Extra Dry. I thanked her ever so much. Proud of my American cosmetic, I rubbed it on my face every night before going to bed. It was only years later that I learned I'd used deodorant as a night cream on my face, not exactly what the good WAC had in mind for this unwashed German girl.

Christmas was close, and Oma thought of her sons and of times gone by. I also missed our former family holidays, my uncles, and my Aunt Margaret. Things were worse now than during the first postwar Christmas. We talked about what had been and that had led to thoughts of the future and what might be again.

Since the war ended, Oma had heard from Uncle Will only once, in early July, when we still lived in Halensee. He had sent her a happy letter, posted somewhere near Bremen, saying he would see her soon. When his ship returned from Norway, his troop had surrendered to the Americans. He was on his way to Mainz, where they would be decommissioned and sent home. Oma looked radiant from that day on, carrying the gift of his life spared in war within her like a cherished gift. But Will did not come to Berlin. Oma waited and waited. She did not know where he was, and as the months passed, she fell back into a depression.

In November, Uncle Richard visited us for a week. He had been taken prisoner by the Americans in Austria and had been released months ago. We enjoyed his brief stay, but then he returned to his family in Leipzig.

Around that time Oma received a letter—forwarded from Halensee—from Hans Gebhardt, an old university friend of Uncle Will's. Hans wrote that Will was in a French POW camp, and he continued his letter with a bizarre story.

Hans was half-Jewish, and just before the war, he had taken refuge with his older sister in Bordeaux. In the mid-1930s, his sister had married a French citizen who owned his own vineyard, and Hans became the vineyard's overseer. Then, of all the strange ironies of war, or of the postwar period, several German POWs were assigned to help with the grape harvest in

Hans's brother-in-law's vineyard. Will was one of those German POWs sent to Bordeaux. I imagined the surprise when the two old friends recognized one another. They knew they were being watched, though, so they had concealed their pleasure at meeting again.

Hans wrote that the labor camp was grim and that Will had lost forty pounds off his normally one hundred and seventy pound frame. Oma would not see her son anytime soon because the French planned to keep the prisoners for several more years of labor. Hans promised to smuggle food into the camp for Will. He would have to bribe a few of the guards—a few aged bottles of wine would do the trick—and although he might get into trouble, he was willing to do this for his old friend. His own position in this region was precarious. People in the village might look upon him as an enemy sympathizer. After all, he was a German, and few of the villagers understood that he had come to France for political reasons.

When Oma read the letter, the pink of her cheeks deepened into a dark crimson, a sign that her blood pressure had risen. I was afraid she might have a stroke and ran to fetch Dr. Stortz, an eminent cardiologist who lived a block from us. He was at his house, and he followed me home. We found Oma in shock, but nitroglycerin revived her.

A few days later we visited Uncle Victor and Tante Wanda and told them Will's story. "Since Will was taken prisoner by the Americans," Uncle Victor said, "Handing him over to the French to do labor is strictly against the terms of the Geneva convention."

Oma shook her head, "Then how could they do this? Why would they have shipped him to France? Americans always abide by international law," Oma said.

After speaking with her boss about this issue, Mother explained the situation to us. The colonel justified the sending of prisoners to France by explaining France's position after the war. Many of that country's young men had been sent to German labor camps during the Nazi occupation of France, and now France wanted retribution. They insisted that the Americans provide them with cheap labor. The French themselves had not taken any prisoners of war, and the Americans' prisoners were to make up this needed labor force, as part of war reparations that Germany owed to France.

Mother disputed the colonel's argument, telling him she had known several French prisoners who had worked in office jobs and who had more food than Germans, thanks to the Swiss Red Cross. The colonel dismissed Mother's tales as fantasies, since the Germans' abuse of war prisoners, mainly of Russians and Poles, was well known.

The colonel's justifications did nothing to calm the rising anger Oma felt against her beloved America. Keeping prisoners for any length of time after an armistice was against the rules of the Geneva convention, which stated prisoners were to be sent back to their homeland as soon as a country had capitulated and the fighting had stopped.

Oma and Mother kept discussing Will's circumstances. They remembered Fernand, one of the French prisoners Mutti had become acquainted with. Mother's friend Gwendolyn (my godmother) had translated Rilke with one of the prisoners—a professor of literature—into French. That prisoner had introduced Fernand to Mutti. I had met him once. He was a handsome man in his midtwenties from Marseilles, with an unruly shock of black hair. When he laughed, he exposed a slash of white teeth. He kissed Mother's hand—I thought a bit too much—up to her elbow and called her *ma reine*—my queen. The POWs had office jobs and a certain amount of freedom; they had more food than we did, some of which Fernand shared with us. One of Fernand's Swiss Lindt bars was the last chocolate I tasted until the magical day when one of the Americans entering Berlin threw a Hershey bar in my direction.

The French held Will and the other prisoners in harsh, unfair conditions. He was not even allowed to write home to his mother for Christmas.

Later, when Will was back in Germany, he wrote to Oma about his ordeal. In his letter, he mentioned one episode that explained a lot. After two years of hard, backbreaking labor in a stone quarry, Will was sent—because of his skills in drawing and architecture—to work as a draftsman for an architect who was designing new facilities for the partially destroyed harbor nearby. The architect spoke reasonable German, having learned it in Germany as a prisoner of war. The Frenchman had spent several years on a farm working for an elderly couple whose sons were fighting in Russia. He had become fond of the couple who'd treated him like a son. When Will asked him, "Why don't you tell your countrymen that not all the *Boche* were monsters?" The architect replied, "*Mon cher* Keller, if I were to defend Germans, my countrymen would call me a *collaborateur*. They would never believe me. I would not be allowed to complete this project."

We faced the prospect of Christmas without a tree. There were no trees for sale, not anywhere. This second postwar Christmas looked as if it would be even more bleak than the last.

Then Mother had a plan that she whispered to me, so Oma would not hear. She and I were going to sneak into the woods after dark and cut down a tree.

The night was almost black, and there was no moon at all. Only the stars cast a cold blue light onto the snowy path. Mother and I stole off armed with a rusty saw and a small axe. Steamy breath flags preceded us as we slinked off from the main paved road, ducking into the undergrowth. My heart pounded, and even the icy snow crunching beneath our footsteps sounded exciting to me, as I listened for animals or imagined dangers. I loved every minute of it. We looked the trees over, shining a flashlight on them for a second or so, taking care not to be discovered. We found most of them too tall or too stunted. Then we saw one that was my height, about five feet five, and began cutting. We had selected a symmetrical silver-tipped fir, a beauty of a Christmas tree. We sawed and sawed with this dull blade, and then I gave it a last whack with the axe and over it fell. I was happy, but in a strange way, I also felt sad. I remember crying. Here was this little tree, a moment ago it had stood above the needle-strewn snow, decorated with glittering ice crystals, and now it was lying on its side, never to grow to its full size.

The only sweets we had that year were some brownish-looking cookies made partially with oats and sweetened with awful tasting molasses. Even Oma's cooking skills and little tricks, in this case, spreading tiny globs of four-fruit jam on cookies, didn't help; they still tasted terrible. There is a saying in German, "*Der Hunger treibts rein*"—hunger shoves it in. How true. It was only hunger that let us eat the cookies. The only presents I received were several notebooks, which I needed for school, and a pair of socks and a pair of mittens Oma had knitted for me, using the wool from an old moth-eaten sweater she'd unraveled.

There were nights when I was so hungry that my stomach hurt with it. I thought of the adage, "Hunger is gnawing in your stomach." Yes, hunger was gnawing and biting. The gnawing kept me awake. I turned and turned and thought of the hungry rats that had taken bites out of Aunt Margaret's arm in the Great War. It felt as if rats were inside my stomach now, chewing me up from the inside. And then there were times when that strange animal of a stomach growled. I was kept awake by the noise it made, the saliva pooling in my mouth, the beast clamoring to be fed. In all my life I have never forgotten those terrible, aching pangs of hunger.

Oma kept a small fire lit in the kitchen stove throughout the night. Black and ugly, it sat next to the stainless steel electric stove top built into a white-tiled counter. But ugly was our salvation.

On the stove sat a cracked blue enamel pot, filled with perpetually warm *mucke-fuck*—the infernal acrid tasting coffee substitute—now containing fewer and fewer grains of barley. When hunger kept me awake, I pulled on a second pair of heavy woolen socks over the ones I wore to bed and tiptoed down to the kitchen. There I poured some of the black brew into a cup and filled my stomach with this bitter drink. Then I crept back upstairs and crawled under the covers again. For a little while my stomach stopped growling and allowed me to grab a little round of sleep.

In the new year, our sewer lines froze and broke. A messy brown goo flooded the basement, then a swill of foul liquid from the burst pipes in our toilet inundated even the hallway.

But Oma had a few cigarettes left. She was "rich." A handyman came to help, but it meant he had to turn off the water flowing into the house. He explained that because of the extreme low temperatures, and the house not being centrally heated, repairing the pipes while it was this cold would be useless. They would soon freeze and burst again.

There were no musical parties that winter. Mother spent more time at work. I didn't blame her; I would have liked to escape as well. It was a good thing the snow was piled many meters thick in places. We used this snow for water. I shoveled and carried bucket after bucket into the house. I washed with snow and put snow into my chamber pot for cleanliness purposes. I thought it funny when my morning pee hissed and steamed and melted the snow into a little yellow valley. This had to be carried outside. I also helped Oma with her functions. When nature of a more serious sort called, we went into the cellar where aluminum buckets filled with snow stood ready for that purpose. We burnt the dirty paper in the oven. The waste itself froze within minutes to a hard mass that we later threw into the garden, where fresh snow soon covered it. It seemed paradoxical that we stayed healthier than ever that year, considering the cold, the hunger, and the lack of hygiene.

The following summer, our tomatoes, beans, and climbing peas were the most abundant the little plot of land behind the house had ever yielded. Asters and roses wore their brightest colors—splashes of happiness. Was last winter's fertilizer the secret?

Oma, 1945. Pastel by
Fräulein von Fournier.

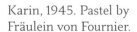

Karin, 1945. Pastel by
Fräulein von Fournier.

Mother, 1946. Charcoal sketch
by Elisabeth Holz Averdung.

Villa at Schopenhauer Strasse 51 in Berlin-Nikolassee. Oma, Mother, and I moved into this house during the summer of 1945. Photo by Karin Finell, 2002.

Oma and me in 1946. Photo by Astrid Kraus.

Uncle Will on a brief visit with
a friend in 1948, just before
the blockade. Photo by Karin
Kraus (Finell).

Veronika Wolfram, my mother's friend
and frequent party guest, shown here in a
newspaper clipping from the 1930s.

Karin, 1948.

Lassie, my beloved dog.

CHAPTER 13

The Winterfelds

Der Tagesspiegel printed a daily report of how many people were found frozen in their beds each morning. There were too many. Two years of minimum rations had left men and women near starvation, and these skeletal bodies could not withstand the icy cold.

It was especially hard on those who had no younger family members to help with cutting wood or hauling coal. Only those who had bought one of the little black iron stoves that puffed black smoke through plywood insets in windows had a chance of survival.

Oma was a true and good friend. Several times a month she made the trek across Berlin to look in on her old friend Frau Winterfeld and her husband. On several visits, she took me with her. Yes, the same Frau Winterfeld I had thrown a plate of spinach at when I was five years old. Thanks to everyone's discretion, the spinach incident was never mentioned.

Before we visited her the first time, Oma told me the story of how Herta Winterfeld had met her husband.

Herta was the sole heir to one of the largest breweries in Berlin, and when she and Oma attended the great seasonal balls, dashing young officers outdid each other to woo Herta. But Herta was smart; the mirror told the young woman that the suitors were courting her father's money. She would have none of them.

Oma suggested to Herta that she take a trip to Switzerland during the summer months, rent a room in a small hotel, using a false name, and pretend to be a schoolteacher. Herta took Oma's advice. And as if arranged by my clairvoyant grandmother, on a sunny day in July, a nice-looking high school teacher in his midthirties from Düsseldorf checked into the same

pension. Each discovered that the other liked to hike, to study rock formations, and to read poetry. They began to speak of a life together. When the
summer ended, each took the train back to their own city. Yearning letters
were exchanged.

Then the young man paid an unexpected visit to his new love's house, or
rather her parents' imposing mansion in Berlin, near the Tiergarten. He
timidly rang the bell at the servants' entrance, thinking Herta was working
there as a tutor. He was shocked, surprised, and terribly dismayed when he
found her to be the daughter of the house. He quarreled with her and
threatened to leave on the spot. He could not understand her deception. But
love won out and the two were married. Oma was maid of honor, and
Herta and her husband had lived happily ever after, until now.

Oma suffered from angina pectoris, and chasing around Berlin doing chores
for others was not what the doctor ordered. Oma felt obliged to help her old
friend by selling some of Herta's jewelry to the Americans, for they both knew
that with her fluent American English, Oma could get a better price.

I remembered Frau Winterfeld's pearls, the huge cream-colored globes I
had detested those many years ago. I often wondered what happened to
them. She wanted Oma to sell a sweet little ruby ring, several bracelets, and
some gold chains with inserts of tiny diamonds and sapphires for her, but
this was not the fantastic jewelry I would have expected from someone as
wealthy as Frau Winterfeld. Perhaps she had placed the valuable pieces in a
bank vault or hidden them in a safe place in the cellar of her mansion in
Tiergarten, which, like so many buildings near it, had become a heap of
rubble and ashes. The bank vaults that had survived the bombs were looted
by the Russians, and by the time the Americans arrived in Berlin, the vaults
were empty.

Late one morning, we climbed the three flights of stairs and, with Oma
still huffing from exertion, found Frau Winterfeld standing in the open
doorway. Her eyelids were swollen and red. She waved us in. She and Oma
did not speak a single word, and I followed silently. I felt a shiver of fear. We
followed her to the bedroom. Her husband of forty-some years lay still on
the bed. He had died during the night, and he was stiff, like a figure carved
from bleached birchwood. I had seen dead people before, but he looked like
the skeleton in a doctor's office. Only he was real, not made of dangling yellow bones connected by wires. His pajama top was unbuttoned, and I
guessed that Herta had opened it to listen to his heart. The bones stuck
against his skin, which was thin, like pale blue tissue paper, and dry, resembling parchment that could crack at any moment. There were minuscule ici-
cles where his nose hairs joined his mustache, as if his very breath had

frozen. Oma drew the duvet up, covering him to the top of his head. She seemed surprised when she discovered I was in the room and waved for me to leave.

We helped Frau Winterfeld with arrangements for the funeral. The ground was frozen rock hard for many meters down, so only a shallow grave could be dug. There were no coffins available. Herr Winterfeld would have to be buried in a box made of roughly nailed together planks.

The love story of Herta Winterfeld and her husband moved me, and though years ago I had disliked her very much, I wept when she died. She outlived her husband by only a few weeks. She was old—the same age as Oma, sixty-seven—but she had no one to look after her.

After Frau Winterfeld's funeral, Oma put her arm around my shoulder and said, "For all the riches she once owned, in the end, she was so very poor." She hugged me. "I have you, and your mother. I have so much to be grateful for." And then she planted a big kiss right smack on my cheek.

CYANIDE

Mother's cousin Maria died that spring. Maria's brother Horst had died at Leningrad, and Tanta Wanda had now lost a second child. Of her three children, only Victor, the idiot savant, was still alive. They buried Maria in a makeshift plywood coffin, and her grave too was shallow in the frozen earth.

Maria had survived the war despite having been stigmatized for being half-Jewish. She had worn the golden amulet containing cyanide around her neck for the duration of the war, but now when leukemia caused her constant pain, she opened the amulet and bit down on the pill.

She had taken care to present an aesthetic picture in death. Tante Wanda found her daughter dressed in her most becoming evening gown of champagne-colored satin, her red hair brushed to a silken sheen, fanning out on the pillow, and her hands folded on her chest. Maria looked like an angel, Tante Wanda said, with tears choking off her words.

Maria had been saddened by her cousin Elisabeth's suicide. Elisabeth had also bitten down on the little cyanide pill she'd carried within her golden amulet, worn like Maria's, on a golden neck chain. Both of their deaths had been quick and painless.

Elisabeth, also half-Jewish, had been protected by her Aryan husband, Walter Schulze-Mittendorf, who had kept his position as the head of stage design at Ufa, the film studio Goebbels had nationalized after Hitler came to power. Goebbels needed him in the film industry and forgave him his half-Jewish wife.

In the early 1940s, Walter had fallen in love with a young Ufa film actress. But he knew that if he divorced Elisabeth, she might be sent to a labor camp. After the war ended, and when Elisabeth was no longer in danger from the Gestapo, he felt free to leave her for the other woman. He asked for a divorce.

Tante Wanda said it had been too much for Elisabeth. The many years of staying out of sight and the constant fear of being arrested had frayed her nerves, and she could cope no longer.

Her death made me think of those Nazi years again and what they had done to Elisabeth and so many others on the periphery of the greater horror of Auschwitz, Buchenwald, and Dachau.

An infinite sadness rose in me. Elisabeth's death was so unnecessary, so ironic. Now that she was safe, she deemed life without the man she loved to be not worth living. The cyanide had provided a way out.

And now Maria.

Oma and I helped Tante Wanda sort through Maria's belongings. Tante Wanda sent some clothes home with us. Among them was the blue silk dress I had admired on Maria so many years ago, which had been a perfect foil for her Titian hair.

Around this time Oma resumed corresponding with her sister-in-law in America. Oma had always emphasized the importance of keeping in touch with relatives, especially those in foreign countries. The letter exchange with Aunt Freda, the widow of Arnold, Oma's brother, had been interrupted twice: once by the Great War and then again after 1940. Now the letters crisscrossed the ocean once again. I eagerly awaited these blue one-page, onion-skin aerograms, with the prepaid postage on the envelope, bearing the spidery script. I wanted to go to America and hoped we would be invited. Then one day, Aunt Freda and her daughter Frances asked if Oma would like to come back to the United States and if she would, perhaps, like to bring me along?

Would we? When Oma read that letter, she grabbed me and we whirled about, laughing and crying at the same time. I was afraid she'd have a heart attack.

It took a while before we were able to apply for immigration visas. Mother still hoped that she would hear from her great love, Päule Carlson, and didn't want to leave Germany. Oma was divided in her feelings as well; she wanted to see Will and wondered where he would relocate once back in Germany. For me, the future was clear: I would go to America.

Mother's dreams of Päule would not be realized; she never heard from him again. He and many other scientists disappeared in the vast expanse of Russia and were, perhaps, working on Russia's nuclear program or in a rocket plant beyond the Ural Mountains. German scientists, such as Werner von Braun, were brought to the United States to help with the American rocket program. Oma commented on the irony of the situation: with the help of the Germans, the erstwhile enemy, the arms race between former allies, the U.S. and the Soviets, was able to accelerate.

Oma and I did not realize that it would take years to process our immigration papers. I blamed Oma's parents for waiting so long to immigrate to America. Had they only arrived six months earlier, Oma would have been born in Utah; she would have been a U.S. citizen and our immigration would have been an easy matter. Oma laughed when I told her. "Karin," she said, "That's why they waited, until I was six months old and able to withstand the hardship of travel. Can you imagine, a pregnant woman with two small children traveling on an early steamship for three weeks in rough seas? Being thrown about on the boat? Your aunt Margaret told me it was difficult enough for them to travel with me, a baby. Our mother was seasick the entire time. Her milk dried up. I almost died. Then they found an immigrant, a nursing farm woman from Pomerania, and she saved my life by sharing her baby's milk with me."

Now our American relatives had become our saviors. We had "eaten" most of Oma's jewelry, when they rescued us with the first of the CARE packages.

The house next to ours had been built years ago by Dietloff von Hake, Oma's second cousin, and the house we lived in was owned by Dietloff's daughter. Dietloff's villa, which was much grander and almost twice as large as ours, had been requisitioned by an American colonel from Alabama. By summer, the colonel's wife and two teenage daughters had arrived in Berlin and were living with him in the villa.

The colonel and his wife remained invisible, but their daughters were a different matter. The situation was a bit awkward. I was living next door to girls my own age, girls whose language I spoke, but because of the law of nonfraternization, we were not allowed to visit one another and could only sneak around and talk through the fence. I would have liked to have seen more of them, to learn about America, and I think they would have liked to know more about me as well.

They were pretty girls and wore pretty clothes. Their legs were tanned, and I envied their white socks and their saddle shoes. I noticed their strange accent and tried my best to imitate the singsong quality of it, believing I'd sound more American.

I had read *Gone with the Wind* and imagined the girls sounded like Scarlet

O'Hara. But my English teacher thoroughly chastised me for speaking with a southern drawl. She had me stand up in front of the class while she lectured me. Speaking in English with her harsh German accent, she said, "Karin, you must speak the King's English. I insist. Where did you pick up this abysmal way of speaking? I want you to pay attention to my pronunciation. I will teach you the King's English yet."

My hand shot up to cover my mouth, trying to hide my giggles. At the same time my lips quivered because I also felt like crying.

The King's English indeed. She might know English grammar, but her pronunciation was atrocious. I felt challenged, and although I knew it was stupid of me to fight back, I could not restrain myself. "Fräulein Gross," I said, "I think it's better for me to speak the way real Americans do . . ."—from my exaggerated southern drawl I went into mimicking her *z* sounding *th*—"than to talk with a tcherman accent." Again switching to the southern drawl I continued, "At least some people whose native tongue is English talk the way I do. Back in Alabama." My classmates laughed, and Fräulein Gross's eyes contracted to slits as she stared through the window ignoring me. Trying to be the class clown had earned me the affection of my classmates, but at the end of the school year, I paid for it with a nearly failing grade in English from Fräulein Gross.

The Alabama girls listened to AFN Berlin (American Forces Network), blasting Glenn Miller and Tommy Dorsey tunes from a little radio on their terrace. The songs were the same songs I'd heard with Erich before the war ended, when we had listened to the forbidden BBC. We had two radios downstairs, one in the kitchen, and one that migrated between the living room and Oma's room. I asked Mother if I could take one of the radios with me to my little room under the roof. After all, Oma didn't use it and Mother was rarely home. At first she demurred, saying it was not necessary, but then she gave in when I "mosquitoed" her, as she called my pestering her, as if I were a buzzing insect.

I cherished my radio. When we had electricity, I woke up to Glenn Miller, brushed my teeth to "In the Mood," and went to bed listening to *The Whistler,* my favorite program, especially after I snuggled under the covers. I liked to be frightened by those stories. They helped me go to sleep and drove away the images of war that haunted me and often led to nightmares.

DOG OF A FEATHER

One of our neighbors gave me a dog. He was a boxer and his name was Max. Mother was at work, so I had a good excuse for not asking her for permission to keep him. I felt certain Oma could be persuaded. All I remember now is that Max needed a home because the man who owned him was leaving for Australia. Max was a sleek, elegant-looking beast, and Oma immediately liked him. She did ask, "What will you feed him?"

This was the first dog I had owned, and I didn't have the slightest idea of the amount of food he would eat or the care he would require. The first night he slept next to my bed, he snored, and I fell asleep with my hand resting on his smooth brown fur, absorbing his animal warmth. At breakfast, I gave him half of my slice of hard black bread with a little margarine on it, which he devoured in one quick gulp. At dinner, I shared my meager portion of pea soup with him. The small bits of bacon floating in the thin green liquid were the only meat he would get. The soup made him want to "go out" all evening. He pulled me down the dark street, with me holding his leash with all my strength, while he tried to race away from me, maybe embarrassed by the jet of green shooting out of his rear during jarring stops.

When the girls next door saw Max, they broke out in *oohs* and *aahs*. "He's so gorgeous," they said in unison. After a few days of our prison food, his bones began to mark outlines in his pelt. I summoned the courage to ask the girls if they would like to have Max. They looked at each other, giggled, and shrugged. Before they could muster up an answer, their father's GI driver—who had overheard our conversation—hollered over the fence, "Yes, for sure! I'd love that dog." Within less than a minute the driver was in our garden. I kissed Max good-bye on the white star of fur on his forehead, then I went to my room and cried. I saw him once in a while and was pleased that he seemed happy and looked well fed.

A little later someone gave me a six-week-old miniature Scottie I named Lassie. I hoped she would have a miniature appetite. The GI driver from next door asked why I would name a Scottie Lassie. I told him that the registry had listed her as "Astrid," but that was my mother's name, and it wouldn't do to call "Astrid" and have both Mother and dog come running. She was a Scottish girl, so I called her Lassie.

The driver said, "Hey, you wrong gal. Only collie dogs are Lassies. Ain't you heard of *Lassie Come Home*? She went over rocks and dales and swam lakes, just to go home. And she's a collie. Sore 'nuff."

"Sorry," I said, "I never heard of that movie. Anyway, Scottish girls are lassies. Don't you know that?"

The driver gave up arguing with me. But he was grateful for the gift of Max and offered to help me feed Lassie. He brought me a box of canned dog food. In addition, from time to time he smuggled bits of food, a half-eaten hamburger or other table scraps, over the fence.

That was my first encounter with the famous American hamburger, a half-eaten discard from the girls next door. The partial hamburger was a big temptation. The smell of charcoal burned meat was something unusual, its scent rich and exotic. The meat was brown and the juice had moistened the bun, making me drool with hunger just by looking at it. But that was all: I watched, I drooled, and Lassie ate.

One day Lassie was absent all afternoon. Looking out of Oma's window, I saw her crawling through a hole she must have dug underneath the fence, and when she arrived back at the terrace, she looked checkered, black and white. When I got hold of her, I noticed wisps of white feathers stuck in the black of her fur.

"Where have you been?" I scolded. She wouldn't say. But she looked guilty and satisfied, with a wild gleam in her eye.

Oma later discovered a dead chicken on the threshold of our front door. Who would have brought us a chicken? Oma took this most welcome present into the kitchen and soon the delicious aroma of chicken soup filled the downstairs. We had not eaten chicken in years.

The following day, Lassie disappeared again. I worried when she stayed out all night. Morning came and still no Lassie, and all day long we were frantic. I walked up and down every street in the neighborhood, calling her name. I rang doorbells, but no one had seen her. Then a note arrived from an older couple who lived far down the street that said we could have our dog back if we were willing to pay for three chickens and two dozen eggs.

They were holding Lassie hostage.

We did get Lassie back that day, with help from the police. We did not have to pay what the chicken owners demanded, but the police arranged to have the case heard in court.

Oma and I discussed the scenario that lay ahead, and I prepared for it as if I were making an acting debut at a local theater. I looked forward to role-playing again.

We had to appear in the equivalent of a small claims court. I planned to take the accused, Lassie, along as evidence—all black, no feathers, wearing a red leash.

Oma chose her one and only, by now nearly threadbare, navy gabardine suit, complemented by a soft pearl gray blouse with a chiffon ruffle around the neck. The pearl necklace she wore was one of the few pieces of jewelry not yet sold for cigarettes. She had swept her silver hair up into a French twist, and I looked at her with admiration.

I was a teenager and chose to dress young, but not childish, in a good pre-war blue wool dress that had once belonged to Mother. She had altered it for me and fixed a large white sailor collar to it. Before dressing, I washed my hair, a major procedure. I had to shampoo my below-shoulder-length hair in the kitchen with water heated on the coal-burning stove. Then it took a long time to brush it dry in front of the stove.

My heart pounded and my fingers twitched when the bailiff seated Oma, Lassie, and me in the front row of the courtroom. The plaintiffs sat a few seats off to our right, throwing us venomous glances. "If looks could kill . . . ," I whispered into Oma's ear.

The man's and the woman's faces were so similar in expression, they might have been twins. Their features were sharp and haggard and their skin sallow. Of course, many people were bone thin and had sagging skin in our starving Berlin. But in addition to being bony, these people looked as if they had never been happy. Their foreheads were deeply engraved with a perpetual scowl. Their mouths were drawn in a downward curve, showing contempt for Oma, contempt for me, and, it seemed, contempt for everyone else in the courtroom. I wondered if they had ever laughed or smiled, even long ago when they were young. They were married. Had that man ever kissed this tight-lipped woman? Did couples like that ever embrace?

The man wore a quilted jacket, dirty pants, and boots. The woman was similarly dressed, but she also wore a babushka covering her stringy hair. She pulled out a grimy handkerchief and loudly blew her nose. Then she scowled at us again. Oma smiled at them, and I elbowed her, signaling her to keep looking ahead, not at those people.

When the judge entered the courtroom, my heart leapt into my throat. He wore a long black robe and wire-rimmed spectacles that kept sliding down his long nose. A fringe of gray circled his balding head.

The bailiff called for order in the court and read from a paper to the plaintiffs and to us, the defendants: "The animal Lassie, opened the latch to the chicken house, then closed the same behind her and commenced to slaughter three chickens."

I rose from my seat, handed Lassie over to Oma, and objected. The judge allowed me to have my say. This amazed Oma.

Pointing to Lassie, I began, "Your Honor, I do not think you or anyone could believe a little dog such as this one would open a latch, close the same behind her, and then commence to kill, kill, kill. Could anyone believe this little dog to be capable of that? No, your Honor. These people accusing Lassie and living on our street are indeed keeping chickens. This is excusable— after all there is a shortage of food—though there are strict ordinances against keeping barnyard animals in our neighborhood. The chickens, I believe, were kept in a ramshackle lean-to. When my Lassie chased the chickens from their front yard into the chicken coop, these people locked Lassie up."

I pointed to the little miscreant, who stuck out her pink tongue as if on cue, making her look like an innocent toy.

"Yes, your Honor, they locked Lassie up. Why? Because they thought they could blackmail us to pay black-market prices for chickens. These people are trying to profit from other people's love for their pet and their fear of the courts. These people intend to profit by demanding payment for chickens we never saw.

"We, my grandmother and I, came to court today because we have nothing to fear. We ate one of the chickens—a very tough old hen, by the way—that appeared out of nowhere on our doorstep. We've never objected to paying for that chicken. That's only fair. But we should not have to pay for the other two chickens, chickens we never saw. Perhaps figments-of-the-imagination chickens. And the dozens of eggs these hens would have laid? How many eggs did they lay before? Where is the proof of there having been three hens to begin with? Your Honor, my grandmother and I plead with you to set a fair price for the eaten chicken and to settle the case here and now."

The judge raised his brows and looked at me over the rim of his glasses. I thought I detected a faint smile around his lips. He raised his gavel, then he pounded the thing a few times, declaring that since we had eaten the chicken we had to buy another live hen for the plaintiffs to compensate them for their loss. And we had to pay a small sum for ten eggs the "chicken soup" chicken might have laid.

Oma and I hugged. I was filled with the rush of victory. For some time thereafter I wanted to become a lawyer, rather than an actress.

Chapter 14

"Isms"

In the winter, Mother's musical parties resumed. Perhaps people flocked to our house because, despite the size of the huge room, it was warmer than other places, but I suspect it was actually the warm, welcoming personality of Oma that attracted them.

Mother had also bought a larger coal-burning stove and installed it near the piano, passing the smaller one on to Oma. Every so often, when the wind gusted from the west, the smoke would cloud the room, making everyone cough. The guests' coughing spells then put a stop to their singing, but they filled the pause by replenishing their teacups with more vodka and with lively conversations, thus warming their insides. Vodka was one of the items readily available at little cost, and while Berliners had little to eat, they always had enough to drink.

Elisabeth Averdung, an artist friend of Mother's, often joined the crowd. She braved a long ride on the S-Bahn from the Russian sector across town; Mother had thought her crazy to move there a year ago from Halensee.

Mother and Elisabeth knew each other from their student days at the art academy, about twenty years earlier. While Mother was studying costume design, Elisabeth was studying under Käthe Kollwitz in the fine arts program.

I had leafed through Mother's art books since I was a young child, and the dark realism of Kollwitz's charcoal drawings, her renderings of dying children in the Great War, had deeply moved me.

Käthe Kollwitz had met the young Elisabeth while on a trip to Silesia's brown-coal mines, where Elisabeth's father slaved as a miner. Elisabeth was fifteen, and the photos of her from that time show a skinny girl with huge brown eyes.

Elisabeth had been lucky. Someone in town showed Kollwitz several of her pencil drawings, sketches the child had made of her father and of other miners. Kollwitz was so impressed by the talent of this serious young girl that she had sponsored Elisabeth's education, paying for her tuition to a boarding school for gifted children in Berlin. Kollwitz herself instructed Elisabeth in drawing. By the time my mother met her at the academy, Elisabeth was no longer a shy country girl but a young and spirited intellectual. She was knowledgeable not only about painting but also about literature and music.

Elisabeth introduced my mother to socialism, and Mother began reading Karl Marx's *Das Kapital.* Those ideas didn't sink in deep with my mother, who was given to flitting across life as if it were a canvas painted by Renoir. During the Hitler years, Elisabeth kept her leftist sympathies hidden. Some of her friends and comrades were sent to prison and concentration camps, and some went into exile. Käthe Kollwitz's work was no longer shown in galleries. Elisabeth painted occasional portraits and flower still lifes in the style of Cézanne. She married a printmaker and they had two sons, and in secret, they designed and printed pamphlets for the underground. Had they been caught, they would have been executed for treason. But they were careful and lucky, and they survived the Hitler years and the war.

When I met Elisabeth her eyes were still huge and brown, but they were also filled with sadness, and I wondered if they had always held such sorrow. But her mouth—in direct contrast to her eyes—showed a generous slash of full red lips that could at any moment break out in spontaneous laughter, showing an appetite for life.

Now Elisabeth was again part of Mother's circle of friends, and I saw her often. I listened to them talk about the Berlin of the late 1920s, and sometimes I fantasized about what it would have been like to have lived in that period of time.

It was only now, after the war, that I could study Berlin's rich cultural history. Books banned under Hitler found their way back into libraries, and abstract and expressionistic paintings were again exhibited in museums. Imitations of 1920s cabarets opened, and although I was too young to visit, I heard the adults talk about them and longed to go. I would have liked the Berlin of Georg Grosz, a friend of my aunt Oda, and the Berlin of political cabarets and Kurt Weill. Others had experienced the Berlin of innovative movies, such as Fritz Lang's *Metropolis* or the *Cabinet of Doctor Caligari,* and the Berlin of books, such as Thomas Mann's *Der Zauberberg,* before I was born. In all, I would have like to have lived in a Berlin of spirited thinkers, a Berlin of individualism. That period was short-lived. It was hard for me to understand how someone like Hitler, a person with an ordinary mind and a lack of taste, could sweep ideas and ideals from the German landscape with such speed. But I had to be honest with myself, I too—not very long ago—had been one of the ordinary horde that had admired the Führer. Only three years had passed since I had thought of Hitler as our savior. When I now questioned adults about how it was possible and how they could have allowed Hitler's rise to power, no one would answer me.

I once screamed at my mother, "How could you have allowed it to happen?" Mother slapped me. Then she turned deathly white and left the room.

The Russians, whom we regarded as bestial conquerors and oppressors, were seen as liberators by Elisabeth. She tried to convince my mother, and anyone else who would pay attention to her litany, that Russia would save the world from the evils of capitalism. When she joined the Communist Party, she tried her best to get my mother to join as well. Mother declined; she was not a joiner, not of any "ism," *ever.*

I was almost fifteen, and Oma allowed me to stay up a little later and to help serve the guests tea and ersatz coffee. During these evenings, I often went to sleep—or pretended to go to sleep—in the living/music room. The sofa in the far corner of the living room was quite comfortable, especially since I huddled underneath a *plumeau,* a huge down pillow. Oma nodded off in her wing chair by the fire, her waxen fingers folded on a plaid blanket. I listened to the adults, and when I overheard our guests speak of new concepts and a new Germany in the making, sleep would be drawn from me like smoke out of a chimney. We were all hoping so desperately for a peaceful new world to follow our old one, which now lay in shambles.

I was excited about many ideas at that time. One of them was being a *citizen of one world.* This thought was put forth by an American named Gary—I've forgotten his last name—who was issuing passports to those who joined him. He seemed to be more phantom than reality and lived somewhere in the western part of Germany, but no one knew where. I wanted to be such a citizen of one world with no borders.

They talked about Willy Brandt, and everyone became excited when he returned to Berlin from exile in Norway. Mother knew some of the people who prepared him for his reentry into politics in a free Germany. Elisabeth did not share in Mother's enthusiasm for Brandt, and she regarded him with aloofness. He was a Social Democrat, not radical enough for her taste. The excitement of political talk around me was like mental coffee, strong and black, and I could not find sleep while these discussions were going on.

The talk of art and politics was interspersed with song.

I loved Mother's voice. Sometimes as I was dozing off, the sound of her mezzo would reach my ear, caressing me as she sang a *Lied* by Schubert or the haunting song of the Lorelei, a lovely maiden who sat high on a rock above the River Rhine, combing her golden hair, enchanting poor fishermen, who, mesmerized by her beauty and by her song, ran their ships onto the rocks. She was a supernatural being, akin to a mermaid, and I loved her. After the war, the song was again acknowledged to have been written by Heinrich Heine, a nineteenth-century German poet of Jewish ancestry—he had converted to Christianity—whose works were not published under the strict Nazi regime. During those years, his "Lorelei" was assigned to "anonymous" in my songbook. Or when Mother sang Orpheus's aria from Gluck's *Orfeo ed Euridice,* in which Orpheus laments his lost wife, Eurydice—a man's part sung by a mezzo—I knew she was thinking of Päule Carlson. "Oh, I have lost her, all my happiness is gone forever," she sang, putting the depth of her feeling into this song of a lost love.

On some late evenings the musicians who liked American jazz began imitating jam sessions they'd heard about. Upturned kitchen stools became drums and the ivories of the Bechstein got a beating. By that time I could no longer pretend to be asleep. One evening I jumped from my sofa and sang Gershwin's "Summertime" and drowned the others out.

Veronika and Karl Wolfram, and now Elisabeth, formed the cornerstones of these gatherings. They brought others into the circle, all espousing new ideas or discussing what the architecture of a new Germany should be.

But sometimes someone would express fear. The war had ended almost three years ago. How much longer could we go on existing on our meager rations? How long could we, as a country, exist without a valid currency? Cigarettes had served as a substitute for legal tender all these years. The black market grew and provided people like Oma and me with necessities, but it had also created gangs of muggers and thieves.

When I arrived at the S-Bahn station in our suburb, half an hour by train from the center of town, I had to run the gamut of gesticulating men—foreigners, perhaps former slave laborers from Poland and Russia—their hands outstretched, nearly grasping me, asking in fractured German, "*Ha'm se was zu verkaufe*"—Do you have something to sell? When I answered "no" and shook my head, they became pushy. At times one or another would come so close I could smell the garlic on his breath as he whispered words I didn't understand. Words I didn't want to understand.

It became quite clear that there could be no rebuilding, no business, no commerce, and no production of goods until Germany had an internationally recognized currency. But no one knew when that would be. Many of Mother's friends saw the future as bleak.

Sometimes arguments began between Elisabeth and others. The Russians were accused of having caused this sorry state by their looting of Berlin. In fact, they had looted all of the German lands they had occupied. The factories had been stripped, and lorries, building cranes, heavy trucks, and entire railroad trains had been shipped to Mother Russia. Elisabeth argued that we owed this reparation to the Russians, since we had lain waste to their land on our army's march eastward and later during our retreat, leaving a "scorched earth."

One day Elisabeth arrived at our house in jubilant spirits. She told Mother of the new commission she'd received from the German Communist authorities. She was excited about being paid handsomely to travel to Moscow to paint an official portrait of Shostakovich. More and more of her paintings found their way into museums in East Berlin. But Mother slowly withdrew from her old friend. I overheard her tell Oma that she was saddened by Elisabeth's selling her talent to communism. She now was no longer free to paint the themes that had drawn her to radical socialism in the years before Hitler: the poor and their hunger, the plight of workers, and social injustices. Mother found that her paintings of cheerful workers waving red flags were no different from the propaganda paintings of Nazi workers marching with arms outstretched in the Nazi salute. The same blue sky formed the background, the same red-cheeked faces smiled at a benign and unseen leader. Only the flags and the uniforms were different. The austerity and the power that Elisabeth had once expressed in her paintings—her link to Käthe Kollwitz—was gone. It had disappeared underneath the sugarcoating of political art.

And so by keeping my ears pointed, *Ohren gespitzt* as we called "heightened listening" in German, I learned that beliefs should be well examined: they may seem ideal, but they often bear a darkness within.

I felt like the ink blotter on Oma's desk. I was the absorbent felt paper on the mahogany wooden curve sucking up all the black and the red ink that was splattered on the blank sheet of my mind. I tried to form these random patterns into a worldview of my own, but I was too immature to integrate these inky marks.

OF SHOES AND OTHER VANITIES

Even before Mother had overheard the colonel and his guests talking about a planned currency reform for Germany, rumors had circulated around Berlin about such a change. The colonel and the other high-ranking officers had kept their voices just above a whisper, and when Mother entered the living room, carrying a tray with coffee and sandwiches, they had broken off their talk. But Mother had good ears—though not as good as mine, the expert in eavesdropping—and had already heard the important points. She told Oma that the rumors seemed to be true: soon there would be a change in our currency. It seemed that the new German money, the deutsche mark, was being printed in the United States for security reasons.

The Soviets were vetoing the new currency and the reconstruction of Germany, and their opposition had to be dealt with first. The French, in control of the southwestern part of Germany, had not forgotten Germany's past wars of aggression against France, and they also tried to hobble the American and British plans.

It was maddening for Mother to hear only parts of what was so vital for us to know. She, like all of us, clung to anything that would give us a tangible hope. But she could not ask. She was a German, a former enemy, a housekeeper, and a servant. When she was sent from the room, sometimes by a harsh voice, she was reminded of her lowly position. My mother was strong willed and, to a degree, arrogant, and it was difficult for her to endure this treatment. She told Oma that at times she felt like taking off her apron and running from the house, but then her anger would pass and she would realize how important this job was for Oma and me.

We longed for the *Währungsreform,* the currency reform. Would it happen soon?

Our correspondence with our relatives in America flourished. Oma's family in Santa Monica were Democrats, and they wrote of their hope that Truman would be reelected that year. My eighteen-year-old second cousin Totty in New York began to correspond with me, and in our letters, we discussed silly, girlish things.

I asked idiotic questions: "Do you eat using fork and knife like we do here in Germany," or "Do you cut all your meat first?" To which she answered, "I eat the way Europeans eat. Mother insists on that. But I grew up in Japan, and often go to eat Chinese where I can use chop sticks. When you get here I'll take you to my favorite Chinese restaurant and I'll teach you how to eat with them." I asked her about her hobbies and her plans for the future. She wrote me about the incidentals of her life. She was born in Japan where her father represented Twentieth Century Fox in the Orient. She and her family had returned to the States a few months before the bombing of Pearl Harbor. Totty had attended a finishing school (I thought that was amusing, a school to finish you off?), and now, rather than furthering her studies at a university—to the chagrin of her parents—she had turned to modeling as a career. She was in demand as a high fashion model in New York City and worked for Mainbocher, New York's most celebrated designer.

A few years later, her face would smile at consumers from Maine to California on thousands of Clairol containers, but that was still in the future. I was in awe of my beautiful cousin, whose photo, showing her dark brown almond-shaped eyes and glossy brown hair, I admired. Totty's full name, Paula von Hake, was the same as our mutual great-grandmother, and like her namesake, this Paula was five feet nine and as lithe as a young birch.

I wondered why she took such an interest in me, her younger cousin, poor and unsophisticated, living in a bombed-out city. But Berlin was a faraway and exotic location in her mind, and she was interested to hear how life in Germany had been affected by the war. She also corresponded with a friend in Japan, and later she told me about what those people had gone through in the firebombing of Tokyo. Totty had a tender heart, and the deaths of so many mothers and children in war touched her.

When I told her about Elisabeth, Mother's friend, she wanted to know more about her painting and her connection to Käthe Kollwitz. "Dear Karin," Totty wrote,

> I can hardly wait to meet you and I hope you get your visa soon. We have so many things in common. When you get here I'll take you to Harlem, that's the most exciting part of New York. Mainly Negroes live there and my mother would die if she knew, but I go there sometimes on weekends to sketch. The colored people are very poor. The women look haggard, and some of the children have these huge, sad brown eyes. I showed my sketches to one of my former art teachers, and she said they resemble Käthe Kollwitz's art. I was flattered. But galleries here are not interested to show any of my drawings. They look at me and tell me I'm too young for an artist, I'll have to mature. Did I tell you that's what I want to be, an artist? I love Harlem, it's so real. I get my inspiration there. Sometimes I go there with friends to listen to jazz. You would love it too, Karin.

Then she added a PS, "I also like classical music. Do you like Bach? Or Brahms? I share an apartment with another model who owns a baby grand, and I often play until three or four in the morning. Until a neighbor bangs on their ceiling, that means: stop."

I wrote back, "Don't you know I'm too young to go to night clubs?" Then I told her I wanted to be an actress, and I described my mother's musical parties and asked her to come and visit us. But she wrote back that travel to Germany was not possible at that time.

Soon I began receiving packages from Totty: a pink angora sweater set (which made me sneeze), a red chesterfield coat with a black velvet collar, white socks, underwear, and saddle shoes. Oh yes! Shoes exactly like the ones the Alabama girls wore. All of these wonderful clothes made me feel as if I were an American teenager already.

Then a pair of penny loafers was added to my American wardrobe. Penny loafers! I had dreamt of having a pair of these shoes, but I never expected to actually own them. I had, in a sense, won these shoes.

I had entered a contest held by the movie magazine *Modern Screen.* They would pay ten dollars to anyone who had a true story about meeting a movie star. In addition to being true, the story had to be told in less than fifty words. To be a witness to something this "Hollywoodsy" would be, under most circumstances, rather difficult for someone like me, living in war-torn Berlin, but I was lucky or not so lucky, depending on how you looked at it.

Sometime earlier, I had come upon a movie crew filming *Berlin Express* in the city center. Of course, I didn't know what they were filming at the time.

The movie was being shot on a street where the buildings consisted mainly of empty facades, where stately apartment houses had been reduced to burned out shells. The dense gray sky peered like ever so many large sad eyes through empty window frames. It had rained, and the black asphalt reflected objects like a distorting mirror. A voice boomed commands through a bullhorn, but I couldn't fully understand what the voice was saying—the words were spoken in a mangled and mushy foreign-accented German. The street was nearly empty and clear of pedestrians. I seemed to be the only one left. Dressed in my shabby brown blanket coat, I felt invisible and had no intention of leaving. Curious about what was going on, I squeezed closer to an open doorway leading to a rubble-strewn space, where a house had once stood, that was surrounded by a half-caved-in wall. I thought I could escape through the opening, if need be.

In the center of the street, men in blue pants and bulky sweaters, some wearing peacoats against the drizzle, relaxed around camera equipment, smoking and chomping. Americans, I thought, they're chewing gum. The crew looked bored. They must have also been cold, for some kept rubbing their palms together with vigor or blowing into their cupped hands, while others were pushing their hands deep into their coat pockets.

I stared with fascination at the red tip of the cigarette one of the men was smoking. I was mesmerized by how this little dot of gleaming brightness stuck between two clenched lips would suddenly intensify its glow, from bright orange to red and then grow dull again, each time the man sucked on the white cylinder.

A long black car drove up, and I lost interest in the cigarette. I inched along, my back to the wall, watching. The rear door opened and a pair of elegantly shaped legs, sleek in nylon stockings, stretched out of the opened door. A woman followed the legs. On her feet were spiky pumps. I stared at her and stopped breathing for a moment, taken with the beauty of her face, exotic and delicate with wide-set slanted eyes and dark hair. She was wearing a perky hat with a veil that half covered her high forehead. The woman stepped out of the car, and I stood awestruck by this apparition. I later learned her name was Merle Oberon.

She hadn't taken more than two steps when a pothole on the street made her twist her ankle, propelling her in the direction of the rain swollen gutter. I rushed to her side to catch her, but suddenly there was a scuffle. Two men appeared out of the fog and pushed at me. Leaning on the two men, the woman kicked me in the shin with a well-aimed spiked heel. I stumbled and found myself in the gutter. I felt dazed. Why did she do that? Why? When I looked up, I saw her hanging between the two men, limping off, glowering at me over her shoulder. She narrowed her eyes to slits. Eyes I had thought of as being so exotically beautiful only moments ago now threw me a look that said, "Stay away from me you disgusting creature." Or maybe it said, "You disgusting Nazi."

I hurt from the kick, but the water welling up in my eyes did not come from the pain in my leg. I tried hard to stifle the tears and bit my lip instead.

Modern Screen sent the ten dollars for my little tale to my aunt Frances. It just so happened that a pair of loafers cost ten dollars. Penny loafers for having met a movie star.

With Totty's clothes, I was becoming well dressed and looking quite American. I suppose if Merle Oberon had met me while I was wearing my red chesterfield coat, she would not have kicked me and shot me such a look of hateful disgust.

Totty's shoes were a size too small for me, but vanity made me squeeze my feet into these lovely, graceful American shoes. I was the envy of all my girlfriends. But if I walked any distance at all, I felt like one of Cinderella's stepsisters. Vanity is a great motivator, but in the end, vanity ruined my two healthy feet.

Almost thirty years later, I ran into Merle Oberon again, this time in a fashionable restaurant on Wilshire Boulevard in Beverly Hills.

The maitre d' had seated my husband and me near a window, next to a table beneath an oversized indoor palm. Fitting in with the restaurant's decor, the couple at the other table looked dressed for the tropics. The woman wore a formfitting white dress that was low cut and that showed off her deeply tanned, perfect shoulders and arms of polished bronze. The man looked to be years her junior, and although I could tell she was not young, her face and body showed no visible signs of age. She wore her dark hair pulled back and knotted into a chignon, and large golden hoops pierced her earlobes. She was beautiful. I stared.

It was Merle Oberon.

I was no longer a poor German girl in a ratty coat, but a grown woman dressed in an orange silk Geoffrey Beene dress. I was wearing earrings almost identical to hers, and my blonde hair was also fastened in a bun. When my husband and I sat down, she looked toward our table and smiled. My husband knew my Berlin story and read my turbulent thoughts.

"Forget it. No, don't say anything. There's nothing to be gained. She won't remember the incident. Let it go."

I did.

Money and the Marshall Plan

Mother came bursting into the living room where Oma and I sat reading.

"Turn on the radio. Quick, maybe we can catch it on the news."

"What . . . what's happening?" I asked, twisting the knob of the radio.

"I heard that Truman signed some pact. Something important . . . it should be on the evening news," she said. It was a little after seven o'clock, and after the radio had warmed up, the voice of the newscaster came on.

We heard that President Truman had signed the Foreign Assistance Act. He was in fact signing the plan that George C. Marshall had designed more than ten months ago, making it a reality. The plan would pump money into the German economy.

We sat stunned. Tears appeared in Oma's eyes, and I knew they were tears of happiness. She smiled and shook her head. "The Americans! I knew it. I knew they would help us. President Truman. I wish I could vote for him. He is a good man, a man who sticks to his principles."

"I told you he fought for this," said Mother, who'd overheard much in the colonel's villa. "Now he signed it. The recovery will begin. Maybe there's a future for us after all."

"We're still going to America, aren't we, Oma?"

"Yes, Karin. After your Uncle Will comes back, we're going to America. But it would be nice to leave Germany on its way to recovery."

And then, coming as a complete surprise to us, Will arrived. The door-bell rang, and there stood Uncle Will, Oma's long-awaited son. He seemed so narrow, standing in the doorway. His clothes hung on his bones, still he was as tall as I remembered him. His hair was thick and wavy, and his eyes twinkled behind horn-rimmed glasses. I threw my arms around his neck, and dangling off his tall frame, I hugged him. I had opened the door, but Oma, having heard my shriek, was by our side and in his arms within sec-onds. She sobbed and laughed, and luckily, the surprise did not cause her to have a heart attack.

It was only two days earlier that Uncle Will's letter from Baden Baden had arrived. I had brought it to Oma, who was standing in the kitchen by the stove. I was happy for her and impatient for her to read it. Oma's hands made the paper quiver like a fluttering bird. She pulled the thin paper from the envelope and held the page close to her eyes. Tears ran down her cheeks, and I knew she wasn't be able to read a line.

"Read it, please," I said, impatient to hear what was in the letter.

At last Oma's hands steadied, and she wiped her eyes and read. Then the letter went limp in her hand. She leaned against the cupboard. Her eyebrows contracted, her face pulled into a strange grimace, and then she sagged into herself. Holding on to the furniture, she pulled herself over to the kitchen table. There she fell into a chair, letting out a deep sigh. She pushed the let-ter to the other side of the table and let her head sink onto her folded arms.

Her behavior puzzled me. "Isn't he coming?" I asked.

She shook her head. It was difficult to understand her because her tears muffled the words. "He's recuperating. People there are helping him. He has lost so much weight, he only weighs sixty kilos. He must be a skeleton. He's not coming, couldn't get a pass for Berlin. One good thing, he had a job offer the third day after he arrived from France. Editing a magazine. That's something to be grateful for. He's happy to be back in Germany, out of that horrible French prisoner of war camp." She took a deep breath and dried her cheeks. "I have to be patient. He'll come when he gets his papers but only for a visit. He'll stay in the West."

Oma stood up to walk back to the stove to check on the bubbling soup. She walked bent over, as if she were carrying a load of wood on her back. She had shrunk in these last minutes. Or had I not noticed that the years had whittled away her height? My Oma, she had been brave and strong through all of our tough situations. When I looked at her now, I saw an old, fragile woman. Again I admired her for not breaking down and letting go, for con-cealing her pain and disappointment.

She had worried about Will for so many years and cried at night knowing that he was facing hardships and dangers. She had missed him and had not seen him for four years. Now he was free, and still he did not come to see her.

I was angry with my uncle. I felt he could have had his discharge papers signed with the destination of Berlin, where his mother lived. And later he could have gone to where he had friends who would help him get established. Oma should have come first.

The mood was still gloomy when Mother came home. He was her younger brother, the "golden boy" of the family. He was everyone's favorite and could do no wrong, until now. How could he not come home first and see his mother? I remembered the American captain who had dreamed of going back home and sleeping the first night in his mother's bed. He had demonstrated love and caring. But Will? I didn't expect him to sleep in Oma's bed, but he should have come home, to her and to us.

But all this was forgotten in an instant. *He was here.* And Mother happened to be home as well. This was a true homecoming, with only the cake missing. I was humming the American tune "Had I known you were coming I'd have baked a cake . . ." Oma laughed, "But Karin, we don't have the proper ingredients. We'd have to get them first on the black market."

Uncle Will had hoped the mail would be slower, that he would arrive before the letter, but the sadness the letter caused now dissolved in joy. But it was not a homecoming: the West would from now on be his home. His friends in the magazine business had arranged for him to get a seat on a British military transport plane to Berlin, but the plane would return the following afternoon and he had to be on it.

However short the visit, Oma was able to hold her son in her arms (which also meant feeling his bones underneath the jacket that was several sizes too large). Her anxiety was calmed for the moment, knowing that his future looked bright.

At this time, the colonel Mother worked for returned to the United States, but Mother found new employment with a Colonel Murphy from Texas, who was a part of the military police in Berlin. He was a red-faced, jovial man who liked Germans and beer. He invited me in for hamburgers bought at the commissary, and when he learned about my little Scottie, he brought me dog food from the PX. Although Mother's new employer was also a colonel, I noted that there were some differences between Colonel Murphy and her previous employer. Since Colonel Murphy seemed to be of lesser importance in the military hierarchy, he was less formal and had fewer high-ranking officers visiting his house.

It was not long before Mrs. Murphy and their two-year-old daughter,

Amber, arrived from the States. I often visited and played with Amber in their garden. The little girl enchanted me, with her head full of blonde Shirley Temple curls and big blue eyes. I offered to take her to the park or the lake nearby. "An American child?" Mrs. Murphy drawled in disbelief. "You want to take her out of the safety of our home? No way, no way. Who knows what goes on behind some of those ole' broke-down walls, those ruins. Lil' Amber will stay right here, where she's safe." Mrs. Murphy left the room and no more was said about my suggestions. I felt sorry for poor Mrs. Murphy who saw evil lurking behind every bombed-out facade.

Their garden was spacious, and Amber and I played ball; rather, I threw it and she tried to catch it. In the late afternoon, when the other military wives would come over to the colonel's house to slurp martinis on the terrace, Mrs. Murphy and my mother were relieved that someone, namely me, paid attention to the little girl. Mrs. Murphy was usually reeling by the time dinner came around, then she'd kick off her shoes, wiggle her perfectly pedicured toes that sparkled with bright red Revlon polish, of course, and dance. But more often she lurched and fell. Mother was usually in the kitchen cooking. She had never been a good cook and had only a few recipes in her repertoire. By the time the guests were seated, they were all in such high spirits that whatever she served was well received. Alcohol had effectively numbed their palates. Upstairs, little blonde Amber sat on my lap while I read her stories from her picture books or told her stories of mermaids who lived in palaces made of coral, pearls, and golden amber, like her name.

I spent several weekends at the house, sharing Amber's room. I loved the Sunday morning breakfast, made Texas style, with sausages, bacon and eggs, pancakes, and, something new to me, biscuits with butter and honey. I was amazed by the amount of food the Murphys consumed, while their waistlines remained slim.

One Saturday night, after some heavy drinking, the music was blaring and the guests were dancing. Colonel Murphy barged into Amber's bedroom and woke us. He took the child, drowsy with sleep, down to the living room. I sneaked down the hall to see what was going on.

The colonel placed Amber on the cocktail table. "Come on now," he coaxed, "You want to be in movies? (Is he crazy? I thought. She's much too young to understand 'movies') Let's see you dance." Amber was a graceful child, but at this moment, she looked awkward, still half asleep, as if she didn't know what was being asked of her. I wanted to take her in my arms and run upstairs with her. But I was a coward. I hugged the wall and watched.

The father turned the music up by several decibels and clapped his hands. That seemed to be a signal, and Amber began to gyrate. The guests squealed and clapped their hands in rhythm as she tossed off her pajama top. Round and round she went, holding her hands over her nonexistent little breasts. When the music's tempo increased, Colonel Murphy clapped his hands again. Her little face looked up at her father's, and he nodded. She then removed her pajama bottoms, whirled them around her head like a flag, and threw them into the applauding crowd and danced naked.

I noticed Mother stepping uncomfortably from foot to foot and could see that she was holding back her anger. I admired her restraint. But when Mrs. Murphy passed Mother on her way to the bathroom, my mother burst out, "I don't think it is suitable for a little girl to dance naked in front of these men."

Mrs. Murphy giggled. "She's just an innocent lil' ole' baby," she drawled. "Now don't you go puttin' things in your mind. There's nothin' wrong. Just nothin'. She won't be doin' this when she's older, but now, she's so cute. Just too cute not to share with our friends here."

Mother replied, "She'd be just as cute dancing with her pajamas on," which earned her a reprimanding look from Mrs. Murphy. Mrs. Murphy then demanded that another bottle of Jack Daniels be brought to the guests. The two-year-old's gyrations continued.

Little Amber Murphy stripped, while I dressed—like an American. I wore my red chesterfield coat, saddle shoes, and bobby socks, and soon discovered that I could ride the S-Bahn, trams, and buses for free, if I pretended to be an American.

On one of my S-Bahn trips, as I sat reading an issue of *Modern Screen,* two military policemen began checking the ID cards of the Americans in the compartment. I didn't have a ticket stub, and I certainly didn't have an American ID card.

I opened my American leather purse, a gift from Totty, and rifled through it, pretending to look for something that I knew very well was not there. In the process, I dropped my American hairbrush. Then my eyes lifted to the soldier closest to me, and I said, imitating a Texan accent, "Ah'm so sorry, I must 'ave left my *idee* at home. I just arrived here a few weeks ago, ya know? I'm Amber Murphy, Colonel Murphy's daughter."

The MP clicked his heels and said, "Yes, ma'am. From Texas, we know."

Ma'am? I smiled at that. "Golly," I said, and I thought, still in a Texan mode, I've just gotten me a whole bunch older in a hurry. I said, "But don't you tell my Daddy on me? Forgettin' my *idee* and all that. Ya hear?"

Both of the MPs smiled, saluted, and left the compartment of the train. I breathed a sigh of relief and got off at the next station. From then on, I bought my tickets.

Oma chided me for being dishonest and for being stupid. How could I do something so brainless and risk my chance to go to America by impersonating an American? If caught, I might have wound up in jail. I wondered for a long time if the soldiers ever found out that Colonel Murphy's daughter was only two years old.

In June, the long-awaited currency reform took place. We read in the newspapers that the Soviets felt insulted by this move. They were outraged and angry that despite their maneuvering against this reform, they had failed. But the printing of the deutsche mark for West Germany in the U.S. had not remained a secret. The Russians were prepared: they had printed their own German ost mark in their eastern territory. Their money appeared at the same time as the new deutsche mark.

Oma said, "Thank God the Americans were not fooled, did not negotiate. Just think, if the Russians could have had their way, the ost mark would have been legal tender in all of Germany. Then the Russians would have controlled our economy." She took a deep breath. "My God, we could have been another Poland or Hungary, all under Soviet rule."

The following day I accompanied Oma and Mother on their walk to the Deutsche Bank to exchange their allotment of money. Long queues had already formed. It was a hot early summer day, and I offered to stand in line for Oma, but she would not hear of it. Adults could each exchange sixty reichsmark for sixty new deutsche mark. The new bills Oma and Mutti now clutched would have to do until Mother received her pay, and Oma, her pension. I could not exchange anything, since I was a dependent, and my father's child support payments had stopped in January 1945. Oma's and Mutti's savings accounts were now worthless. It didn't matter, though, it hadn't been much. We were all glad that the big *Schieber,* the racketeers who had amassed fortunes in the black market, were now, from one day to the next, as poor as we.

It was strange in a way that now everything had to be paid for in the new currency. It was as if someone had said, "abracadabra," and just like that, things were back as they had been before the economy collapsed. The Berlin money had a little stamp on it, a *B* in a circle. This could be spent only in West Berlin or, of course, in West Germany. If we wanted to attend an opera or a stage performance in the Russian sector, we had to first exchange our new deutsche mark for the new ost mark at the official ratio of one to one. On the black market, however, one new deutsche mark would bring four ost mark.

The tirades on the East Berlin radio against the Western Allies were relentless, as were the editorials in the *Tägliche Rundschau,* the Berlin communist newspaper.

"Those Russians. Acting so innocent, so surprised, as if they had been taken advantage of. They have spies all over the place. Only yesterday another one of their spies was arrested. Did you read that, Karin?" Mother asked.

"No, I didn't. They act like sulking thirteen-year-olds," I said.

"Ha! They'll retaliate," Oma warned. "They can't be trusted. And remember, they are superb chess players, these Russians. Thirteen-year-old children they are not."

A day later, while Oma and I were eating oatmeal, the news exploded on the radio, spoiling our breakfast: "The Russians have blocked all access routes to Berlin." All access to the city by train, road, or barge via the railway, the autobahn, or the rivers and canals was blocked. The Russians justified their breach of guaranteed access to the Allied sectors of Berlin by claiming that the bridge over the River Elbe was damaged and in need of repair. At the same time, they closed the Avus, the major freeway artery connecting the western zones to Berlin for roadwork, and used similar ruses to close down the access by train as well. Berlin was in effect closed off from the West.

On June 24, 1948, the blockade had begun.

Berlin was now an island, swimming in a sea of red.

CHAPTER 15

Airplanes over Berlin

SUMMER–FALL 1948

They came at ninety-second intervals, the same planes that had bombed us only a few years earlier. Now they flew in with food and coal. I stood in our garden, craning my neck toward the blue sky and wishing away the occasional cloud that might obscure visibility. I watched these planes, these marvels, and I could not get my fill of looking at them.

Some Berliners called them *Rosinen Bomber,* these planes that flew in "raisins," so to speak, rather than bombs. The airlift brought us food; but still our rations were cut to nine hundred calories a day—too much to die of starvation but too little to keep alive for any length of time. The allotment of coal for cooking and heating that we received was also very small, and we feared the coming winter.

Oma and I could no longer go on our occasional treks, our *Hamster-Touren,* to the countryside to barter for eggs and vegetables. But we were grateful for the flown-in egg powder and milk.

I often stood on the terrace looking at the highway in the sky, where silver birds moved like a chain, bringing us food and the coal to generate electricity. The Americans, with their huge cargo planes as well as converted B-17s and B-24s, flying over the crowded city and landing at Tempelhof Airport, and to a lesser degree, the British, flying four-engine Sunderland seaplanes onto Gatow Lake, risked their lives, day in and day out, flying supplies into Berlin. I read in the *Tagesspiegel* that the Russian fighters harassed the American pilots, buzzing them, and if the Americans strayed a few meters out of the free-fly corridor, the Russian pilots would practically fly their MiGs onto the wings of the American planes in near suicidal attempts to frighten the pilots. During night flights, the Russians often tried to blind and disorient the American pilots by flashing strobe lights into their cockpits. There was more involved than economic aid when Americans flew into Berlin. Oma said, "The United States has taken up the gauntlet thrown down by the Soviets."

Churchill said on the radio, "We are now in a new war. *The Cold War.*"

Oma stood by the kitchen table mixing powdered milk with water. The doorbell rang, and when I opened the door, a dark figure stood there, Tante Wanda. I showed her into the kitchen. Oma was all aflutter. Tante Wanda rarely came to visit us, and Oma thought something must be wrong.

"Go on with what you are doing, Elsa," she said. "Don't let me disturb you. No, Victor is fine. I just needed a little outing."

Oma looked at Tante Wanda, maneuvering her eyebrows into strange winged shapes. To me that meant she didn't believe her. There was something Tante Wanda wanted. But meanwhile Oma indicated that I should put water on the stove to boil for tea, while she went on with what she had been doing. The powdered milk tasted quite bad, but Oma tried her best to make it palatable by whirling it with her *Quirl,* a wooden star-shaped, whisklike utensil, and by adding a few spoonfuls of sugar and a few drops of artificial vanilla to the mixture.

Tante Wanda looked wide eyed at Oma's quirling, and Oma explained to her that this improved the taste of the powdered milk. But Tante Wanda had only used her French cookbook, which was useless now, and she never invented anything, in contrast to Oma who experimented and tried to improve the taste of food on a daily basis.

I brewed the fragrant English Breakfast tea that had been a present from Lilly Penske. Tante Wanda inhaled the aroma with obvious pleasure, then savored the taste, taking tiny sips. The women talked about the blockade and how much longer it might last. Then Tante Wanda said, "It can't go on much longer. Victor is down to sixty-three kilos, the poor man. With his one-meter-ninety frame, he's a mere skeleton. He couldn't survive the cold of another winter."

Oma nodded and looked worried. Tante Wanda coughed nervously. She broke the silence, "You know Victor's stamp collection. He has some very rare stamps. One of them is the . . . ," she broke off what she was going to say and wiped her face with an embroidered handkerchief.

"Does he want to sell the collection?" Oma asked.

Oma had guessed right: Uncle Victor wanted to sell his stamps. It embarrassed Tante Wanda to talk of their needs. They had been our well-to-do relatives. Oma had already sold most of Tante Wanda's jewelry, but now that the new deutsche mark had become legal tender, Uncle Victor decided it was time to find a buyer—preferably an American—for his stamps.

I had first seen the collection when Uncle Victor showed it to an old military friend while Oma and I were visiting. He also showed him his military medals: his *Pour le Mérite,* which people called the "Blue Max"; his two Iron Crosses; and a few of his other medals. I was dutifully impressed by his memorabilia. I asked to look at the stamps and he proudly showed them to me, singling out the pages of American stamps, with a wink in his eye toward Oma. The stamps were in a book larger than our burned family bible.

I found the medals more beautiful than the stamps, but because the medals had been awarded to him in the Great War for valor, he would never part with them. I envisioned myself wearing the *Pour le Mérite*—this delicate fabrication of blue cloisonne with touches of gold—hanging from a velvet ribbon on a low-cut sky blue ball gown. I wondered if women ever wore medals like these as jewelry? The Iron Crosses looked more warlike and would be unsuitable for that purpose. Frederick the Great, the great German military leader and Prussian king, had commissioned the *Pour le Mérite* in 1740, and although it was a medal commemorating German bravery, he gave it a French name. I found that strange. But every educated German knew that Frederick was a Francophile, that he had personally known and admired Voltaire, and that he had named his summer palace in Potsdam *Sanssouci,* or "Without Worry." And I should not worry about the *Alte Fritz*—that's what we called him—loving French things.

I thought about these medals: they were handed out for bravery, but they represented death. Compared to looking at war medals, it was a pacifist undertaking to be sitting at a table looking at stamps. Some of Uncle Victor's stamps reminded me of miniature paintings. But, strangely, the stamps pointed out to me as the most valuable had dull colors and uninteresting depictions. My favorites were the American stamps from the nineteenth century: one was an 8-cent green stamp, showing a tall rock, with a river below it, and the word *Zion;* the other was a 2-cent stamp that showed the Grand Canyon. Oma said both the rock and the canyon were in Utah, though most of the Grand Canyon is actually in Arizona. She told me again how beautiful Utah is and how she regretted that she had not seen either one of these natural wonders.

"Why didn't your father take you to see them?" I asked.

"Travel to those parts was very difficult when I lived there. It was all very wild. I think now it would be easy, with trains and buses. Wait till we go to America, then we'll see all the great beauty that is to be found in the American West."

Tante Wanda, who was in the room with us, looked up somewhat surprised. "You are planning to go to America, Elsa?" she asked.

"Yes," Oma said simply. "If we can obtain our visas, Karin and I will go to America."

Tante Wanda looked disbelievingly at us out of her large brown eyes. I went back to looking at the American stamps, imagining myself in California with my relatives, writing letters to my mother and to friends in Berlin. I would buy the prettiest and most colorful stamps I could find and paste them on white envelopes. I would never use the blue, prestamped letter envelopes my relatives sent to us.

A few days after Tante Wanda's visit, an acquaintance of the Alabama colonel next door honked the horn of his car in front of our house, and Oma and I rushed out. Lassie scampered on after us, and as soon as the major had opened the door for Oma, Lassie jumped into the jeep.

"Out, come out, Lassie. You're not going," I said, shooing her back into the garden. There she stood behind the garden gate, barking.

"You can let her come along," the major said. "I like dogs, reminds me of Fala."

"Who is Fala?" I asked.

"That was Roosevelt's dog."

"I like President Truman," I said. "He's my hero. He brought us the Marshall Plan and is now defending us from the Russians." The major smiled at my remarks. I then explained that Lassie had a little accident the last time at Uncle Victor's and therefore she had to stay home. Oma and I had entered the car by now and were seated in the back. The major sat next to the GI driver in front.

He turned and asked, "What did she do?"

"It's too embarrassing,"

By now we had passed the blue shadow of the Schlachtensee, the lake nearest our home, shimmering through the thicket by the shoreline. Then the car took us through the Grunewald, in the direction of Charlottenburg. The green of the woods swallowed us. The major looked out of the window, shaking his head. "Berlin sure is beautiful," he said.

"Was beautiful," Oma corrected him.

"Yes . . . but go on, tell me the story of your little dog and your uncle," said the major, eager to change the subject of Berlin before the bombing.

"Uncle Victor knew we had this new Scottie, Lassie," I said. "And he'd asked me to bring her along. He likes dogs. Tante Wanda despises them and claims she is allergic, so the general was never allowed to own one. That day I walked Lassie on her red leash into the apartment, and Uncle Victor found her adorable. He picked her up, held her on his lap, and stroked her pink belly. Maybe she didn't dare jump down and go to the door and bark to let us know she had to go out. Anyway, she sat there looking comfortable and then she piddled onto his elegant cashmere dressing robe. We knew there were no cleaners in Berlin to take care of the mishap. But Uncle Victor was so sweet. He gently put the dog down and excused himself, saying, 'Sorry, I have to change clothes, I feel somewhat damp.' That was funny. But also awful. Oma wanted to take the robe home, saying she was sure she could clean it, but Tante Wanda would not hear of it. And so we've never taken Lassie back."

We arrived at the turn-of-the century apartment building in the Reichs Strasse in Charlottenburg, one of the most elegant apartment districts of Berlin. The American major gaped when we entered the building. He marveled at the spotless foyer, with its white marble walls and grayish black and white mosaic marble floor, and ran his hands over the intricate ironwork on the open-cage elevator. Hesitating for just a moment before entering it, he asked, "Does this thing work?"

"Yes, it works just fine," Oma replied. "When we have electricity. And the power is on right now, but later we may have to walk down."

We rode the creaking iron cage to the third floor, the major still shaking his head. "I'm just so amazed," he said, "everything is bombed to rubble and here you have this perfectly preserved building."

"The entire street was hit by bombs," Oma said. "But General Keller acted like a military commander when the bombs hit near his house. He organized a brigade of old men and women to fight the fires. The neighboring house was burning. It must have been strange, the old general taking over, giving orders again. They broke down the walls in the attic, and everyone fought the neighboring fire. That done, more fire bombs hit his own apartment house, and again he marshaled the people to fight it. He saved both buildings."

The major, an air force man, nodded, his eyes fixed on the floor of the elevator. "Some story," he said, as the elevator shuddered to a halt.

I wondered if he might have been one of the bombers. But that was then, and now he was eager to see the stamp collection.

Tante Wanda ushered us into the library where Uncle Victor stood before the long wall of glass-enclosed, leather-bound books. He held his hand out to greet the major. I stood fascinated when the general of the Great War met the major, a former enemy in the most recent war. The American seemed impressed by Uncle Victor's stature, his straight military bearing, but I saw Uncle Victor as a man much diminished during the last years. He had grown shorter, thin, and frail.

I liked being in the library far more than I liked being in the living room. The library's windows let in the afternoon sun, and the electric bulbs in their alabaster bowls hanging from the ceiling gave off a diffused, pleasant light.

Oma, the translator, sat down between the two men; all three were ensconced in leather armchairs. To be near them, I pulled a small stool up to the square table where they sat. Tante Wanda marched past us as if she were walking in a procession, her eyes fixed on the corner bookcase. She unlocked the bookcase, took out the book of stamps, and brought it to the table. She placed it solemnly before the major. I sat looking over the major's shoulder as he opened the yellowing pages edged in gold, and in my mind I turned them with him, leafing the wispy silk paper, which protected the stamps. The men looked as if they were old friends, a professor and his younger student. The round yellow glow from a standing lamp cast a theatrical light onto the prized stamps.

The major looked serious and kept very quiet. I thought he might be disappointed by what he saw. What I saw were beautiful stamps from many lands and countries that I hoped to travel to one day.

Aunt Wanda served French cognac in crystal snifters. They thanked her. She nodded for me to follow her, but I did not want to go. Oma rescued me by asking me to sit on the sofa and read a book. That was better than leaving the room with Aunt Wanda. I picked up a book of poetry from a shelf and opened it. I did not read a line but sat watching the major and my uncle. The American took a sip. I noticed his right hand quivered just a little and a drop of sweat appeared on his brow. Why was he nervous?

Then an agreement was reached that satisfied both. However, we had to return with the major one more time to conclude the transaction, since he didn't have enough money with him. The American paid Uncle Victor in both in deutsche mark and in U.S. dollars. He paid a lot of money. Only Oma knew how much, and she wouldn't tell: it was all illegal for the American to have that much Germany money and for Uncle Victor to receive U.S. dollars.

I wanted to see the medals again and said, "Uncle Victor, I'm sure the major would like to see your Blue Max and the other medals. Why don't you show them to him?"

"You were awarded the *Pour le Mérite*?" asked the major.

Only the jaw bones in Uncle Victor's face moved as he stared out of the window and ignored my demand as well as the major's question.

Later, I noticed him blink away a tear as he handed over his beloved stamps. There was a tremor in his fingers, and his movements dragged. He had wrapped the large book in a burgundy velvet shawl, and it looked as if he were handing over a sacred object. The major received the stamps with a small bow and a salute. His face was serious, and if he felt like smiling for getting such a prized collection, he concealed it well.

The men shook hands and thanked Oma for translating, and we left. We rang for the elevator, and at that moment, the electricity went off. The hall and stairway were thrown into semidarkness. It was lucky that the lights had not gone out earlier. We walked down the flights of stairs, with the major carrying his velvet wrapped treasure under his arm.

Oma said later she could tell by the major's speech pattern and, of course, by his manners that he was an educated man. He had mentioned Yale. I knew it was one of the respected old universities in the eastern United States. Totty had written that her father had gone to Yale and that her brother was expected to attend Yale in a few years.

Oma said this educated Connecticut Yankee—he was from New Bedford—did not try to take advantage of our hardship by bargaining for the stamps. He was fair with Uncle Victor, as one gentleman to another, and he still managed to get a rare stamp collection for a fraction of its U.S. value.

Operation Little Vittles

That fall everyone in Berlin was talking about the little parachutes filled with candy bars that the American pilots dropped shortly before landing. One of the pilots had dreamt up this idea: he made tiny parachutes from handkerchiefs, attached these to baggies filled with sweets, and dropped them near the landing fields before touching down. Other pilots followed suit, and the children of Berlin went wild.

I was afraid at fifteen I would be too old to join the children, but I was desperate for a taste of chocolate. It had been a long time since I had had any candy, and I decided to try my luck. I took the S-Bahn and transferred to a streetcar to the airport at Tempelhof. Children crowded all around. Overhead the planes flew so low they barely cleared the rooflines. It was a bit of a shock to see them so close, the huge silver wings right above me as if I could almost touch them, and to hear the deafening roar of engines beat into my ear. It was similar to the sound I had heard when Oma and I were on the train and had been shot at while traveling from Wiesbaden to Berlin. Those planes had been close, but then I had not seen them. Now, I forced myself to look.

The wonder of it.

The parachutes appeared, white little pyramids floated slowly to earth. Children shrieked, ran, and shoved. More parachutes, more and more, until the sky was filled with silver wings and tiny white floating clouds.

It seemed like a miracle. Some of the children caught three, others none. It reminded me of carnival in Frankfurt, when costumed people in the main parade had thrown candies from the floats.

There were too many children, so I hung back. I could not elbow the little ones and had to be satisfied being an observer.

Oma said, "You see, Karin, this shows it. Americans have big hearts. They're generous. Would any other nation ever think of anything like this? Pilots making these little things with their own hands? Buying the candies with their own money and dropping them to children they would never meet? Children of the former enemy. Just think, unknown pilots to unknown children. That's America for you."

Of course, it was the children who were most impressed and most grateful. For a few moments, as they scampered to collect one of the sweet white gifts from above, these children were happy. Our days were so miserable that these parachutes were the one light moment in a time filled with hunger, doubt, and fear. Yes, fear. We were afraid that the United States could not sustain the airlift and would pull out and leave us to the Russians.

We continued our daily dance on the edge of a sword.

I had come home with empty hands the day I went to the airport. But a few weeks later, about three miles from where we lived, I happened to look up when I heard the drone of a plane. In the sky, I saw the tiny speck of a balloon wobbling, growing larger and larger until it was a big white globe, floating down to earth. A strange apparition it was. I had read *Li'l Abner* comic strips in *Stars & Stripes,* the U.S. Army's newspaper, and was amazed when I saw this thing, this Shmoo, hovering right above my head. I opened my arms as it came nearer. A few children crowded around me, but I was taller and able to grab the creature. It was about three feet tall and looked as if it had jumped right out of the pages of the comic strip: white and shaped like a bowling pin, with black whiskers drawn on its face. But instead of having a bubble with a message coming from its mouth, the creature had a small card attached to it: "A Shmoo will turn into anything you need it to be. For you it will turn into a CARE package." The card gave the address of the center where the exchange could take place.

While I read the card, I pressed the Shmoo so close that I punctured its skin, and with a hissing sound, the air escaped. Oh no! Would the center still give me the CARE package for a shriveled up white piece of rubber?

I took the remains home. I had to show my find to Oma and Mutti. This incredible gift that had drifted down from the skies right into my arms, a CARE package. We had not received any of these packages since the start of the blockade.

"Just in time," Mother said when we were on our way to pick up this present from a heavenly Li'l Abner. "I quit my job. I couldn't take the Murphys any longer. This will tide us over."

We entered a low building on the Kronprinzenallee, now called the Clay-allee for the beloved General Clay, West Berlin's "governor" for so many postwar years, and found a line of people hugging Shmoos. It was a strange sight, all these Berliners, this entire motley group, hugging white balloons. Some women were wearing plain print housedresses, others were in skirts and proper suit jackets, and some came in brown socks and sandals. There were men in pieced-together shirts, jackets, and pants that were obvious mismatched items bought for a few cigarettes on the black market. The sight made me afraid that perhaps my deflated balloon would no longer count as a bona fide Shmoo/CARE package. But I need not have feared. I saw another person with a piece of deflated rubber approach the counter and leave with a package and a smile.

I hadn't yet asked Mother why she had given up her job with the Murphys, but now I asked. Mother said, "Because I have a new job. A much better job."

"Where?" This turn of events did not please me; I would miss Amber. "Does Oma know?"

"Yes. She encouraged me when I got the offer."

Someone pushed at me from the rear, and I almost fell into an elderly woman. Before I could say "Excuse me," the woman turned around, eyeing me up and down. Her darting eyes were filled with hostility. "You girls, pushing, always pushing. Your generation has no manners."

Mother spoke up and told her it was a man behind us who had pushed me into her. "Excuses, excuses," growled the woman, tugging on the apron covering her dress.

The large beige gray boxes with CARE printed on them in huge letters were disappearing at an alarming rate. The queue that had been orderly when we arrived had become a knotted ball of scrambling people, all trying to get to the counter before the packages ran out. I bucked the shoving man behind me and braced myself against the floor with both feet firmly planted and my posterior extended. When he shoved again, I kicked backwards, hitting him on his shin. He yelped and hopped on one leg. I turned and flashed my sweetest smile at him and said, "I'm so sorry. I didn't mean to step on you, but you pushed and I lost my balance." He grumbled and allowed me a bit more room.

We had to be vigilant to keep our place in line, and this made a conversation difficult. But I needed to know more about Mother's new job. "Where are you going to work? For someone higher up, a general?"

"No," Mother laughed. "No more housekeeper jobs. I'm going to be the director of the girls program in a GYA club. You could come and visit, though most of the girls are a bit younger, twelve to thirteen."

"GYA? What's that?"

"Oh. You don't know? It's a place for young girls to go to after school. GYA, you know, 'German Youth Activities.' It's a terrific idea. The military is keeping the children off the streets while teaching them to do useful things and about democracy."

We had almost reached the counter and were being shoved at again. This time it was a young woman, tall, with frizzy red hair. I turned around and asked her to stop, but she squinted her eyes and pushed some more. In the process she squashed her Shmoo and deflated it. "Now, see what you did," she shouted, raising her hand as if she were going to hit me. I lifted my arm to shield my face, and then I felt a tug on my sleeve as Mother pushed me ahead of her. Only the aproned woman was left in front of us.

Then she too was gone.

Mother told the soldier handing out the packages that I had found the Shmoo. He smiled. I told him I loved the *Li'l Abner* comic strips.

"No kiddin'?" he said. "Bet you're the only one here who knows what they are."

"Really? I love this white ghost. The Shmoo becomes anything you want it to be, right?" The soldier nodded. "If you have no food, he becomes food. If you need shoes, his skin becomes leather for shoes."

Mother tugged at my arm, "Come on, you don't have to go through the entire Shmoo litany. The soldier knows and the others want to get their CARE packages."

"Oh Mutti, they should know." I looked around me, wanting to address the entire crowd. "What an idea. And now they drop these things and have them transform into food for us."

That remark settled the soldier's smile even deeper into his cheeks, in fact his dimples appeared. Meanwhile Mother presented her German identification card and began filling out a form in receipt for the package. The soldier leaned over, eager to continue the conversation with us, I think with me, for he liked that I spoke American English and was familiar with *Li'l Abner*.

"You know what? The minute Al Capp introduced the Shmoo—not so long ago, just a couple of months—people went crazy back home. My sister wrote me that clubs opened named for the Shmoo. They sold Shmoo clothes, and they even dance the Shmoo Rumba."

"My goodness. I'd like to see that. What do the clothes look like? White sacks?"

"I don't think so. They were just clothes and were called Shmoo this, Shmoo that. So, when the Berlin Airlift commanders heard about this wonder animal, they cabled Al Capp and asked him to design an inflatable Schmoo and to send it over here, so's we could drop them along with 'Operation Little Vittles.' Fits right in with the candy in the toy parachutes."

"I tried to get one of those, but the children were so young. I didn't want to fight them for it. But this Shmoo floated right into my arms."

"Well, good luck, little lady. Here's your Shmoo, happy eatin'," the soldier grinned as he handed me the CARE package.

Mother lifted the package, all twenty pounds of heavenly food. The crowd pushed from all sides, and I was afraid someone would grab it from Mother's arms and run with it. I walked next to her, shielding her from people getting too close. I should not have worried, we were within an American compound and soldiers were nearby.

We took the S-Bahn home, and every eye in the compartment was fastened onto our package. All hungry eyes.

"Mutti," I said. "I'm bursting to know. What are you going to do in this club?"

"I have to keep the girls busy after school. When winter comes, it will keep them warm until they go home at night. As for busy, I'll teach arts and crafts, water coloring, things like that. The club is buying a loom, so I'll teach weaving. There's cross-stitching . . ."

"Boring," I interrupted her.

"You don't have to come," she said, her voice testy. "But there'll be one thing I am looking forward to. I'm encouraged to start a choir." She sounded happy, and when I looked at her, she seemed to glow. I hadn't seen her smile like that for a long time. "I'd be the conductor. There will be choir competitions. Are you happy for me?"

"Yes, I am. Could I sing with them? And could I visit Amber once in a while?"

"I'm afraid not. On both counts. Only the boys and girls belonging to the club will sing in the choir. And the Murphys, that's another story. She wasn't happy when I left. Mrs. Murphy will have to wash her own dishes for a few days, until she finds a replacement. She was quite upset. My God. Before she married, she sold buttons and such at Woolworth's. Never had an inkling of household help, and now she acts as if she can't wash out a martini glass by herself. I apologized for the lack of notice and explained that I had to take this job right away, or risk losing it." Mother's mood had changed, and she sounded angry, "I don't care if she breaks one of her long red finger nails doing the dishes."

I hugged Mother, big with CARE, and I was happy for her. At last she had found work in a capacity she was trained for.

The train arrived at our stop. We left the station, and I asked Mother if I could carry the heavy box. No, she could manage, thank you very much. Okay. It was at least two kilometers to our house, and while we walked, the box grew heavier. I offered again and this time Mother let me carry it for a while. We should have brought a piece of rope to sling around it, so both of us could have shared the load.

Oma's intuition again surprised me. She often knew what was going to happen long before it did. Now she had felt when we would arrive, and she had come out to wait for us in the open door as we were walking toward our house.

She clapped her hands when she saw us. This was not our first CARE package, but we were hungry, and opening and discovering this food was as novel as the first package had been.

The big black scissors pried the box open, the cardboard lids unfolded in four directions, and there were the contents. I was most interested in the chocolate, an entire pound of dark, rich chocolate.

Oma smiled at the golden tin of American margarine, which tasted like butter. We thought of it as "gold" to be eaten. Oma grabbed the pound of coffee and immediately locked it in her personal cupboard. Coffee was pep-up medicine for her heart condition. There were other delicious things, such as a pound of beef in broth, to which Oma would add potatoes, carrots, and onions to make a stew that would last us for days. There was a pound of steak and kidneys. I would leave the kidneys to Oma and Mutti, but I welcomed the half a pound of liverwurst and the Spam for my school sandwiches. Mutti didn't much care for the Spam, but I loved its taste. The pound of bacon would be a welcome addition to many of Oma's pea soups, and then there was lard, apricot jam, sugar, flour, rice, egg powder, and raisins, which Oma would soon use in a cake; the cake would be prewar yellow because of the egg powder and rich American margarine. And there was laundry soap and twelve ounces of toilet soap, called Macy's—and the wonder of it, when I took a bath in Miss Hemet's tub, the soap floated on top of the water. We could have a full stomach and be clean as well. What a heavenly gift this package was. (The contents varied in CARE packages, so each was always a surprise.)

We were rich. Thank you Shmoo, and thank you Al Capp.

APPLE PIE DEMOCRACY

The GYA club was located in Zehlendorf, two stops on the S-Bahn from where we lived. One late autumn day, when I was visiting Mother, I smelled a pervasive aroma of apples and cinnamon, something that made my mouth water. I followed the scent down the hall, and there, on a long table, sat about eight round cakes. They looked different from any of the German cakes I was familiar with. The edges were formed into little waves and the crust was a golden brown, and I knew something delicious was hidden by the top layer.

"Apple pies, they are. Never had one?" The sergeant asked when I came near, inhaling. I shook my head. "Got a treat ahead, young lady," he said.

The U.S. soldiers in charge of teaching German boys about America, baseball, and democracy had brought us these delicious desserts. The sergeant who had offered me a slice of pie brought a tub of vanilla ice cream in from the kitchen. The kids who were members of the club, the girls from Mother's classes, and the boys who had completed their baseball game or lessons in democracy filled the hall. I never thought anyone would eat ice cream in this cold autumn weather, but here we were. One of the soldiers had switched from baseball coach to server, and all of us grabbed paper plates and got into what he called a "chow line." The pies were still steaming, and the apple filling was juicy and syrupy with sugar and spices. The scoop of ice cream topped it off, and the taste combination was sheer heaven. We didn't have pies in Germany, only tarts and cakes. Even Austria, the land of pastries, didn't have this particular taste sensation.

The kids in the GYA club were taught English and learned about American customs. They even ate hot dogs at their baseball games. *Hot dogs?* What a terrible name. In my imagination I saw little Dachshunds skewered and grilled and served while hot. Ugh. But I had no quarrel with apple pie. The pies symbolized an appropriate supplement to the lessons on democracy: democracy tasted sweet.

Later I heard the soldiers say that June Allyson—an actress I had seen in the movie *Good News*—was as "American as apple pie." I also wanted to be as American as apple pie, but I suppose I didn't quite make the grade and remained, for another few years at least, a German *Apfelstrudel*.

It was November, and heavy fog shrouded Berlin on most days. The poor visibility made it extremely difficult for planes to land, and there were several crashes. The two airports used for the many planes coming and going were insufficient: a new airport had to be constructed to allow additional planes to fly in and out while keeping a safe distance. Rubble women were hired to build the runways using the debris from bombed buildings, which was crushed and then covered with asphalt. (A series of artificial hills were built around Berlin from the rubble, and after these were covered by vegetation, most Berliners thought they had always been part of the landscape.)

There were problems building the airport. German heavy equipment and machinery had been looted and shipped to Russia. Mother wondered how the Americans could possibly build an airport and runways? Planes could not transport the huge cranes, steamrollers, and other machinery necessary for such an undertaking. But we soon experienced firsthand the innovative spirit of Americans. The solution was to cut up the heaviest pieces of machinery and number the parts like in a giant erector set, then fly these separate parts into Berlin where German machinists and technicians would weld the pieces back together again. Soon dozens of cranes and bulldozers grew into a defiant army to build whatever was necessary to keep the Russian bear at bay and Berlin free.

My friend Robert stood at the door, dripping rain from his wooly cap. I took his soaked peacoat and shook it out in front of the door. Behind him the skies were thick with swollen clouds and the rain came down in squalls.

Robert was a family friend, especially liked by Oma. Her American roots attracted many young people. They practiced their English with her, and because she was open to things new, such as jazz, Robert and his friends congregated at our house, bringing along their instruments for jam sessions. Robert banged on the drums and Toby hammered on the piano. There were others with guitars and trumpets. One person even had a saxophone.

Robert was a few years older than I and a history student at the "Lindenuniversität," in the Russian sector. With pressure from the Com-munist Party increasing, many of the liberal professors were let go or left of their own accord. Members of the SED, the official name of the Communist Party, rose to advanced positions, even though they were often unqualified.

For the sake of learning and teaching in a free environment, the students and some of the faculty had prepared to break away from the yoke of communism and establish a free university in West Berlin. That was precisely the name they gave their university: Freie Universität Berlin (F.U., for short).

Now as Robert hung up his dripping coat in the vestibule, he shouted, "Karin, we've done it. I didn't think we could, but we've done it." He strode into the kitchen, embracing Oma with a hug and lifting the cover off the pot bubbling on the stove. "*Hmm,*" he sniffed. "Lentil soup?" He rolled his eyes in anticipation of being invited.

"Pull up a chair and get yourself a bowl. Soup's almost ready," Oma said.

"But what have you done?" I asked.

"The new university will open officially this Saturday. We did it, hurrah!"

"Congratulations!" I said.

Oma's eyebrows went up, perhaps she was not sure what exactly we were hurrahing about, but she unlocked the cupboard and brought out a bottle of German Sekt to celebrate.

We clinked glasses, watched the bubbles dissolve, and sat down to eat. The meal was a strange combination: German champagne accompanying lentil soup, floating a ham hock. Oma cut off little slivers of meat from the bone, there wasn't much, and put them in Robert's bowl. I didn't mind that he got this special treatment; he was our hero of the moment and skinny enough to warrant Oma's mothering him.

Robert went on with his story. "The free university opens officially on December 4, in the Titania Palast," he snickered, "Of all places."

"Makes sense," Oma said. "It's about the only hall big enough to seat a lot of people."

"Yes, but still. It's a movie palace. But let me tell you. Here we are, the students, the actual founders of this new university. We took our motto from America: 'Freedom, Truth, Justice.' It will be engraved in the stone over the entrance: *Freiheit, Wahrheit, Gerechtigkeit.*" He turned to me, explaining the Jeffersonian ideal. Then he went on, "Here we are, and these old, timeworn rectors are telling us we have to sit way in the back of the auditorium. The first twenty rows or so will be filled with dignitaries, visiting professors, Americans, you name it. Imagine, we, the students who founded the university, will have to sit behind all the others. Is that the new democracy? Ha. You know what we did?" I frowned and shook my head. "We banded together and told them that in that case we would not be present. You should have seen the faces of those silver heads. They were so sure they could talk us into doing what they wanted. But no! We would not give in. After much palaver back and forth, they decided we would be seated on stage. Is that funny or what? From being relegated to back rows to suddenly be elevated to the stage. We'll sit there like a goddamn—pardon my language, Frau Keller," he shrugged to my grandmother. "We'll be sitting there like a choir. I just hope someone won't pelt us with rotten cabbage if we don't sing."

Saturday came and I thought of Robert when the weather turned its most beastly. He and another two thousand dripping people would fill the theater.

Luckily, we had electricity. We turned on the radio to listen to the ceremonies taking place at the Titania Palast. There had been several more accidents in the airlift, and one plane was lost. We were still afraid that at any moment the Americans might find the losses too high to justify defending Berlin. We feared they would leave. Oma, Mutti, and I were tense, and I could imagine the tension in the Titania Palast, when the commander of Berlin, General Lucius D. Clay, mounted the stage. He spoke a few phrases relating to the new university, then he cleared his throat and declared, "My headquarters will remain in Berlin. Any rumors of Americans leaving are false."

The deafening roar of applause coming from the radio was so loud that I got up and turned down the volume. Oma, Mutti, and I hugged. No matter what the weather, no matter what the risk to planes, no matter what the cost of this airlift, the Americans were staying.

We felt a rush of love for America, and the radio seemed to transmit the love of the two thousand people present at that moment. It was astounding. When I think about the emotions we felt, of love mixed with gratitude, I believe they were unique in the annals of war.

We, the people of Berlin, were loyal. We were hungry, and although the Russians allowed us to buy rations such as fresh vegetables, fresh eggs, and milk in their sector, only a few people took the Soviets up on their offer. We knew we would be playing into their hands, and they would use our purchases for their propaganda. We, and 97 percent of the population, preferred our meager rations of dried egg powder and milk powder to anything the Russians might have to offer.

Thornton Wilder came to Berlin at that time, bringing us his play *The Skin of Our Teeth*. Mutti took me to the Renaissance Theater on opening night, when Wilder stood on stage and announced that he was honoring the steadfast will of the Berliners and paid homage to our will to survive. The applause was akin to thunder, and many in the audience brought out their handkerchiefs, wiping at tears of emotion. I was so enthused that I convinced Oma to see the play with me again. In German the title is *Wir sind noch einmal davon gekommen*—We have survived. We Berliners had survived. Every Berliner saw him or herself in the play, and every performance quickly sold out.

Christmas came and went. This one was as equally miserable as the previous one, especially since Uncle Will was in Germany and unable to visit us in Berlin. Studying for school became more problematic: we were running out of candles and the electricity was only on for two hours in the middle of the night. I began a schedule of napping in the late afternoon, getting up to read my schoolbooks from two to four in the morning, and then going back to bed so that I could get up at seven to get ready for school. It was winter, and the water in the wash basin was frozen once again.

One afternoon in March, Robert picked me up from my singing lessons in Zehlendorf, and we bicycled around the shore of the Schlachtensee, the lake near my house. We took a break and sat on the log of a fallen tree. We conversed rather than talked. Yes, that's what you did with Robert: you conversed about life and its complications and our existence on earth. Robert encouraged me to read Kierkegaard and Heidegger—existentialism was en vogue—but I confess, although I read the words, their philosophies remained a mystery to me.

That afternoon we talked about the play *The Flies* we had recently seen. (Sartre's existentialism via a play was more accessible to me.) As Robert explained Satre's ideas, my eyes wandered to the shimmering water, watching ducks swim past in pairs. The air smelled like a promise of spring, and only patches of snow remained. Small crocuses pushed their heads of yellow and white through the black earth.

Robert fell silent. He stared at me, making me feel uncomfortable. Then he put his arm around me and I knew he was about to kiss me. I swung myself back up on my bicycle and off I rode.

Kissing or not, we remained friends. One day he invited me along when he and his friend Otto visited Otto's much older sister. She lived in a villa by the Wannsee. When she opened the door, she smiled a toothy smile. Addressing her brother but looking at me, she said, "How nice Otto. You brought a young lady to visit me." Then she said, "Karin, I have something for you to see, but later, later . . . ," and she waved us into the house.

What could that "something" be, I wondered?

When we crossed the threshold, the former elegance of her villa made me shiver as if I had entered a tomb. The entry hall was wallpapered in a shade of deep brown. As she ushered us into the salon, I noticed that the walls in this room, though black–green, were covered in the same textured paper. This large room had tall French doors, hidden by heavy dark green velvet drapes. I walked to the doors and peered out onto the stretch of lawn leading down a slope to the lake and wished someone would open the curtains to let in some light.

Otto's sister was most gracious and served us tea and dainty finger sandwiches. She then rose and asked me to follow her. "I have something unusual to show you. I'm so happy you came along, the young men aren't interested in my collection."

A collection of what?

She preceded me to a sitting room. A heavy curtain separated this from a chamber. She opened the drapes with a "Voilà!" as if she were opening the curtain to a stage. Sitting on a long table, on shelves, and on chairs were dolls: old dolls and new dolls, baby dolls and dolls of all ages, celluloid dolls and porcelain dolls. I stared at them. Some were dressed in velvet, some in satin and taffeta, and some were without clothes, pink and naked.

"Karin, don't you want to come closer and see my collection?" she asked.

I stood, staring. I did not see what was before me; I did not see harmless dolls. My mind blurred reality with a mental replay of the bombing in Wiesbaden. And I saw as clearly as I had those many years ago, my dead schoolmate among the corpses on the floor of the pharmacy. The dolls were transformed into dead bodies. I pressed my hand against my mouth and raced through the salon to the French doors and down to the water. By the lake, I threw up, over and over again.

I was never invited back.

Children waving at a "Rosinenbomber" (Raisin Bomber) as it brings food to the people of Berlin during the Berlin Airlift, 1948. (The Granger Collection, New York.)

Rolf, Karin's first love, 1949.

Karin practicing American
songs on the piano, 1949.

Robert and Karin in 1950 by his little sail-boat on the Wannsee.

Cousin Totty, 1951.

Brixie, 1951, before applying
for a modeling job.

Preparing stuffed green
peppers for my father, 1951.

CHAPTER 16

Lilacs

On May 12, 1949, the Soviets removed the barricades from the autobahn, and they allowed freight trains to travel from West to East Germany. The blockade was lifted. People streamed onto the streets and greeted the first trucks rolling in with food. Others, waving little flags, welcomed the first train that arrived with coal from the West. I hoped that now the electricity would be on for additional hours.

The Americans had succeeded in keeping Berliners alive during the blockade, and the Soviets had given in. It was springtime and the air was sweet with the scent of blossoms. I felt lighter. I felt like dancing rather than walking down the street. In fact, I felt as if I could spread my arms and fly.

I met Rolf when we were both buying milk at the corner grocery store. Now that the blockade had been lifted, we were able to drink heavenly white, rich, liquid milk once again. He dropped his ration cards when I bumped into him, and then we bumped heads when we both bent down at the same time to pick up the green bits of paper. When I straightened up, our eyes met. Could it be that these expressive gray-blue eyes looked at *me*? Could it be that this handsome mouth filled with gleaming white teeth smiled at *me*? When my eyes traveled upward, for he was tall, I saw a high forehead topped by a shock of wavy brown hair. I clutched my chest.

Milk bottles in hand, we walked toward our homes and discovered we were close neighbors. When I looked out from my attic room, I could see his bedroom window beyond our garden and the lilac trees. I was sixteen and he was nineteen, and I felt something so strange in my chest and my stomach that I knew I must be falling in love.

Since we had no telephones, we would hang towels from our upstairs windows to signal that we were home. The moment he saw my towel, he would dash over and toss a small stone up to my window. I would run down to meet him, and we would stroll down the street hand in hand to the Rehwiese, a small park where the lilacs were blooming. I regarded lilacs as symbols of renewal, since they were among the first bushes to bloom after the fires and destruction of Berlin. Rolf liked poetry and always carried a book with him. We'd sit on one of the park's benches while he read to me from Rilke, Hölderlin, or Goethe.

But one day he closed the book. His expression became soft and his eyes dreamy, and he pulled me closer to him. As his hand caressed my hair, his lips lowered to touch mine. We kissed. We didn't speak any more, just kissed, longer and longer. I did not want him to stop, did not want his lips to leave mine. His lips, half open, were soft, and I could feel the velvety smoothness of his mouth and the lightness of the flicker of his tongue. It all seemed so natural and so right.

We kissed until my lips burned. We kissed until the sun hid behind clouds and a shower chased us beneath the sheltering branches of an old chestnut tree.

I began to crave the scent of lilac, and I associated it with Rolf. To me, the scent of lilac became part of the odor of maleness. Along with the scent of shaving cream, it all blended into something akin to pheromones, exciting me.

While his mother was out of town—she had taken one of the first trains to West Germany after the blockade had lifted, but how she accomplished that miracle he never told me—I tried to prove my domestic side and offered to iron his shirt. Like a fool I began with the front near the collar, and I scorched it. There it was, a big brown splotch right near the buttons. I cried and was so embarrassed that I wanted to dissolve into the air, but Rolf took me into his arms and said it didn't matter.

"But it does. I am so sorry. I can't even buy you a new shirt, I don't have any ration cards for it."

"Don't worry. I'll keep this shirt forever, as a memory. When we're old, we'll laugh about it."

When we're old? Thoughts of marriage at our age were pure fantasy; the future did not exist. The world outside of his apartment did not exist. What existed were our feelings for one another, in this space and in this time.

Minutes melted into hours as we held each other on the sofa and kissed.

Before my next visit to Rolf's house, I put on my best panties, one out of a set of "Days of the Week" panties my cousin Totty had sent from New York. I was hoping Rolf would discover them and be impressed that I had chosen the right day, "Thursday," stitched in pink along with dainty rosebud garlands. When I put them on, I thought of my girlfriend Ellen's little trick. She slipped into torn, dirty underwear before meeting her boyfriend. They served as her shield to remain a virgin, or so she told me, since she knew she would rather die than allow him to discover those disgusting knickers.

I put on a plaid skirt and a red sweater over my pretty underwear. Unlike Ellen, I did not want to preserve anything, especially not my virginity. I loved Rolf, and I wanted to be one with him on his brown and beige patterned sofa.

Later I sensed him wanting me too, feeling his body grow hard when I arched to meet every part of him. But he suddenly stood up and went to the bathroom. He returned a little while later with a glass of water and sat down and gently kissed me on the forehead. He respected me, he said, and after all, I was so young that it would be better to wait.

"I have to go to Switzerland in a few days," he said. "That's what Mother is arranging right now. I have tuberculosis. A clinic in Davos has accepted me."

I bolted upright. Tuberculosis was an almost always fatal disease in pre-penicillin Germany. "I don't want you to go."

"But you want me to be cured, don't you?"

The night before he was to take the train, we scrambled eggs over fried potatoes. He held me tight and whispered gently, "You're like a crystal goblet filled with a rare golden wine." I thought of the Tokay wine at the Esterhazy château, and although this comparison seemed silly to me, it was also romantic. Then he said, "I don't want to drink the wine until I have time and health to savor it fully."

"Rolf," I said. "Tomorrow you leave. I love you. I want to . . ."

"No, Karin. No, it will have to wait."

He walked me home, faster than usual. His stride was long and I had to take two steps to one of his. His lips were soft and yearning when we kissed beneath the purple lilac bush. My tears made the kisses taste like salt.

And then he left.

I could not stop crying. Two weeks had passed, and my eyes were still red. Oma wondered what was wrong, and I confessed. Mother shot from her chair. "I knew that boy had consumption."

"He looked so healthy," Oma said. "Such good color in his face, who would have thought?"

"I saw him buy milk. No one over eighteen would get that kind of a milk ration. Did he kiss you?"

"Yes."

"Then you might be infected. Oh my God."

"Mother, stop it. Everything is a big drama for you."

"Has he written to you?"

"Yes. Two letters so far."

She made me bring them to her. The first one was written like a fairy tale, and Rolf again used the metaphor of the goblet of wine. In the second, he told me about the difficulties of his trip and his missing me. I flashed the letters at her, and when she made a grab for them, I rushed from the room to hide them. Mother chased me to the kitchen, trying to tear them from me. She was strong and wrestled them away. She lit a match. I tried to grab them, but she had been fast. They caught fire and went up in flames. I snatched at them again and the pages fell to the floor. I stomped out the flames and gathered up what was left of the scorched papers. The writing in blue ink had been blackened by fire, and the goblet of wine was undecipherable.

"You are crazy!" I yelled at Mother. "Why did you burn his letters?"

"You are so stupid. The paper is full of bacteria. Do you want to get ill?"

"Yes. Then I could go to Switzerland and be with Rolf in the clinic."

Mother slapped me, hard. "Go to your room," she said.

I never heard from Rolf again. Other letters may have been intercepted by Mother or he might have died in the clinic in Davos. Perhaps he thought I'd forgotten him when I didn't write, but after Mother burned the letters, I no longer had his return address.

But his memory is alive in the scent of lilacs.

Some weeks had passed since I had been so desperate to lose my virginity to Rolf. School taught me that Mother was right: kissing Rolf posed a health threat to me. My gym teacher, to whom I confided my exposure, sent me to see a doctor working for the schools. I had to be tested immediately. Mother had been pestering me to go and be examined. Now she would have her way, since the school requested it.

During one of the classes involving the subject of health, our biology teacher lectured that Berliners were in grave danger of contracting numerous diseases. She warned that we were still undernourished, even now, four years after the war had ended. Our bodies had little strength to fight invading bacteria or viruses. To raise our awareness of those dangers, she would show us an American film.

Fräulein Dr. Schwänzner (her name said it all, meaning one with a *Schwanz*, a tail, synonymous with both the devil and a penis) herded us, a group of sixteen- and seventeen-year-olds into the auditorium. We were told that the movie was in Technicolor. The only American movie in color I'd seen was *Good News,* with the apple-pie actress, June Allyson. I was hoping to see *Gone with the Wind* soon, but the movie we would see was not *Gone with the Wind.*

Dr. Schwänzner, like many of the teachers I'd encountered throughout my school years, was gifted with a certain sadism. Our lyceum was for girls only, and perhaps the teachers believed, since we were not in mixed company, that it would be all right to show us this film, which had been made by the U.S. Army as a warning for the troops. But we were not young and naïve soldiers whose testosterone levels placed them in jeopardy in foreign lands. We were young German girls, living with our parents. Most of us lived sheltered lives, and many of us had survived the Russian's rape immediately after the fall of Berlin as virgins, even though others among my schoolmates had not been so lucky. Now our biology teacher wanted us to see the ravages of syphilis on screen.

Why had the film producers chosen black men to be filmed? Their skin color emphasized the gore—the festering lesions of yellow puss, the red open wounds, and the whitish canker sores—all in full glorious Technicolor, with great attention given to detail. We stared in disbelief. The message "Penicillin fails one in seven times" was heard over and over again in the film. The voice sounded like the one I'd heard on AFN Berlin, the U.S. Army radio station, where that message was broadcast every hour on the hour. For us Germans, a cure for syphilis would more than likely fail seven in seven times because we could not get penicillin.

During the Nazi years, when the police state severely punished prostitutes, syphilis had almost been eradicated. After the Russians raped thousands of women, the illness had made a triumphant comeback. There were only outmoded and painful medicines available for a cure, one of which I remembered from having visited Siegrid, when she had lain on the floor writhing in pain from sulfa injections.

The film's images stayed in my head. Could something so horrible and full of sores insert itself into a woman? I got sick and headed for the toilet. Several of my classmates also left the room, and soon I heard a chorus of heaving. Later we sat on the wooden benches outside the auditorium.

"I'm not going back inside. Let the old *Schwanz* give me a failing grade, I don't care. I'm sick," I said.

"She's cruel, showing that disgusting movie," Helga said.

"I'm never going to get married," Ingeborg said.

"Not me either," said Lilo.

"I don't think I could ever sleep with a man, so I can't get married either," I said.

"Let's swear to it then," Ingeborg said with a grave voice. "Here, put your hand on my hand, and you, Karin, put yours on top, now let's all say this together. We will never ever go to bed with a man. We will remain untouched virgins all of our lives."

A chorus of voices rang out, "We will never go to bed with a man. We will remain untouched virgins all of our lives."

"Now swear to it," Ingeborg said.

"By what?" I asked.

"By our mothers," said Ingeborg.

"I don't want to swear by my mother," I said. "Why not swear by our own bodies? We will hold our bodies sacred."

"Oh Karin. Sacred bodies. All right then. We swear by our health and our bodies that we shall remain virgins. Forever," said Ingeborg.

Fräulein Dr. Schwänzner would have been elated had she known the effect the movie had on us.

I couldn't believe that just a month or so ago I had wanted to make love with Rolf. When I thought of him, I still felt little birds fluttering in my tummy and still longed for him, wanting to be held by him. But I shook my head. No, I would never make love to a man.

I later told Oma about the film and the pact my friends and I had made. A shy smile appeared on her cheeks. "Oh Karin. Remember, forever is a long long time."

THE BLUE DRESS

Oma was usually happy when Will's letters arrived, but on that day, her eyes filled with tears. She dabbed at her face with her embroidered handkerchief as she read his explanation for his continued absence. I did not like his letter; he wrote as if he were writing to an accountant, numbering the many obstacles he faced. A permit to travel through the Russian zone was still difficult to obtain. Will had worked for the *Funkwelt* but had been in negotiations to launch a new woman's magazine, *Die Frau*. He had assumed the helm as the chief editor a short while back, and now that the first issue was ready to go to press, he could not get away.

Of course it pleased Oma that Will had found interesting work so quickly after his release from the prisoner-of-war camp, but even if these were valid excuses, she longed to see him and was sad. Some days her lips twisted strangely, telling me that she thought he didn't try hard enough. Berlin was free. Trains arrived daily, and other people got permission to travel. He had managed to visit us for a day and a half a year ago. Why not a few days now? She counted on her fingers, if he only took three days off, one day each for travel to and from Berlin and one day to spend with her, it would be balm for her heart. He could spare that much time, couldn't he? She voiced all this to me, but in her letters to him, she kept silent about her misgivings. She even tried to get a pass for herself to journey to the West, but because of her age and because she didn't have proof of lodging, the authorities refused her travel papers. There were few hotel rooms available in 1949, and most of the small boardinghouses and villas that had previously taken in guests were occupied by refugees. Uncle Will did not have a place of his own but shared a small apartment with a woman friend.

As the weeks passed, Oma's head seemed to sink deeper into her shoulders and her back became more bent. She aged visibly, her chin sagged, and her pink skin turned sallow. She was not yet seventy years old, but she had become a very old woman.

While visiting Mother in the GYA club, I heard of an audition for musicians and singers to perform in Saturday night floor shows at officers' clubs. When I told Oma, she limited her response to one word: "No." But Mother was in favor of it, and this was the first time I went against Oma's wishes. Even though Mother would accompany me to the audition, I didn't want Oma to see me leave in fancy clothes, so with my dress over my arm and shoes in a bag, I tiptoed past her room and out of the house to change clothes at Brixie's house.

Mother had loaned me one of her dresses, a black prewar silk dress with a V-neck. There was some empty space in front that my budding breasts tried in vain to fill. The dress was a little too matronly for me, but I felt sophisticated and elegant wearing it. My hair fell free to my shoulders, and Mother suggested that I tuck one of our garden's dahlias behind my left ear. She had probably seen that in a magazine. I picked one in a shade between pink and magenta. Mother was right: it made the severe black of the dress look more lively. I lacked nylon or silk stockings, but Brixie came to the rescue. My legs were fairly tanned from sunbathing by the Wannsee, but Brixie suggested that I darken them even more by slathering them with oil mixed with iodine. That also gave them a shine like silk. Then Brixie held a sheet of cardboard against my calves and, with an eyebrow pencil, drew a dark line on them to simulate the seam in nylons. I squeezed into a pair of black high heeled ankle-strap pumps from Totty. The shoes were sheer agony, but I thought they looked sexy.

There I was, with Mother by my side, waiting for my audition. I felt awkward and somewhat embarrassed, sitting on fragile, gold-leafed chairs in the foyer of the club, staring and being stared at by the other would-be performers. There were two clowns with red noses somewhat askew, and two women in their late twenties with low décolletages and lots of bosom showing. One had brass-yellow hair, and the other's was a deep black. The hair of both looked enhanced. They looked me up and down as if they were evaluating my worth. I felt as if I were a rabbit in a meat market. Several men with instrument cases sat on a wooden bench. Next to them, on one of the small chairs, sat a very fat saxophone player. His silver instrument lay on his lap, and he kept fingering the knobs as if he were itching to play. His posterior was too wide for the chair and hung over the edge. I heard creaking and thought that at any moment man and chair were going to succumb to the laws of gravity and crash. Another of these band members had teeth that protruded like a dilapidated fan, so much so that he couldn't fully close his lips. He breathed in and out through his teeth, making whistling sounds. I also noticed his violin case. Good, he would not be at the piano, whistling while I sang. Then there was a young boy, maybe ten or so, and I wondered what he would be doing for his audition. Another thirty-something woman stood apart, disdaining the chairs. She looked like a proper performer to me, carrying her full bosom high and holding herself erect like an opera diva.

The yellow-haired woman was called first. Her song floated through the door, which had been left slightly ajar. Her voice wasn't bad, but she sang in English, which proved to be a mistake. Her accent was so "tcherman" that I'm sure the officers would have preferred "Lilly Marlen" sung in the original German, rather than in mangled English. They excused her after one song. The clowns didn't last long either. I thought Americans liked clowns. When it was the young boy's turn, I sneaked to the door and looked through the narrow opening. The boy removed his shirt and then his trousers, revealing a pair of bright green tights. I had wondered why such a young boy wore long pants. His chest was bare, and I was amazed at how white his skin was. The boy supported his torso on his forearms and bent his body in a curve so his legs wrapped over his shoulders and around his neck. Holding my breath, I wondered if he would ever be able to untangle himself, as I watched the white torso and the green tights transform into a coiling snake, but then he slowly unwound. He was hired.

I was called next. Mother and I stood up at the same time. Mother, ever superstitious, spat "*Toi-toi-toi*" for good luck over my left shoulder. Inside the room, three officers sat behind a long wooden table. They smiled when they saw how young I was and said something to reassure me that they were not going to bite my head off. Mother walked over to the piano and I stood next to her. She played a riff leading into my song, and I began with one of the selections from my "American Hit Parade" song sheets. "Blue Moon, you left me standing alone . . ." I thought of Rolf when I sang the lyrics and put all of my longing for him into the song. The officers applauded. Then the officer in the center asked how many American songs I knew. He said I needed to have a large repertoire because when it came time for encores, some of the officers were certain to request their own favorites. I was hesitant, should I lie? I smiled and said, "I only know a few songs, but I can learn quickly. These songs are a lot easier to memorize than an aria from a Mozart opera." One of them said, "Guess that's right," and the other two grinned. I sang a few more songs: "The Best Things in Life Are Free"; "Chattanooga Choo Choo"; and "Shoo Fly Pie and Apple Pan Dowdy." The three officers whispered to each other, then scheduled me for next Saturday night to give me a first tryout. I had to know at least ten songs by then, plus "Goodnight Irene," which would end the floorshow.

I was told I would make fifty mark a night for working from eight to ten o'clock. In addition, my chaperone—necessary because of my age—and I could eat dinner at the club. If they employed me every Saturday, it would be two hundred mark a month. This amount of money seemed like a staggering sum to me.

My potential earnings went to my head. I hated school more than ever. Why did I need to put up with those terrifying teachers when I could earn my livelihood by singing? But Mother would not let me drop out of school; she insisted I keep going to that institute of torture where I would run into Frau Dr. Schwänzner and suffer her scowls.

A sergeant, ready to burst out of his uniform, waddled over to me. He informed me of the restrictions: I was not to socialize with any of the officers, and I was not to accept gifts, drinks, or even a single cigarette. I snarled into his face, "Hey, I'm only sixteen. I don't drink, I don't smoke, and I don't want to have anything to do with the military. All I want to do is sing."

Oma was not reconciled to my singing in the club and had daily arguments with Mother. She thought it outrageous to imagine her granddaughter in a club on a small stage, singing in a smoky room. No, this was too much, and she was utterly disgusted with both Mother and me. She would not accept my apology for having gone behind her back. I tried my best to kiss and tickle her and to lift her up and whirl her about, but she kept her angry mien and refused to be reconciled.

Mother, on the other hand, was excited about my having been hired. Saturday was fast approaching, and I had to learn the lyrics and music to more than eleven songs by then and decide what I was going to wear. I opened the doors to my wardrobe and looked through my clothes. Nothing seemed pretty enough or appropriate for evening wear. Then Mother thought of the blue silk dress Aunt Wanda had given us after Maria's death.

I remembered the color, forget-me-not blue. I would wear this dress and Maria would not be forgotten. The dress hung in Oma's wardrobe. Mother retrieved it, and I put it on. She pulled out a wooden stool and had me climb on it. Scissors, pins, needles, and thread appeared as if by magic. It was like old times. But I remembered the jabs with needles and warned Mother, "Please don't stick me. You know how I hate that." Mother quickly ripped open several seams. She looked up at me with an expression that said, trust me.

She pulled, tucked, shortened, and cut off some material and lowered the neckline just a little, rounding it out more and making it come slightly off the shoulders. When she had time and was motivated, my mother could work magic on clothes.

Oma entered the room. She stared at us and shook her head.

"Oma, don't you think it's pretty?" I turned in a circle for her. "I think Maria would like to see her dress put to good use."

"Maria is dead. Remember when she wore it, she also wore the cyanide around her neck. Just there." Oma stuck her finger on my neck. "You call this good use? It's not much better than singing in a bar. *Pfui Teufel,*" she spat on the devil—as if he were present in the room and the cause of this perceived evil.

"Mutter, you are taking this much too seriously. Karin is only singing in an American officers club, with a chaperone. It is quite harmless."

"Harmless? To expose a young girl to that atmosphere? Singing in a smoke-filled room? Don't you care at all about her voice? You know what the singing teacher said: she is not to sing where people smoke. Bah. You are selfish, Astrid. You want your dream realized in her. Because you could never face an audience."

Mother's face flooded a deep crimson. She stuck me with a pin and a small dot of red blossomed on the blue below my waist. But I saw the apology in her eyes and knew it was an accident. She was flustered and getting angry. "Mutter," she said, "You are spoiling Karin's big chance . . ."

"Big chance for what? Maybe to become an American officer's fräulein?"

Mother took a deep breath. She blew up her cheeks, making a sort of frog face. I was afraid she would not be able to control her temper.

"Oma," I said, "Don't you think I know better? Don't you trust me?"

"Karin, you are young and easily influenced."

"But Oma, maybe the band will hire me for other occasions? Maybe I can get to sing on RIAS, like Rita Paul? You like her singing, and you said you like my voice even better than hers. Wouldn't you like to hear me on the radio?"

Oma shook her head. Now Mother got into the fray again. "Karin will make a lot of money, that's something to consider."

"Money has never been important to us. To have enough food, yes. Astrid, for you to be speaking of money? Shame on you. If your father were alive, he'd be deeply disappointed. And just look at you," Oma now grabbed my neckline and pulled it down. "Why don't you lower it some more? Make her look even more like a cheap little cabaret singer? *Ach . . .*" She threw her hands up and left the room, banging the door shut.

Mother ran after her, yelling down the hall, "You've gone crotchety. You're too old to judge what goes on today. The world has changed. What was improper fifty years ago is quite another thing today."

Oma brushed Mother aside, as she returned to the room. "Please, Astrid, don't shout through the house like a fishwife. If you accuse me of being old, then be happy I am. If I were not old, I'd be dead."

"*Omchen,*" I said. "Please, Mother . . . , we're all saying things we don't mean. To me you are young, Oma. Robert and all of his friends say that you are the most modern of all grandmothers. You even like jazz."

"Nonsense. Your grandmother is hopelessly stuck in her own time." Mother then turned and shouted in Oma's face, "You better look out so the potato soup won't burn and, please, allow me to get on with fixing Karin's dress."

"Did you hear yourself, Astrid? You told me I'm an old, over-the-hill woman and ordered me into the kitchen like hired help. Who do you think you are speaking to?" Oma stormed out of the room. I wanted to go after her and make her smile again, but Mother wouldn't let me off the stool.

Here I stood in front of the mirror, watching the blue silk dress take shape. A tuck here and a tuck there gave me a waistline, the hem reached halfway down my calves, and I marveled at the transformation from shapeless blue silk into a lovely dress for my debut. I kept looking at myself in the mirror. I liked the reflection of this young woman looking back at me, and I am ashamed to say, I forgot about my grandmother's humiliation.

CHAPTER 17

Oma's Heart

FALL 1949

In the fall, Oma suffered a heart attack. As she lay in the hospital, I felt guilty, thinking it had been brought on in part by our continued arguments about my singing engagements.

Oma had accompanied me to the club several times, much against her better judgment, because I had to have a chaperone and Mother was busy. Oma hated the club, the smoking officers, and the women who blew smoke through both of their nostrils, as if blowing smoke from two chimneys; it all disgusted her. Most of the women in the club were military personnel, but there were also a few wives. German girlfriends, if any of the officers had them, were not allowed. Oma didn't like that; it made it plain to her that we were second-class citizens in our own country. Poor Oma, who always thought of herself as an American, it must have been awful to feel so demoted.

While Oma was in the hospital, Mother accompanied me to the club one night. Of all people, Mrs. Murphy waltzed into the club on the arm of the colonel. I almost didn't recognize her. She wore a teal blue satin dress in the new midcalf length. The dress had a cinched waist bodice that ended in a peplum, and Mrs. Murphy wore her hair in a marcelled upsweep. An amazing change had taken place. She had gone from being a plain woman in Sears, Roebuck & Company mail-order catalog clothes to looking svelte, as if she had been following Paris fashion trends and had been inspired by Christian Dior's "New Look."

The floorshow was in progress when the Murphys arrived, and I was in the midst of a song. Mrs. Murphy stared at me. Her finger shot out, pointing at me, and then she shouted, "What in the hell are you doin' in here in our club?" I froze. The words I was about to sing, "the best things in life are free, . . ." stuck in my throat. Then she saw my mother who was partially hidden by the piano and waiting for me to finish my performance. Now she shrieked, still pointing, "Get that woman out of here. Get her out, get her out."

The colonel grabbed her arm as she marched toward us. I ran behind the piano. Mother just sat there, not moving, while the colonel dragged Mrs. Murphy toward the exit. He spoke to someone behind him, one of his guards, I think. Would he call his MPs to restrain his wife or to have us forcibly removed?

While the colonel had his wife in his grip, she elbowed him in the ribs and freed herself. She took a few fast steps in our direction, then lurched and lost her footing. She sailed toward a couple of WACs sitting at a small table, upsetting their drinks, turning over the table, and landing in the lap of one of the women. The other WAC rose and nonchalantly brushed off the spilled drinks with a napkin. Colonel Murphy was by his wife in a second. This time he took a tighter grip on her and pulled her to stand upright, then he dragged her out of the club, apologizing to the WACs on his way out while ordering new drinks for them. Through the slammed door, we could hear Mrs. Murphy yelling, "Goddamn German bitches . . ."

People sat in shock. Everyone's eyes were on my mother and me. I imagined they all wondered what those terrible German women had done to that poor and naïve lady from Texas?

The piano player hit the keys again and some of the musicians joined in, but I sat stunned. The club manager reached my side while I was still debating if I should try to sing or call it a night. Mother tugged at my arm and whispered, "Time to go home."

"It's best you take your Mother's advice," the manager said. "We'll let you know when to come back."

I shook my head and murmured, "I don't know why she did this. I babysat her little girl. We were friends. I've done nothing to her. Nothing."

The manager cleared his throat and repeated that he would let me know when the club would want me to sing again.

I went to visit Oma in the hospital the next day. The small oval of her face seemed to disappear in the fluffy white pillows. Her hair was all silver and lay in loose waves, the strands meeting in a thin braid. I bent over to kiss her and whispered in her ear, "Oma, this will make you happy. I'm not singing at the club any longer."

She smiled, and it seemed as if this good news brought on a flush of pink to her pale skin. Then I told her the story. "So they let you go?" she asked, sounding disappointed.

"No. They called Mother at the GYA club and apologized for Mrs. Murphy's behavior. Colonel Murphy is a decent chap. He told the manager that his wife was still upset with Mother for leaving them and that they still had not found a good replacement. Hard to believe. Mutti a good housekeeper," I had to chuckle "But why would she be mad at me?" I shrugged. "Anyway, everyone in the club must have realized that Mrs. Murphy has an alcohol problem. They wanted me to come back this Saturday." I stroked Oma's hair and kissed her on the cheek. "You know, you are right, that's not a good place for me. I'm young, I have time, and I'll sing in better places. I told the manager I have to concentrate on school, on my studies. No more singing in his club." Oma smiled.

Oma was back in her bedroom. The doctor who had released her from the hospital told her to stay calm and to take her medication, and he had cautioned Mutti and me to take good care of her. She must have no upsets, not even happy ones. Happy ones? That would only be if Uncle Will would suddenly appear.

"You must get strong to go to America," I told her.

"*Ach,* Kind, I think it's too late for that."

"You must, Omchen, you must. What would I do there without you? Please, drink this, it will make you strong," I said, holding the broth, which I had made from a marrow bone, to her lips.

She waved it aside. "Maybe later. I can't get anything down now," she said, closing her eyes. I knew she wanted to rest, so I tiptoed out of the room.

Mother stood outside the door, tears running down her face. She made me angry. "Why are you crying?" I asked. "She's going to be all right. We're going to America together. She'll be strong again, you'll see. Stop your crying!"

Mother threw me a pitying glance. "Huh," she said and went to her room.

Another letter from Uncle Will arrived. He still could not come. Mother had told him that Grandmother's heart was getting weaker and that he must come right away. Yes, he wrote, I will come. Soon.

I was glad that I no longer sang at the club because I had made Oma happy with my decision to quit. But it was painful to see her diminish daily, as her life force had ebbed, leaving her drained.

I slept on a small sofa in her room now, to be near her in case she needed anything during the night. Water, that was the only thing she called for, repeatedly, as if she had an unending thirst. One morning she surprised me by asking for a *Schrippe,* a crispy Berlin-type bun, and liverwurst. I was pleased when I heard her strong teeth crunch the bread with relish. (She never had a cavity. She claimed her teeth were healthy and strong because, after all, horses have great teeth and eat oats and because she had eaten a lot of porridge growing up in Utah.) She ate every last morsel. She's eating again, I thought, she'll get her strength back and will walk again. I had hopes. But her asking for that one *Schrippe* was the only time she showed an appetite. It was ironic, now that we had enough food, she wouldn't eat.

"I'm so tired," she said each time I tried to tempt her with food.

She did perk up a little when she drank her cup of coffee in the morning and in the afternoon, but I worried. She had to get strong to travel to America. I wondered if the American consulate would issue a visa to someone who appeared to be ill. In another three weeks, on November 14, Oma would celebrate her seventieth birthday. Surely Uncle Will would come home to celebrate her birthday with us, and then she would get well. He would be the needed shot in the arm to give her energy and the will to live. She had called Lassie, my Scottie, her little *Lebenselixier,* an elixir that gives energy and life. But I thought her elixir would be Will: he would arrive and Oma would rise from her bed and be my old singing and dancing Oma again.

October ended, and no news came from Uncle Will. Then, on a Friday night, Oma's snores suddenly stopped in a gurgling sound, as if she were suffocating. I jumped out of bed and switched on the light by the nightstand. Oma was deathly white and her eyes were wide open, and she was clutching her heart. Then she cried out in pain, a penetrating sound, not loud, but high in pitch and like nothing I had heard before.

I woke Mother, grabbed a coat, and ran down the street to fetch the doctor. The night was dark gray and heavy with mist, except for round pools of yellow-green light the streetlamps painted on the sidewalk. My mind was clouded, but I ran by instinct, knowing the way to the doctor's house well.

Meanwhile, Mother was able to get Oma to swallow her digitalis, which was next to the water carafe on the nightstand. The doctor rushed to our house with me, after having telephoned for an ambulance from his home. By the time we arrived at the house, the ambulance attendants were already pushing the gurney with my grandmother into the open jaw of the vehicle. Mother and I were allowed to come along. On the way to the hospital, the doctor sat next to Oma, holding her wrist and counting her pulse rate.

Oma went into intensive care.

When Mutti and I returned to the hospital the next day, Oma was still asleep. Mother who was always full of nervous energy found it difficult to sit by Oma's bed. She left to send telegrams and to run errands.

When we'd first walked into the room, I was surprised and full of hope, seeing Oma look like she had years ago. Her skin was glowing, and her face, which had sagged before, had filled out. I sat down next to her, quite close, and when she opened her eyes, I whispered that I loved her. "I'm so happy to see your color has come back," I said. "I'm sure you're going to be well. Soon we'll go to America."

"My sweet, sweet child. You will have to go to America without me. I'll be with you, you know? You can show me all the wonderful things you'll see."

"Only if you get well and come with me."

She shook her head. "I'm very tired, *mein liebes Kind,* I want to go."

"Yes. You want to go to America . . ."

She shook her head. "Karin, here, take this ring." With these words she pulled her wedding ring off her finger and put it into my hand, closing my fingers over it. I looked at the ring, not knowing what to do. "I want you to have this ring," she said. "I want it to protect you." Oma read my face; she always knew what I was thinking. "Your mother will have my brooch from America, the big bowknot you know, the one I hung onto and would never sell." Her smile deepened, thinking of those hungry times when we sold our few possessions one by one to survive. "The brooch is nice for her, a memento from Utah. But this ring is to be yours. We are so close, you and I. As if you were a child of my body, not a grandchild. So guard it. Think of me when you wear it. You have been the warmth of my . . ." Her slender ivory fingers shot up and grabbed her nightgown, clutching it above her chest, pulling it askew.

"Oma, what is it?"

"Nothing. Where's your mother? Send a telegram to your Uncle Will. I just started to get maudlin, you know, thinking of how much joy you brought into my life."

"Mother went to send telegrams, she'll be right back."

"Karinchen, come closer." She breathed in and out a few times, belabored breaths. She waved me nearer to whisper in my ear. "I don't want others to know . . . I saw your Aunt Margaret this morning, promise, you won't tell?"

"Aunt Margaret? What did she look like? Oh Oma."

"I saw your grandfather, too. But I was so happy to see Aunt Margaret. She looked radiant. I think she wanted to let me know she was happy. We should not think of her sad death any longer. She wanted us to know that. She loves you very much. So, Karin, if I am no longer here with you . . ."

My thoughts reeled and my head spun. I tried to force my mind into some kind of order. What was Oma trying to tell me? Had she really seen them? Were they ghosts? A thousand thoughts flitted by and I could not catch a single one of them to try and make sense out of Oma's words. I looked at her for an answer, but she remained silent.

She looked peaceful now, and her new serenity affected me. It had to be caused by her seeing Aunt Margaret, knowing that she was happy and had gone beyond her cruel death. I wanted to believe Oma's vision. It made me feel as if something heavy from the past had been resolved. Having received my beloved Aunt Margaret's message, a feeling of peace filled me. I understood that she had come to Oma to let her know she was well. But my grandfather, why had he come? I had heard that our deceased loved ones would greet us when we pass from life to death. But Oma was not going to die, not now, not yet. Oma was here and she would stay here for many more years.

"It's wonderful . . . that you saw Aunt Margaret," I whispered.

"I am tired, *Liebchen,* it's time. But I will be with you, I will. Always."

I panicked, suddenly understanding *everything.* I grabbed her hands. "Omchen, I love you so much. Please, I need you."

She closed her eyes. Her breath came shallow but regular. Where was my mother? I rushed out of the room to find her. She was walking toward me in the hallway, returning from having sent the telegrams to her two brothers.

"Come, Mutti, come."

When she heard the tone of my voice, she picked up her pace and didn't ask questions. We entered Oma's room. She had fallen asleep and looked serene. Her skin color was as it had been earlier in her life, a very light peach color, and there were only a few wrinkles on her face. I sat on one side of her bed, and Mother pulled up a chair at the other. We both held her hands. I stroked Oma's right hand, the now ringless hand. I showed Mother the ring and indicated that Oma had given it to me. Mother nodded. Oma was breathing, but her shallow breath came in small spurts as if she were trying to swallow bites of air. She made no sounds indicating that she was in pain. We both kept holding and stroking her hands, those loving hands.

Oma opened her eyes, round and blue. They were luminous as if lit from within. She smiled at Mutti and at me. Then she closed her eyes and her breathing stopped.

Empty Rooms

It was late when Mother and I returned home from the hospital. Leaves rustled beneath our feet, and there were rainbow haloes around the streetlamps that lit our way. Mother said it might rain. I hoped for rain: let nature cry with me.

I crawled into Oma's bed and snuggled into her pillows, trying to breathe in her scent, trying to stay connected through her essence. She had said she would be with me, but I wanted to feel her and to see her. I waited for her, but sometime during the long night I fell asleep. I did not dream.

When I awoke, the sun smiled from above, mocking my sadness. The kitchen felt strange; there was no Oma bending over the stove, nor would there ever be again. I could not understand what I was feeling, the sensation of utter abandonment, alternating with anger. How could she leave me? I loved her. Did she die because Uncle Will did not visit her right after the blockade was over? She loved me. Was I not enough for her to go on living? She had promised to go to America with me. She had given me her ring, but I didn't want it. I wanted *her.* Her. I pounded on the kitchen table with both fists.

Mother looked up. She was making coffee; the aroma reminded me of Oma and her weak heart. She was the one who should be drinking the coffee. Mother offered me a cup, and I took a sip. But it tasted bitter and I pushed it aside. I shook my head when she asked if I wanted something to eat. Mother didn't eat either. Her eyes were red and puffy and she kept wiping them. When she looked at me, I saw anger in her too, as well as sorrow. Mother and I often fought, and Oma had always taken up my defense. Now Mother seemed angry with me for still being alive while Oma was gone. I shook my head and dismissed the thought. I wanted to go back to bed and breathe in my grandmother again.

"Karin, we have to find your Oma's special nightgown, you know the one she had made in Potsdam."

"The white one with lace?"

"Yes. We'll take it to the hospital for Oma to wear. She has to look beautiful when your uncles arrive." She saw my questioning look and said, "I expect them tonight. Uncle Will can sleep in Oma's bed and Uncle Richard . . ."

"No. I'm sleeping in Oma's bed. Uncle Will can sleep upstairs, in my bed. He didn't even come to see her after the blockade was over. He's not sleeping in her bed."

"Karin, I decide who sleeps where."

"No! No you don't! If you put him in her room, I'll make a scene. I'll scream so loud the neighbors will call the police. I'm sleeping in Oma's bed. That is final!"

Mother left the room.

I remembered that the nightgown was packed away in an old trunk stored next to my attic room. I clambered up the stairs and arrived on the upper floor struggling for breath as if I had been climbing the Zugspitze. I leaned against the wall in the hallway, remembering the times Oma had climbed these stairs, carrying food for me when I had the flu or waking me up for school. By the time I reached the trunk, my eyes were brimming with tears, and I could hardly find the keyhole for the key.

When I opened the trunk I first came across Oma's navy silk dress wrapped in white tissue paper. I remembered the theater evenings when she had worn it and the Christmas party at the Esterhazy's palace in Eisenstadt. I rustled around and found the white nightgown. The same seamstress who had made dresses for Brixie and me had made this gown from a long piece of dotted Swiss material for which we had traded cigarettes. Oma had later added cascades of lace to the oval neckline and around the wrists of the long sleeves. I tried to think of a time when Oma had worn it. I shook my head. Oma had never worn this gown, and it even smelled new. When I lifted it carefully from the trunk and held it up I wondered if she had intended it to be her burial shroud?

I put the gown aside and replaced the navy dress. Something bright red caught my eye. I pulled at the cloth and saw it was the American flag we had made.

After a long while I heard Mother's footsteps coming up the stairs. "You found the gown? Why didn't you come down?"

I couldn't answer. The gown and the flag were in my arms and both were wet with tears. Mother took a few steps toward me, and I was afraid she'd be angry, perhaps jealous. But she surprised me by kneeling on the floor and putting her arms around me. I put my head on her shoulders and we both wept.

Dressed in her gown, Oma lay on the white satin pillow from her bedroom. While the wide ruffle of lace on her gown played in graceful waves around her thin neck, hiding her sagging skin, the lace framed her long thin hands. Her hair had been brushed and coiled into a silver braid that lay on her shoulder. I had placed the American flag on her chest, and someone else had folded her hands above the little stars that we had so laboriously cut and sewn. When? Was it more than four years ago? It had been such a barbaric time, but thinking back on it, we had been happy that day, making the flag, talking about Oma's beloved America.

When Uncle Will first walked through the front door, he appeared as a stranger to me. He was wearing a raincoat, which was two sizes too large—probably bought from a war widow—and a hat. I had never seen him wear a hat before. It was one of those big floppy hats Humphrey Bogart wore in his detective movies. The rim dripped the pouring rain onto Will like a gutter spurts rain from a slanted roof, making him look altogether miserable.

I mumbled when he came toward me and did not hug him as I had in earlier days.

"Ah, the past year has transformed you into quite a young lady. The duckling into a swan. What's this, no kiss? Do you feel you're too grown up now to kiss your uncle?"

I nodded, not wanting to tell him that I was angry with him for not coming sooner. Uncle Richard's arrival made it easier to be with both of them, but I mostly stuck to the side of my older uncle. When we walked as a group to the mortuary, I kept to myself. Uncle Will noticed my withdrawal and tried to charm me by paying me compliments. I had grown into a pretty young woman, he said. I could see he felt guilty, and I also realized he was genuinely sad. He admitted to having been selfish, but at the same time, he defended himself by saying that he thought Oma would live for many more years and that he had planned on coming for her birthday. Now he had to come two weeks earlier for her funeral. I still couldn't look at him, but I didn't want to make him feel even worse, so I kept silent.

Everything was happening, and at the same time, nothing was happening. It was as if time were going forward and backward simultaneously, every moment shrouded in fog.

The small church in Nikolassee where the funeral service was held was filled to capacity. I was surprised that Oma knew so many people. Our immediate family was there and, of course, Uncle Victor and Tante Wanda with "young" Victor. But most of the people present were Mutti's friends, who had all loved Oma's generous spirit. There were also many of my school friends, Brixie, Erika, Robert and his jazz musicians, and others, all crowding into the church. Lilly sang Handel's "Largo." My mother had sung it in the Gedächtniskirche so long ago, when I first became aware of the special timbre of her voice. Oma had sat by my side then, but now she lay in her coffin. Karl Wolfram sang the Lord's Prayer. Otherwise I don't remember much of anything, except the coffin disappearing through the double oak door under a load of white chrysanthemums. I wanted to run after it but remained motionless on the hard, wooden bench.

Uncle Will sat next to the driver of the hearse and accompanied the coffin to the house of cremation, where he had to sign the official forms. He stayed with us for a few more days until he could collect the ashes and take them to the family burial plot near Frankfurt. Here Oma would rest next to my grandfather and my aunt Margaret.

My thoughts returned to the time when Oma and I took Aunt Margaret's ashes to that grave. Oma had insisted her sister be buried on the side of my grandfather that was nearest to a butcher's grave in a plot adjoining theirs. Grandfather would be in the center of both sisters. I asked why this was important. She said, "I'll be safe on *that* side, when my time comes."

"Safe from what?" I asked.

She had waved her hand rather dramatically. "Karin, I don't want to lie next to a butcher. Maybe he's got a huge carving knife next to him . . . ," she broke off, shrugging and half laughing at herself and her ridiculous thoughts.

"That is the silliest thing I ever heard," I said, eleven years old at the time.

Day after day, it rained, with only brief interludes. Of course, it was November and this was typical late autumn weather in Berlin. Richard had gone back to his family in Leipzig, and the house felt empty. Will gave in to Mother's pleading and agreed to stay until Oma's birthday. On what would have been her seventieth birthday, it rained all day. Our Lutheran church was closed during the week, and there was no grave we could visit. Mutti suggested we go to a small Catholic chapel to pray and to concentrate our thoughts on Oma.

Candles flickered, and I thought I could smell the years of burned incense ingrained in the walls. I thought I could feel generations of prayers still lingering in this sacred space. I slowly walked to a side niche and knelt beneath the statue of the Virgin. I lit a seven-day candle in a red glass. When I turned, I saw Oma standing in the entrance of the chapel. She was dressed in dark red and was wearing a crimson shawl over her shoulders. She smiled at me; she was radiant. I thought the red garment was odd since my grandmother had always worn navy, gray, or black, but I did not for a moment think it out of the ordinary to see her. I rose to go to her, holding my hand out to touch her, but I encountered only empty space.

Uncle Victor and Tante Wanda were expected for tea and reminiscences later in the afternoon to "celebrate" Oma's birthday with us. Mother surprised me by baking a walnut cake that tasted much like Oma's own. Maybe Oma was all around us. I had seen her, and now Mother baked like her. The cake was one of my favorites, but I could only force down a bite of it. Sipping my tea and looking over the table surrounded by sad faces, I silently asked God why he had taken my Oma and left dour old Tante Wanda. She always spoke of looking forward to death and of seeing her children, Maria and Horst, again. But my Oma had loved life and had wanted to go to America. God was not fair.

On Tuesday morning, Mutti and I took Uncle Will to the train station. I was still angry with him, but I was also sad that he was leaving. He still looked like a stranger to me in his civilian clothes, since in most of my memories he had worn a uniform. He carried a large parcel wrapped in brown paper and twine under his arm. He and Mother had packed the box carefully. They had spent hours placing old books in a battered carton, hiding the urn with Oma's ashes in the center.

It was strictly forbidden to transport human remains through the different zones of Germany, and he had to traverse three of them: the British sector, the Russian zone, and the American zone, where Oma's ashes were to be laid to rest. From there, he would go back to where he lived in Baden Baden, which was in the French zone. If found out, Will risked being arrested and thrown in jail, but it was a chance he had to take. "If anyone makes me open it and sees these tattered books, they'll have me close it again in a hurry. I'll be all right," Uncle Will tried to reassure me. "I'll tell them that these are books my sister kept for me. Don't worry," he said, lifting up my chin and kissing me on the tip of my nose. I reached up and kissed him on the cheek, no longer angry with him.

When Mother and I returned from the train station and walked through the front door of the house on Schopenhauer Strasse 51, I was met with an unfamiliar feeling of despair. My heart raced and I had difficulty breathing. The reality of Oma's death became palpable. Life would go on but not life as I had known it. I searched for Mother's warm, comforting hand. Then we got out of our dripping coats and entered the living room slowly, as if afraid to encounter more of this nameless feeling.

We were alone now, Mother and I, and the emotion was new and overwhelming.

Our rooms were as they had always been, and yet they were vastly changed. The soul of our house, the woman who sang while making a tasty soup, the woman whom I still saw in my memory grabbing one of the delicate chairs and waltzing with it in the living room, the woman who had upheld our flagging spirits through the worst of times, my Oma, was gone.

CHAPTER 18

The Mermaids' Room

After Oma's death, Mother moved us into a bright apartment near the Nikolasee S-Bahn station. I was sad, having to leave the house where I had such warm memories with my grandmother. But that house also weighed on me because every corner of it reminded me of Oma.

Since housing was scarce and still allotted by the housing authorities, we had to share the apartment with another tenant. But this time, it was much better than sharing rooms with Frau Kuhnert in Halensee had been. We and another formerly bombed-out woman were on an equal footing, and when shown the apartment by the authorities, neither one of us could claim prior rights.

My walk to school from Teutonen Strasse 11 was a bit farther, but I walked through the Rehwiese, the lovely parklike green space where I cherished my "lilacs and kisses" memories of Rolf. But I worried that if he came back to Berlin, he would not know where to find me.

We had to leave most of the furnishings behind, since they belonged to the Schmidts. Mother bought beds, chairs, and tables at flea markets, and little by little we furnished the three rooms in "gypsy" fashion. Mother's taste and ability to transform discards into exotic sofas and end tables or to brighten old lamps with silken shades soon transformed our apartment into a cozy space.

We didn't have a piano, and much to our regret, the musical evenings had come to an end. The Wolframs relocated to Düsseldorf, and Elisabeth rarely crossed from East Berlin into what she considered the "corrupt and materialistic" West. And the musical group that had been linked by the piano and Oma's benevolent spirit disintegrated.

Robert came to visit on a Saturday in late February, waving two tickets for the famous *Bunte Zinnober,* the art academy's costume ball before Lent. This was carnival as celebrated in Berlin, three whole nights of it.

To my surprise, Robert invited me to the ball. I had fantasized about going to a costume ball for years, but now that I was old enough, I accepted the invitation with mixed feelings. Less than four months had passed since Oma's death and I doubted the dancing and fancy costumes could cheer me up. But at the same time, I looked forward to a change of routine, and I felt the need to at least get out of the apartment and think of something other than my grandmother.

Robert said he would dress as an Apache dancer. I didn't know what that was, but he explained it was a dance from Paris that was all the rage in the 1920s, when men imitated the dance of the underworld and slammed women around the dance floor doing something like a tango number. "If you think you can slam me around, forget it. Just try," I said, flexing my pitiful biceps.

He laughed. "Don't worry. I just happen to have clothes that I could make into that costume. And people always tell me I look as if I come from Marseilles. The costume would go well with my dark coloring."

I never could have afforded these expensive tickets to the ball, which Robert had won in a student lottery. The tickets were for Shrove Tuesday, or Mardi Gras, the last of the three fund-raiser balls for the academy. The following day, on Ash Wednesday, many celebrants would receive the ashen smudge on their foreheads and promise to sin no more.

The revelry took place at the art academy in Charlottenburg. The academy occupied a former palace, and I imagined that elegant ladies wearing taffeta gowns had floated up the marble stairs into this magnificent building before the academy had taken over. Mother and Elisabeth had attended classes here in saucy flapper dresses, but in our postwar days, students, wearing paint-spattered clothing and carrying canvases, ran up and down these same stairs.

I asked Mother if she had ever attended a costume ball there, and she shook her head. When she was young, she did dance at several costume balls in Frankfurt, where we used to live. "And when you were a student?" I asked. "I didn't have much money for extravagances," she said. "When I went to the academy and lived with Veronika's parents, we attended costume parties in friends' homes."

The tickets were our passport into a fantastical world of plenty. Champagne and other libations, as well as canapés and bite-sized foods, were included in the price of admission. And no one cared how young I was.

Mother made Robert promise to keep an eye on me and to meet up with me every hour. He promised, and she trusted him. I think she hoped it would take my mind off thoughts of death. I had immersed myself in Theosophist and Rosicrucian literature and ideas of the afterlife. Reincarnation and death held a great fascination for me. I told Mother I could hardly wait to die, to experience passing through the veil of existence. And, of course, I hoped to see my grandmother again. Mother reminded me that Oma, our loving pragmatist, would have frowned upon these fruitless speculations. Life was to be lived *now,* with decency and humanity. There was to be no filling one's head with fantasies of "other lives"; death would come soon enough. Mother's reasoning surprised me, since it was she and her friend Lilly who had aroused my interest in the theories of reincarnation in the first place. I did not want to tell Mother that Oma had told me about Aunt Margaret's unearthly visit. That was our last secret. I knew Oma dismissed the theory of reincarnation, but she did think that the soul would go on living on another plane. She obviously believed, or had in her last hour come to believe, that the soul could take on its previously known form and make itself visible. I reasoned that if the soul was indestructible, it would, after a certain time, elect to be reborn and to live again in another body.

For now, I had to put these thoughts aside, though, and choose a costume for my almost seventeen-year-old body.

This led to a big argument. I had selected a gypsy-style, bright orange skirt and a white off-the-shoulder peasant blouse. When she saw me, Mother said one word, "*Nein.*" The outfit was pretty, she conceded, but it was not a "real" costume and was much too revealing. She then pulled my ballet leotards and tights from a drawer. "This is what you are going to wear," she said, holding the clothes in her hand.

"That's dumb, Mother. And talk about revealing. It shows more than the skirt and the blouse."

"But you'll be fully covered. And it will keep you warm. Those halls are drafty, I know." Smiling at me, she said, "I'll make you into a cute devil. If you don't want that, tell me now. Then Robert can find someone else to take to the ball."

When I began dressing for the evening, I smelled onions frying in butter and heard the splattering of potatoes being dropped into the hot skillet and a spatula scraping eggs into the pan. My stomach was aflutter. As Mother stirred diced ham into the omelet, I said, "I can't eat all that. I hope you're making it for both of us."

"Karin, eat what you can. This will have to last you all night."

Mother watched as I washed the food down with a huge glass of milk mixed with heavy cream. "This is too rich," I burped.

"Eat. And mind your manners."

My stomach felt heavy, and when I put on my devil's costume, I felt as if I were stuffing a sausage into its casing. I put on black tights and a black, long-sleeved leotard. I grabbed the long tail Mother had sewn onto the derriere of the bottom of my leotards—she had fastened a red triangle on the tip to make it look properly devilish—and held it in front of me to hide my pouching stomach that made me look as if I were four months pregnant. Mother put the finishing touch—a little cap sprouting two red horns—on my shoulder-length blonde hair.

Robert arrived looking very French in a black felt beret and a red scarf knotted around his neck. He unbuttoned his peacoat to reveal a tight-fitting black-and-white-striped jersey top that showed off his well-toned chest. Tight black pants that flared at the bottom emphasized his long legs. I wondered where he had gotten these clothes. He was right, though, with his dark brown eyes and black hair, the Apache look was perfect.

Transportation was a problem. We lived in the suburbs and did not have a car, and taxis were too expensive. The first S-Bahn would not run before 5:30 a.m., which meant we had to stay at the party until dawn.

That night was one of those clear, cold February nights aglitter with distant stars and ice crystals. The cold attacked my ears, which were not protected, and they turned a bright red to match the devil's horns on my cap.

We arrived at the Kunst Akademie. Holding on to Robert's arm, I stopped to stare in fascination at the building. I had never seen it lit up after dark. It was a beautiful early nineteenth-century building that took up much of the city block. My eyes followed the graceful lines of columns and the scrolled ornamental stone decorations, which in the lamplight glowed in soft shades from peach to ocher. I had a hard time tearing my gaze away from the many windows that looked as if they opened onto a brighter world of peace, leaving the dark phases of the war far in the past.

We checked our heavy coats and my bulky shoes in the cloakroom. I slid into my ballet slippers, and we stepped into the great downstairs hall. I felt like Cinderella at the ball. A double winged marble staircase led to the upper floor, where I had been told the students had decorated their classrooms in competing designs. A domed ceiling spanned the interior space. Down in the great entry hall, a big band played. Robert told me that smaller combos performed in individual rooms upstairs.

My eyes widened as I looked around the hall; I had entered a surreal world of fantasy. This was the first time I had celebrated carnival as an adult, but at sixteen, I would find that I was much too young. Robert said he would meet me every hour on the hour on the upstairs balcony.

One thing struck me as strange: the older the women, the less clothing they wore. Décolleté costumes were plentiful. Men kissed bare shoulders and tried to pull down tops. At times, they succeeded, and several women were dancing bare breasted. Had Mother known, I'm sure she would not have allowed me to come. I felt out of place, but I was trapped. I envied Cinderella. She had to leave at midnight, but I had to stay until five o'clock in the morning.

I saw Robert at eleven o'clock and again at midnight, but then I missed him at one o'clock and at two o'clock. Where was he? Searching for Robert, I noticed a voluptuous woman, wearing a scanty two-piece outfit. Several young men began to torment her. One of them tore off her top and threw it off the balcony, guffawing as the bright triangles floated down the marble stairs. Her spiked heel connected with the man's groin. Ouch! Now another grabbed her, pulled off the offending shoe, and winged it down. I rushed into one of the rooms, looking for someone to help her. I tried to get the attention of an older man, but he was more interested in nibbling on a harem girl's ear. By the time I returned, the young men had ripped off the bottom part of the woman's costume and that too floated down, fluttering like a piece of bright plumage, to the white marble of the entry lobby. Below the balcony, the big band played "In the Mood," and the woman's purple panties landed on the drummer's head. The woman wailed and tried to cover her nakedness with her hands. She called the men animals, but they answered merely with sardonic laughter and left her hiding behind a pillar. I quickly marched in another direction, too ashamed to help.

Werner Egk's ballet *Abraxas,* showing frontal nudity of both sexes, had recently been performed at the opera house. The critics remarked that it reflected the newfound freedom after years of Nazi repression. Was tonight's behavior part of this rebellion against old restrictions? What would Oma say? I felt her watching, and it embarrassed me to be here.

A short, fortyish man with juglike ears, who reeked of cologne, grabbed me. He proceeded to step on my feet as he pretended to dance with me. I freed myself and ran off. Then another took my arm. His cologne was even more pungent than the first man's, and it made me slightly nauseous as he tried to kiss my ear, tickling me with his mustache. I got away from that one and ran from classroom to classroom looking for Robert.

These classrooms were marvels of inspiration and talent: painting classes completed with sculpture or printmaking classes to create the most fantastical decorations in order to win top prize for originality and artistry. Students had transformed a room into one of exotic splendor. Veils in purple and gold hung from the ceiling and low couches were covered in Oriental fabrics, and a trio played Middle Eastern music. I smelled incense and heard the gurgling of water pipes. In another room, students had re-created a tropical island reminiscent of a painting by Gauguin, replete with palm trees perhaps on loan from the Berlin Botanical Gardens. Then there was a room where huge Picasso-like images were projected onto the walls. Ever changing geometric shapes in primary colors depicted faces with noses moving from the left to the right and one eye opening while another eye slid down the cheek. The room was disorienting because tables and chairs were placed at odd angles, and it was next to impossible to sit down. I felt as if I were in a cubist painting. An ensemble played Bach and Vivaldi here, of all places.

The room I entered next depicted hell, with mirrors reflecting orange and red lights leaping up walls as if fires were burning. Masks and devilish visages grinned down from corners and appeared to move in rhythm with the jazz combo. I smelled a slightly sulfurous scent, but perhaps that was my imagination. In my devil's outfit, I should have felt right at home.

But where was Robert? I was sure I'd find him here because he liked jazz. I looked beneath a table laden with hors d'oeuvres but didn't find Robert. Thank God, Robert was not one of the two writhing bodies I found. I stared. The bodies were intertwined, making weird groaning noises rising above the canapés. I fled, my face as red as the décor of the artists' hell.

I grabbed another glass of champagne from the table, to blur what I had seen. But Mother's food fortifications kept me sober.

The night had almost passed when I found Robert, slightly tipsy and dragging a thirty-something woman to the dance floor. "Robert, where have you been?" I held onto him since he didn't stop, and when he shook me off giving me a "get lost" look, I shouted above the din that I'd wait for him in the Mermaids' Room, near the Inferno.

I knew I had behaved badly; after all, he was not my boyfriend. He had a right to flirt and to dance with whomever he chose. But I felt miserable. The price of admission was expensive. The students who had won tickets danced with older women, and most of the men who wanted to dance with me were foreigners or racketeers and older than my mother. The smoke of the perfumy Turkish and Greek postwar cigarettes made me cough. And the sweat-and-garlic reeking people in these overheated rooms nauseated me.

The Mermaids' Room offered refuge with its otherworldly music. I

sipped more champagne as a trio played on strange, dreamy-sounding instruments. There were gurgling sounds, the trill of a flute, and the swooshing
of waves. The sounds soothed, as did the room itself, swimming in ocean-
colored gauze. Layers of tulle and toile hung from the ceiling, the lights were
dim, casting reflections of silver, turquoise, and a soft lavender onto the fabrics. I staked out a corner in this room, claiming it as my cocoon. I would lie
dormant here until morning, until a sliver of gray light released me from the
bacchanalian night, allowing me to go home.

Away from the forbidding world of grown-ups.

By the Skin of My Teeth

I decided to quit school. It took a lot of persuading to convince Mother,
but this time, after a lot of begging and explaining, she conceded that I was
right.

Our new principal, Fräulein Dr. Schwänzner, had called me into her office to tell me that my English teacher was going to give me a failing grade
for the year. This was the same teacher I had taunted a few years earlier by
mimicking the Alabama accent I'd learned from the girls next door, and
whose tcherman accent I had made fun of. If she gave me a failing grade, I
would have to repeat not only the course in English but the entire year. If I
agreed to leave school, however, the principal would persuade the teacher to
give me a passing grade. I would get a certificate, the so-called *Einjährige,* of
early completion of the lyceum. To get the coveted *Abitur,* which would en-
title me to attend a university, I would need two more years of lyceum. In
short, the principal's ultimatum cut me off from advanced education in Germany.

I could not comprehend a failing grade in English when my English, at
least my pronunciation, was better than the teacher's. This was pure chicanery,
and if my grandmother had been alive, she would have gone to the principal
and teacher and fought for my rights. Mother was not interested, and she told
me I didn't need the *Abitur* if I wanted to be an actress or a singer.

Brixie also left school. Neither one of us was loved by our teachers. They
assumed that because we sang American songs in the schoolyard and often
spoke English with each other, we were fraternizing with American soldiers.
The irony was that other girls, who did not sing songs from the "American
Hit Parade" and who did not speak English as well as we, did have American
boyfriends. We did not, but the teachers were blind to the truth.

Years later, after I was married to a Harvard graduate and living in California, I came across a tattered schoolbook containing essays that my former English teacher had marked in red ink. My husband leafed through it. "That's outrageous," he said, "Your teacher miscorrected some of your well-structured sentences."

After I left high school the Berliner Schauspielschule admitted me to study drama. This school, founded by Max Reinhardt, was heaven compared to the rigid hell of the lyceum, and learning became pure joy. I studied role after role and read play after play, loving the curriculum and the pace. My fencing and voice lessons were a plus now. However, I could not pronounce the rolling *r*'s, so necessary for speaking in dialects, try as I might, which frustrated Hans Eisolt, one of my teachers. He showed me how the tongue had to curl and roll on the back of the teeth to produce this sound, but I still could not duplicate his *r*'s. He must have thought me obstinate, for he lost his temper and crashed a thick volume of Schiller's collected plays over my head. Despite that incident, I loved drama school and did well there.

Summer quickly turned to autumn. Shortly before the first anniversary of Oma's death I applied for a job at an American PX and was hired. I divided my time between drama studies and work. Mother had misgivings about my working as a salesgirl at the PX. I would be exposed to military personnel on a daily basis, and I would not be protected by a chaperone as I had been at the club. I thought she was foolish; after all, I felt quite capable of protecting myself.

The job was perfect. The Truman Hall PX was located on what is now Clayallee 135 and the Allied Museum. It was close to where Mother and I had gone to pick up the Shmoo CARE package. It was not within the soldiers' barracks as other PX stores were, and it was mainly frequented by civilians and officers. It took me less than thirty minutes to reach the low-slung white building where I worked. We, the salesgirls, entered through the basement. We left our purses and our coats in a small room and slipped into navy blue smocks that we wore over our clothing.

Next door to the PX was the American movie theater. Mr. Arnsen, the manager of both, knew I was available to work there most weekends since I did not have a boyfriend, and he scheduled me to sell candy bars and Coca Cola. This was a dream job. I managed to see every new American film release that came to Berlin. And while I watched, I munched on candy bars, which I sold for three for a dime or one for a nickel.

I had not only a dream job but also a dream boss. Mr. Arnsen was a civilian, but he had been in the military. During the Italian campaign, he had fallen in love and married a woman from Naples. They had two small children. His wife was a Gina Lollobrigida look-alike, but he was unhappy since he could not converse with her. Her English was limited to a few sentences, and she made little effort to learn. He spoke a little Italian but worried about what would happen once they were living in the United States. His ancestry was Norwegian, and he lived in Minnesota where hardly anyone spoke Italian. He kept seeking out my company, perhaps because he could joke around with me and talk to me about movies and American books.

When Christmas neared, he assigned me to the toy department. An elevated model train track was installed in an oblong loop on a wide shelf running about twenty feet in length of the rectangular room. One of the famous Böcklin trains zoomed around the track. There was a second, smaller track set up on a Ping-Pong table. The table was covered by a long white cloth on which green fields and little villages sat, much like the ones I had played with in the captain's apartment several years ago. Mr. Arnsen put pellets into the locomotive and the engine steamed and blew smoke. Its whistles blew, and I often was torn between serving the customers who inquired about dolls and stuffed animals and obliging Mr. Arnsen who kept me busy attending the trains.

The windows on one side of the room were concealed by floor-to-ceiling linen drapes. To herald in Christmas, the janitors decorated the store by pinning golden cardboard stars on the white cloth of each panel. After the store closed, Mr. Arnsen would stride into the toy department and throw me a BB gun, his eyes twinkling. Grabbing one for himself, he would challenge me to a shooting race, saying, "Hey, Karin! You take the left and I'll take the right, and let's see who can shoot these suckers down the fastest." I aimed my pellet gun at the stars of the left panel and fired—*bang, bang, bang.* They hit the floor with a light sigh. He won, but then again, he always won. I offered to pin them back up, but he dismissed that notion. "That's what the janitors are for," he'd say.

We laughed a lot during those times in the toy department. His laugh reminded me of Erich's, the boy I'd gone stealing apples with, the laugh of a mischievous boy, but then his coal black eyes crinkled and a myriad of little crow's-feet appeared. I told him I thought it was strange, that a Scandinavian like him had dark hair and slanted eyes. He laughed and said that one of his ancestors had probably married a Laplander, a Norwegian version of an Eskimo.

Mother once picked me up from the PX, accompanied by Lassie. When Mr. Arnsen saw Lassie, he crouched low to pet her. She stuck out her pink tongue and made *Männchen*—that is, standing on her hind paws. After that, he gave me permission to buy dog food in the PX. He never asked me how I acquired the U.S. dollars, and I did not volunteer to tell him.

My American dollars came from a side business I had selling coffee to my neighbors. I bought coffee in the PX, which cost me one dollar per pound, and sold it to my neighbors for sixteen mark, or four dollars, making a profit of three dollars per can of coffee.

One evening on a rainy day, I had been late in closing my register, and I hurried down to the changing area. Most of the salesgirls had already gone. I grabbed my net bag and stuffed coffee cans wrapped in packing paper into it. I felt uneasy this time and slunk out of the room, tiptoeing down the long, dimly lit hallway. The sound of voices came from one of the side cubicles of this storage cellar. I recognized Mr. Arnsen's voice. Whoever was in there with him had seen me and called for me to come in. I trembled. He was the big brass from Heidelberg, the headquarters of all post exchanges. Mr. Arnsen introduced me, "This is Karin, our mascot. The youngest of our girls. Speaks perfect English." Waving toward the tall man in the Macintosh and the dripping hat, he introduced him as Mr. O'Hoolihan, the chief of operations.

This Mr. O'Hoolihan eyed my net bag. However, only one of his eyes was looking at the bag, the other of this pair of walleyed, watery-blue orbs wandered off searching for answers on the ceiling. I stood fascinated by his eyes, but at the same time they made me uncomfortable, because I didn't know which eye to look at.

Pointing to the net bag, he asked, "And what do we have in here, little lady?"

I bit my lips and hesitated for a moment. I felt myself get very hot, blushing, I suppose. "Well," I said, "I have coffee in here."

Now Mr. Arnsen blushed. Poor man, I had embarrassed him, but if I were caught in a lie, I might not get my American visa.

Mr. O'Hoolihan looked somewhat bemused. I kept staring at him. He looked so different from the rest of the Americans I had met. The skin of his face was soft, loose, and pink, like the color of a baby's bottom. Strange. A man with pink skin and wandering watery eyes. He was tall, probably a foot taller than Mr. Arnsen. But he had a strange pear-shaped figure, with shoulders that sloped downward. He held out a whitish hand and waved for me to come nearer. At that moment, Mr. Arnsen got up from the wooden crate he had been sitting on and walked over to me. He put his hand on my shoulder and said, "It's all right, Karin, you don't have to kid around." Then he looked at Mr. O'Hoolihan. "Karin has a Scottie," he said, "I let her buy dog food here with dollars her relatives send from California."

Mr. O'Hoolihan nodded and released his formerly tight lips into a half smile. "You have relatives in California? Where? My brother just moved to San Francisco from Boston, that's where I'm from."

"My relatives live in Santa Monica. I'll be moving there when I get my visa."

I knew Mr. Arnsen was anxious for me to get out of there, because he was dancing a little nervous jig, hopping from one foot to the other. Mr. O'Hoolihan's smile deepened and his pudgy hand waved me good-bye.

"See you tomorrow. Go feed that dog of yours," Mr. Arnsen said.

No need to tell me twice.

A month later, several generals and other high-ranking military personnel were expected to arrive from the Heidelberg headquarters for an inspection of the soldiers' barracks nearby. It was unusual for soldiers to shop in our PX, but they all seemed to be in a hurry that day to buy essential supplies, and they outnumbered the officers and civilians. Mr. Arnsen asked me to help out at the cosmetics counter because it was understaffed and there were no customers in the toy department.

The amount of merchandise was overwhelming. Perfumes, deodorants, shaving creams, and every imaginable item a drugstore might carry were arranged on dozens of shelves. I couldn't possibly learn the names of all of these many items in one morning, but Gudrun, a girl who had worked there all along, calmed me down when she saw how jittery I was. "Most of the soldiers want shoelaces," she said. "Here are the sizes: twelve inch for regular, then the longer ones for boots, and the real long ones for the boots that go halfway up the leg. They need to have their footgear in tip-top shape for the inspection. Don't worry, Karin. It's easy."

Soldier after soldier bought the laces. It was a breeze. Then a tall sergeant came in, and looking at me with squinty eyes, he said, "Gimme some of them *dimdi didim* . . ." The last word in the sentence was lost to me because of his thick Texan drawl.

"Yes, sir," I said. "What size, sir? Twelve inches, twenty-four, or longer?"

I watched with amazement as this man's face turned purple. He leaned over the counter, and I thought he was going to hit me. I backed into Gudrun, stepping on her foot and making her cry out. The sergeant screamed at me and hollered for the manager. Within a flash, Mr. Arnsen appeared.

"What's going on?" he asked.

"That goddammed fräulein is making fun of me. Where do you get these Krauts from anyways? Asked me what size I am when I want some Silvertex. Goddamn nerve."

I shrugged and looked at Mr. Arnsen, whose face twitched, as if he were trying hard to suppress a laugh. What did I do? The sergeant pointed at me, still yelling.

Mr. Arnsen signaled to Gudrun to give the sergeant the desired merchandise, a packet of condoms, then steered him away from the counter, stopping him from any further verbal assault. He explained to the sergeant that I had not meant to be sarcastic and that I was an innocent girl who had up to now worked in the toy department. "She knows nothing of Silvertex," I heard him say. "Everyone so far has been buying shoelaces. Please accept my apology for the misunderstanding."

The sergeant grumbled, paid, and left.

"When are you leaving?" I asked Mr. Arnsen when he explained that he had to go to Heidelberg on business and that he would be gone for about five days.

"I want you back in the toy department. No rowdy GIs bothering you there."

He was taking care of me, and I felt as if he were one of my uncles.

"You look sad. Will you miss me?"

"Well, I wish I could go to Frankfurt. I used to live there. I'd love to see my old friends again. And one of my uncles lives there now."

"Hey," Mr. Arnsen slapped his thigh. "I've got an idea. I'll take you along. I can drop you off in Frankfurt. It's on the way. Or you can come to Heidelberg with me."

"No, I couldn't do that."

"Okay. When I'm finished in Heidelberg, I'll zip by and pick you up again. Would you like that?"

"Would I? Are you kidding?" But I thought about it and shook my head. "I don't know if my mother would let me go. Besides, I'd need a pass for traveling through the zone. What reason would I have for traveling? Getting a pass is nearly impossible."

"You said you once lived there, and you have friends . . ."

"Wanting to visit friends and relatives is not a valid reason."

"Tell you what. If you think you can survive in the trunk of my car for an hour or so, I'll put you in there. You don't have claustrophobia, do you?"

"I'd have to squeeze into the trunk? I'd suffocate."

"No, there's plenty of room. Plenty of air."

"I don't know," I shook my head, remembering the time I was locked into the hanging closet when the Russians came. Closed spaces terrified me. But maybe this would be different. "It sounds crazy. If the Russians catch us, they'd confiscate your car. They'd put me in jail. You can imagine what they'd do first. I think it's too risky."

Suddenly Mr. Arnsen looked like a little boy who had lost his favorite toy. "I'm willing to take the risk," he said. "I'm sorry. I thought you and I were alike. Fearless. Okay. I'll go by myself."

"I wouldn't be much company anyway, crouching in the trunk."

"You'd only be in the trunk while we cross through the Russian zone. A little more than an hour. After the checkpoint at Helmstedt, you'd come inside."

"I can't." I was sad and thought of Nunu and Guggi whom I'd love to see again after all these years. Uncle Richard had "defected" from the Russian zone and moved to Frankfurt a few months ago. I could see him and sleep on a sofa at his place. The memories of Frankfurt became vivid flashes: the corner house where we'd lived, the parades down the Hansa Allee with Nunu walking in the procession dressed in white, the horse chestnuts and their blossoms like cream-colored candles, making the trees look like sacred objects for the occasion. I shook my head, but this time it was in agreement. "I'll go," I said. "But I have to ask my mother. If she says no, then . . ."

"I'll take you home today and talk to her. She'll see I'm serious and to be trusted."

I burst out laughing. "She'd trust me more than she would a man. No need to take me home. It would look strange for my boss, a married man, asking for permission to take me to Frankfurt. You give me your word. You drop me off in Frankfurt and pick me up exactly five days later. Okay?"

When Mother complained, I promised her that there was nothing funny going on and that every night away from home would be accounted for at Uncle Richard's place. Travel fever infected me, and I counted the hours.

Mr. Arnsen picked me up after dark. Mother was still working, and although she had given me permission to go, she did not know that I would be crossing the border in the trunk of the car. Mr. Arnsen had lined the trunk with an army blanket, and I found it quite comfortable after I climbed in and pulled the blanket like a cover around me. Mr. Arnsen was right. The trunk of this huge American car, a four-door Oldsmobile, was large and I could breathe. In fact, it was so comfortable, I fell asleep. I was vaguely aware when Mr. Arnsen stopped at the Russian checkpoint in Wannsee, before going onto the autobahn through the Russian zone. I pulled the blanket higher over my head and continued to sleep.

Mr. Arnsen was livid when he opened the trunk after the border crossing in Helmstedt. When he extended his hand to help me out of the trunk, he jerked so hard he almost wrenched out my shoulder.

"How could you go to sleep? I thought I could trust you."

I rubbed the sleep from my eyes, blinking into the bright beam of the flashlight Mr. Arnsen was shining on me. "What do you mean, not trusting me? What did I do wrong?"

"You snored. That's what you did wrong. Snored like an old woodcutter. Louder than a saw," he said, shaking his head. "Incredible for a young girl to snore like that. You almost gave us away. The Ruski came around the trunk and I was scared to death he'd hear you snore. He looked worried, probably wondering what those noises were, coming from the rear of an American car. I tried to make light of it and hoped he'd understand some English when I told him the car was passing gas. Then when he came closer, I stepped on his toes. He hopped on the other leg and rubbed his foot. I guess he had tight boots and I'd stepped on a corn."

The small smile dropped off Mr. Arnsen's face, and he fell silent, glowering at me. "I told him I was sorry, very sorry. Meanwhile he filled out the forms and then, the next time he came near the trunk, I said I had to go to the toilet. He couldn't let me go unsupervised, so he came along. I was loud on purpose, girl, certain some of the racket would wake you up and stop you from your goddamned snoring. But no, I came out and there you were. Snoring, gurgling, Christ!"

I began to cry. "I'm sorry. I didn't know. I warned you it would be dangerous."

"Well, it never dawned on me you might go to sleep on me and snore like a drunken sailor. That snooze could have cost me my car."

"And me my future in America. I didn't go to sleep on purpose. You never said I had to stay awake. I was tired and it was comfortable with the blanket and all. You don't have to take me back. I'll try to get a pass and take a train."

"No, I'll take you back as promised. But I won't put you in the trunk, that's too damn comfortable. We'll hide you between the seats."

That did not sound good at all. But I didn't want to argue. I considered the alternatives. Getting a pass was next to impossible. How could I prove to be legitimately in West Germany? I depended on Mr. Arnsen to get me back to Berlin.

I regretted the darkness during the rest of the trip. I would have liked to see the landscape. But once we left the autobahn and neared Frankfurt's north end where Uncle Richard lived, streetlights illuminated the skeletons of bombed-out buildings and fields of rubble. I believed Berlin had borne the brunt of the bombing, and for some reason, it surprised me to find so much destruction elsewhere.

"Heidelberg is beautiful," Mr. Arnsen said, as if reading my thoughts. "Nothing was bombed."

"Yes, so I heard. They say that the Americans had planned long before the war ended to make it their headquarters."

"I'd say that was pretty good planning. Old university town on a lovely river . . ."

"And beautiful Berlin could be sacrificed."

"Hey! Hitler holed himself up in Berlin. That city might not have suffered the last hour's damage it did." Mr. Arnsen reached over to pick up my chin. He gently wiped at a tear rolling down my cheek. "Karin, as I said, Heidelberg is a lovely city. You sure you want to go to Frankfurt? You could come to Heidelberg with me, and we would go to see your uncle a few days later."

I sat quiet, at a loss for words. Is that why he had taken me along, to have a little "trip" with the mascot of the PX? Maybe I had given him the wrong signals; I had laughed with him and flirted with him because I found him attractive and funny.

I could have fallen in love with him, were he not married. My feelings for him were different from those I had had for Rolf. Mr. Arnsen was older, I considered that, but I had a lot of fun with him. However, it did not feel romantic. I thought of Oma's advice about going to bed with a man. "Karin, I will not preach to you what was preached to me fifty years ago. You know, girls remained virgins until they got married. Times have changed, but one thing is important. Going to bed with a man is a very big step. You have to love him. But when you are young, you might confuse physical attraction with love. Think of this, only sleep with a man if you want to have children with him. Remember, before you give in, ask yourself, '*Would I want to have a child from this man.*' If the answer is no, then let 'no' be the answer to the hypothetical man."

I turned to Mr. Arnsen and looked at his profile in the light of a passing car. He had a small straight nose, high cheekbones, a good chin, and a high forehead. I liked him, despite his being my height when I wore flat shoes. I liked his straight dark hair and eyes. I looked away, through the car's window on my right and felt a lump in my throat.

"I promised Mother I would stay in Frankfurt. And even if it weren't for that . . . , I like you so much, but," I shook my head, "It wouldn't be right."

He understood. For a moment he moved his hand from the steering wheel to my thigh and gave my leg a little squeeze, and then he returned his hand to the wheel again. I kept staring through the windshield into the dark of night.

It was close to midnight when we found the house where Uncle Richard lived. He had rented a room from a war widow, until he could find a larger place that would accommodate his family, who were still living in Leipzig. It was awkward to arrive so late, but Uncle Richard received me with a big smile. He wrote down his landlady's telephone number so Mr. Arnsen could call before he picked me up. I waved good-bye, watched the car drive down the dark street, then wiped my eyes.

I found Guggi, who had grown into a tall, buxom beauty. I was surprised that her only interests were going out dancing, acquiring pretty clothes, and trying to catch a wealthy husband. She had spent the war years at a farm in Bavaria, and it became clear that our mutual history had ended when I moved to Berlin. She had not seen the horrors of war and felt no guilt about the evils Germans had committed during the Hitler years. I soon found that the only thing we had in common was the memory of spitting plum pits onto the umbrellas of passersby from our balcony. I could not find Nunu, who I heard had moved to a small town near the Swiss border. I strolled through the bombed-out inner city. At one time, rust-red brick buildings dating from the fourteenth century had proclaimed the wealth of this merchant town, with its once proud medieval center, town hall, and cathedral. But now everything, even the famous Goethe house, was in ruins. Frankfurt was further along than Berlin in clearing its rubble, but the devastation was wide and depressing. I didn't go to see our former house at Hansa Allee 17; I did not want to know if it too had been bombed. In my imagination it was still the graceful apartment house on the corner of the street, with its green wrought-iron balconies intact. This is where I had watched the Corpus Christi procession, waiting for Nunu to walk by so I could run down the stairs and join her in the parade.

I thought of Mr. Arnsen and wondered how much business he had in Heidelberg, and I longed for him to pick me up and take me back to Berlin.

He called, and I was ready at the appointed hour. His car drove up and there he was. I almost fell around his neck, I was so happy to see him. He brought me a fancy box of Swiss chocolates. I was amazed that he had thought of me and that he had bought me a gift. After one last long hug from Uncle Richard, I climbed into the passenger's seat of the big turquoise-blue Oldsmobile.

Shortly before the crossing at Helmstedt, Mr. Arnsen stopped the car. "Okay, my little snorer, you are going to hide yourself between the seats."

He'd told me five days ago that's where I would have to ride. But how? "Can't I go into the trunk? I'll stay awake. I promise. I had some coffee," I said.

"Sorry. I can't take the risk. It's too comfortable for you in the trunk. This will be rough, and I'll guarantee you won't go to sleep. Hop in, crouch down, yeah, like that, lower. Now don't get alarmed, I'm going to heap the suitcases on you. The Russians will think I have a lot of luggage. They won't suspect a thing."

There was a lot more luggage now than when we had left Berlin. Large boxes containing a toy fire truck and a rocking horse sat on the backseat, and the rest were all piled on top of me. It was very uncomfortable, crouching low, trying to fit my body and folded legs over something akin to a camel's hump, rising in the center of the floor of the car. At every sudden stop or jolt, not being able to see and therefore not able to brace myself for what was coming, I would bang my head and shoulders.

Then the car stopped.

"You be very quiet now," Mr. Arnsen said. "Not a peep out of you. The Americans waved us through, but we're at the Russian checkpoint now, going into the Soviet zone. Remember, be very still. And don't breathe so hard. I can see the suitcases moving up and down. Can't you breathe more shallow?"

"You want me to stop breathing? Is that it? One moment you bring me candies and the next you want me to play dead? Maybe be dead?"

"Don't argue. Just don't breathe so hard. Here they come. *Shh.*"

I heard him get out of the car and speak to someone who answered in a deep basso voice. I pictured the voice as belonging to a barrel-chested Russian who would sing the lead in *Eugene Onegin.* I heard Mr. Arnsen's hard heel clicks, as he walked around the car, and the longer footsteps of heavy Russian boots coming closer. I imagined the man with the deep voice looking through the windows at the stack of suitcases. Mr. Arnsen asked the Russian if he wanted to inspect the cases. Would he want him to take them out of the car? *Has he gone crazy?* Then Mr. Arnsen mentioned, in a voice coated with honey, that according to the American and Russian agreements ending the blockade, the Soviets had no right to inspect the private property of members of the American occupation forces traveling on business through the Russian zone. But he wanted to be polite and oblige the sergeant.

I had to sneeze. Oh my God, the tickling in my nose was driving me crazy. I pushed the tip of my nose up, that often helped. Then I felt a scratch in my throat and felt like coughing. I thought of times at the opera, when Oma would punish me with her most severe stare, until I was able to suppress a cough. I managed it now, but it was difficult. While suppressing the cough, I felt my chest move. Knowing that even the smallest movement would show a rising and falling of the suitcases made the situation unbearable. I counted the seconds; I counted an eternity. The Russian argued with Mr. Arnsen. I heard an angry voice but did not understand what was being said.

Someone opened the door, and I froze. I hated to be in hiding and wanted to spring out and grab the Russian by the throat. But I controlled myself. The suitcases remained immobile. The Russian's voice was near, and he was groping for something in the car. He took hold of an object and Mr. Arnsen said, "Yes, these are Swiss chocolates. Would you like to try one?" The Russian laughed and said *spasiva,* a word meaning "thank you," and marched off.

The driver's door opened and Mr. Arnsen slid behind the wheel. He let out a whistling sigh. Then he started the motor and drove off into the Russian zone, into utter darkness. "Well, kiddo, you just lost your chocolates," he said.

"No! Really? Can I come out now?"

"You can move some of the suitcases, but you better stay down there until we pass the next checkpoint into West Berlin."

"This is pure torture."

"Sorry. I owe you. Now I can't even sweeten the ride for you. I offered him some cigarettes. The guy was huge, like a wrestler. Who would have thought he'd prefer chocolates to cigarettes? But hey, you almost did it again. Those suitcases moved up and down like waves in the Atlantic. Just stay very still when we come close to the checkpoint. The papers are displayed in the windshield, the Russians won't stop us. But they'll look into the car when we drive through. So, sit tight. I'll tell you when."

A few minutes after passing Dreilinden, the last checkpoint, Mr. Arnsen pulled up at my house. I jumped out of the car, grabbed my small suitcase, ran to the door, and rang the bell. Mother pressed the buzzer to let me in. Home had never looked so good. Still, when I turned and waved at Mr. Arnsen in the car as it turned the corner, I felt a twinge of sadness.

ASHTRAYS AND BELLS
SPRING 1951

I was working at the cosmetics counter again. I had learned a few things in the meantime, but whenever anyone asked for Silvertex, Gudrun pushed me aside and took over.

I was still the mascot of the PX, though some eyes had rolled when it was noted that both Mr. Arnsen and I had been absent for the same number of days. I couldn't admit to this harmless trip: first, it had been illegal, and second, the other salesgirls would have been quick to point out that I was receiving privileges. I wanted to avoid envy and hard feelings, so I made up a story that I had been ill with an inflamed appendix, which in the end, everyone believed.

While I stood behind the counter arranging merchandise, a lieutenant walked up and leaned toward me on the glass display case. He leaned down from a great height and smiled with teeth out of a Colgate ad and asked—with a slight accent that I could not place—which perfume I would consider to be suitable as a gift for a very special young lady. I chewed my lips and shook my head. I didn't know. He then asked me what perfume I would like. I didn't know one perfume from another, except for Mother's Chanel N° 5, but I did know that Shalimar by Guerlain was the most expensive perfume we carried. And I remembered Oma had said the Countess Esterhazy wore Shalimar.

"I think the young lady would like this one," I said, showing him the bottle. "Would you like to smell it? We might have a sample."

"No, no, thank you. That's fine. Would you please gift wrap it for me?"

I hated gift wrapping. I was clumsy and felt as if I had five thumbs. I wrestled with the golden paper and managed to tie it with a golden ribbon. "Here you are," I said, handing him the present.

"Thank you very much," he said. Then he paid, tipped his cap, and left the PX.

"He is certainly good-looking," Gudrun said. "But he is a bit too tall. A girl would have to climb up a ladder to kiss him goodnight."

"Yes," I laughed. "Has he been in here before?"

"Haven't you noticed him? He's been here a few times, never bought anything though. No Silvertex," she giggled. "I've noticed him looking at you when he came in."

"He did?"

"Yes, he did."

A few days passed and the tall lieutenant came back. This time I was behind the counter in the toy department. He strolled through the wide doors and seemed at a loss. "May I help you?" I asked, holding up a small teddy bear. "This is the symbol of Berlin. It makes a nice souvenir," I said.

He grinned, and he took the bear in his large hands and inspected it as if he wanted to know how it was put together.

"It's well made," I said. "It is a Steiff Knopf-im-Ohr bear. These are the best toy animals made in Germany." While I was making small talk, I thought, how dumb of me. What does he care? But it was so awkward to have him stand there and not know what he wanted.

He introduced himself as Lieutenant Jorge Matos (*Jorge* was pronounced "Hchorchey"), and then he asked, "Would you like to have dinner with me tomorrow evening? At La Maison Française?" And before I could say yes or no, he had found his courage and more of his words gushed forth, like water in a river released from a dam. He said he wanted to take me dancing afterward. He knew a place where they had a wonderful Latin band, and since he was from Puerto Rico, he could teach me the rumba and the tango.

I stood transfixed. Dinner at the finest restaurant in town and dancing afterward? In the company of an officer from an exotic land? Although he was not from Spain, he spoke Spanish, which was the next best thing. I was delirious but controlled myself.

"I'll have to ask my mother," I said. "Here's my phone number. You can call me later tonight and I'll let you know."

He turned to leave, but then he stopped and asked, "What is your name? When I call you, I have to know whom to ask for."

"It's Karin."

"Pretty name. Karina."

I wore the blue silk dress that had once belonged to Maria, the same dress I had worn for my singing debut. It was slightly off the shoulders, and to keep up with fashion, Mother had made me a petticoat to wear underneath, making the bell-shaped skirt resemble a ballerina skirt. I borrowed a pair of high-heeled silver slippers from my girlfriend Brixie, and from Mother, a pair of short white leather gloves, which closed at the wrist with a pearl button. I felt very elegant when Jorge came calling for me.

His eyes opened wide when I answered the door; I think he liked what he saw. He presented me with a gift wrapped in gold: Shalimar. The package showed my own gift-wrapping handiwork.

I opened it on the spot and dabbed some of the perfume behind my ear as I had seen Mother do, but using far too much. Later I was hard-pressed to tolerate my own overpowering, heady, and exotic scent. After a while, I got used to it, and Jorge must have liked it, since he inhaled deeply, actually sniffing and smiling when he parked and when he took my hand to help me out of the car.

La Maison Française was on the Kurfürstendamm. It was off-limits to Germans, but as a guest of an occupation officer, I was allowed to enter. I found it strange that the French club was located in the British sector and that it was frequented mainly by Americans, who crowded the place. The food was, of course, the reason. Even though Americans had all the proper ingredients to make delicious meals in their officers' clubs, it was the French who knew how to make food taste as if it had been prepared in heaven.

"Look, the décor matches your dress and your eyes," Jorge said, pointing to the blue runner and the blue upholstered velvet chairs when we entered through the tall glass doors.

"But my eyes aren't that blue," I said. "They're more green and gray. I wish they were this color."

"They look blue to me, maybe they reflect the dress. I love your eyes. They're different from other German girls' blue eyes. They tilt up a bit. I wanted to have a chance to look into your eyes for a long time. So here we are," he said, beaming big white teeth at me.

"You're making a study of eyes then?" The entire conversation sounded stupid to me, and I thought I had better drop it. We had arrived at a table, and I felt myself blush. After we sat down, I kept my gaze fixed on the roses in a crystal vase.

Jorge ordered two Tom Collins. I loved the cherry and ate it, but when Jorge wasn't looking, I poured the drink into the container of a palm tree behind my seat. (I remembered what the woman in our apartment had done to avoid getting drunk with the Russians.) Jorge ordered another drink for me and then another. He asked how I managed to stay sober, drinking so much, and I confessed.

"I don't like these mixed drinks," I said. "But it's an American custom, isn't it, to drink a lot?"

"No. Some do, but women in Puerto Rico don't drink much at all."

"Oh. But I like the cherries."

He then ordered me a Shirley Temple with six cherries.

"Shirley Temple? That's a strange name for a drink," I said. He explained to me it was like a Tom Collins but without the alcohol. "Like for a child?" I asked. He smiled without answering me. I felt insulted, but I ate the six cherries and drank the drink.

Violins were playing, candles were glowing, and French onion soup was served. A delicate veal concoction with a cream and cognac sauce followed, but later, the crowning culinary experience came in the shape of a Grand Marnier soufflé. I was not used to gourmet food, and to be honest any substantial food tasted good to me, but my taste buds were awakened and I fully appreciated this exceptional dinner.

While we ate, Jorge told me about his father's sugar plantation in Puerto Rico and about how proud his family was when he graduated from West Point. He missed his parents and his two sisters, and he missed the warmth of the sun. He told me about the Caribbean and about the sugar cane, which grew high and wavered golden green in the sunlight. He told me how blue and clear the sea was as it lapped the white sand. He painted word pictures of bright red hibiscus and the purple of bougainvillea, and he told me that palm trees grew right up to the sand on the beach. In Spanish, *Puerto Rico* meant "rich port," and as he explained, this port opened to reveal an island rich in fertile land and in beauty.

I found his accent charming and loved listening to his stories. Again, he spoke about teaching me Latin dancing that night. But I wondered, would he be able to loosen up dancing the rumba? At the table, even while he spoke, he sat as stiff and erect as if he had swallowed a flagpole.

The time came for him to pay the bill. On the table sat a large round silver plated ashtray with the fleur-de-lis and the name La Maison Française engraved on it. I pointed to the ashtray, shiny and clean since neither of us smoked, and with my eyes full of adoration, I pleaded, "Jorge, please, could you slip that ashtray in your jacket?"

"You mean . . . steal it?"

"I wouldn't call it . . . no, not steal. But if you like me at all, Jorge, please, could you take it for me so I could always remember this evening? Jorge, I'm so happy, and I don't ever want to forget this evening. Please?"

There were a few more noes and a few more pleases, and he must have seen a big tear rolling down my cheek. He furtively looked around, and with one quick swoop, he picked up the ashtray and hid it between his jacket and shirt. "Let's go," he said, impatient to leave.

I grabbed my pocketbook and my gloves and stumbled when I got out of my chair. The waiter probably thought I was drunk, since I had emptied four or five Tom Collins. I dropped my gloves, and Jorge bent down to pick them up. The ashtray obeyed the laws of gravity and tumbled to the floor. When it hit the carpet, it rolled all the way down toward the elevator. We kept walking down the long blue carpeted aisle. Near the elevator, the maitre d' picked up the ashtray, handed it most graciously (with a slightly sardonic smile) to Jorge, and said, "Voilà, monsieur, your ashtray."

Jorge grabbed the confounded thing and pushed me rather ungently into the waiting elevator. But we did go dancing.

At the end of the date, when we arrived at my apartment building, he leaned me against the wall of the building to kiss me goodnight. He was no longer flagpole stiff; the tango had loosened him up. He was a fiery Puerto Rican, and his kisses were a revelation. I heard bells ringing and, not only that, lights went on. Then the windows above opened and the neighbors looked down on us, wondering who was ringing doorbells at 2:30 in the morning. I had been leaning against the box where all six of the apartment doorbells were located, and my enraptured back had rung each and every one of them.

Jorge did not ask me for another date.

Karin, November 1951.

CHAPTER 19

Fire and Ice

FALL 1951

One day in August, the doorbell rang. When I opened the door, I encountered an old bent man standing at the threshold, holding on to a cane with trembling hands.

It took me a moment before I recognized him. "Vati?"

He limped past me, handing me his fedora and coat.

"Karin, yes, I made it up the stairs." He took a deep breath and stopped to look at me. "I'm not well," he said, "not well at all. I wrote to your mother, and she agreed to put me up for a few days. Didn't she tell you?"

"No. She didn't." We stood in the entry, feeling awkward. We shook hands, and I motioned for him to follow me into the living room. "Make yourself comfortable. Mutti is still at work." I glanced at my watch, "She'll be back in an hour or so."

"My suitcase is at the bottom of the stairs." He shrugged, as if apologizing. "My strength gave out. It's small, would you please get it for me?"

"Of course," I said and scampered down the stairs, saddened by my father's condition. Why hadn't Mother told me he was coming?

"Thank you, Karin." He smiled when I brought him the suitcase. "You've grown up. Quite a young lady. And no more glasses? How many years has it been since you last visited us in Altenburg?"

"A few. Well . . . ," I tried to think, counting the years. "It must have been before the blockade. And after . . . I mean the blockade, I couldn't get papers to go to the East zone. You know that." I felt embarrassed. Could he read my mind and know I didn't like to visit that dreadful Russian-occupied part of Germany?

He sat down in the overstuffed chair near the table. I was still standing, not quite sure of how to proceed. I asked, "Would you like some tea? We also have American coffee?"

He chose tea. I remembered that in Liegnitz he liked to take it with a shot of cognac and that he drank it strong and with lots of sugar. Tante Erna had used a lovely old Russian brass samovar for making tea, but I boiled the water in a battered aluminum kettle. I placed the silver teapot Mother had saved from the burning house, two cups, spoons, Mother's French cognac, and a silver sugar bowl on a tray.

He smiled when he saw the cognac. "You remember?"

"I remember lots of things." I sat down at the table with him and poured tea, but he allowed only a drop of cognac to escape into his cup.

"I'm not supposed to have any alcohol. Not like in Liegnitz where I had my wine cellar." His eyes grew dreamy, remembering. "When I sent you down to fetch Krövner Nacktarsch, you always blushed and were embarrassed by that name. And by the label, remember?"

I remembered. The label showed a black-cowled monk with a baby over his arm. The baby's naked pink bottom was showing, hence the name of the wine, "naked ass from Kröven."

"Why did you always send me to fetch that particular white wine with that awful name. Why? When I remember you actually preferred red wine."

"It was amusing to see you blush."

"Not to me, it wasn't."

Father smiled, but I frowned and took a sip of tea. We sat in silence. Then I went on babbling about the past, to break the uncomfortable mood. "I remember really far back. Even when I rode on your shoulders on the Pahnsdorfer Lake." When the memory came back, I could still feel his skin touching my bare legs. His shoulders sloped slightly and his smooth skin felt slippery, and I was afraid that I might slide off, especially when he was wet. He had no body hair and very little hair on his head. Sometimes he tumbled me off his shoulders right into the shallow of the lake. I would emerge, laughing and splashing him with both my hands. I don't remember ever sitting on his knees. High up on his shoulders was the closest I ever came to being held by him.

"Vati? Do you remember when you and I and the little wolves crowded into the huge bathtub wearing our bathing suits? You wore that old fashioned black one. The one with a top to it. That was so funny." I laughed out loud, remembering it. "You had a large black umbrella, pretending the water from the shower was rain. I remember lots of things."

"Yes," he smiled. "And do you remember our walks in the woods with the Baba Yaga?" Vati asked, stirring sugar into his tea. Then he lifted his cup to blow on the steamy brew and took a sip. "Ah, yes, and the Po language, do you still know how to speak it?"

"There's no one to *speapoikpo ipot wipoth*."

"You still know it. No one else ever spoke it with me again."

We reminisced for a while, and Father seemed to enjoy these recollections as much as I did. I offered him a Hershey bar, and he took it. I was puzzled when he put it into his pocket. As I took a bite from the half bar I had, Lassie ran up to me and begged—she was irresistible, standing on her hind feet with her pink tongue hanging out and her little black ears that were two tiny triangles lined in pink—and I snuck her a small piece under the table.

Father erupted. "You feed chocolate to a dog? Don't you know that your brothers haven't had any chocolate since before the war ended?"

How could I have known? Now I had yet one more thing to feel guilty about. But I surely couldn't mail one small piece of candy in a letter to Altenburg. I could not mail three candy bars to three brothers either—that was prohibited.

I let a few moments go by and asked, "What brings you to Berlin, Vati?"

"I have a medical problem. It's getting worse and so far the doctors in Altenburg can't diagnose what is wrong with me. I'm hoping they can find out what ails me in the Oscar Helene Heim."

I knew of this hospital in Zehlendorf, a few kilometers from where we lived. It enjoyed a far-reaching reputation in the field of neuropathology. "It's difficult to get an appointment," I said, "but Mother has a friend who works there. Maybe she can help."

"Yes," he said. "She's a therapist. She set me up with an appointment for tomorrow morning."

I felt left out and was furious at Mother for keeping me in the dark. I also felt uncomfortable around my father. I didn't know what to talk about, so we continued to recall the past. Then he asked me what I intended to do with my life. Mother had written that I was in drama school, and he disapproved. He did not want his daughter to become a second-rate actress.

He studied me. "If you are serious about an acting career, I would like to form an opinion for myself and see if you have talent. I can understand your dream. I've always loved the theater."

I reminded him that part of my love for the stage came from him, since I had accompanied him to many of the plays he had critiqued for his newspaper. He looked at me, his eyes thoughtful and earnest. "If you have talent, then maybe I can help you make some connections while I'm in Berlin."

I frowned. *If* I had talent? Some of the tea in my mouth went down my windpipe. I coughed and spilled tea onto my saucer. I put the cup back, rattling it.

"What's wrong?" Father asked.

"Nothing."

"Yes, you look angry. Your face is all red."

"Mother has given me permission to go to acting school. She thinks I'm talented."

He sat quiet. "Karin, I want to help."

Why had Mother told him everything about me? And where was she anyway? If I had to prove myself to him, I'd better do it now, before Mother arrived to watch me with her eyes squinted and with her drawn mouth.

I searched through my books and found Gerhard Hauptmann's fairy-tale drama about a bell on the bottom of a lake, *Die Versunkene Glocke.* I opened the book to a well-worn page and to a scene I loved. I would play the role of Rautendelein, a water sprite—a creature that is akin to a mermaid but that lives in lakes and brooks. I placed the book in Vati's hand, so he could verify that I was letter-perfect. Then I pushed a second large easy chair into position for a make-believe well, pulled the rubber band from my ponytail, and shook out my hair. I settled down on the arm of the chair and spoke my lines into the "well." In this deep well lived my friend, the merman, Nickelmann. I knelt on the armrest and combed my hair, pretending it reached far below my waist. My voice became more childlike, as I conjured the merman to come and help me while the time away. I—Rautendelein—was lost in this world. I was so alone and didn't know who my parents were or where I belonged; I had no one in the world to love. What was I to do?

I felt Rautendelein's isolation. I became this child woman of the lake. With tears rolling down my face, I ended my soliloquy. Vati sat still for a moment and then clapped and clapped. I heard more applause coming from the doorway, and I looked up in surprise to see Mother standing there.

"So you agree our daughter has talent? Am I not right?" she asked, greeting my father with a fleeting kiss to his cheek.

"Yes, yes. Talent she has. I will call Bernt von Kuegelgen. You remember him, Astrid, from our visit to Berlin shortly after we were married? Maybe he can arrange something. He's close to Brecht, the Berliner Ensemble."

Mother poured herself some tea and sat with Father, sipping from her cup. She encouraged me to act out other scenes I had studied in drama school. I basked in her rare approval. One of my favorites was a scene from *Mary Stuart* by Friedrich Schiller. In that scene, the great queens of the sixteenth century confront one another in the Tower of London, where Mary is being held prisoner. First, I was Mary, pleading for mercy from my cousin

Queen Elizabeth, and then, I played Elizabeth, calling Mary a whore and refusing her request for freedom. So it went, back and forth, until as Mary I shouted, "And now a bastard has ascended to the throne of England." End of scene, and soon to be the end of Mary. Father smiled and applauded again.

I chose another piece, a scene from *Romeo and Juliet,* act 4, scene 3. Not long ago, when I had rehearsed it after ten o'clock at night, our neighbors called the police, thinking someone was being murdered in our apartment. Mother also remembered and kept waving her hand to tone down the volume of my voice, but I was no longer myself, I was Juliet Capulet, envisioning the horrors of the vault where I might "die strangled ere my Romeo comes?" Where I imagined Tybalt's ghost and cried out, "Stay, Tybalt, stay!" at which point the apartment reverberated with my shriek. I calmed down and lifted the make-believe vial with its poison to my lips.

I shut my eyes and wiped my sweaty forehead, hearing only faintly my parents' joined applause. I was euphoric.

Father told me that my instincts for choosing the three scenes were right. He said the Rautendelein scene showed longing and alienation and, of course, was age appropriate. The second was brave for me to do, though totally wrong as far as my age and experience were concerned, and the third one, Juliet's scene, showed my passion.

My parents sat side by side smiling at me. I wanted the moment to last forever.

Bertold Brecht had been acquainted with Father's cousin Bernt von Kuegelgen during the Berlin years before Hitler. Shortly after the war had ended, Kuegelgen had returned to Berlin from exile in Soviet Russia, a few years earlier than Brecht, who had come back from his exile in America in 1947. The friendship of the old intellectual idealists resumed. Kuegelgen had become the foremost literary and theater critic in East Berlin, as well as chief editor of the *Berliner Zeitung.*

Father and I took the S-Bahn to meet with Kuegelgen. A tall and gracious man welcomed us into his office, and after a few minutes of small talk about the families, Father told him that I was an aspiring actress and that he thought I had talent. He asked Kuegelgen to help arrange an audition for me at Brecht's new theater, the Berliner Ensemble. Brecht, for the first time in his life, had a free hand to stage his own plays, of which the prolific playwright had an overwhelming number. The theater occupied the former Theater am Schiffbauerdamm, across the border in the Soviet sector of Berlin.

I was ignorant about Brecht's concept of epic theater. I hadn't seen any of

Brecht's plays, and Father had not told me much about him. Perhaps Kuegelgen assumed I knew the works of Brecht, for he too had not given me any insight to prepare me. My generation, having grown up under Hitler, had not read Brecht's stories, poetry, or his plays. Ironically, Brecht was better known in Israel and in France than he was in Berlin. I had read several newspaper articles about epic theater, but I did not quite comprehend Brecht's idea about "alienating" the audience. His aim was to be didactic, to motivate the audience to think, and that was in direct opposition to what had been taught to me, the Max Reinhardt method, in which the actor tried to transmit the emotions inherent in the character he or she played to the audience in order to evoke the viewer's own emotions. Brecht's *Entfremdung*—alienation—was indeed an alien concept to me.

When Brecht left California in 1947, he first went to Zurich, but then returned to his Berlin. He chose to settle in the Russian sector. When I became aware of him in 1951, he had not yet become disillusioned with East German communism, which he later thought had become perverted into a brand of Soviet imperialism.

Kuegelgen did arrange for my audition, but it fell on the same day that my father had to go to the Oscar Helene Heim for another battery of tests. Mother accompanied him, while I went to audition for the Berliner Ensemble by myself.

Had I understood the Brechtian concept at the time of my audition, I would have acted "alienated" from the words, my body would have been stiff, and my voice devoid of emotions. In other words, I would have been dreadful. It is a good thing I was so ignorant.

I came to understand years later, after seeing several of Brecht's plays in London, New York, and in his own theater in Berlin, that Brecht, the playwright, had cancelled out Brecht, the teacher of a new didactic theater. His genius lay in writing plays that were so human, so touching, that despite his new methods, not many eyes in the audience remained dry when seeing his *Mother Courage, The Good Woman of Setzuan, Galileo,* or *The Caucasian Chalk Circle.* The theme in each of his plays emphasized the human condition: living in an imperfect world and feeling helpless to right society's wrongs.

I stood on the boards of the slightly elliptical stage, wearing the pink angora sweater set from cousin Totty in America. I was hoping that the nice clothes would give me confidence and override my stage fright. But my brain acted as if it had been short-circuited. Some of the angora hair tickled my nose and I sneezed, and suddenly I could not remember a single line or the scene I was going to begin with.

The auditorium of the theater was dark and the stage lights blinding. I had asked for a chair for the Rautendelein scene. The stagehand acted as if I'd made an outrageous demand, as if I had asked for a throne of gold. But he relented and brought in a wooden armchair at the last moment. Below the proscenium, several men and women lounged in seats. I peered into the dark, trying to distinguish faces. I wanted to see if Brecht's wife, Helene Weigel, the famous Mother Courage of the play by that name, was among those present. Or if the great man himself was there. But faces remained shadows. I stated my name, my age, and my training, and then it all came back. I announced what I was going to perform. A slight rasp from the auditorium brought back my nervousness. Perhaps they didn't like my choice? Father had said Brecht was the greatest playwright alive. This was his theater, perhaps I should have chosen a part from one of his plays?

I began. The men and women beyond the proscenium clapped after each of my scenes. When I finished with Juliet, they applauded louder and told me I would hear from them within a few weeks.

I went home exhilarated and exhausted.

Father and Mother returned from the hospital, but so far the doctors had not been able to find a cause for Vati's increasing palsy and his escalating weakness. Tests still had to be evaluated. Both asked how my audition went. I shook my head. "I don't know if they liked my acting. I should have chosen a part from one of Brecht's plays."

"Didn't anyone applaud?" Mother asked.

"They did. But don't they always, to be polite?"

Vati shook his head. "No, Karin. If they clapped it means they liked it. If they had you go on with the rest of the scenes, they were ready for more. It's all positive. Now we'll have to wait for the results," and he added, "For mine too."

I wanted to be an actress. But I didn't like that the theater was in the Russian sector. When I told Father, he said, "I told you, Karin, Brecht is the greatest living playwright. You will learn lessons that will serve you well, wherever you go."

I crossed my fingers that the Berliner Ensemble would accept me.

A few days passed, and Vati was still with us. The sun poured through the kitchen window and added a golden patina to the rich green of the Hungarian peppers in the basket. I put the bottle of Revlon's "Fire and Ice" nail polish back onto the window sill and studied my fingers, hoping to impress my father with my perfect manicure. I blew on them, to dry them faster, so I could go on with cooking the special dinner I was making for Father.

Earlier at the outdoor market I had not been able to resist the peppers

with their sumptuous skin that begged to be touched, and I planned to prepare a dish I had made once before: green peppers stuffed with ground beef.
To the meat I added a little rice, some chopped onions, an egg, salt, pepper
and paprika, and, later, to the sauce, fresh peeled tomatoes.

I picked a pepper from the basket, held it in my palm, and played with it,
turning it this way and that, delighting in the contrast of white fingers
tipped with red nails holding the plump green smoothness of the pepper. I
inhaled the aroma, pungent and exotic, so unlike any other vegetable. I
hoped my father would appreciate my efforts.

He was a half-starved man from the Russian zone, and he viewed this
visit to us and our filled meat pots as one would view a visit to the magical
"Land of Plenty."

I had watched with incredulity when Father ate his breakfast. He added a
big dab of butter to the yolk of the soft boiled egg. We still didn't have butter to spare. When I quizzed him, he said, "You know Karin, we still can't get
eggs in Altenburg, only once in a great while. And we can't get butter, only
this terrible tasting margarine. It feels so good to enjoy this luxury—butter
in my egg. Oh, it's wonderful to be eating well."

I'd reached out and stroked his bony hand.

A strand of hair had fallen into my face, and I brushed it aside, concen-
trating on preparing our meal. I mashed the potatoes with butter and sweet
cream and added an extra dollop of cream to the tomato sauce. I wanted the
food to be extra rich for my father. The peppers simmered in a large iron
skillet. When all was done, I spooned the food onto the plates. It all smelled
delicious and was a feast for the eyes as well. The green peppers, offset by the
red of tomatoes and the light yellow of fluffy potatoes, looked as if they were
begging to be painted.

Mother helped me carry the plates into the room. The three of us sat
around the table. Father was the first to take a bite. As I looked at him, hoping for approval, I noticed tears filling his eyes. Was he so touched by our
warm home? Moved by my cooking for him?

Mother took a bite, made a face as if she had bitten into a lemon, and
dropped her fork. I took a bite and said, "*Pfui* . . . what . . ." The food was
so spicy hot that it burned my mouth and throat, and I wanted to spit it
straight out.

"Karin, did you scrape out the little seeds of the peppers before stuffing
them?" Mother asked.

"I thought I did," I said. "I made them once before, remember?"

By now tears of embarrassment ran down *my* face. I had so wanted this
meal to be perfect.

"It's all right, Karin. Don't worry," Vati said. "I'll take out the meat and scrape off any seed I find. It will be very good with the potatoes and the sauce. Everything is delicious, just a bit too . . . well, spicy."

Mother's *Pflaumenkuchen,* made with fresh black plums and served with whipped cream, was perfect, and it rounded out the meal. In the end, Father complimented us both.

Mother and I cleared the table. When I returned to the room, Father sat in the same posture, quite still, his long tapered fingers resting on the white linen cloth. His head drooped slightly to his chest and a low snore came from his half-opened mouth.

I drew a chair and sat near him. The polish on several of my nails looked nicked; I had not given them enough time to dry before cooking. I went to get the bottle of "Fire and Ice" and touched them up. I looked at my hands with their red tips, then at my father's pale, yellowing nails, perfect ovals that stretched toward me. I unscrewed the top. The little brush stood poised in my hand. Carefully, I inched my hand over and began painting the nails on my father's right hand.

Mother had finished in the kitchen. She came into the room, stared at me, then she screeched, "Karin, what are you doing!"

Vati awakened, shook his head, looked up at Mother. He looked down at his hand and then at me.

"What . . . what is this? Why, what have you done?"

"I'm sorry, Vati. I did my nails and . . . I thought you'd laugh."

He wept and tears rolled down his face. Why did my father weep when I had only done this in jest? The man who had liked to play pranks on other people now cried.

"Woga," my mother's voice sounded soft, as if she were speaking to a young child or a lover. I had only heard him called *Woga* years ago by his sister, Aunt Oda. Mother walked to his chair and stood behind him, putting her arms around his shoulders. "Karin didn't mean to be disrespectful, believe me. She didn't."

But my father couldn't stop crying. He turned in his chair so his face rested between my mother's breasts and shook. Mother kept stroking his head, then she took a napkin from the table and wiped his cheeks.

Vati made a noise, like a hiccup, and with that he stopped crying. He looked at Mother's hands and held them, then he kissed them and just sat there.

I caught Mother's eye and I understood I should leave the room. I left the door slightly ajar and listened.

I had become used to my father being here and had been happy during the last week. What had possessed me to paint his nails? It was demeaning, especially since he was no longer the powerful man he once had been. Living in communist East Germany made his life difficult in many ways. He had joined the Nazi Party in 1943, and now he could not get work anywhere. No one would publish his books, no newspaper would hire him. His colleagues in West Germany had an easier time. Even those who'd joined the party of their own free will, long before Vati was forced to join, went through the process of a court hearing, a "denazification." With this new clean slate, they were able to find jobs at newspapers or magazines.

Father was an uprooted man, a man without a position in life. He depended on his wife to earn a living for his family and on the charity of a friend to pay the rent. As if that were not enough, his body had become palsied and his health was failing. And now I had humiliated him.

Through the crack in the door I saw Mother returning to the table. Father's hand lay on a sheet of wax paper, and Mother began taking off the nail polish with cotton balls drenched in smelly acetone. He looked on in astonishment, as if he'd never seen any of these procedures before. His eyes remained riveted on Mother's hands.

"You still have the most beautiful hands, Astrid. Truly aristocratic hands."

"You used to say the same thing about my feet," she said with a small laugh.

"I still do." He glanced at her sandals, narrow strips of brightly colored cloth on thin leather soles. "You have the feet of an Egyptian queen."

Ha, I thought, there he goes with his Egyptian queen. I almost choked on my own saliva, coughing.

"Are you eavesdropping, Karin?" Mother shouted.

"No," I spoke to the split in the door. "I just heard that about Egyptian queens. How does Vati know about their feet? Did he ever meet any?"

"You're rather impudent," said my mother.

"Is the Egyptian treasure back in the museum yet?" Father asked. "I'd like to take Karin and have her meet my first great love, Nefertiti."

I don't know what Mother answered, since she'd lowered her voice, and I could only hear Vati, as he said after a while, "You know Astrid, there were times when I regretted the course our lives took. We could have been happy. We had much in common. You loved the theater, and I could talk to you about books, about James Joyce. Remember when we read *Ulysses* in bed? How long into the night we discussed it? I'm so sorry I hurt you. I've always loved you. *You.*"

"Then why . . . ?"

"You gave me an ultimatum. You were headstrong. And I felt it was my duty to stay with my mother." He was silent for a moment, and all I could hear was his breathing. It sounded as if something rusty were rattling in his chest. His voice changed. "I was headstrong, too. No one had ever given me an ultimatum before. I should have tamed you. Instead I let you go. Astrid, you were all the things I had dreamt of in a woman. I was so proud of you when you were crowned the most beautiful woman in Hiddensee. Remember?"

"Yes, and I also remember that you were livid with jealousy when Fritz Lang wanted to give me a screen test."

My mother? Someone famous had wanted to give her a screen test?

"Silly," Mother said. "I wasn't about to go to Berlin. But I was flattered when he said I had the *Gesicht der Zeit,* the 'face of the time.' And we were on our honeymoon. Actually, I liked you being jealous."

"I would have killed him had you gone."

"But this Lang was generous. Remember? He ordered champagne for . . ."

"Hold it, I ordered the champagne. Cost me a fortune. Did you think all these years that some moviemaker from Berlin paid for the party after you were crowned?"

"Why, yes. I didn't think you could afford it."

"I couldn't, but I loved you. I was proud of you. You were mine. And when you loved me back, ach. Had there been no one else to consider, only you and I, we would have been very happy."

"But you wanted a son, and now you have three." An edge had crept into my mother's voice.

"You mustn't say it like that. I wanted a *Stammhalter.* An heir. We could have had more children." He cleared his throat. "But you are right. I have three sons. Three intelligent and wonderful sons. I have to be grateful to Erna for them and for being a good mother. But my marriage was not always happy. Erna was never interested in the things that interested me. She doesn't understand my family. You are different."

I heard these confessions and wondered what would have happened if Father and Mother had stayed together. If I had been born a son.

For so many years I had missed my father. I so often had wept myself to sleep because my parents didn't live together. Would he have hugged me and maybe even kissed me if he had stayed with my mother?

Then I thought of all the things that had happened to us at the end of the war. If Mother had stayed with him, we would not be in Berlin now. Where would my Oma have lived? Would she have died alone, somewhere in the countryside? Had Mother stayed with him, I would now be living in the communist part of Germany. Had she stayed with him, she would now be married to a sick, old man.

I realized that because of my parents' divorce, life had presented me with a great gift.

Freedom.

Decisions and the Torture Chair

It was as if two trains, carrying my two possible futures, were speeding full steam ahead on diverging tracks. Would I be wise enough to choose the right train, to jump on and follow it in the right direction?

In October, my visa to immigrate was granted. The papers from the American Consulate arrived, stating the date that I had to present myself. There were forms to be filled out beforehand, and I had been given an appointment in the U.S. military hospital for a physical checkup from army doctors.

Two days after I received the news from the consulate, Brecht's theater informed me that I would be hired as an ingénue and that I was to report to the Theater am Schiffbauerdamm for rehearsals on the first of November. This would be the beginning of my acting career.

I felt as if I were being pulled in opposing directions. To add to the confusion, the band leader with whom I had sung at the officers' club contacted me and asked me to join his new "big band" in rehearsals. He needed a singer for a fund-raising benefit concert for the German Olympic team. The concert would take place in the Titania Palast, the same theater where General Clay had earlier made the declaration during the blockade that the Americans would not abandon us Berliners.

Meanwhile, Mother had made plans for us to visit the old fisherman's house on Sylt again. She had already obtained the necessary traveling documents allowing us to pass through the Russian zone.

I was torn. I wanted to go back to this place I had loved so much, but how could I? "Mutti, I can't go now. I have to prepare for the theater, I have to audition with the band, and I have to . . ."

"I know, I know." She held up her hand, cutting me short. "I also know my child. *Meine kleine* Karin. You know I don't want you to go so far from me, but I know you've dreamt of California for years. I can imagine Oma smiling now. She'd want you to go. But *you* have to make up your mind. Brecht or America? You'll have to let the theater know. You can meet with the bandleader before we go to Sylt. The appointment dates for the consulate and the medical exam are next week . . ."

I interrupted her, "No, the physical is scheduled for this afternoon."

"Well then. Take a bath and get ready." She looked at me wistfully with her large gray eyes and added, "It's cold now on the island, but the air is fresh and exhilarating. Not so many people. You and I will be able to spend some time together. Something we will both remember when you are far away over the ocean."

My head spun. Mother had changed her mind. I did not have to cajole and convince her to let me go to America. The expectation of Sylt, even now with winter approaching, of seeing the old house with the straw covered roof again, of walking through the dunes down to the sea, it all began to take hold of me. It would be nice to spend time with Mother before leaving Germany. I loved her very much at that moment. She knew me and she was right: I wanted to go to America much more than I wanted to act on a stage in East Berlin. And Santa Monica was close to Hollywood. Who knew what might await me in California?

"Yes, yes, yes," I laughed, scooping Mother up and whirling her about as I had done with Oma, only Mother was a few pounds heavier and I quickly put her back down.

The U.S. Army hospital was located within the army compound. I had never been inside before now, since the Truman Hall PX was outside the military base.

When I pushed through the heavy hospital doors, an array of odors assaulted my nose; iodine, alcohol, disinfectants, and a variety of other strong smells made me feel ill to my stomach. Oma would have laughed and called me, "Contrary Karin," amused that I, perfectly healthy, could walk into a hospital and feel sick.

The reception area, where I was to wait, was on the second floor. There were many people crowding the room, but I found a space to sit down on one of the upholstered benches. I smiled at the others and that earned me stern looks and several frowns. However, the woman next to me smiled and this reminded me of my grandmother, making me ache with longing for her all over again. Oma should have been sitting next to me.

Then it was my turn. I had to fill out a two-page questionnaire, have my chest X-rayed, and give a blood sample. The blood looked brown. I hoped I was healthy, when I cut myself the blood had always looked red. A nurse directed me to a screen, told me to undress, and threw me a cotton gown. When I asked if the opening was to go in the front or the back, she replied, "It opens in the back," in a tone of voice that made me feel like an idiot. Then a doctor, appearing to be in his late twenties, waved me into an examining room, where I would undergo a thorough physical examination.

The only time I had ever been to a hospital was when I visited Oma after her heart attack. All this was new and unfamiliar to me.

After listening to my heart, registering my blood pressure, and looking into my eyes with a little light, the doctor motioned for me to climb onto a strange-looking lounge chair. What was that contraption? It looked medieval, like out of a torture chamber. I frowned, and the doctor answered my look of confusion with a lopsided smile. He said, "Come on, sit down, put each foot into one of the stirrups and scoot back." I was reluctant.

The doctor's voice grew impatient. "We don't have all day. Scoot on back, yes, put your head down for Christ's sake, and your feet in there."

What had gotten into him? He had been friendly when I first arrived. I was startled by the goggles he wore, with a little mirror and a light projection over one eye. They made him look like a Cyclops. A mask covered his mouth and a small cotton cap hid his hair. He was rough when he pried my knees apart. His head moved down between my legs, and with an object in his hand, which felt round and smooth and cold—I guessed it to be something made of steel—he probed around those parts of myself normally tucked away within my "Panties of the Week." I felt so embarrassed that I wanted to jump up and run away.

Suddenly his head jerked up. Then he stood and went to the door, yelling, "Hey, Alvin, come and take a look at what I've got here."

The *what* was me, caught in this horrifying position on the examining chair. Did he discover a venereal disease? Could I have picked up syphilis from a toilet seat?

The doctor, accompanied by this Alvin, strolled back in. The first doctor stepped aside and let this Alvin, who was also wearing goggles and a mask, take a look at me. I wanted to die.

"I should have bet you ten bucks when you said there aren't any virgins in Berlin over fifteen. Here, just look at that. Perfect hymen, everything intact. And she's eighteen."

I snapped my legs together, almost crushing the face of the second doctor.

"Are you insulting me?" I yelled. "Do I have to go through this before I can immigrate?" I broke out in hysterical sobs and jumped off the chair. The first doctor tried to press me back into it, more gently than earlier. "Let me go," I shouted. "I don't want to go to America if that's the way I'll be treated."

The door opened, and an older doctor, a major, entered. "What's going on here?" he asked when he took notice of my red and tearstained face.

I stood next to the ugly chair and clutched my gown, which was sliding off me because I was shaking so hard. "Sir, the doctors made fun of me. I'm a virgin and they think they can laugh at me. I don't care if I don't get my visa. I don't want to be treated like some circus freak."

The major's face seemed to grow longer and folds appeared, making him look like a worried hound dog. There was kindness in his large brown eyes directed at me.

He barked questions at the two doctors. He understood my health was fine, so why then was a second doctor called in?

I should have kept my mouth shut, but I was angry. Boiling over angry, I said, "The doctor wanted to show his friend a German virgin. He said he should have bet him ten bucks."

It was the major's turn to get red in the face. The veins on his temples pulsed. "Out, out! Leave this room at once," he shouted at the two doctors. "I'll talk to you both later."

The doctors left the room, a few centimeters shorter, or so it seemed, or maybe they just pulled in their necks as we used to do when we felt guilty and got reprimanded by the principal in school.

In a softer voice, the major asked me to go behind the screen and get dressed. When I reappeared, he apologized for the doctors and said there was no excuse for that kind of behavior. He shook his head, "I can't understand this breakdown in discipline and medical conduct."

I picked up my cardigan. "Is my examination finished?"

"Yes, you may go now."

The major saw that I was still shaking and asked if I was all right. I nodded, but I felt like fainting. I was not all right, and the major noticed my lack of balance.

"You wait right here, young lady," he said. "I'll call for my driver and have him take you home." He waved me off when I objected, "No, no. You just sit there. The driver will be here in a minute. That's the least I can do to help you on your way to America."

I dreamt of my grandmother that night. Again she appeared to me wearing dark red, with a lighter shade of vermillion around her shoulders. She no longer looked like the old woman I knew and loved, but she seemed to have no age and no wrinkles when she smiled at me. I woke up with my heart pounding and I knew Oma was happy with my decision.

And again, Good-bye!
November 1951

The train Mother and I took to reach the island of Sylt traveled from Bahnhof Zoo Station in the British sector of Berlin, through the Russian zone, to Hamburg in the British zone. There were no interim stops. After we entered the Russian zone, East German police in tandem with train conductors passed through the compartments and checked our papers and our tickets, making sure we were not defectors.

I looked out through grimy windows onto a pastoral countryside, where forests of pine gave way to farmland, interspersed with lakes and small villages. Winter was approaching, and although the land still appeared fresh and green, the villages looked dismal. Battle scars of the fierce fighting during the last weeks of the war were still evident in the buildings. Most houses were in disrepair and farm equipment rusted near semicollapsed barns. Did no one care enough to make repairs, to replace the wood and cardboard in the window frames with glass? Or were these materials difficult to obtain? People on the streets cast furtive glances at the train as it passed. Children with cheeks the color of ripe apples waved and I waved back, but the adults walked as if in a stupor and kept their eyes to the ground. I pointed to three women outside a bakery and asked Mother, "Do you think all the young people have left? Everyone looks so old."

"It's hard to tell their age. All of them wear these babushkas. Remember when we wore those scarves over our heads in 1945? They slump, hang their heads, and look unhappy. That's why they look old, I think."

Out in *Niemandsland,* in no-man's-land, the train jarred to a halt. There was no station in sight, only a few low barracks that I pointed out to Mother.

"Must be some sort of checkpoint," she said.

A Russian soldier with a bullhorn shouted, "Everyone out, everyone out."

"And leave our suitcases in the compartment?" Mother worried. "What if someone comes by and steals our things?"

"Mutti, come on. The other people are leaving theirs, too. It'll be all right."

We climbed down the high metal steps and stood in line, waiting to be inspected. Soldiers walked up and down the line; men were separated from women. As one of the soldiers walked up to my mother and me, I felt cold shudders and began to tremble with fear, remembering the time in the cellar when the first Russians had entered.

"You go over there," one of the soldiers said to me, pointing to a barracks farthest from the train. I noticed one lone teenage girl walking toward the building. I was to follow her. I shook my head no. He pushed at me, "Go! There!!"

"Why?" I asked. "My Mother has my papers. I am going where she goes."

"You go to there!" He yelled at me and shoved me, pointing to the far barracks again.

"By what authority do you separate my daughter from me?" Mother shouted. "Have you heard of Bertold Brecht, . . ." and she continued rattling off names. I understood something like Elisabeth painting Shostakovitch for the great Soviet Republic, and then she mentioned the communist cousin Kuegelgen and several others. When she finished her word deluge, I stood in amazement when the Russian shook his head and waved me on to proceed to the near barracks with my mother. Mother jabbed me with her elbow, "Come on, don't just stand there," she whispered. "We're lucky." When we were out of earshot of the Russian, she said, "I can't believe he knows any of those names. Well, maybe Shostakovich, but he must have thought we have important communist connections."

I looked around me and saw only women my mother's age and older. When the young girl arrived at the door of the far off barracks, she hesitated and looked in our direction. I had the impression that our eyes met for a second, though we were too far apart to see clearly. She seemed to be asking for help. A Soviet officer with a Stalinesque mustache and an impressive vodka belly stood in the open door and yanked her inside.

Meanwhile, Mother and I had entered the wooden building near the train, and once inside, we went through a thorough grilling from Russian officers who spoke fluent German. We did not tell them we worked for the U.S. Army, I for the PX and Mother for the GYA. I told them I was an ingénue for the Brecht Theater in the Russian sector and Mother said she was the conductor of a children's choir. (Anyone connected with music impressed Russians, most of whom had a profound love of music.) The information we gave them was duly noted in a huge ledger, which led to our worries that the Russians would check out our stories and arrest us on our return trip.

When we reboarded the train, we noticed several passengers were left behind. An elderly East German conductor told us not to worry, they would be put on a later train. What about their suitcases? The luggage would be collected and stored in Hamburg, he said. I asked, "What will happen to the young girl who went by herself into the barracks?"

He laughed, a basso sort of laugh, "Maybe the captain likes them young. No, no, I'm just joking. She'll also be on the next train. She'll be fine."

"Do the trains stop here again on the way back?"

"Young lady, you worry too much. Rest assured, they don't stop on the way to Berlin, only on the way to the West."

When he was gone, Mother said, "That's a relief. The Russians don't want defectors. They go from East Berlin to West Berlin and then hop on a train and leave the Russian zone. We won't have to worry about the checkpoint going back."

We found the house on Sylt much as we had left it years ago. The roof still dripped its strawlike unruly boy's hair. When we entered through the low door, I felt as if I had only returned from a long walk on the beach, a twelve-year-long walk; nothing had changed.

No, there were a few things that looked different. Since it was November, the sunflowers in the garden—no longer a yellow blaze—had withered and now hung brown on dried-out stalks. One dahlia still burned bright crimson near the house, but the others had wilted long ago. I chuckled and pointed to the old *Volksempfänger* still sitting on the kitchen shelf. One thing was certain, we would not hear Hitler's gravelly voice booming through this little radio now.

A half moon hung in the sky, and I was impatient for Mother to walk to the water with me. But Mother was hungry and wanted to go out to dinner. The Kupferkanne, a restaurant pub, was on her list. We saw the sign from afar, which showed a brightly lit copper pitcher above the entrance. The door squeaked when we entered the cozy, low-ceiling room. We were seated at a table near a window. From here we could see the moonlight reflect on the still mirror of the Wattenmeer, the body of water between the island and the mainland. Our heavy hand-knit woolen sweaters did not keep out the damp cold. Mother, who did not approve of my drinking alcohol, surprised me by ordering hot grogs for both of us. It was a drink similar to hot buttered rum, made with black tea, honey, and a large shot of rum.

We ate crisply fried *Scholle,* a local flat fish akin to flounder, which had swum in these waters only a few hours earlier. It was accompanied by parsley potatoes and brussels sprouts. The owner of the restaurant came to our table to ask if we were satisfied with the food, and with his compliments, he sent us a plum dumpling dessert with hot vanilla sauce. He flirted with Mother and then with me, which raised Mother's arched eyebrows.

Two more grogs arrived, also compliments of the house, and for the moment I forgot about going down to the sea. A young man entered, carrying a *Schifferklavier*—accordion—on his chest. His muscles bulged, and he looked more like a wrestler than a musician. A horizontally striped navy and white jersey showed the ripples of his anatomy. Part of his face was handsome, but unfortunately the rest was hidden by an excess of a wheat blond beard and a mustache. Thick waves of hair fell from his forehead. He played nostalgic seamen's ballads and sang with a pleasant baritone. I knew the lyrics to "*Aloha hey, Aloha hey, mein Schiff sticht morgen in die See . . .*" and sang along. The lyrics were poignant and spoke of someone whose ship would go out to sea on the morrow. I had booked passage on a boat leaving on the 4th of January, allowing me to spend one last Christmas with Mother.

My ship would go to sea in a little more than a month, and singing about leaving the country of my birth made me sad, even though I looked forward to my American future.

After Mother went to bed, I slipped quietly out of the darkened house and walked down to the water. My feet remembered each step across the shifting dunes. The waves reflected fragments of the low moon. I sat down on the sand, pulled my heavy sweater higher around my neck, and thought of that time so long ago, when the war, that unspeakable war, had interrupted my daydream of mermaids. Again I watched the foam, silvery and phosphorescent, dissolve on the dark, wet sand. Again I took deep breaths of the iodine sea smell I so loved, and I remembered my girlish beliefs about mermaids and their souls. I smiled. Although I no longer felt the aching loneliness of my younger years, I still felt a connection to the mermaids. They had been the companions of my childhood, and I walked to where the waves broke in a pattern of lacy foam, put my feet into the water, and said, "Good-bye."

Epilogue

The benefit concert for the German Olympic team took place in December. I was told I sang well and there had been a lot of applause. A record was made of the band and my singing, "Again, this couldn't happen again . . . ," and sent to President Truman. The song's title, even though it was a love song, summed up my feelings about what had happened to me in these past twelve years.

War. I certainly did not want that to happen again, not to me or anyone else.

There was magic in the last Christmas Eve I spent with Mother. We walked home through the forest, returning from a midnight candlelight service in the Nikolskoe Kirche, in the Grunewald by the lake. The night was lit by distant stars reflecting on snow-laden trees hanging from the branches resembling ornaments. The snow crunched beneath our boots and the waning moon cast an eerie blue light onto the land.

Soon after New Year's Day 1952, I left Germany. When I arrived in Hoboken, New Jersey, ten days later, a telegram awaited me. It simply read, "Your father died on January Fourth. He has been freed from his pain and suffering."

My father died the same day I left my Fatherland.

346

Index